Shaker Fever

A VOLUME IN THE SERIES

Public History in Historical Perspective

EDITED BY

Marla R. Miller

Shaker Fever

....

America's Twentieth-Century
Fascination with a Communitarian Sect

William D. Moore

University of Massachusetts Press
Amherst and Boston

ISBN 978-1-62534-509-7 (paper); 508-0 (hardcover)

Designed by Jen Jackowitz
Set in Minion Pro and Directors Gothic
Printed and Bound by Books International, Inc.

Cover design by Kristina Kachele Design, llc
Cover photo by Barbara Morgan

Library of Congress Cataloging-in-Publication Data
Names: Moore, William D., 1963–author.
Title: Shaker fever : America's twentieth-century fascination with a
communitarian sect / William D. Moore.
Description: Amherst : University of Massachusetts Press, 2020. | Series:
Public history in historical perspective | Includes bibliographical
references and index.
Identifiers: LCCN 2019044478 | ISBN 9781625345080 (hardcover) | ISBN
9781625345097 (paperback) | ISBN 9781613767566 (ebook) | ISBN
9781613767573 (ebook)
Subjects: LCSH: Arts, American—20th century—Themes, motives. |
Shakers—United States—Public opinion. | United States—Intellectual
life—20th century.
Classification: LCC NX504 .M66 2020 | DDC 700.88/2898—dc23
LC record available at https://lccn.loc.gov/2019044478

British Library Cataloguing-in-Publication Data
A catalog record for this book is available from the British Library.

Portions of chapter 2 were previously published as "'You'd
Swear They Were Modern': Ruth Reeves, the Index of American Design,
and the Canonization of Shaker Material Culture," *Winterthur Portfolio*
47, no. 1 (Spring 2013):1–34. Portions of chapters 5 and 6 were previously
published as "Interpreting the Shakers: Opening the Villages to the
Public, 1955–1965," *CRM: The Journal of Heritage
Stewardship* 3, no. 1 (Winter 2006): 49–69.

FOR CHARLOTTE, MY BELOVED

CONTENTS

· ·

ACKNOWLEDGMENTS   ix

INTRODUCTION
Shaker Fever   1

CHAPTER 1
Visualizing the Shakers   13
The Early Museum Exhibits at the New York State Museum,
the Berkshire Museum, and the Whitney Museum of American Art

CHAPTER 2
"A Native Tradition with a Future"   73
The Shakers, the New Deal, and National Design

CHAPTER 3
"Using Material from Our Own History in the Arts"   138
Performing the Shakers, 1930–1950

CHAPTER 4
Instituting a Shaker Museum   185
The Shaker Museum at Old Chatham and the Yale University Art Gallery

CHAPTER 5

"Real Americana" 216

Shaker Pageants, Adapted Sites, Folk Music, and Heritage Tourism

CHAPTER 6

Opening the Villages to the Public, 1955–1965 288

POSTSCRIPT

"Borrowed Light" 313

Persistent Symptoms of Shaker Fever

NOTES 329
INDEX 423

ACKNOWLEDGMENTS

· ·

I first became intrigued by the twentieth century's Shaker fever while serving as the director of the Enfield Shaker Museum in Enfield, New Hampshire, as I developed an awareness that popular conceptions of the sect differed in detail and emphasis from the understanding I gleaned from documentary, photographic, and artifactual sources. The path from those initial inklings of dissonance to this volume has been long and circuitous. On this journey, I have incurred debts both personal and intellectual. I could not have completed this project without the goodwill of a larger community.

I would like to begin by thanking the many individuals at museums and Shaker heritage sites who have assisted me by facilitating access to holdings while also discussing institutional history and interpretation. This group includes Bridget Enderle, Jerry Grant, Lesley Herzberg, Tommy Hines, Sharon Koomler, Sarah Margolis-Pineo, Karen Quinn, Lacey Schutz, Lisa Seymour, Linda Steigleder, Scott Swank, and Darryl Thompson. Christian Goodwillie has consistently been a stalwart friend of this project and generous beyond expectations. My initial contacts at the Enfield Shaker Museum, including Galen Beale, Barbara and Earl Brady, Dick Dabrowski, Michael O'Connor, and Steve Powell, were vital for the genesis of this undertaking.

A number of organizations and offices have provided financial and institutional support. The Department of History of Art and Architecture and the American and New England Studies Program (AMNESP) at Boston University are supportive and collegial intellectual communities and have inspired me in my toils. Julia Kline, within AMNESP, has contributed significantly with her competence and unerring sense of humor. Karl Kirchwey, the associate dean of the Faculty for the Humanities within the College of Arts and Sciences at BU, generously provided a subvention toward publication of this book as well as expressing persistent interest in the topic. The Boston University Center for the Humanities (BUCH) similarly awarded a Publication Production Award to the volume as well as granting me a Jeffrey Henderson Senior Research Fellowship in the Humanities to draft portions of the text. At the BUCH, Christine Loken-Kim, Tamzen Flanders, Susan Mizruchi, and the late James Winn all worked to make this book a reality. Rhoda Bilansky, Boston University's interlibrary loan supervisor, has frequently provided solutions to research problems that seemed intractable.

The Winterthur Museum and Gardens in Winterthur, Delaware, generously provided me with a short-term research fellowship and a National Endowment for the Humanities Winterthur Fellowship, both of which were crucial for this volume. The community of scholars with whom I interacted while at Winterthur was remarkable and included Gretchen Buggeln, Katherine Grier, Emily Guthrie, Amy Henderson, E. Richard McKinstry, and Jeanne Solensky. While I was at the University of North Carolina Wilmington, this project was supported by two Moseley Fund Grants from the Department of History and a Charles L. Cahill Award from the College of Arts and Sciences. The Filson Historical Society of Louisville, Kentucky, also awarded me an invaluable Filson Fellowship to allow me to work in their collections.

Portions of three chapters of this book have previously been published as articles. "Interpreting the Shakers: Opening the Villages to the Public, 1955–1965" appeared in the winter 2006 issue of *CRM: The Journal of Heritage Stewardship* and has been incorporated into chapters 5 and 6 of this work. I am indebted to Antoinette Lee, the editor of *CRM*, for her help with this article. It is unfortunate that this vital journal produced by the National Park Service, which promised so much to the preservation and public history communities, has been discontinued. *Winterthur Portfolio* published "'You'd Swear They Were Modern': Ruth Reeves, the Index of American Design, and the Canonization of Shaker Material Culture," in the spring 2013 issue. That article forms the basis of chapter 2. I offer to Amy C. Earls, the managing editor of *Winterthur Portfolio,* my greatest appreciation for her unfailing enthusiasm and support for this work.

The Vernacular Architecture Forum (VAF) has provided me with a vibrant intellectual home throughout my career. Colleagues from this organization have been instrumental in shaping my thinking surrounding this topic. Among my many VAF compatriots, I wish to thank particularly Catherine Bishir, Richard Candee, Lisa Davidson, Claire Dempsey, Andrew Dolkart, Paul Groth, Kim Hoagland, John Larson, Louis Nelson, Abigail Van Slyck, and Michael Ann Williams.

Others who have contributed to making this work possible and whom I wish to recognize and thank include Louise Anderson Allen, Bill Atwill, Simon Bronner, Marjorie Carr, Walt Conser, Robert Emlen, Tammy Gordon, Karen Haas, John Kirk, Nancy Lee, Gerald Marks, David Martin, Nancy McDowell, Gordon McIntosh, Keith and Elizabeth Morgan, B. Matthew Neiburger, Daniel Patterson, Patricia Hills, Peter Reznikoff, Roy Skodnick, Stephen J. Stein, Virginia Stewart, Penny Stillinger, and Nick Wankowicz.

Marla Miller, Matt Becker, and Margaret Hogan at the University of Massachusetts Press have graciously shepherded my manuscript from initial proposal to published form. Thank you. It has been a pleasure working with you.

Finally, this work is the product of a loving and encouraging household. I am so fortunate to be married to Charlotte Emans Moore. This book would not have assumed the form it did without her input as interlocutor, editor, and proofreader. Charlotte and our son, Gideon, shaped this product through their patience, indulgence, insight, and understanding. I could not offer either one of them "more love" than I already do.

Shaker Fever

INTRODUCTION
SHAKER FEVER

....

A t Barack Obama's presidential inauguration on January 20, 2009, in
front of television cameras broadcasting to an audience of millions, the
French-born Chinese American cellist Yo-Yo Ma led a quartet performing
John Williams's "Air and Simple Gifts." Composed specifically for the occasion, this piece featured variations on the melody of a nineteenth-century
Shaker song written by Joseph Brackett, Jr., of Alfred, Maine. The celebrity
quartet, which Ma assembled, featured Itzhak Perlman on violin, Gabriela
Montero on piano, and Anthony McGill on clarinet. The ensemble was artfully balanced to represent the cross-generational, gender-inclusive, racially
diverse, multicultural coalition that the new president believed would characterize the nation he would lead.[1] One newspaper account of the event
reported that the performance was meant to "demonstrate the message of
inclusion that President Barack Obama conveys."[2]

The familiar melody, which Ma's quartet played to usher in what many
hoped would be a new chapter in America's national story, had been introduced to the public's ears more than six decades earlier. In 1944, Aaron
Copland, a Jewish composer seeking to create a modern music rooted in the
nation's culture, had appropriated the Shaker song for use as a score of a ballet choreographed by Martha Graham.[3] Copland, whom the national press
repeatedly identified as Obama's favorite composer, subsequently reworked

1

this material into *Appalachian Spring*, an orchestral suite that ultimately gained broad popularity and became his best-known composition.[4]

In organizing this twenty-first-century inaugural celebration, Obama's team had charged Williams with revisiting the melody of a sacred song created within a marginal American religious sect. Yet, in the hands of a twentieth-century composer, it had been transformed into a melody closely identified with national identity. Many Americans who watched the inauguration probably recognized the tune, introduced by McGill's clarinet, as reprising Copland's beloved work, redolent of Franklin Roosevelt's New Deal optimism; some subset of that group presumably understood its Shaker origins. By using this musical theme, the inauguration's organizers celebrated America's diverse heritage but also signaled to the cognoscenti ideas concerning pious labor, modest self-sacrifice, honorable communal effort, and elegant yet humble artistic production, all attributes popularly associated with the Shakers.[5] For Obama's reformist Democratic administration, this Shaker melody provided an evocative signifier of a shared political vision.

The inauguration's organizers drew on a national understanding of the Shakers that had been established in the middle decades of the twentieth century. Between 1925 and 1965, a wide range of Americans experienced what one participant termed "Shaker fever."[6] Sufferers of this malady became fascinated with the sect, its theology and practices, and its cultural products. Victims of this fixation included local history buffs, government bureaucrats, museum professionals, artists, writers, and choreographers. Shaker fever spread across the nation but was experienced most fervently in geographic areas surrounding former Shaker villages in eastern New York State, western Massachusetts, New Hampshire, Ohio, and Kentucky. Although the fascination gripped a gamut of individuals, members of liberal Protestant denominations including Unitarians and Congregationalists were particularly susceptible, as were individuals influenced by the Progressive educational philosophies and practices of John Dewey and John Cotton Dana. An individual's association with the nascent American Studies movement within American institutions of higher learning, including Smith College, the University of Michigan, and Yale University, also tended to affect the intensity of the enthusiasm.

In the second third of the twentieth century, Americans who had caught Shaker fever radically reshaped the nation's understanding of the sect and its history, music, and material culture. Prior to this moment, the United Society of Believers in Christ's Second Appearing, as the group was known more formally, functioned as a pietistic communitarian religious organization little recognized beyond the immediate geographic vicinities of its villages. When individuals outside these areas were aware of the Shakers, they primarily perceived them to be either bizarre religious fanatics following heretical familial and sexual practices or producers of quality consumer commodities including seeds, patent medicines, chairs, brooms, collegiate letter sweaters, and ladies' cloaks. By 1965, however, the Shakers were viewed widely as quintessentially American, personifying the nation's finest qualities of piety, ingenuity, simplicity, sobriety, and self-denial.[7] Shaker material culture, in particular, was broadly appropriated to embody such elevated ideals. In the middle of the twentieth century, public and private collections dedicated to Shaker objects were established, images of Shaker items were published broadly in both popular and scholarly contexts, Shaker villages were preserved as pilgrimage sites, and household furnishings based on Shaker antecedents were featured in ladies' magazines and marketed in department stores.

This book documents and analyzes the transformation in America's understanding of the Shakers within the context of twentieth-century American social and cultural history. The six chapters of this volume argue that the taste for "things Shaker" must be understood in the context of mid-century nationalism, modernist artistic movements, and the politics of the Cold War. This study's period is bracketed by the first serious interest in the Shakers by Charles C. Adams, the innovative director of the New York State Museum in Albany, New York, and the opening of Shaker villages in Massachusetts, Kentucky, and New Hampshire as tourist attractions in the 1960s.

Established in North America at the end of the eighteenth century, the Shakers were a religious society with historical roots in the British Isles. Under the leadership of the charismatic prophet Mother Ann Lee and her successor, Joseph Meacham, the group congregated in celibate, communitarian villages and lived according to a set of strictures, known as the "Millennial Laws," which guided both public and private behavior. According to these codes, all economic resources were shared, individuals worked for the common good, and pairs of male and female leaders attempted to steer the community to spiritual perfection and economic self-sufficiency. The Millennial Laws, grounded in Protestant avoidance of temptation and abhorrence of excess, also guided believers in their material life, leading to architecture and furniture that tended away from extravagant design and ornamentation.

Following the Second Great Awakening, and as a result of thoughtful and deliberate missionary efforts, the society grew to comprise eighteen villages located from Maine to Kentucky. Within these communities, the Shakers organized themselves into families composed of individuals who were biologically unrelated. Men and women who espoused, and attempted to practice, celibacy slept in chambers in sexually segregated areas of communal dwellings but ate, socialized, and worshipped together. Ecstatic and inspired trembling and shaking during worship, from which the group's popular name was derived, developed into a ritualized liturgical dance practiced by the community as a whole during Sabbath religious services. The group's emphasis on communal labor as an expression of religious devotion led to prosperity in many communities, as well as to innovative agricultural and manufacturing processes. Shaker villages produced packaged seeds, medicinal compounds, furniture, clothing, and agricultural equipment, including wooden buckets and other containers, which were sold in the regions surrounding their settlements. The sect reached its largest membership of more than four thousand members in the 1840s and subsequently declined.[8]

Shaker fever, as expressed in the resultant twentieth-century American popular reevaluation of Shakerism and the Shaker legacy, coincided with a painful and prolonged collapse within the institution itself.[9] Journalists frequently predicted the sect's demise. In 1922, a newspaperman reporting on the closing of the Shaker village in South Union, Kentucky, commented that the "picturesque colony of Shakers, that unusual religious sect which takes its name from the peculiar motion they manifest when wrought up to religious ecstasy, at South Union . . . will soon be but a memory. Most of the quaint and deeply religious people who once made up the colony have died."[10] Similarly, in describing the end of the Shaker settlement in Alfred, Maine, Karl Schriftgiesser of the *Boston Evening Transcript* wrote in 1931, "Their buildings will be deserted, their farms let go to seed, and an even more deathly silence than usual will settle over their little community where they have worked so hard and lived so long."[11] Schriftgiesser's prediction proved accurate: by 1951, only three active communities remained, containing a total of just forty members of the faith.[12] This collapse has continued until, at the time of this writing, there are only two individuals who self-identify as Shakers residing at the village in Sabbathday Lake, Maine.[13]

This book, however, is not about the lives, labors, and beliefs of the Shakers. Rather it is about the individuals who celebrated them, collected their furniture, reveled in their music, and were inspired by their history. *Shaker Fever* examines the various ways in which nonbelievers found meaning and value in Shakerism and its legacy. It explores and explains how twentieth-century individuals from the profane world outside the boundaries of the Shaker villages refashioned the Shaker experience to make sense of it for themselves and to share their insights with others.

The decline of Shakerism during these years also coincided with a more general surge of interest in American history and material culture. Collectors such as Henry Mercer in Pennsylvania and Edna Hilburn Greenwood in Massachusetts, Electra Havemeyer Webb in Vermont, and many others gathered artifacts that spoke to them of the country's past, and preservationists, including William Sumner Appleton of Boston and Reverend William A. R. Godwin of Williamsburg, Virginia, organized to protect buildings and sites that could be used to educate the public about America's history.[14] The celebration of the Shakers, their history, their music, and their theology chronicled in this book interweaves intricately with the broader investigation of American national identity taking place in the middle decades of the twentieth century. Shaker fever was experienced within the interrelated contexts of the Colonial Revival, the New Deal's embrace of the common man, regionalism in both art and literature, the folk music revival, and the burgeoning popularity of historic preservation.

Interpreters wrestled with the conflicting ideas that the Shakers represented what was praiseworthy in American culture and that they existed outside the national mainstream. Paradoxically, the Shakers could serve as both icons of Americanism and as critiques of national shortcomings. Interpretations of the Shakers proved problematic in that the group could be appropriated to argue for American exceptionalism, but in doing so interpreters celebrated individuals who rejected many foundational aspects of the nation's common culture, including individualism, monogamy, and property ownership. Because of this dichotomy, Shaker fever struck a varied group. Some like David Potter, a conservative consensus-school American historian who taught at Yale University, and John S. Williams, a wealthy stock broker who established the Shaker Museum at Old Chatham, were drawn to the sect because they believed it manifested the Anglo-Saxon Protestant work ethic and fostered religiously motivated entrepreneurs. Simultaneously, individuals such as Miriam Cramer, a Unitarian choreographer from Cleveland, Ohio, and Jerome Count, a left-leaning educator, embraced the group's communalism, pacifism, and heretical worship practices. Celebrants from the entire political spectrum embraced the Shakers' perfectionism while finding it difficult to reconcile themselves to the ideology of celibacy.

Twentieth-century Americans' fascination with the Shakers assumed many forms across various media.[15] Museum directors and curators formed collections of Shaker objects and mounted exhibitions about the believers. Artists and photographers created two-dimensional representations. Choreographers and pageant organizers produced living three-dimensional enactments of Shaker worship and historical events. Authors wrote books and pamphlets meant for both popular and scholarly audiences. Choral directors and composers created musical performances and, ultimately, audio recordings of music both written by and inspired by the sect. Designers, furniture manufacturers, and milliners created consumable Shaker-inspired goods for American consumers. Each of these cultural products contained coded messages concerning the group, their beliefs, national identity, and the existential dilemmas of human life.

Recent historical and art historical analyses of the early twentieth-century fascination with Shaker material culture have largely credited Faith and Edward (Ted) Deming Andrews, authors and antique dealers from Pittsfield, Massachusetts, with shaping public reception of the Shakers in these decades. Hugh Howard and Jerry V. Grant, for example, claim, "Almost by themselves, Ted and Faith Andrews . . . secured for the Shakers . . . honored places in the pantheon of American art."[16] Similarly, Kory Rogers, a curator at the Shelburne Museum in Vermont, has credited the Andrewses almost exclusively for linking Shaker furniture to modernism.[17] In a less hyperbolic mode, the historian Stephen J. Stein writes, "[Edward] Andrews was a leading force in the revival of interest in the Shakers and deserves to be recognized as the most significant scholar of the twentieth century."[18]

Although the Andrewses were indisputably important disseminators of Shaker fever, their role has been overemphasized at the expense of other actors, in part because the Andrewses were inveterate self-promoters and jealously guarded their status as experts on all topics relating to the

Shakers.[19] The couple went so far as to refer to themselves as "the only recognized authorities in this . . . field."[20] On another occasion, they described themselves as "instruments" divinely chosen to promote and interpret the Shaker heritage.[21] Historian Mario S. De Pillis characterizes the couple, with whom he was acquainted, as "proselytizers."[22] Less sympathetically, in the early 1960s, Robert F. W. Meader, director of the Shaker Museum in Old Chatham, New York, expressed his antipathy toward Ted Andrews's self-proclaimed expertise by mockingly referring to the collector as "the G. A." or "the Great Authority."[23]

Throughout their careers together, Faith and Edward Deming Andrews established a pattern of currying favor from those in positions to assist them in publicizing, celebrating, and marketing the sect's cultural materials before ultimately, like apostates, turning against these same associates and decrying them as polluters, exploiters, or adulterators of the Shaker tradition. The Andrewses' self-regard frequently led to conflict with those around them and hampered them from reaching desired goals. The scholarly literature's historiographic emphasis on this couple has resulted in the activities of other figures of the same period being overlooked, thus creating a skewed and inaccurate representation of how Americans came to understand the Shakers and their legacy. One goal of the present work is to recognize the contributions of individuals whom this pair systematically attempted to push out of the spotlight.

This work is meant to be interpretive and stimulating rather than encyclopedic. I have not attempted to include every artist who created images of the Shakers and their villages, every author who published a book about the Shakers, every composer who worked with a Shaker theme, or every preservationist who valued Shaker buildings and landscapes. Shaker fever's contagious quality during this time period would make it foolhardy to pursue such a goal.[24] Similarly, this work is not meant to be an exhaustive survey of the Andrewses' career and publications. Rather, this volume examines the primary modes through which culture workers introduced the Shakers to the American public while also explicating the interpretive tropes linked to their methods.

My approach is essentially semiotic. During the period of this study, the Shakers, their practices, and their material culture had symbolic relevance for many Americans. This work attempts to untangle the Geertzian "webs of significance" in which midcentury enthusiasts entangled the believers.[25]

Folklorist Henry Glassie warns us that, while interpreting culture forms the very center of humanistic study, meaning remains elusive. In his poetic phrase, it is "the unverifiable issue of unknowable intention with unknowable response."[26] While heeding that warning, by presenting historically contextualized thick descriptions of photographs, museum exhibitions, pageants, musical scores, preserved villages, and other cultural texts, this study attempts to sketch the varied meanings projected on the Shakers by the diverse group of individuals who presented the sect in these decades. Understanding how twentieth-century participants interpreted the Shakers provides insights concerning how these individuals understood their role in the world and the existential dilemmas that they faced.[27]

The process of attempting to comprehend the enigmatic meanings inscribed into the artistic, literary, and cultural performances of these historic figures necessarily renders a group biography of those who experienced Shaker fever. Glassie asserts that "biography is the epistemic entrance for the historian."[28] Understanding the fascination that Shakerism held for these individuals frequently requires delving into their formative experiences and cultural training, including examining their religious, educational, familial, and professional backgrounds. In doing so, we begin to understand why these individuals living in the profane world of twentieth-century America found themselves drawn to a millennialist, communitarian faith to which they did not subscribe. While these diverse individuals cannot easily be described as constituting a movement, embedded together in a particular national and historical reality they used their various talents, resources, and perspectives to create a lasting understanding of the Shakers that continues to influence American civic discourse.

This interdisciplinary examination of the rich and varied corpus of materials inspired by the Shakers in this period is organized into six chapters and a postscript arranged both chronologically and thematically. The initial chapter examines the first significant exhibits of Shaker materials mounted by museums between 1925 and 1935. In creating a collection at the New York State Museum and supporting a seminal exhibition with accompanying publication, the ecologist Charles C. Adams brought together Ted Andrews with William F. Winter, Jr., an industrial photographer who lived in Schenectady, New York, and worked for General Electric. Andrews and Winter subsequently were both involved in Shaker exhibitions at the Berkshire Museum in Pittsfield, Massachusetts, and at the Whitney Museum in New York City. Almost a century later, these individuals' activities profoundly impact how Americans understand the Shakers and the objects they created. This chapter also offers a detailed analysis of the photographs of Shaker objects and spaces Winter created before his premature death from cancer.

The activities of the Index of American Design, a New Deal government agency, are central to the second chapter. Under the leadership of Holger Cahill, an influential arts administrator, and Ruth Reeves, a textile designer who found herself underemployed because of the Great Depression's downturn in manufacturing, this federally funded bureaucracy undertook to create a record of the nation's artistic heritage. Because of modernist aesthetics and nationalist ideologies, the agency found Shaker material culture particularly appealing. Artists on the federal payroll created numerous watercolor paintings and photographs of Shaker objects in collections from Kentucky to Maine. These images subsequently were exhibited across the country, influenced popular conceptions of the Shakers, and inspired artists, furniture designers, milliners, and other aesthetes.

The third chapter moves from visual and material culture representations of the sect to study the efforts of four women who produced choreographic and theatrical presentations between 1930 and 1950. Doris Humphrey, Miriam Cramer, Marguerite Melcher, and Clarice Carr were all educated, middle-class women who had been raised in the liberal Congregational and Unitarian denominations. These advocates, some of whom defined themselves as dancers and others who thought of themselves as writers and educators, separately used their diverse talents to educate Americans about the Shaker faith by convincing individuals to don costumes and give public performances interpreting Shaker history and worship. In venues that ranged from Broadway theaters to Midwestern college campuses, and from folk festivals to New York experimental drama workshops, these women situated a small, eccentric regional religious sect as worthy of international attention, while simultaneously working to further their own artistic ambitions and expand the boundaries of the sphere of activity dictated by their class and gender.

Chapter 4 compares and contrasts two midcentury attempts to establish institutions that would steward permanent collections of Shaker artifacts so that they would be available to scholars and the general public. John Williams, the scion of a prominent New York mercantile family, had both the financial strength and the social connections to successfully establish a nonprofit institution to maintain and interpret his private collection of Shaker artifacts. In stark contrast, after promising negotiations, Faith and Ted Andrews, were unable to convince Yale University to commit to permanently accession their holdings and validate their status as erudite scholars of this American faith. This chapter illuminates varying understandings of the Shakers during this time but also examines the impact of wealthy donors and collectors on the practice of American Studies, an intellectual field of study that was expanding both inside and outside universities in the decades following World War II.

The fifth chapter returns again to Shaker music, this time with a focus on Shaker musical productions and pageantry between 1950 and 1965. In these years, as one manifestation of a national folk music revival, increasing numbers of Americans, many of them teenagers or college students, dressed in supposedly Shaker garb and performed the faith's dances and music. These musical performances and pageants frequently were linked to individuals attempting to restore and interpret Shaker villages in New York State, Massachusetts, and Kentucky. Jerome Count introduced generations of teenagers to Shaker music at his Shaker Village Work Camp, a liberal summer educational institution located in the South Family compound of New York's Mount Lebanon Shaker Village. In the winter of 1961, Shaker Community, Inc., the nonprofit corporation founded to preserve Hancock Shaker Village in Massachusetts, worked with the Smith College Art Museum to present a Shaker pageant on that college's campus. Similarly, Julia Neal and Deedy Hall, the founders of the Shaker Museum in Auburn, Kentucky, cooperated with faculty from Western Kentucky State College to produce an annual pageant entitled *Shakertown Revisited*. Each of these efforts resulted in audio recordings of Shaker music, making the sect's musical repertoire available to a broad popular audience for the first time. The recordings these groups made under the influence of Shaker fever, some still commercially available today, have had a profound impact on subsequent treatments of Shaker music.

The final chapter discusses and analyzes the efforts to transform Shaker villages into educational, cultural tourism sites in the years between 1955 and 1965, focusing on Hancock Shaker Village in Massachusetts, Pleasant Hill Shaker Village in Kentucky, and Canterbury Shaker Village in New Hampshire. It demonstrates that these compounds underwent distinct historical processes of preservation and thus present visitors with slightly varying interpretations. Hancock, located near aesthetically sophisticated urban audiences, followed the lead of seminal curators and presented Shaker architecture and material culture as antecedents to American modernism. Because of a local tradition of treating history and cultural heritage as an economic driver, Pleasant Hill in Kentucky presented the village as a premodern, agrarian resort serving as a respite from the cares and tribulations of the present. Canterbury, which Shaker associates transformed into a museum while still housing members of the faith, benefited from offering visitors the chance to interact with living exemplars of the disappearing sect. Each of the villages in their own ways manifested messages carved into the landscape by both the Shakers who inhabited the compounds and by the administrators who preserved them and opened them to the public.

The postscript examines the persistent impact of Shaker fever on American arts and culture in the decades surrounding the end of the twentieth century and the beginning of the twenty-first. In these years, although the flurry of innovative and transformative activity of the earlier period had subsided, the American public continued to purchase Shaker inspired furniture, attend performances of music and dance derived from Shaker traditions, and visit preserved Shaker compounds. The meaning of these works, however, was transformed by the nation's continuing economic and cultural histories.

As a whole, this volume documents the efforts of women and men who lived in the middle of the twentieth century and valued, collected, interpreted, and preserved the Shakers' legacy. These individuals, from Charles Adams to Doris Humphrey, and from John Williams to Jerome Count, deserve to be recognized. While acting individually and without coordination, as a group they brought the Shaker experience to the attention of Americans and individuals around the globe, they offered the Shaker faith and way of life as an alternative to the alienated existence lived by many Americans under the thrall of materialism and an unreliable capitalist economy, and they created an astounding body of Shaker-inspired cultural works. Their enthusiasm for this American, millennialist, communitarian, celibate sect made it possible for Obama's inauguration organizers in the first decade of the twenty-first century to appropriate the melody of a nineteenth-century Shaker hymn as a nonverbal signifier of a reformist vision of an inclusive, egalitarian, caring nation built on consecrated labor and combined effort.

Simultaneously, this text also seeks to contextualize and problematize the understanding of the Shakers that this cohort bequeathed to us. In the middle decades of the twentieth century, when modernism and nationalism formed lenses to transform the ways in which Americans viewed the world, the humanity of individual Shakers and the complexity of their communities became obscured. Shaker fever led to a multifaceted, romantic, nostalgic understanding of the celibate, perfectionist, millennialist believers. Enthusiasts in this period created an understanding of the past that was useful for the era in which they lived.

In the present, when the global economy and international migration has called nationalism into question and when modernism itself is a subject of antiquarian interest and museum study, we can appreciate the artifice of the figures who created the works chronicled in this volume, but we may also wish to move beyond their constructs to seek more nuanced historical representations of the men and women who followed the teachings of Mother Ann Lee. By more fully understanding the sect's representation that we have inherited from the twentieth century, perhaps our generation will forge a new synthesis that more accurately represents the concerns of the Shakers while speaking to the anxieties and biases of the twenty-first century.

CHAPTER 1
VISUALIZING THE SHAKERS

•••••••••••••••••••••

The Early Museum Exhibits at the
New York State Museum, the Berkshire Museum,
and the Whitney Museum of American Art

The American people initially became aware of the Shakers largely as the result of a series of three seminal museum exhibitions held between 1930 and 1935. Mounted by the New York State Museum in Albany, New York; the Berkshire Museum in Pittsfield, Massachusetts; and the Whitney Museum of American Art in New York City, these landmark exhibits featured the photographs of William F. Winter, Jr., and the collection of Faith and Edward Deming Andrews. By the time the exhibition at the Whitney closed in December 1935, the various actors involved with these exhibitions had created an aesthetically appealing and visually compelling vision of Shaker material culture and thus of the sect's identity. More than eighty years later, this constructed vision endures and continues to inform the public's understanding.

The few scholars who have addressed these exhibitions have treated them as essentially analogous and interchangeable since they all took place between 1930 and 1935, contained many of the same materials, and featured apparently similar installations.[1] Their historiography has also tended to privilege the roles that Faith and Edward Deming Andrews played in mounting them. Understanding these installations as the homogenous intellectual output of the Andrewses, however, ignores the organizational histories of the sponsoring institutions and fails to recognize others' contributions. In each case, rather than being the dynamic force and creative auteurs behind the exhibitions, the Andrewses were contractors brought in to promote an administrator's vision. Thus, instead of being pure expressions of the Andrewses' interpretation of the Shakers, these shows must be understood as complex undertakings created collaboratively by individuals with multifaceted motivations.

This chapter offers a detailed historical account of these three early exhibitions, created in the years following the onset of the Great Depression, while recognizing the contributions of Charles C. Adams, the director of the New York State Museum; Laura Bragg, the director of the Berkshire Museum; and Juliana Force, the director of the Whitney Museum. These remarkable individuals all offered the Andrewses opportunities to contribute to exhibitions about the Shakers in their galleries. However, each of these administrators had their own professional and ideological objectives in sponsoring the installations and thus contributed to both the sect's institutional interpretation and its public reception. These exhibitions reflected the intellectual backgrounds and professional experiences of the institutions' directors: Adams as an ecologist interested in geography, Bragg as a Progressive educator, and Force as an art impresario.

None of these figures, it is worth noting, was a theologian or particularly religious. Therefore, the Shakers' faith was not central to their interests. Adams was concerned with how the sect functioned economically within New York's cultural and physical environment. Bragg promoted Shaker artifacts as products of the region surrounding her institution. Force saw the Shakers as purveyors of a distinctly American aesthetic and as artistic precursors to the work of early twentieth-century modernists. Shaker religion was of interest to these individuals only in as much as it caused the membership to create particular physical forms.

This chapter also foregrounds William Winter, a remarkable figure whose creative contributions the Andrewses sought to marginalize. Following their lead, other chroniclers have chosen to understand this reserved man, who died prematurely, as a product of the Andrewses' enthusiasm.[2] By close examination of Winter's photographic oeuvre and an expansion of his biography, this chapter argues that his talent and vision were central to the creation of a canonical "Shaker style" during this time. Winter's influential images were the product of his professional identity as a photographer for General Electric as well as his desire to transcend the limitations of his professional identity.

Understanding these Shaker exhibitions within their institutional contexts also provides insights into patterns within the Andrewses' careers. The manner in which they gained, and later rejected, the patronage of first Adams, then Bragg, and then sequentially Force foreshadows their later interactions with the Index of American Design, Yale University, and eventually Amy Bess Miller, the founding president of Shaker Community, Inc., the nonprofit that preserved Hancock Shaker Village. In each instance, the collectors opportunistically sought institutional backing that would advantageously showcase their ever-changing collection of Shaker artifacts and promote their careers as experts with specialized knowledge of the Shakers. As they worked with, and learned from, Adams, Bragg, and Force, over time Faith and Edward Deming Andrews cemented their status as Shaker experts and increased the monetary value of their holdings.

CHARLES C. ADAMS AND THE NEW YORK STATE MUSEUM

When in 1926 the New York State commissioner of education appointed Charles C. Adams to serve as the director of the New York State Museum in Albany, the institution, located on the top floor of the State Education Building near the state capitol, was largely a scientific enterprise that held zoologic, botanic, and geologic specimens.[3] An influential ecologist, having earned a B.S. from Illinois Wesleyan in 1895, an M.S. from Harvard University in 1899, and a Ph.D. in zoology from the University of Chicago in 1908, Adams was well qualified for this position.[4] He had previously served from 1903 to 1906 as museum curator at the University of Michigan and as director of the Cincinnati Society of Natural History from 1908 to 1914.[5] Immediately before taking the post in Albany, he had served on the faculty of the New York State College of Forestry in Syracuse.

Adams was a prolific scholar with an impressive publication record. His *Guide to the Study of Animal Ecology*, published in 1913, was particularly influential.[6] In 1956, the respected zoologist Ralph S. Palmer observed that this volume ranked "among the most important pioneer ecological treatises done in North America."[7] Adams focused particularly on zoogeography, the scholarly investigation of the spatial location of animals. One of his most important studies examined distribution patterns of different varieties of snails within the *Io* genus, which lived in the waterways feeding into the Tennessee River in Virginia, Tennessee, and Alabama.[8] He was similarly the lead author (possibly because his last name began with A) of an extensive article, appearing in three parts in the first volume of the journal *Ecology*, which addresses the plants and animals of New York's Mount Marcy.[9] In this article, Adams and his coauthors explained that they endeavored to "learn more of the relation of plants and animals to their environment."[10] Adams's interdisciplinary approach to scholarship is indicated by the fact that he was a founding member, and later president, of the Ecological Society of America; an active contributor to the Association of American Geographers; and a charter participant in the American Association of Museums.[11]

When he arrived at the New York State Museum, Adams found the institution's historical and archeological collections disappointing. Although Theodore Roosevelt had asserted in 1916, at the opening of the museum's new space, that it should be a "museum of arts and letters as well as a museum of natural history" and that the collections should offer "a full representation of American history since the time when New York cast off its provincial character and became an integral portion of the American republic," Adams communicated in his first report as director that "these collections have not grown . . . as their merit would lead one to expect."[12] The historical collections languished at least in part because the museum budget did not provide funds for acquisitions or to pay for a staff member dedicated to the state's heritage.[13] Much of the historical material the museum held had been transferred to the institution in 1901 by the New York State Fair Commission and was composed of artifacts collected by the New York State Agricultural Society for a museum that was later suspended. Since the institution did not have staff dedicated to either history or art, Chris A. Hartnagel, the assistant state geologist, voluntarily oversaw the historical collection when he could spare time from his other duties.[14]

During the spring of 1927, as part of the recognition of the sesquicentennial of the Revolutionary War, New York State legislators began to advocate for an alternative and separate state-sponsored historic institution that would assume responsibility for the museum's historical collections. As an administrator, Adams rightfully saw this as a threat to the future of his institution. He indicated that such a plan, if it had succeeded, would have "seriously injured the Museum."[15] To reinforce his museum's position and secure its future as the repository for the state's historical artifacts, Adams began to build collections and pursue more robustly that aspect of the institution's mission. He hoped that the celebration of the nation's sesquicentennial would arouse the public's interest in the past and secure the museum's stability as a repository for the state's heritage.

Within a few months, Adams was presented with a remarkable opportunity to build a noteworthy collection of artifacts and thus stave off this threat to his institution. Dr. A. C. Flick, the state historian, shared with Adams a letter written by Caroline Mallary Marvin Spicer that had been printed in the *Troy Record*. She bemoaned that no proper authority was managing the records belonging to the Shaker village of Watervliet, just outside of Albany, which was closing down and being repurposed by the county.[16] Adams read Spicer's complaint as a call to action and an opportunity that would allow him to fulfill the museum's mission of collecting and interpreting the state's history while strategically improving the institution's holdings of artifacts.[17]

Albany County had acquired portions of the declining Watervliet Shaker Village in 1924 so that the real estate could be used as a charitable home and regional airport.[18] Adams contacted Leo M. Doody, the county commissioner of charities, who was responsible for managing the property. Doody understood the materials in the Shaker village to be excess goods cluttering up buildings that he was about to demolish.[19] Adams thus deputized Hartnagel to gather artifacts.[20] Almost from the beginning, Adams envisioned presenting this material to the public. In July 1927, he wrote, "At some future time, a good exhibit could be prepared."[21] Between July and November 1927, the museum repeatedly dispatched trucks to Watervliet to "harvest" Shaker materials and "place [them] under lock."[22] During these months Adams similarly instructed Edwin J. Stein, the museum's photographer, to record the compound and its contents.[23] As the fall progressed, Adams became increasingly aware that he was involved in an important undertaking. In November he wrote to William Thompson, the museum's regent, "The more we see of this, the more we are impressed with its real importance as an industrial exhibit."[24]

Individuals including John Patterson McClean of Ohio, Wallace Cathcart of the Western Reserve Historical Society, and Clara Endicott Sears, a wealthy resident of Massachusetts, collected Shaker materials before Adams. McClean and Cathcart both focused on published and textual materials while Sears added local materials from the Shaker village in Harvard,

Massachusetts, to an idiosyncratic installation of utopian and antiquarian materials on her hillside country estate.[25] Sears had also published a small volume entitled *Gleanings from Old Shaker Journals* in 1916.[26] Adams, with the institutional capacity of the New York State Museum behind him, surpassed all previous enthusiasts in the number, diversity, and scale of Shaker materials collected.

Adams's approach to the Shakers was essentially ecological.[27] He sought to understand how this community of religious believers functioned within its geographic, environmental, and economic contexts, just as he investigated how snails and mountain flora interacted with their surroundings. The Shaker artifacts Adams accessioned into the collections were meant to undergird the museum's historical mission, but they were also comparable to bivalve shells or moose antlers; they were remnants left behind by living things that provided evidence of how organisms were related to their environs. Thus, Adams built a collection that he described as "a very large number of objects, including looms, spinning wheels, several herb presses, handmade objects of wood and metal, old glass and stone ware and a series of samples of herbs in their original packages."[28] This accumulation of artifacts, which as early as March 1929 Adams strategically bragged could probably not be matched in any other museum in the country, was particularly rich in materials illustrating the Shakers' economic activities.

Stein, the museum's employee who had experience photographing biological specimens and wampum belts for the museum, produced workmanlike, documentary, black-and-white images of the Shaker village. His portraits of the Shaker meetinghouse and of a stone house that served as a sisters' workshop, both taken in three-quarter view to record two facades, provide visual references for the appearance of structures about to be demolished (figs. 1.1–1.2). His interior documentation of the village's schoolhouse illustrates a wall's lathe construction while also exhibiting the results of years of neglect. A photograph of a room crammed full with spinning wheels, baskets, trowels, flax breaks, work benches, and other artifacts serves as an inventory of the kinds of materials the museum acquired while documenting the disarray of a compound vacated by a failing organization (fig. 1.3). His rendering of a tape loom, taken outside on one of the village's walkways, provides insight into a manufacturing process by depicting the device's mechanisms, but the viewer's reading of the image is compromised by the overgrown grass and shuttered clapboard structure in the background (fig. 1.4). Although he produced seventy-seven useful and legible

FIGURE 1.1. Edwin J. Stein, "Old Church at the Shaker Settlement near Albany, N.Y.," 1927. Stein's photographs created for the New York State Museum document the buildings at Watervliet but did not seek to represent them artistically. Published by Charles C. Adams in the "Twenty-Third Report of the Director of the Division of Science and the State Museum." Courtesy Library of Congress, Prints & Photographs Division, Historic American Buildings Survey (HABS NY, 1-COL, 36—1).

FIGURE 1.2. Edwin J. Stein, "A Stone House at the Shaker Settlement near Albany, N.Y.," October 1927. Stein's photograph of Watervliet's Church Family sisters' workshop documents the facade of a building threatened with demolition. Published by Charles C. Adams in the "Twenty-Third Report of the Director of the Division of Science and the State Museum." Courtesy Library of Congress, Prints & Photographs Division, Historic American Buildings Survey (HABS NY, 1-COL, 28—1).

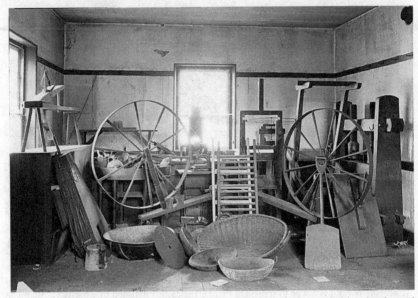

FIGURE 1.3. Edwin J. Stein, "A Part of the Historical Collection of Household and Industrial Materials, Secured for the State Museum from the Original American Shaker Settlement near Albany, N.Y.," 1927. Stein recorded surplus property that the New York State Museum was in the process of acquiring. Published by Charles C. Adams in the "Twenty-Second Report of the Director of the Division of the State Museum and Science Department." Courtesy New York State Museum, Albany, NY.

images, Stein was primarily concerned with recording ethnographic specimens, rather than with visual aesthetics.[29]

Similarly, Adams did not find beauty in the items he was acquiring. While
publishing Stein's photographs in his annual director's report to accompany
his account of the growth of the institution's Shaker holdings, he referred to
the items he was accessioning as "homely objects" and suggested that few
antique collectors would find much interest in them. He asserted, however,
that because of the Shakers' role in the region, the artifacts that had "accumulated about the farm" were of "considerable historic interest and value."[30]
In his next annual report, Adams proudly boasted that "the Shaker collection in the New York State Museum is the largest and the most important
one in any museum."[31]

Adams hired William L. Lassiter to assist with the expanded burden
of managing and caring for the museum's historical collections, including the newly acquired Shaker material. Lassiter, an Albany native who
had attended Hamilton College and Cornell University, was employed as

FIGURE 1.4. Edwin J. Stein, "Loom Used for Weaving Narrow Braids or Tapes of Cloth or Straw," 1927. Stein photographed Shaker machines as anthropological evidence and with little concern for photographic composition. Published by Charles C. Adams in "The New York State Museum's Historical Survey and Collection of the New York Shakers." Courtesy New York State Museum, Albany, NY.

a teacher at the school on the Shinnecock Indian Reservation on Long Island.[32] Because of his professional responsibilities during the school year, and because of the State Museum's limited budget, Lassiter was originally employed only during the summers.[33] A history buff with interests in whaling and Native American material culture, Lassiter had in his youth been acquainted with Watervliet's Shakers, including Elder Isaac Anstatt.[34] From his temporary seasonal employment, Lassiter eventually rose to the position of senior curator of art and history at the New York State Museum, becoming a recognized expert on Shaker history and culture.[35]

WILLIAM F. WINTER, JR.

Adams would later credit William F. Winter, Jr., with sparking his interest in and appreciation for the Shakers and Shaker material culture. Adams, moreover, claimed that Winter was his "chief adviser on Shaker matters."[36] Winter, who was born in Albany on October 10, 1899, was a resident of Schenectady, New York. His father was employed by General Electric (GE), a corporation that played a dominant role in that city's economy.[37] The 1920 U.S. Census indicates that the younger Winter, who was twenty at the time and had been educated in the public schools, also was working at GE as a clerk.[38] The 1930 census lists both men still in the company's employ, the elder as a model maker and his son as having advanced to the status of electrical engineer, reflecting the fact that he had taken courses offered by the corporation.[39]

While working at GE, however, William F. Winter, Jr., developed an interest in photography that would define his identity for the rest of his short life. According to Adams, Winter photographed the scenery of the Adirondacks as an avocation. "Possessed of a reflective mind," Adams wrote, "he devoted much thought also to the perfection of his technic [sic], no doubt greatly aided by his years of experience in the research laboratory."[40] The 1933 Schenectady directory indicates that Winter had successfully transformed his hobby into a vocation and lists his profession as photographer.[41] He continued to work for GE in this capacity, producing machine-age images of industrial equipment, products, and processes.[42] At this time, GE's institutional hierarchy included a Photographic Department, which employed photographers to generate images for a variety of public relations purposes. These industrial photographers used viewfinder cameras to create 8 x 10 inch plates that American Studies scholar David E. Nye has described as seemingly "more objective than artistic photography." GE's industrial photographs were produced with an aesthetic that emphasized sharp focus, a clear subject, and a composition which allowed the viewer to ignore the fact that the photographer had acted as a mediator.[43]

Winter's photographs represent the products and mechanisms of General Electric's plants within the parameters of the company's industrial photography. However, they also demonstrate an awareness of the two-dimensionality of the picture plane and celebrate form and massing. An image of voltage meters, published in GE's promotional pamphlet *When You Can Measure*, exhibits both Winter's fascination with repeating geometric forms and his utilization of shadows as compositional devices (fig. 1.5). A photograph of an electrical shunt manufactured by the firm shows Winter's love of shadows and uses an angled composition to emphasize the parallel and perpendicular lines inherent in the mechanism's fabric (fig. 1.6).

FIGURE 1.5. William F. Winter, Jr., "Small Panel Instruments—Dozens of Them, All Identical," ca. 1935. Winter's industrial photographs demonstrate an interest in geometry and repeated forms. Published in General Electric Company, *When You Can Measure: Story of General Electric Measuring Instruments* (Schenectady, NY: General Electric, n.d.). Courtesy MiSci, Museum of Innovation and Science, Schenectady, NY.

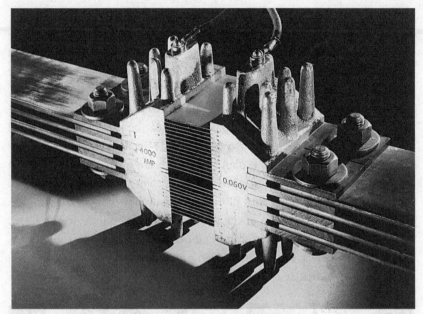

FIGURE 1.6. William F. Winter, Jr., "Massive but Accurate Shunts," ca. 1935. Even when photographing electrical equipment, Winter used lighting and cast shadows to positive effect and emphasized forms and lines intersecting at right angles. Published in General Electric Company, *When You Can Measure: Story of General Electric Measuring Instruments* (Schenectady, NY: General Electric, n.d.). Courtesy MiSci, Museum of Innovation and Science, Schenectady, NY.

Similarly, Winter, like other early twentieth-century modernist photographers, including Edward Weston and Barbara Morgan, created botanical images that demonstrate an awareness of pattern, symmetry, and organic form. Overall, his oeuvre shows that, although trained as an industrial photographer, Winter was aware of the modernist photographic conventions being created in the early twentieth century by artists including Weston, Morgan, Paul Strand, and Charles Sheeler.[44]

Although Winter created photographic compositions of machinery, flowers, tools, and other subject matter, his artistic output primarily focused on the Shakers, their buildings, and their material culture.[45] Beginning around 1923, the photographer visited with his camera the Shaker villages of Watervliet and Mount Lebanon in New York. In doing so, he recorded the villages while simultaneously training himself as a photographer. He would say later of what he called his "Shaker Portfolio" that its "growth and development coincided with the growth and development of the photographer himself as a photographer," and that it led "through a series of events almost miraculous in nature, to a complete and happy change of profession."[46] He also became acquainted with a number of the Shakers in these communities, notably Eldress Sarah Collins of the Mount Lebanon South Family, who gave him access to buildings that the community no longer used.[47]

In contrast to Stein, who was a professional charged by his employer to create a documentary visual record of the Shakers' material remains, Winter was using Shaker materials to explore the capabilities and inherent qualities of an artistic medium. He was not recording specimens; rather, he was seeking to use photography to express the majesty that he found in the Shaker villages.[48] Adams explained, "Winter was one of those who have been able to recognize the unusual values in our immediate environment. He saw beauty in the Shaker handicrafts and recognized the importance of their contribution to American life."[49] Winter, however, expressed this beauty in the conventions of the medium and the moment in which he was creating. His photographs of Shaker spaces revel in formal compositional devices, particularly flat surfaces, geometric forms, symmetry, and empty spaces.

During his explorations of New York's Shaker villages, Winter created stunning, carefully crafted compositions on large photographic plates with long exposures.[50] His April 1925 portrayal of the northwest corner of the second Shaker meetinghouse in Watervliet, New York, for example, is a particularly good sample of Winter's ability to represent Shaker architecture as abstract geometric compositions (fig. 1.7). The divisions of space created by the spindles of the railing echo the vertical rectangles of the doors and windows, which in turn are subdivided by mullions. The sun shining through the windows plays on the plane of the floor to create bright parallelograms stretching away at an acute angle from the dark wainscoting. Rectangular interior windows, meant to allow the Shaker ministry to observe the believers at worship, punctuate the far wall, adding yet another set of forms to this austere concatenation of quadrilaterals. This remarkable early photograph, which eloquently expresses Winter's aesthetic, presages the many later Shaker images reproduced repeatedly on which the photographer's artistic reputation rests.[51]

An image from approximately the same time of the interior of the carpenter's shop in New Lebanon, New York, although representing a cluttered

FIGURE 1.7. William F. Winter, Jr., "Northwest Corner of Meeting Room," April 1925. Meet-inghouse (second), Watervliet, NY. This early photograph, created five years before Winter met Faith and Edward Deming Andrews, demonstrates many characteristics he would later develop more fully. Courtesy Library of Congress, Prints & Photographs Division, Historic American Buildings Survey (HABS NY, 1-COL, 27–5).

space, similarly celebrates geometry (fig. 1.8). Symmetrical twelve-above-twelve sash windows flank a Shaker cabinet, which itself is divided into a series of balanced rectangular drawers and cabinet doors. Sets of built-in drawers on either side of the frame harmonize with the picture's central massing while the peg rail below the ceiling further geometrically divides the plane of the far wall. The stove in the foreground introduces curvilinear elements into the work, with its semicircular lip and tubular flue. Although the stove's cylindrical pipe stretches upward, before reaching the ceiling it bends to the right at a ninety-degree angle, thus forming a rectangle with the bottom and side margin in the lower right corner of the composition.[52]

Winter's April 1925 photograph of the herb press at the Watervliet village, which was subsequently also recorded by Edwin Stein, is concerned with the interplay of circles and rectangles (fig. 1.9). The press's grooved shafts and the teeth of the gears provide visual interest, while the brightly lit solid wooden beams contrast strikingly with dark, vacant, negative spaces. Yet,

FIGURE 1.8. William F. Winter, Jr., "Interior View of Carpenters' Shop," 1920s. Church Family Brethren's Workshop, New Lebanon, NY. Winter's image of a cluttered vacant Shaker workspace demonstrates his experimentation with symmetrical rectilinear compositions. Courtesy Library of Congress, Prints & Photographs Division, Historic American Buildings Survey (HABS NY, 11-NELEB.V, 4—4).

for all of its elegant composition, this image tells the observer almost nothing about the purpose of the machine or its function. While resembling one of Francis Picabia's Dadaist images of fanciful imaginary machines from the previous decade, Winter's photograph sheds little light on the agricultural or economic activities of the sect.

In photographing the sisters' workshop of the Watervliet Church Family in April 1925, Winter positioned his camera such that only a fraction of the near facade was included and the intersection of two walls created a border between light and shadow that almost equally divided the view (fig. 1.10). Unlike Stein's photograph of the same structure from two years later (fig. 1.2), Winter did not accentuate symmetry but once again filled the composition with multiple light and dark quadrilaterals, the granite lintels contrasting with the recessed, glazed fenestration. The bright lighting from the left creates a three-dimensional quality to the roofline while simultaneously obscuring the details of the building's eave facade by casting mottled

FIGURE 1.9. William F. Winter, Jr., "Interior View with Herb Press," April 1925. Church Family Herb House, Watervliet, NY. In this image from the middle of the 1920s, Winter has created a geometric composition of circles and rectangles. Courtesy Library of Congress, Prints & Photographs Division, Historic American Buildings Survey (HABS NY, 1-COL, 31—4).

tree shadows on it. While Stein provided Adams with a portrait of the same Shaker building, Winter produced an argument for the monumentality and grandeur of the sect's architecture.

Winter displayed a gift for creating strong compositions, even when producing intimate images of modest domestic spaces, such as his portrait of an iron stove located in the sewing room of the sisters' workshop of Watervliet's South Family (fig. 1.11). Created in the summer of 1930, this image emphasizes the geometry of the stove, with its planar and semicircular features punctuated by a cylindrical stove pipe emerging from its top. Although the stove's form is the primary focus of the photograph, the image demonstrates a strong verticality since Winter included multiple light and dark upright planes that harmonize with the metal flue, as does the wallpaper's pattern. The door, the door jamb, and the corner moulding (to which a match safe has been attached) all stretch upward out of the picture on the left side of the composition. Similarly, the partition on the right creates

FIGURE 1.10. William F. Winter, Jr., "View from Southwest," April 1925. Church Family Sisters' Workshop, Watervliet, NY. Unlike Stein's image of the same building, Winter's composition plays with light and shadow to emphasize geometry, line, and form. Courtesy Library of Congress, Prints & Photographs Division, Historic American Buildings Survey (HABS NY, 1-COL, 28—3).

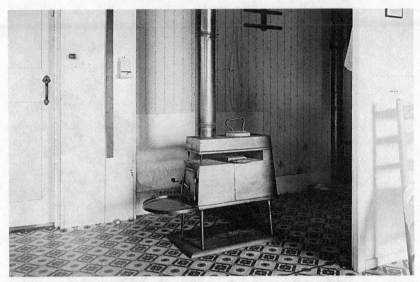

FIGURE 1.11. William F. Winter, Jr., "Stove in Sewing Room," summer 1930. Shaker South Family Sisters' Workshop, Watervliet, NY. This image by Winter documents the Shaker's use of wallpaper and patterned linoleum while simultaneously exhibiting the photographer's love of planes, shadows, and geometric forms. Courtesy Library of Congress, Prints & Photographs Division, Historic American Buildings Survey (HABS NY, 1-COL, 17—2).

a bright vertical plane. The ladder-back chair, just barely included in the lower right corner, generates a series of Winter's beloved rectangles, echoed by the rectilinear form of the clothes hanger, which intrudes down into the image from the top. Notably, when this image was created in 1930, this Shaker space, rather than being spare, was augmented with striped wallpaper and intricately patterned linoleum.

Although Winter was quiet and reserved, he and Adams became close through their mutual interest in the Shakers. Together they traveled around the region visiting Shaker villages so that Adams could augment the museum's collections and Winter could add new locations and vistas to his growing portfolio of images. Adams's daughter, Harriet Dyer Adams, recalled picnicking with the two men in the meadow below the New Lebanon Shaker Village.[53]

FAITH AND EDWARD DEMING ANDREWS

While pursuing their related, but distinct, fascinations with the Shakers, Adams and Winter eventually encountered Faith and Edward Deming

Andrews, who were pursuing a parallel journey.[54] How Adams and Winter came into contact with the Andrewses is unclear. Faith Andrews asserted that her husband met Winter at a Shaker village, although at different times she offered conflicting accounts that this meeting occurred in New Lebanon, New York, and in Hancock, Massachusetts.[55] A letter at the New York State Museum from Adams to Winter, however, indicates that the Andrewses sought out Adams in February 1930 after Sister Jennie Wells of Mount Lebanon informed them of the museum's growing collection of Shaker materials.[56]

Natives of Pittsfield, Massachusetts, the Andrewses had been aware of the Shakers their entire lives. Having received a B.A. from Amherst College in 1916, Edward married Faith Young in 1921.[57] While he taught at private schools and pursued a doctorate in education at Yale University, the two made ends meet by buying and selling American antiques out of Ted's family home in Pittsfield.[58] In Faith Andrews's words, at first the couple focused on "colonial and post-colonial artifacts."[59] In the Berkshires they bought and sold the American domestic materials, including Queen Anne furniture, highboys, and paintings, for which collectors, dealers, and institutions had created a market in the preceding decades.[60]

Christian Goodwillie, a former curator at Hancock Shaker Village and one of the Andrewses' most recent biographers, asserts that the couple's fascination with the sect and its material culture began in late 1923 when they stopped at the Church Family dwelling house in Hancock, Massachusetts, to buy a loaf of bread. From that moment, over the ensuing decades, the Andrewses were actively engaged with, according to Goodwillie, "buying, selling, and trading Shaker materials."[61] With a business in Pittsfield, they were well situated to secure excess furniture from the villages in Hancock and New Lebanon and disperse it at a profit to those without such easy geographic access.[62] In 1981, Dorothy Miller, who served as curator of the Museum of Modern Art and knew the couple for decades, remembered that the couple were "constantly buying and selling."[63] Ted and Faith Andrews may have sought out Adams at the New York State Museum in 1930 with the hope that his institution would buy objects they had acquired and wanted to peddle.

The couple, who functioned as an economic and social unit, worked within an early twentieth-century patriarchal view of marriage. Although Faith was ambitious, competent, and had strong opinions, Ted held the high-status educational degrees and served as the couple's public face.

Together they revealed complex personalities and pursued multiple motivations. While serving as conduits through which Shaker materials moved from declining villages into the profane, public realm, they inspired both admiration and condemnation.[64]

As antique dealers, the Andrewses initially focused on the Shaker domestic furnishings (what Ted Andrews called in 1957 "household furniture"), which had the closest analogs to commodities with already proven resale value.[65] The antiques market privileged items that could be used in buyers' homes. Shaker chairs, trestle tables, candlestands, and case pieces all could be resold as attractive, useful, and less expensive than high-style antiques or new designer furnishings. Herb presses, tape looms, and the other manufacturing equipment that Adams was gathering for the New York State Museum's collections, however, could not be resold as easily and thus was not initially as interesting to the Andrewses.

The Andrewses retailed items to individuals but also served as pickers who supplied stock to other established antique dealers.[66] Eventually, the Andrewses even came to place their "Old Shaker Furniture" in "Altman's Country Shop," located in the B. Altman & Co. Department Store in New York City.[67] Dorothy Miller purchased from Altman's antique furniture department what she described as "an extraordinary tall narrow chest of drawers" that had passed through the couple's collection.[68] At times the dealers refinished Shaker items to make them more marketable.[69] Later in their careers, as they attempted to burnish their image, the Andrewses would disavow their entrepreneurial roots. In 1961, for example, Faith Andrews told the *New Haven Register,* "We bought only to collect, never to sell."[70]

As their business began to focus exclusively on Shaker material, the Pittsfield couple sought to educate themselves about the items that comprised their stock. In doing so, they discovered that the secondary literature on the topic was exceedingly sparse. As they recounted in their memoir, "No one knew the history of their chair industry, nor when and by whom the furnishings of the community dwellings and shops were produced."[71] They therefore turned to other collectors and to primary sources. In a 1926 letter, Clara Endicott Sears, who had acquired Shaker artifacts as part of her fascination with New England's alternative religions and utopias, informed them that her holdings had not been documented in book form and suggested to the couple that they might visit her compound on Prospect Hill in Harvard, Massachusetts, when the weather improved.[72]

As subscribers to the *Magazine Antiques,* founded in 1922 to provide reliable information to collectors, dealers, and connoisseurs, the couple corresponded with Homer Eaton Keyes, the journal's editor.[73] Keyes, a former English professor and astute businessman, nurtured writers who could contribute to his periodical. He recognized that these dealers from western Massachusetts had developed a specialized knowledge and solicited text from them.[74]

With Keyes's assistance, the Andrewses published two seminal articles about Shaker furniture in the *Magazine Antiques* in August 1928 and April 1929, just as the American economy was unwinding. Entitled respectively "Craftsmanship of an American Religious Sect: Notes on Shaker Furniture" and "The Furniture of an American Religious Sect," these articles, illustrated with items from the Andrewses' holdings, provided the journal's readers with an introduction to Shaker furniture.[75] The articles emphasized how little was actually known about the topic and provided examples of various forms, information about the time period and region in which the furniture was produced, and data concerning the colors of the objects' patina. The first article, in which Ted Andrews's middle initial appears incorrectly, boldly asserted that Shaker objects were the "direct expression of the life and thought of a whole group of people" while also claiming the designs were "a natural expression of a natural need."[76] The authors thus simultaneously linked these objects to religious identity and mystified their production by deemphasizing the agency of the individuals who made them. Indicating progress in the dealers' research while also providing attributions that might raise the value of individual articles, the second essay listed the names of "men of skill," allegedly "attuned to the Shaker spirit of simplicity," who trained apprentices who thereafter anonymously copied their masters' work.[77] Decorative arts scholar John Kirk has noted that the first of these articles functioned to embed Shaker furniture within larger American joinery traditions, while the second intellectually separates the Shakers and their furniture from the outside world.[78]

Purporting to deliver fresh scholarly information related to a newly discovered aspect of the American patrimony, these articles, written by dealers and published in a magazine for collectors, exude an air of refined salesmanship. The first text celebrates the "high standards of excellence" of anonymous Shaker craftsmen and notes the existence of "many enthusiastic collectors of specimens of this interesting craft."[79] The second concludes by calling attention to the "restrained charm and sound workmanship which resides in even the commonest of Shaker pieces."[80] In addition to providing historical insight, these texts promoted consumerist desire in readers and thus boosted the market for Shaker furniture.

Although they illustrate examples of what would become canonical Shaker forms, the images accompanying these two early articles are surprisingly unsophisticated (figs. 1.12–1.15). They are neither Stein's documentary views of ethnographic specimens nor Winter's stylized geometric photographic compositions. The chairs, tables, beds, and case pieces that form their subject have been removed from any historical context and placed against neutral backgrounds. Consistently photographed from a position above the right front corner of the object being documented, these naive black-and-white images were probably produced by the couple themselves, possibly in their house in Pittsfield. In many of the images, folds and ripples are evident in the cloth draped under and behind the furniture. These photographs, like others that the couple produced of Shaker furnishings in

FIGURE 1.12. "Shaker Chairs," 1928. This naive, amateurish photograph demonstrates the visual competence of the Andrewses before they met Winter. Illustration from Edward A. and Faith Andrews, "Craftsmanship of an American Religious Sect: Notes on Shaker Furniture," *Magazine Antiques* 14, no. 2 (August 1928): 132. Courtesy *Magazine Antiques*.

and around their house in Pittsfield, might have been useful for communicating to their clientele about the latest acquisitions available for purchase.[81] Keyes subsequently queried Andrews, "Have you any idea where we could get hold of a competent photographer?"[82]

Thus, when Adams took Winter to Pittsfield to meet the Andrewses in the spring of 1930, the group convened with a shared interest in Shaker material culture but with three distinct backgrounds and perspectives on it. Adams, the museum director, understood Shaker material culture as an ecological response to the human geography of New York State and sought to preserve evidence of what he perceived to be a disappearing culture. He simultaneously endeavored to strengthen and expand his museum's historical collections. William Winter found beauty in the Shaker environment and used the Shaker villages to create modernist, two-dimensional

FIGURE 1.13. "Small Tables or Light Stands," 1928. Shaker tables presented unimaginatively in a photograph from the *Magazine Antiques*. Illustration from Edward A. and Faith Andrews, "Craftsmanship of an American Religious Sect: Notes on Shaker Furniture," *Magazine Antiques* 14, no. 2 (August 1928): 134. Courtesy *Magazine Antiques*.

FIGURE 1.14. "Wall Table," 1929. Curious shadows and wrinkles in the cloth under the table distract from the viewers' appreciation of this Shaker table. Illustration from Edward D. and Faith Andrews, "The Furniture of an American Religious Sect," *Magazine Antiques* 15, no. 4 (April 1929): 293. Courtesy *Magazine Antiques*.

compositions that both brought recognition to the sect and advanced his career transition from electrical engineer to photographer while employed by GE. Faith and Edward Deming Andrews through their activities as dealers had become aware of an unexploited aspect of the American antiques market and, with the assistance of Keyes, had taken initial steps toward establishing themselves as experts in this arcane specialty.

FIGURE 1.15. "Tailor's Bench, from Hancock," 1929. The amateur quality of the photograph makes it difficult to understand this tailor's bench as a desirable antique. Illustration from Edward D. and Faith Andrews, "The Furniture of an American Religious Sect," *Magazine Antiques* 15, no. 4 (April 1929): 293. Courtesy *Magazine Antiques*.

THE COMMUNITY INDUSTRIES OF THE SHAKERS

Together this group decided that it would be advantageous to mount an exhibition of Shaker materials at the New York State Museum. In his annual report for the period ending June 30, 1930, Adams wrote that the show occurred "at Mr. Winter's suggestion and with the hearty cooperation of Dr. and Mrs. Edward D. Andrews," however it benefited all the parties.[83] For Adams, the exhibition demonstrated that the museum was fulfilling its mission and allowed him to spotlight the collections he had been building. For Winter, it showcased his work and provided institutional validation for his developing pictorial abilities. For the Andrewses, the exhibition provided an opportunity to exhibit the materials that they had gathered, and confirmed their status as experts on the Shakers, although they were not paid for their involvement. Ted Andrews completed his doctorate in education in 1930, and from that point onward employed the honorific "Dr." before his name, but did not immediately find employment.[84] In the harsh economic climate following the crash of the stock market in October 1929, when jobs for academics and for teachers were scarce, the Andrewses, who were never economically secure, had free time to invest in the project.[85] While the group collaborated on the exhibition, Adams and Winter were also otherwise employed.

As the group was preparing the exhibition, the museum simultaneously continued to collect Shaker objects from Watervliet, with the assistance of Eldress Anna Case and Sister Jennie Wells, and also from the Mount Lebanon Church Family through Sister Sadie Neale and Sister Emma Neale. Both Winter and the Andrewses assisted in securing objects from Mount Lebanon. Again, Adams emphasized in his reports that he was salvaging "large amounts of industrial materials, which do not interest antique dealers."[86] At the same time, the museum augmented its collection by purchasing items directly from the Andrewses.[87] As had happened previously, during the summer, Lassiter assisted with processing and cataloging these acquisitions.[88]

The Community Industries of the Shakers opened to the public on June 17, 1930, in the museum's space atop the State Education Building. Walter Rendell Storey of the *New York Times* would later assert that it was "the first exhibition devoted to [Shaker] works."[89] Photographs of the installation by Edwin J. Stein, the museum's photographer, reveal a show that uneasily balanced the priorities of the collaborators. Photographic, industrial, and household interpretations of the sect were displayed in parallel, largely segregated spaces. Winter loaned photographs of Watervliet and New Lebanon, which were mounted on vertical exhibition furniture and displayed in glass-top cabinets (fig. 1.16). The museum's collections of materials relating to the herb industry were installed to present a simulacrum of the interior of an industrial workshop (fig. 1.17). A third space was filled with materials, largely loaned by Dr. and Mrs. Andrews, to illustrate the sect's "household arts" (fig. 1.18). This third area, defined by coverlets and other textiles hung around the walls, also featured items that formed the backbone of the Shaker antique trade including chairs, tables, case pieces, a cast-iron stove, peg boards, and a spinning wheel, the most important icon of the American Colonial Revival. The latter two components of the exhibition can be read as gendered, with the economics of the herb industry and its engagement with the outside world of commerce coded as masculine and the "household" area surrounded by textiles and focused on life within the community understood as feminine.

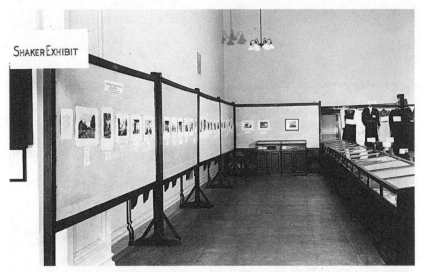

FIGURE 1.16. Edwin J. Stein, "Photographs Displayed by William F. Winter in Connection with the State Museum Temporary Exhibit Illustrating History and Industries of the Shaker Colonies in New York," 1930. Winter's photographs comprise a distinct segment of the New York State Museum's Shaker exhibit. Published by Charles C. Adams in "Twenty-Fifth Report of the Director of the Division of Science and the State Museum." Courtesy New York State Museum, Albany, NY.

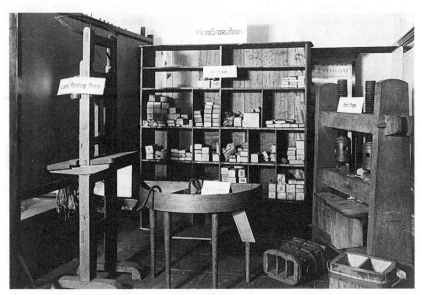

FIGURE 1.17. Edwin J. Stein, "Objects Illustrating the Herb Industry at the Shaker Settlements in New York," 1930. Because of Charles Adams's interest in human ecology, the New York State Museum's early Shaker exhibition sought to reproduce Shaker industrial spaces. Published by Charles C. Adams in "Twenty-Fifth Report of the Director of the Division of Science and the State Museum." Courtesy New York State Museum, Albany, NY.

FIGURE 1.18. Edwin J. Stein, "Another View of the Room Showing Shaker Household Arts, as Displayed in the State Museum Temporary Exhibit," 1930. In the New York State Museum's early Shaker exhibit, the sect's furniture and decorative arts were displayed as examples of local economic history rather than as art or fine antiques. Published by Charles C. Adams in "Twenty-Fifth Report of the Director of the Division of Science and the State Museum." Courtesy New York State Museum, Albany, NY.

In publicity materials and text labels mounted on the exhibit walls, the museum identified the chronological scope of the exhibition as spanning the period from 1800 to 1825. Yet there is no indication that Adams or the Andrewses had firm evidence for dating the objects on display to this era. Many of Winter's photographs were actually of structures built after this period. Moreover, the exhibit did not engage, explicitly or implicitly, with historical development over this time frame. Rather than being based on transformative historical factors, this eccentric periodization seems to have served primarily to identify the sect as being representative of a distant, romantic, preindustrial, and apparently ahistoric past.

In describing the exhibit for the *New York State Museum Bulletin,* Andrews claimed that the show called "attention to one of the most significant experiments in communistic living ever attempted on this continent." He also emphasized the "merit and variety of the work done by Shaker sisters" in producing textiles. Although his description of the exhibition is largely a list of its contents, the preliminary and rudimentary interpretation he offered tends toward local history or history of technology (although in both cases without hard dates), with an emphasis on manufacturing processes and economic niches.

Andrews's description of the exhibit is as noteworthy, however, for what it does not say as for what it argues. Most strikingly, although Winter's photographs filled almost a third of the exhibit's square footage, Andrews made no mention of them. This oversight might be the result of Winter's curating his own section of the exhibition and thus Andrews not feeling invested or involved in that portion, or it may be the result of an obsession with Shaker objects which meant that Andrews could not recognize or value Winter's photographic contribution. Andrews's commentary on this early exhibition is also remarkable for the absence of the rhetorical flourishes concerning simplicity, austere beauty, and clarity of design that later were commonplace. Although his description includes an inventory of objects in the exhibit, they are listed by function and category, rather than as exemplary specimens of decorative art.[90] As an introduction to the first significant exhibition of Shaker material culture sponsored by an established museum, this text by Andrews indicates that he had not yet begun to think of his collection in terms of aesthetics and formal qualities. Under the influence of Keyes and Adams, he understood the items in his collection primarily in terms of their historical significance and economic function.

Stein's installation photographs support this reading of Andrews's description of the exhibit. In our own time, viewers are shocked by the primitive state of museological practice represented in these images, with hanging historic textiles supporting their own weight and handwritten labels affixed directly to the objects on display. Design historians Stephen Bowe and Peter Richmond describe the installation as "cluttered and . . . poorly arranged" and note that "the exhibit designers do not seem to have been tempted to place everything into room settings."[91] Stein's images, however, also indicate that the artifacts, arranged to resemble period rooms or demonstrate use, are not being displayed as art objects. In these jumbled and disorderly settings, they are evidence of a culture but not manifestations of an aesthetic sensibility. Winter's photographs, with their modern compositions that used Shaker materials to emphasize form and tonality, were demarcated from the rest of the exhibition by a line of wooden display cases and rendered invisible in Andrews's introduction to the exhibition, thus marginalizing the photographer's artistic rendering of the Shaker legacy.

In October 1930, the museum published a pamphlet to accompany the exhibition.[92] Entitled *The New York Shakers and Their Industries,* this brochure is composed of text by Andrews, who is identified as holding a Ph.D., and images by Stein of the installation and of the Shaker village of Watervliet. Andrews's words focus on textile manufacture and the herb industry and conclude with a bibliography of eight items. Furniture is not discussed, except to say that the chairs, table, and stool on display were made at Mount Lebanon and were "characteristic Shaker products." Surprisingly, but following the pattern established by Andrews's description in the director's annual report, the author made no mention of Winter or his photographs, even though Stein's image of their installation is included as the brochure's first figure.

Although originally conceived as a short-term, temporary installation, this tripartite show was successful enough that its run was extended for a full two years. This first, important Shaker exhibit at the New York State Museum finally closed on July 1, 1932.[93] However, its influence was increased by a second publication suggested by Andrews, which he planned to not be a "superficial survey" but rather a "definitive investigation which shall be comprehensive in scope and complete in detail."[94] Adams lent the museum's backing to this publication because, as he asserted, he was eager to have "such studies printed in our . . . series."[95] Although Andrews and Adams planned the publication early in 1931, because of financial constraints the museum did not publish it until 1933.

The Community Industries of the Shakers, with authorship credited to Edward D. Andrews, was released by the New York State Museum as number 15 in its series of handbooks. This volume was the first in the series dedicated to a historical topic; all previous handbooks had addressed botany, geology, zoology, or paleontology.[96] In their memoir, the Andrewses claimed that writing this volume moved them forward as scholars and taught them the discipline of using primary sources as evidence.[97]

Having been stripped of the regional and period specificity of the exhibition and its earlier brochure, *Community Industries of the Shakers* expanded and built on the earlier publication to create a compendium of data concerning Shaker economic activity. Based largely on data related to New Lebanon, it sought to depict a larger reality by arguing "each of the Shaker Villages was like the others."[98] Using a variety of sources, including many manuscripts in his own possession, Andrews discussed agricultural pursuits and manufacturing. Within the former category, he documented the sale of packaged seeds, medicinal herbs, and dried and preserved food. The latter included the production of brooms, containers (such as baskets, boxes, and buckets), brushes, and furniture. Along the way, he also touched on the production by "the Shaker sisters" of textiles and clothing. Throughout, Andrews celebrated what he called "the continuous economic success of every branch of agriculture and manufacturing."[99] The author apparently was not struck by the irony of the fact that the sect whose success he was trumpeting had been shrinking and becoming increasingly moribund for decades.

Written in the midst of the collapse of the American economy, *Community Industries of the Shakers* presented the Shakers as a praiseworthy industrial system and an example of "progressive business enterprise, on the plan of joint interest."[100] Possibly foreshadowing Franklin Delano Roosevelt's New Deal ideology, Andrews suggested that American industrialism would be improved if it more closely resembled the Shakers and adopted reliance on cooperative methods and a "religious actuation" of economic life.[101] Moreover, Andrews contended that Shaker prosperity was based on an economy managed by conscientious leaders guided by devotion to God and to the good of the community. This critique of the free-market capitalist economy is particularly piquant when it is placed in the context of the Hoovervilles, breadlines, and nascent dustbowl migration of the period in which it was written.

Andrews's text was generously illustrated with sixty-five black-and-white figures, most of them photographs by Stein and Winter. *Community Industries* included many images that had previously appeared in New York State Museum publications, including Stein's photographs of Watervliet and of the 1930 exhibition installation (figs. 1.1, 1.17). The book also, however, incorporated new images, possibly produced specifically for the publication, which set a new standard for how Shaker material culture would be represented.

The most noteworthy of the book's new figures were William Winter photographs of Shaker objects owned by the Andrewses, which place these artifacts within austere, geometric Shaker rooms. Figure 23 from the book, for example, presents a Shaker cobbler's bench from New Lebanon's Second Family, identified as being from the Andrews collection (fig. 1.19). As with the photographs that the Andrewses used to accompany their articles in

FIGURE 1.19. William F. Winter, Jr., "Early Cobbler's Bench, with Lid of Cabinet Down, Showing Drawers and Compartments," ca. 1931. In this image, Winter and Andrews have recorded objects from the Andrewses' collection within a vacant Shaker building. Published in Edward D. Andrews, *The Community Industries of the Shakers*, fig. 23. Courtesy New York State Museum, Albany, NY.

the *Magazine Antiques,* the item being documented has been photographed at an angle from above the right front corner. Rather than being placed against a wrinkled sheet or other blank background, however, this bench has been located within a spare architectural space defined by a wooden floor and white plaster wall. The diagonal position of the bench cuts across the parallel lines of the floor's planks. Cobbler's lasts are lined up carefully in alignment with the bench, thus also rebelling against the geometry of the floor. A shaker peg rail slashes across the work, both identifying the ascetic space as belonging to the sect and dividing an elongated white rectangle from the main section of the photograph. As this rail could easily have been edited out if the photographer had desired a close shot of the bench, it must be understood as an important element of an artistic composition. This deceptively simple documentary photograph of a cobbler's bench, redolent of Winter's love of quadrilaterals and planar surfaces, elevates its subject matter through its artistic construction. The contrast between this work and the amateurish photographs the Andrewses submitted to the *Magazine Antiques* is telling.

Winter similarly photographed a wool spinning wheel in the corner of a Shaker room with white walls and a wooden floor and included it in *Community Industries* (fig. 1.20).[102] Like Winter's earlier photograph of the herb press (fig. 1.9), this composition is an investigation of the geometric interactions of circles and rectangles. Within the visual context of the receding wall planes, the string that connects the large wheel to the base of the spindle suggests an optical illusion of a cone. While a photographic representation of a spinning wheel within a bare room, the multiple geometric shapes, including the cone, the circles, the rectangles of the walls and floor, and the truncated acute triangle formed by the ceiling (which is echoed by the white space below the spinning wheel's body) easily dissolves into abstraction if the viewer loses focus on the pictorial content.

Figure 60 in the book, an image of a slat-back rocking chair, has all of the common elements of this series (fig. 1.21). The Shaker object is positioned on a wooden floor in front of a white wall punctuated at the top by a peg rail. The negative spaces created by the chair's legs, stretchers, and splats form quadrilaterals that harmonize with those of its surroundings. In this incidence, however, the photographer has introduced an additional compositional element by placing a rectangular rug under the chair. The dark stripes in the rug, along with the cracks in the floor and the back stiles of the

FIGURE 1.20. William F. Winter, Jr., "Shaker Spinning Wheel, Sometimes Called a Wool or Great Wheel; from New Lebanon," ca. 1931. Winter photographed this spinning wheel from the Andrews collection against the backdrop of a vacant Shaker building to create a modernist geometric composition. Published in Edward D. Andrews, *The Community Industries of the Shakers*, fig. 34. Courtesy New York State Museum, Albany, NY.

FIGURE 1.21. William F. Winter, Jr., "Arm Rocking-Chair from the New Lebanon Church Family," ca. 1931. By combining a rocking chair with a rug and placing it within a vacant Shaker room, Winter and Andrews created a complex image that is a geometric photographic abstraction while also gesturing toward interior design and historical documentation. Published in Edward D. Andrews, *The Community Industries of the Shakers*, fig. 60. Courtesy New York State Museum, Albany, NY.

chair, form vertical elements in the composition that create tension with the horizontal lines formed by the near edge of the rug, the foot moulding, the chair's splats, and the peg rail.

The rug's placement transforms the photograph in another fashion as well. While the images of the cobbler's bench and the spinning wheel are still obviously documentary photographs of furniture taken within an empty room, the composition of the chair and rug begs to be understood not as a portrait of a chair but rather as representing a room. This image, with its multiple related furnishings within a defined space, can now be understood as interior design, as not recording craftsmanship but as portraying an aesthetic.[103] The spare, plain, austere taste conveyed in this image did not originate with the Shakers, however; Winter, the photographer, contrived it by arranging Shaker materials within an unused and unoccupied Shaker space.

The aesthetic Winter created out of Shaker objects within a Shaker space is not an artistic construction inherent to the sect itself. This can be

FIGURE 1.22. William F. Winter, Jr., "Sewing Room," ca. summer 1930. Shaker South Family, Sisters' Workshop, Watervliet, NY. Winter's image of a Shaker room with patterned linoleum, ornamental carpets, and jigsaw woodwork in the archway contrasts with the spare simplicity of figure 1.21. Courtesy Library of Congress, Prints & Photographs Division, Historic American Buildings Survey (HABS NY, 1-COL, 17—1).

understood by comparing the image of the chair and the rug within a sparse room to a photograph that Winter took in the summer of 1930 of the South Family's sewing room at Watervliet (fig. 1.22). This room, which includes the stove seen in figure 1.11, has patterned materials applied to the floor, walls, and ceilings but has the characteristic peg rail only in the antechamber. Jigsaw-cut foliation ornaments the door, and the room includes no less than three patterned ornamental throw rugs. Shakers lived in this space, not in the ascetic rectilinear fantastic composition with the rocking chair and the rug that was published in a guidebook meant to explain the Shakers to the American public. Having developed an appealing visual formula for powerful, attractive simulations of Shaker interior design for this 1933 publication, Winter (and the Andrewses) reproduced it repeatedly in the years to come.

LAURA BRAGG AND THE BERKSHIRE MUSEUM

Following the success of *The Community Industries of the Shakers*, Andrews and Winter collaborated on a second exhibition installed at the Berkshire Museum in Pittsfield, Massachusetts, from October 10–30, 1932.[104] This exhibition, once again combining objects from the Andrewses' collection with Winter's photographs, was organized by Laura Bragg, the museum's progressive and iconoclastic new director.[105]

In 1931, Zenas Marshall Crane, a local philanthropist and industrialist, hired Bragg to revitalize the Berkshire Museum, which his family had been funding since the first decade of the twentieth century.[106] Bragg, a Massachusetts native and daughter of a reform-minded Methodist minister, was trained as a librarian at Simmons College in Boston, graduating in 1906.[107] While at Simmons, she was influenced by the Museum of Fine Arts, the Museum of the Boston Society of Natural History (where she interned), and the institution being formed in the Fenway by Isabella Stewart Gardner.[108] Bragg's first job after graduation, as a librarian on Orr's Island, Maine, convinced her that public institutions could be active agents of education and uplift. While there, she collected examples of local flora to create the Orr's Island Museum.[109] In 1909, Paul Rea, a biology professor at the College of Charleston who simultaneously served as the director of the Charleston Museum, in Charleston, South Carolina, recruited Bragg to work with that museum's collections of books and natural specimens.[110] She quickly rose to positions of responsibility at the institution by organizing and building collections while also instituting programs informed by the progressive educational ideology of John Dewey.[111]

A New Woman of the early twentieth century, Bragg was not constrained by patriarchal gender roles or traditional family structures and never married.[112] In 1920, she succeeded Rea as the director of the Charleston Museum, becoming the first woman in the nation to head a publicly supported museum of history and science.[113] Using the Charleston Museum as a bully pulpit, she rose to national prominence. With a grant funded by the Laura Spellman Rockefeller Memorial, she conducted a survey of southern museums, she taught museum administration at Columbia University, and she was brought in as a consultant to revitalize Richmond's Valentine Museum.[114] She also advocated for professional training and status for museum workers. In 1927, the *Charleston Evening Post* quoted her as claiming that "a modern museum must have a well trained staff . . . so that the public may learn of the peoples who created the art, and not look upon it as a dry example of work long since accomplished."[115] Bragg argued that museums could become a vital factor in the life of a community if they created an environment in which the public learned about the art and artifacts being displayed.

As the director of a municipal museum, Bragg became involved in the local art and culture scene and became a proponent of the importance of regional identity and material culture. She was active in Charleston's Society for the Preservation of Old Dwellings and worked to get the Joseph Manigault House donated to the Charleston Museum so that it could be opened for tours. Under her leadership, the museum also became a repository of local architectural fragments from structures being demolished.[116] Bragg's efforts brought regional and then national recognition to the work of Dave Drake, an enslaved potter of the antebellum period, and the ceramic products of South Carolina's Edgefield District.[117] As she had on Orr's Island, Bragg used indigenous resources to assist the local population in educating themselves about their surroundings.

Upon her arrival at the Berkshire Museum, Bragg sought to transform a sleepy repository of paintings and biological specimens associated with the local public library into a functioning educational institution encompassing art, culture, and natural history. She quickly instituted educational programming and implemented a schedule of rotating exhibitions. An early installation, which the *Springfield Republican* trumpeted as opening "a new era" in the Berkshires, featured contemporary American art loaned by New York's Grand Central Art Galleries.[118] This show included works by John Singer Sargent, Hunt Diederich, Daniel Chester French, Frederick Mac-Monnies, and F. Luis Mora.[119] The next summer she opened an exhibition of eighty-eight modern paintings by fifty artists from twenty-one countries.[120] Pittsfield was close enough to New York, and had enough wealthy summer residents from the metropolis, that Bragg's activities in the provincial city received attention from the New York press and from the New York art scene, garnering coverage in the *New York Times*, the *New Yorker*, and *Art News*, among other periodicals. In the *New Yorker*, Lewis Mumford celebrated Bragg's accomplishments, claiming that she represented "a new type of director" setting "the pace in showmanship and interest" with "admirable zeal and taste."[121]

Thus, by opening an exhibit of Shaker materials in the fall of 1932, only three months after *Community Industries of the Shakers* closed at the New York State Museum, Bragg was continuing her career trajectory. She was using local materials exhibited in a museum setting to draw people together and educate them about their environs. On Orr's Island, she had created a museum of local vegetation. In Charleston, she found value in architectural fragments, iron work, and pottery. In Pittsfield, the region offered Shaker materials. Bragg also may have been attracted to the Shakers because of their espousal of gender equality and the leadership roles they allocated to women.

Since she contracted Shaker fever in the 1930s rather than the 1920s, unlike Adams, Bragg did not need to amass a collection for her museum; the material was readily accessible. Winter had compiled a portfolio of his Shaker images, and the Andrewses could provide her with a recognized collection. Bragg, Winter, and the Andrewses thus cooperated on an exhibition that served each of their needs. Bragg understood Winter's photographs and the Andrewses' holdings as regional resources that would be useful in promoting her museum and assisting in ushering it into a new chapter. Winter sought a place to exhibit his work, and the Andrewses viewed Bragg as a new patron with an institutional budget, museum expertise, and a national reputation.[122] In turning from Adams to embrace Bragg, the Andrewses established a pattern they would repeat recurrently in ensuing years.

The Berkshire Museum's Shaker exhibition was held under the auspices of the museum's "department of culture history," which benefited from Bragg's particular attention.[123] Although her exhibition featured both Winter's photographs and the Andrewses' collection, the two components were distinct enough that they received separate billing. The invitation to the opening reception indicated that the show featured "Furniture, Industrial Material, and Textiles of the Shakers of New England and New York" lent by Edward D. Andrews, Ph.D., and Faith Andrews of Pittsfield, Massachusetts, as well as "Camera Studies of the Shaker Communities of Hancock, Mass. and Mount Lebanon, N.Y." created and lent by William F. Winter of Schenectady, New York.[124] As was the case at the New York State Museum, the printed material accompanying the exhibition contained scant information about Winter's contribution, so although twenty-three of his images were displayed, it is unclear exactly which works were included.

The text that Ted Andrews prepared to include with the invitation to the opening reception indicates that his Shaker antiques were exhibited as a series of compositions meant to invoke spaces within a Shaker village.[125] Andrews noted that these constructed environments represented "artificial rearrangements."[126] A sisters' retiring, or bed, room included a large pine case of drawers, wash-stand, towel rack, mirror, two cots, a table, and a wood-burning stove. A sisters' work room was furnished with three different forms of sewing cabinets, textile samples, and equipment for producing and maintaining fabric, including a spinning wheel and swift. A trustees' office was portrayed as including a large desk, chairs, a chest with drawer, and a candlestand. A brothers' workshop included a cobbler's bench, broom-making equipment, baskets, buckets, and labels related to the seed and medicinal herb industries. A mockup of a Shaker dining room included a "rare sideboard," a trestle table, examples of various forms of Shaker chairs, a cabinet, candlesticks, and pewter serving dishes. Lastly, a Shaker kitchen, including a cast-iron stove and a drop-leaf table, and schoolroom were also represented, although it is unclear what was included in the latter space.[127]

Although the Berkshire Museum's exhibition was similar to and drew on the same collections as the New York State Museum's earlier show, the emphasis was somewhat different. While the Berkshire show included a few manufacturing artifacts, such as the cobbler's bench and the broom-making equipment, the exhibition placed a greater emphasis on Shaker domestic settings. Without the New York State Museum's collections and Adams's involvement with human geography, large-scale Shaker economic activity was essentially missing from the later show's interpretation. Printing presses and seed-sorting equipment were not displayed. Moreover, while the Albany museum had labeled their show with a rather specious date range of 1800 to 1825, Bragg's exhibition did not attempt a specific historical analysis. At the Berkshire Museum, spaces within the village were portrayed as timeless and unchanging, as outside of chronology. Similarly, while the New York State Museum had offered a geographic specificity, the Berkshire Museum exhibition, in its attempt to present characteristic or representative Shaker objects, brought together material that Andrews identified as being from New Lebanon, New York; Hancock, Massachusetts; Canterbury, New Hampshire; Alfred, Maine; and Canaan, New York.

Bragg's exhibition, with its lack of economic, chronologic, or geographic specificity and its focus on artistic photography and artfully recreated spaces, should not be understood as a history exhibition. Rather, Bragg, Andrews, and Winter celebrated an aesthetic vision and showed Shaker objects that could easily be incorporated into the homes of the museum-going public. Sewing cabinets made for Shaker sisters would make quaint additions to a suburban sewing nook, just as a Shaker trustee's desk could serve as an appealing surface on which to pay the monthly bills. While the museum claimed that the antiques had been arranged according to the sect's Millennial Laws as revised in 1843, the vignettes resembled furniture displays in department stores and interior design showrooms. Following the lead of Homer Eaton Keyes and the *Magazine Antiques*, the Berkshire Museum exhibit promoted Shaker materials as desirable commodities to be collected and preserved.

Installation photographs indicate a more sophisticated exhibition strategy than the earlier show (figs. 1.23–1.24).[128] The settings in which the furniture was shown are roomy, spare, and uncluttered. The form and line of the furnishings could easily be read and admired. Even with a cast-iron radiator intruding into a composition (fig. 1.23), these rooms, with their white walls and applied peg railings, could be mistaken for actual Shaker spaces. They exhibit the aesthetic that Winter was developing for his photographs in *Community Industries of the Shakers*. Rocking chairs in the museum's rendition of the sisters' retiring room rested on woven rugs just as does the rocking chair in Winter's composition for that publication (fig. 1.21). Noticeably absent from these artificial arrangements are the patterned

FIGURE 1.23. Installation photograph of Shaker exhibition at the Berkshire Museum, 1932. As noted on the wall, this arrangement of furniture at the Berkshire Museum was meant to represent a trustees' office. Note the museum's radiator intruding in the composition in the lower right corner. Courtesy Berkshire Museum, Pittsfield, MA.

FIGURE 1.24. Installation photograph of Shaker exhibition at the Berkshire Museum, 1932. This arrangement of furniture was meant to represent a community dining room, yet it could also be interpreted as an attractive option for a familial domestic space. Courtesy Berkshire Museum, Pittsfield, MA.

linoleum, striped wallpaper, and oriental carpets that were present in the actual sisters' sewing room which Winter documented at approximately the same time (fig. 1.22).

Because of Bragg's professional and social connections, the Berkshire Museum's 1932 exhibition received better press coverage than had the earlier show in Albany. The *New York Times* ran an article by Walter Rendell Storey in its weekend magazine illustrated with a Winter photograph of the museum's installation of the sisters' retiring room. In this 1932 piece, Storey made one of the earliest comparisons between Shaker furniture and contemporary design. "Shaker furniture, if more widely known," he wrote, "should furnish a definitely native inspiration that should be appreciated especially by the contemporary designer, who stresses function and simplicity of line and surface."[129] Similarly, writing two months later, Charles M. Stowe, an antiques expert and journalist, suggested in the *New York Sun* that previously, when he had considered Shaker furniture, he had understood it as the product of a country industry interested in selling inexpensive goods. More recently, however, he and his wife had come to understand "the close kinship between the products of the Shakers and some of the extremely modern craftsmen. . . . Emphasis upon the straight line is characteristic of both."[130] Although Andrews's writings had claimed that Shaker furniture exhibited fine craftsmanship, the comparison of Shaker furniture to modern design, which subsequently became commonplace, may have been explicitly articulated for the first time as a result of Laura Bragg's exhibition at the Berkshire Museum.

Bragg's connections also brought important cultural figures to Pittsfield to see the exhibition. The show's opening reception drew a number of Massachusetts luminaries, including Elizabeth Paine and Dorothy Daly of Smith College's Tryon Gallery; Charles R. Green, librarian of the Jones Library at Amherst College; Donald E. Richmond of the Williams College Mathematics Department; Lillian Sanford Proctor, an heiress related to the fortunes created by Proctor & Gamble who owned an estate in New Ashford, Massachusetts; and Edna Hilburn Little, an important collector of regional antiques who worked with George Francis Dow at the Society for the Preservation of New England Antiquities (now Historic New England).[131] A more select group was invited to Bragg's home in Pittsfield's South Street Inn for dinner to meet the Andrewses and Winter and his wife. This group included, along with Zenas Crane, the museum's primary benefactor,

Charles Sawyer, director of the Addison Gallery at Phillips Andover Academy (who later served as the dean of fine arts at Yale University), and Juliana Force, the director of New York City's Whitney Museum of American Art, whom Bragg may have known through their mutual involvement with the American Association of Museums.[132] In Juliana Force, Faith and Edward Deming Andrews recognized their next patron.[133]

The Shaker exhibit at the Berkshire Museum was by all accounts a success. The *Berkshire Eagle* reported near the end of its short run that over nine thousand visitors had viewed it.[134] This total included a number of Shakers including Eldress Sarah Collins of Mount Lebanon, and Brother Benjamin De Rue and Sisters Alice Smith, Olive Hayden, Elizabeth Belden, Rosetta Stephens, and Sadie Neale of the Hancock village.[135] Sister Emma Neale and Elder Walter Shepherd of Mount Lebanon even presented interpretive lectures in the galleries, drawing an audience of 125 and emphasizing the exhibition's local character.[136]

Bragg hoped that she could institutionalize the outpouring of public interest in Shaker culture her exhibition generated. In late October 1932, she announced a meeting to found a society to preserve Shaker antiquities. She proposed forming a museum, based on the Andrewses' collection, in an "appropriate environment," probably meaning within a Shaker compound.[137] Bragg, however, had misjudged the collectors. Having already leveraged their holdings into two museum exhibitions and a forthcoming book, the unemployed academic and his wife had no intention of depositing the source of their status with a local nonprofit. Even as Bragg publicly proclaimed her intention to establish a Shaker museum in the Berkshires, Faith and Ted Andrews were in correspondence with Juliana Force concerning bringing their collection to Manhattan.[138]

JULIANA FORCE AND THE WHITNEY MUSEUM OF AMERICAN ART

Force, who had been born Juliana Reiser in Doylestown, Pennsylvania, in 1876 to German immigrant parents, was one of the most influential figures of her generation in American art. With a professional background as a stenographer and social secretary, she was hired in 1907 by Gertrude Vanderbilt Whitney, the sculptor, heiress, and art patron.[139] Having married Dr. Willard Burdette Force, a dentist, Juliana Force quickly made herself indispensable to Whitney's art activities, even though she had no formal training or background in art. She subsequently directed Whitney's art undertakings as they evolved from the Whitney Studio to the Whitney Studio Club and finally, in 1931, to the Whitney Museum of American Art. Through her affiliation with Whitney and her dispersal of her employer's money, Force befriended and ultimately patronized a generation of influential American artists including Edward Hopper, Henry Schnakenberg, Charles Sheeler, Stuart Davis, and William Zorach. After Force's death art administrators Hermon More and Lloyd Goodrich wrote of her, "Her likes and her dislikes were strong. . . . She had an unerring sense of quality in whatever form it occurred, and her professional taste was unusually broad."[140] Flora Miller Biddle, Whitney's granddaughter, remembered Force as "a decisive vibrant woman with pretty clothes and red hair, who made up for her lack of training in art history with her intelligence, informed opinions, steely will, and wit."[141] Together, Whitney and Force were prodigious advocates for American art.

Partly because of strong family attachments to Bucks County, Pennsylvania, Force was an early collector of American folk art.[142] With her husband, in 1914 she bought an eighteenth-century stone house on a sixty-acre property near Doylestown, which she called Barley Sheaf Farm. She furnished this personal retreat with materials she gathered during forays into the countryside in her station wagon. Visitors were charmed by her portraits by itinerant artists, hooked rugs, country furniture, Pennsylvania German artifacts, Jacquard coverlets, quilts, and trade signs. Avis Berman, her biographer, asserted that Force understood the materials she was collecting as a "manifestation of the indigenous American culture she and Gertrude were working . . . to legitimize."[143] Like the contemporary art that the pair advocated, folk art represented a rejection of the tyranny of the academic artistic tradition as promulgated by the National Academy of Design.

Force shared an attraction to American antiques with many of the artists who circled Whitney and the Whitney Studio Club. In February 1924, the realist painter Henry Schnakenberg organized an exhibition at the Whitney Studio Club entitled *Early American Art*, featuring oil paintings, including two paintings of Hudson River steamboats by John and James Bard, but also a cigar-store Indian, a chalkware cat, and a pewter pitcher and sugar bowl. Schnakenberg's associates, including Force, Sheeler, Yasuo Kuniyoshi, Charles Demuth, and Alexander Brook, loaned these objects. Both Sheeler and Force occupied apartments in the Studio Club building at the time of the exhibition.[144] Although the press was cautious in reviewing the show, subsequent commentators have suggested that this was the first formal public exhibition of American folk art.[145] Three years later in 1927, the Whitney Studio Club similarly exhibited paintings from the collection of Isabel Carleton Wilde, a collector of early American paintings and antiques based in Cambridge, Massachusetts.[146]

As Force gathered objects for her personal collection that spoke to her of a unique American artistic tradition and contributed aesthetically to her New York City apartment and her Pennsylvania farmhouse, she acquired a number of Shaker objects, possibly as the result of her personal relationship with Sheeler.[147] In his attempts to document what he envisioned as a plain American tradition that stood in contrast to Europe's ornamentalism, the precisionist painter began collecting Shaker materials in the early 1920s, with Shaker decorative arts beginning to appear in his paintings around 1927.[148] Over time, Force became so enamored of the Shaker aesthetic that when in 1928 she purchased a house in South Salem, New York, near where Sheeler, Brook, and Peggy Bacon lived, she named it Shaker Hollow. After meeting Faith and Edward Andrews at the opening of Bragg's exhibit, Force discovered that the Andrewses had sold a piece of Shaker furniture to the dealer in Ridgefield, Connecticut, from whom she had purchased it.[149]

When the Andrewses met Force, she was in the process of inventing the Whitney Museum of American Art. In 1929, Whitney had offered to donate her entire collection of American art to New York's Metropolitan Museum of Art (MMA) along with $5 million to build a wing to house it. When the conservative decision-makers at the MMA rejected this offer, Whitney opted to establish her own museum with Force as the director. The new museum, which opened on November 18, 1931, less than a year before her trip to Pittsfield, had a mission of celebrating contemporary American art while simultaneously, in the words of the *New York Times,* telling "the whole story of American art, from early days to the present."[150] As the director of the first public institution dedicated to American art, Force was charged with answering the question that the critic Edward Allen Jewell, among others, posed: "What is American art?"[151] With art historian Lloyd Goodrich as the institution's research curator, the Whitney began a process of exhuming, rediscovering, and reevaluating forgotten, little-known, or underappreciated American art as a means to validate contemporary art by providing it with an identifiable national lineage.[152]

Thus, Bragg's 1932 exhibition, and the Andrewses' collection of Shaker material, ideally fit the needs and desires of the young museum's director. The impresario immediately began planning with Winter and the Andrewses for a Shaker show at the Whitney and placed them all on monthly retainers. By staging a Shaker show, Force followed the precedent of the Schnakenberg and Wilde exhibits of folk art and featured a specifically American genre of art with which she was already intimately familiar. Presenting Shaker material at the Whitney offered an ancestry for the kind of linear abstraction that many of the artists in her orbit, including Sheeler and Davis, favored while showing simultaneously images of the nation's life that resonated with the works of Thomas Hart Benton, John Steuart Curry, Grant Wood, and Edward Hopper, all of whom were represented in the Whitney's collections.

SHAKER HANDICRAFTS

The Whitney Museum offered an exhibition, entitled *Shaker Handicrafts,* from November 12 to December 12, 1935. The title once again indicates a change in emphasis by the sponsoring institution. Rather than focusing on the sect's community industries or on their "furniture, industrial material, and textiles," the Whitney drew on the language of art history to emphasize the Shakers as craftspeople. Notably, the exhibition focused on finished products, such as chairs, tables, and cupboards, rather than on process. This show, unlike the previous two, did not include looms, spinning wheels, or printing presses.

The approximately eighty objects in the show, selected and arranged by Faith and Edward Andrews, were displayed in constructed vignettes in two galleries and a hallway on the second floor of the museum. The majority of the pieces were from the New Lebanon village, with a significant number of items also from Hancock. Two or three objects were included from each of the villages of Alfred and Sabbathday Lake, Maine; Enfield, Connecticut; and Watervliet, New York. The community in Canterbury, New Hampshire, was represented by a single case piece. The exhibition was largely composed of chairs, tables, and cupboards, along with desks, clocks, and benches. A number of smaller items, such as oval boxes, tinware, sconces, baskets, and costumes, were included to expand visitors' understanding of Shaker crafts and to add verisimilitude to the artistic arrangements of furniture.[153] Many items had previously been shown at one, if not both, of the earlier installations. The Whitney exhibition, dependent on what the Andrewses had amassed through their trade over the previous decade, did not include any material from the Shaker communities in Ohio and Kentucky.

As had been the case at the New York State Museum and the Berkshire Museum, William Winter's photographs were included to provide context for the "handicrafts." However, in addition to exhibiting architectural photographs, the Whitney showed formal black-and-white portraits that Winter had created of five Shaker sisters, including Eldress Anna Case, Eldress Fannie Estabrook, and Sister Sadie Neale (figs. 1.25–1.26).[154] Although Winter's compositions were exhibited on the museum's third floor, his contribution to this enterprise was marginalized even more than previously. The catalogue did not recognize him by name or enumerate the images; it simply noted the presence of "a group of camera studies" while also indicating that "no works in this exhibition are for sale."[155]

This exhibition differed from the earlier shows in that it included two-dimensional Shaker artworks which had not been previously exhibited. Nineteen Shaker "inspirational drawings," which scholars have more recently referred to as "gift drawings," were hung in the two galleries, as were six views of Shaker villages, including two signed and dated by Joshua Bussell (figs. 1.27–1.28). These colorful, decorative, graphically intriguing flat works of art would have appealed to the folk art enthusiasts on the Whitney's staff and among its audience, who might have noted stylistic similarities to Pennsylvania German Fraktur, samplers, overmantels, and other familiar genres.[156] By including them in this exhibition, the Andrewses and the staff of the Whitney Museum significantly expanded the public's knowledge of the sect.[157] The cover of the catalogue of *Shaker Handicrafts*, for example, was decorated, with an ornamental design derived from an inspirational drawing. This may represent the first time that Shaker sprit drawings served a graphic designer as inspiration. Subsequently, it would be commonplace for individuals to incorporate elements of these inspired artworks into printed materials related to the sect (fig. 1.29).

Geography separated the Whitney show from its predecessors. The museum staff and local visitors to the earlier shows knew the Shakers as their neighbors. In Albany, Lassiter had an early acquaintance with members of the group. In Pittsfield, Shaker sisters and brothers offered their own interpretive lectures in association with the installation. In New York City,

FIGURE 1.25. William F. Winter, Jr., "Sister Sadie Neale," ca. 1935. Winter expanded his photographic vocabulary from representations of Shaker buildings to include portraits of living believers. Courtesy Collection of Hancock Shaker Village, Pittsfield, MA, 1988–3090.

however, because the living Shakers were located at a greater physical distance, the sect was more easily romanticized. At the Whitney, the believers were not three-dimensional living, breathing humans; they were quaint, pious, elderly figures represented in black-and-white portraits. Rather than being a show about a local religious group, *Shaker Handicrafts* was an exploration of the artistic output of a disappearing group of American forbears

FIGURE 1.26. William F. Winter, Jr., "Eldress Anna Case," ca. 1935. Winter's portraits of Shaker sisters were included in the 1935 exhibition at the Whiney Museum of American Art in New York City. Courtesy Collection of Hancock Shaker Village, Pittsfield, MA, 1991–5397.

imagined as distant in both time and place from the twentieth-century gallery visitors. The detachment between the Shakers and museum-goers was further accentuated by the polyglot nature of New York City, shaped by waves of immigrations. While the Shakers historically were a Protestant

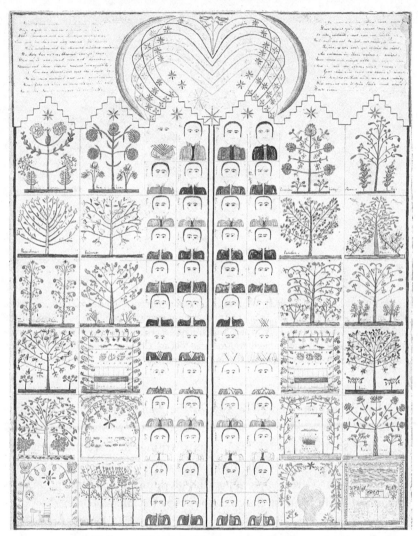

FIGURE 1.27. Polly Collins, *An Emblem of the Heavenly Sphere,* 1854, ink and watercolor on paper, 31⅗ x 26⅛ in. Shaker gift drawings were first exhibited to the public in 1935 as part of *Shaker Handicrafts* at the Whitney Museum of American Art in New York City. Courtesy Collection of Hancock Shaker Village, Pittsfield, MA, 1963.113.

religious sect largely composed of individuals descended from the British Isles, New York City museum attendees were increasingly ethnically and religiously diverse. The Shakers thus could be understood as representing a remnant of a previous America.

FIGURE 1.28. Joshua H. Bussell, "Plan of Shaker Community at Poland Hill, Maine," 1850. Shaker village views were first exhibited to the museum-going public in 1935 through the show *Shaker Handicrafts* at the Whitney Museum of American Art in New York City as part of the institution's early commitment to American folk art. Courtesy Winterthur Library: The Edward Deming Andrews Memorial Shaker Collection, SA 1532.

Edward Deming Andrews's text for the *Shaker Handicrafts* catalogue also differed from what he had contributed to the publications prepared for earlier shows. Although his previous writings had been workmanlike and exemplified someone who had earned a doctorate writing a historical study, they were nevertheless somewhat plodding and dependent on facts and narrative. In contrast, the collectors' copy for Juliana Force's show glistened with *bon mots* and clever turns of phrase. He identified the Shakers as "practical idealists" and suggested that Mother Ann Lee's successors expanded Shakerism into "a philosophy in which transcendentalism was strangely infused with Yankee common sense." Moreover, as befitting an exhibit at an art museum, Andrews's introduction exhibits newfound facility with the language of aesthetics. He wrote that Shaker retiring rooms "had the unmistakable 'Shaker look,' a reticent impersonal quality of pure usefulness unobscured by superfluous detail." Similarly, in discussing Shaker furniture in general, he asserted, "Custom and law forbade surface embellishment, carving, inlay or excessive turning; the merit of the finished

SHAKER HANDICRAFTS

NOVEMBER 12 TO DECEMBER 12, 1935

WHITNEY MUSEUM OF AMERICAN ART

TEN WEST EIGHTH STREET · NEW YORK

FIGURE 1.29. Designer unknown, cover of *Shaker Handicrafts*, 1935. The cover of the exhibition catalogue for the Whitney Museum of American Art's 1935 exhibition may be the first printed object to draw on Shaker spirit drawings for graphic elements. Courtesy Frances Mulhall Archives Library, Whitney Museum of American Art, New York, NY. Digital image © Whitney Museum of American Art / Licensed by Scala / Art Resource, NY.

piece must depend on form alone, on rightness of proportion and linear composition."[158] Scholars probably will never be able to determine whether Andrews's increased flair with the language of decorative arts and modernism was the result of interaction with Force and her coterie or the product of a skillful museum-affiliated editor.

In either case, however, this exhibition at a burgeoning, nationalistic museum located at the nexus of the country's art and publishing worlds had a far larger public impact than either of the previous shows. The periodical press was full of notices even before the show opened. The *New York Times* remarked that, with the Shaker exhibition, folk art had "come to the fore again."[159] Homer Eaton Keyes, the Andrewses' longtime backer, published a long gallery note trumpeting the show in the *Magazine Antiques*. His rhetoric reflected the Whitney's desire to create a lineage for contemporary American artistic output. "I shall be particularly interested," he wrote, "to observe the reactions of the modernistic tribe. . . . As a whole this furniture comports, in theory at least, with the ideas of sundry contemporary designers. Furthermore, many of its visible features will at least faintly remind the observer of latter-day creations in the domain of domestic equipment."[160]

Celebratory coverage of the show continued once it had opened, with journalists and editors dutifully transmitting the interpretations the museum had fed them positioning Shaker handicrafts as a form of American folk art presaging machine-age functionalism. Writing in the *Brooklyn Daily Eagle*, Harriet Dyer Adams, Charles Adams's daughter, reported, "Many will find that this furniture fits into the modern scheme in a most persuasive manner, because Shaker crafts resemble Colonial types in general, although they are easily distinguished from them by their even greater simplicity."[161] The *New York Herald Tribune*, after presenting an extended quote from *Community Industries of the Shakers* that posited the Shakers as a model for creating an industrial system, noted, "The present exhibit at the Whitney Museum shows that they were . . .—quite unconsciously, it may be, certainly self-instructed—masters of design."[162] In the *Christian Science Monitor*, the domestic science columnist Helen Johnson Keyes informed her readers that Shaker functionalism resulted in "the same orderliness and tranquility that one feels today in contemporary interiors. Among the Shakers the concept was not esthetic but religious, yet the effect is identical."[163] In the *New York Times*, Walter Rendell Storey suggested that "the professional designer of today" might benefit from studying the "ascetic simplicity" of the "old-time Shakers."[164] Similar rhetorical points were made in articles in *Art News,* the *New York Sun,* the *Springfield Union and Republican,* the *Albany Times Union,* and the *Boston Evening Transcript.*[165] As far away as Texas, the *Dallas Morning News* made note of the exhibition.[166]

While Winter's photographs were inadequately recognized within the museum's catalogue, critics commented favorably on them. The *New York Times* called them "especially good."[167] Harriet Dyer Adams noted that Winter's "fine craftsmanship, as well as his rich artistic gift, resembles the Shakers own spirit and qualities."[168] A reporter for the *New York Sun* suggested, "Look at the camera studies made by William F. Winters [*sic*]. . . . Mr. Winters has caught the spiritual quality that comes . . . to those who have earned peace."[169]

Even more significantly, newspaper articles about the show were accompanied not by installation photographs of the exhibition but by Winter's constructed photographic compositions of furniture from the Andrewses' collection within sparse, white-walled spaces.[170] On November 24, 1935, for example, the *New York Times* published an image of two chairs and a table in a room of the South Family dwelling house at New Lebanon (fig. 1.30). These items were augmented with rugs, a candlestick, a wall sconce, and a book artfully arranged as though a believer had just exited the room. The image, which the *Times* attributed to Winter and captioned "Ascetic Simplicity Marks the Furniture of the Shakers," displays the artist's love of geometric forms and emphasizes the tension between the monumental verticality of the built-in cupboard and the horizontality of the peg-rail and tabletop. These lines are echoed in the stiles and splats and chair seat on the far right of the image. This photograph also appeared in the November 30, 1935, issue of the nationally distributed *Christian Science Monitor* to accompany Helen Johnson Keyes's review of the Whitney show entitled "Thus Spake Shaker Crafts."

Keyes's article also included a Winter photograph of an attenuated tall-clock, a splayed-leg drop-leaf table, and a chair (fig. 1.31). This image, which Homer Eaton Keyes entitled "Shaker Simplicity" when he published it as the frontispiece of the December 1934 issue of the *Magazine Antiques,* does not use a corner of a room to create perspective but rather employs the architectural fabric of the building along with its furnishings to create a two-dimensional abstraction of geometric form. The diagonal lines of the chair back, the table legs, and the folded table leaf slash across the

FIGURE 1.30. William F. Winter, Jr., "Ascetic Simplicity Marks the Furniture of the Shakers," ca. 1935. Winter's beautiful photographs of Shaker furniture in sparse white settings were used to publicize the Whitney's *Shaker Handicrafts* show in 1935. Published to accompany Walter Rendell Storey, "Folk Art Inspires the Designer," *New York Times*, November 24, 1935, this image was later reproduced in Edward Deming Andrews and Faith Andrews, *Shaker Furniture, the Craftsmanship of an American Communal Sect* (New Haven, CT: Yale University Press, 1937), plate 27. Courtesy Winterthur Library: The Edward Deming Andrews Memorial Shaker Collection, SA 572c.

rectangular grid created by the frame of the picture, the wall moulding, the peg rail, and the clock.

To accompany its article about the Whitney show, the *Springfield Union and Republican* published a Winter photograph of a Shaker trestle table surrounded by eight low chairs with woven seats. The editor labeled this illustration "Shaker Austerity" (fig. 1.32). This image also included a window subdivided into rectangles by mullions and bifurcated by a rectangular cloth blind, one of Winter's favorite devices for introducing additional rectangles into a composition. The rows of four chairs on either side of the table resonate with the four panes of glass in the exposed bottom sets of window lights. The pewter wares on the table provide a false sense of domesticity without detracting from the stark geometry of the composition. The floor, which has been polished, reflects the lines of the furniture legs extending

FIGURE 1.31. William F. Winter, Jr., "Shaker Simplicity," ca. 1934. Many Americans confused Winter's carefully arranged photographic compositions with factual statements about Shaker life. Published to accompany Helen Johnson Keyes, "Thus Spoke Shaker Crafts," *Christian Science Monitor,* November 30, 1935, this image was later reproduced in Andrews and Andrews, *Shaker Furniture,* plate 41. Courtesy Winterthur Library: The Edward Deming Andrews Memorial Shaker Collection, SA 583b.

FIGURE 1.32. William F. Winter, Jr., "Shaker Austerity," ca. 1935. Furniture historian John Kirk has argued that Winter's images speak of modernism and resemble dealers' photographs. Published to accompany "Crafts of Shakers, Nantucketers, Reveal Two Kinds of Americans," *Springfield Union and Republican*, November 24, 1935, this image was later reproduced in Andrews and Andrews, *Shaker Furniture*, plate 3. Courtesy Winterthur Library: The Edward Deming Andrews Memorial Shaker Collection, SA 547c.

them to the picture's edge. Shadows of the chairs against the far wall indicate that an artificial light source was introduced to heighten the photographic effect.

These images continued the trajectory of Winter's photographs published in *Community Industries of the Shakers*. Folk art scholar Elizabeth Stillinger notes, "The finished photographs showed pieces from the Andrewses' collection arranged in room settings that were spare and beautiful, as Andrews and Winter imagined golden-age Shaker rooms to have been."[171] Like the rocking chair and rug photograph (fig. 1.21), these pictures are compositions that document Shaker craftsmanship, but they are also abstract artistic compositions created by a talented photographer and disseminated by an institution seeking to create an ancestry for contemporary American art and design. They appear to be documentary evidence of the Shaker's use of space, but they are actually the result of collectors who sought to elevate the importance of their holdings and a photographer who was building a professional career by creating compelling images. As David E. Nye has argued about General Electric's manipulated industrial photography, these images "make apparently factual statements about the world" while suppressing the dynamics of their creation; the same could be said of the images which Winter created for other patrons.[172] Furniture historian John Kirk has said of these images that "they speak of modernism, and they look like dealers' photographs."[173]

The images that Winter and the Andrewses created, which quickly became the canonical visual representations of Shaker architecture and material culture, were the result of a process that reached beyond the photographer and the collector. They are the products of extended interactions with Adams, Bragg, Force, and others. As this chapter has shown, each exhibition and publication was created within its own institutional context while also building on those that had preceded it. Charles Adams, as an ecological geographer, recognized the Shakers as a regionally specific group within New York State that provided him with the opportunity to create a significant historical collection to contribute to his museum's vitality. As the director of the New York State Museum, without a professional staff of trained historians, he assembled a team that included William Winter, Edwin Stein, William Lassiter, and the Andrewses to create an exhibition which interpreted the economic life of the sect within its cultural and natural environment. As a result, he brought together the Andrewses, who had already discovered through Homer Eaton Keyes that an expertise in Shaker materials could prove lucrative, and Winter, who understood that Shaker objects and spaces could be manipulated to create aesthetically pleasing modernist compositions. In seeking to recreate the success that she had experienced at the Charleston Museum, Laura Bragg understood that Shaker artifacts could be displayed as local aesthetic objects within a modern regional museum. As an educator and a champion of modern art, Bragg hoped to capitalize on the Andrewses' collection for long-term benefit to her community but also to build a robust national reputation for her institution. In pursuing these ends, she served as a conduit by which Winter and the Andrewses came into contact with Juliana Force, who sought to manufacture a lineage for a national artistic style while also nurturing a nascent museum to collect and exhibit art in support of a unique American identity.

As Winter and Andrews maneuvered their way through this byzantine institutional labyrinth, they improved and polished their images and their writing. The Andrewses' early images as published in the *Magazine Antiques* are amateurish and naive. Winter's preliminary negatives, while attuned to form and geometry, display cluttered and visually busy spaces. Subsequently, in *Community Industries of the Shakers* and then in promotional photographs for *Shaker Handicrafts,* the team mastered the formula for visually appealing, geometric photographic representations of spare, simple spaces. Simultaneously, Andrews's interpretative text advanced from basic factual introductions to the Shakers, to a researched local historical and economic understanding of their industries, to a polished art-historical presentation of Shaker material culture as an American precursor to twentieth-century international modernism in which religious devotion resulted in aesthetic functionalism. This collaborative vision, buffed and polished by competing agendas, created a compelling narrative and beautiful images while overlooking the richly detailed human history of the sect, disregarding the particulars of the sects' religious beliefs, and misrepresenting the lived reality of these communal societies.

CHAPTER 2
"A NATIVE TRADITION WITH A FUTURE"

••••••••••••••••••••••

The Shakers, the New Deal, and National Design

The preceding chapter examined how Shaker materials were exhibited to the public in three seminal museum exhibitions in the years between 1930 and 1935. These exhibits culminated with the American public being introduced to an understanding of the Shakers as "practical idealists" whose religious beliefs led them to produce furniture that predicted international modernism's embrace of functionalism. This interpretation of the Shakers was reached collaboratively by a group of individuals with distinct motivations working together. Charles C. Adams, Laura Bragg, and Juliana Force produced Shaker exhibitions to benefit their institutions as well as to make contributions to human geography, regional identity, and American art history. William Winter, a talented photographer, created images of Shaker buildings, furniture, and material culture to expand his professional capacity while also creating beautiful, modernist photographic compositions. Faith and Edward Deming Andrews participated to build their reputations as Shaker experts while simultaneously elevating the importance of the objects they owned.

The individuals promoting Shaker material culture in these years functioned within the context of regional museums. Charles Adams served as the director of the New York State Museum, a publicly funded institution meant to serve the people of New York State. The museum's cultural activities were largely pursued in and around the capital city of Albany; it did not maintain satellite galleries or travel its exhibitions. Laura Bragg's Berkshire Museum was supported by individuals like Z. Marshall Crane and Lillian Sanford Proctor, who either lived or summered in western Massachusetts and whose families had amassed wealth through industrial and commercial activities. Juliana Force's Whitney Museum of American Art was a unique case in that it was a local institution funded by a single individual drawing on an industrial fortune, but because of its location in New York City, the publishing and art capital of the country, it had an amplified impact.

In the years in which these exhibitions were being mounted, the nation was mired in the economic and political turmoil of the Great Depression. The stock market crashed in the time between Edward Deming Andrews's first article for the *Magazine Antiques* and the opening of the seminal Shaker exhibit at the New York State Museum. Franklin Delano Roosevelt was initially elected president in the month after Laura Bragg's Shaker show closed. Roosevelt's famous first hundred days, during which he passed the Emergency Banking Act, created the Federal Emergency Relief Administration, established the Civilian Conservation Corps, and largely reimagined the federal government's role in the nation's life, transpired while Force, Andrews, and Winter were planning *Shaker Handicrafts*.

Roosevelt's New Deal touched almost every aspect of American life, and unsurprisingly it influenced the expanding interpretation of Shaker culture. With the establishment of the Federal Art Project of the Works Progress Administration, the federal government became involved in arts administration on a national scale. While local, regional, and state institutions remained vital, they now functioned within a context in which federal agencies brought resources to bear in pursuit of specific agendas.

The New Deal's Index of American Design, in particular, revised how the nation conceived of Shaker objects. This transformation resulted from the concerted effort of many individuals from the world of art and design who, through this agency, became active interpreters of Shaker material culture to the American public. Spurred by various motivations, this cohort made choices that influenced how the Shakers and their products were represented. They decided which examples to celebrate and, in doing so, codified a canon. Because their efforts were backed by the federal government, these individuals and their activities had a national, rather than regional, impact. The Index of American Design brought Shaker material culture to the attention of Americans from New York to California and from Maine to Louisiana. The artists, museum professionals, and arts administrators involved with this effort promoted an agenda, both aesthetic and political, that conflated Shaker design and modernism to promote an exceptionalist American nationalism. Their semiotic manipulation of Shaker material culture in the decade before World War II continues to inform how Americans view the sect.

The Index of American Design's central role in disseminating information about Shaker design to a broad audience has largely been underrepresented in the secondary literature. In particular, Ruth Reeves, while she was employed as an administrator of this federal government agency during the summer of 1936, played a central but undervalued role in coordinating the agency's recording and promotion of Shaker artifacts. By placing Reeves and her activities with the Index of American Design within their historical context, including examining her interactions with Faith and Edward Deming Andrews, this chapter introduces a nuanced, revisionist understanding of the process by which the current popular conception of Shaker material culture was invented and codified. This chapter also explores the legacy of this New Deal agency by examining furniture and fashions created by designers inspired by the drawings and photographs of Shaker objects generated under its auspices.

RUTH REEVES AND ROMANA JAVITZ

The Index of American Design, a program of the Federal Art Project of the Works Progress (later Works Project) Administration during Roosevelt's New Deal, functioned from 1935 to 1942. During this seven-year period, the index employed approximately one thousand people in thirty-four states and the District of Columbia. These artists, photographers, and administrators produced over seventeen thousand images—pencil drawings, ink sketches, photographs, and watercolors—of American objects.[1] Although conceived as a national undertaking, the Index of American Design was most active in the Northeast and mid-Atlantic states and weakest in the Southeast and West.

The index was the brainchild of Ruth Reeves and Romana Javitz, two participants in New York City's art scene.[2] Both believed that artists and designers had inadequate access to visual references for indigenous American design traditions. Together they envisioned a collection of images of American objects that would inspire artists and designers to create products within a national tradition.

Reeves was a prominent and influential textile designer. Born in Redlands, California in 1892, she trained at the Pratt Institute in Brooklyn, the California School of Design in San Francisco, and the Art Students League in Manhattan. Reeves subsequently studied in Paris under the influential modernist painter Fernand Léger.[3] Accomplished as a painter and lithographer, Reeves specialized in printing abstracted designs on fabric.[4] In 1931, the Brooklyn Museum exhibited her textiles with the products of leading American modernist artists and designers including Donald Deskey, Rockwell Kent, and Gilbert Rohde.[5]

During the 1920s and 1930s, Reeves established her professional reputation by creating abstract representational designs that drew on diverse sources of inspiration, including motifs from the cultures of Central America and Polynesia.[6] Reeves, led by this interest, embarked on a study trip to Guatemala funded by the Carnegie Institution in 1934.[7] Upon her return, she mounted an exhibition at New York's Rockefeller Center showcasing both Guatemalan textiles and the designs that her trip had inspired.[8] In this period, the furniture historian Marta K. Sironen noted, "Reeves has contributed greatly to American knowledge of primitive design through her interpretations in textiles of the various countries she has visited."[9] For the rest of her life, Reeves sought ethnographic design sources for her textiles, including Persian ceramics, Patagonian silver, and Maori artwork, ultimately leading to an extended sojourn in India to study batik during which she died in 1966.[10]

Although Reeves was inspired by global indigenous cultures, during the late 1920s and early 1930s she was best known for designs derived from American landscapes, culture, and history. In 1934, the art critic Elisabeth Luther Cary noted that Reeves's "efforts to incorporate in her designs distinctively American materials have been constant."[11] A textile designed for the W. & J. Sloane department store in 1930, variously referred to as *Manhattan* or *Canyons of Steel*, is perhaps her most recognized work and expresses the dynamic energy of the American city by incorporating icons of the industrial skyline, including the Woolworth Building, the Brooklyn Bridge, and the Statue of Liberty, with modern forms of transportation and communication such as streamlined railroads, trucks, ocean liners, airplanes, and telephone exchanges within an energetic diagonal composition.[12] Other designs within the suite of ten upholstery fabrics that Reeves created for W. & J. Sloane at the time celebrated diverse aspects of the American experience.[13] *Homage to Emily Dickinson,* for example, honors one of the most beloved individuals in American literature.[14] Figures play tennis, construct buildings, share meals, and frolic in the water in *American Scene* (fig. 2.1).[15]

In 1934, Reeves built on her appreciation for the American landscape by producing a series of fabrics for McCutcheon's department store in New York City displaying views of the Hudson River inspired by the nineteenth-century landscape paintings of the Hudson River School. Cary, critic for the *New York Times,* called these textiles "a modern and thoroughly American variant of the Toile de Jouy of France" and explained that they were "patterned with scenes from American places in the early stages of the historic."[16] The Gardner School Alumnae Association supported Reeves in the production of these designs through a fellowship meant to encourage excellence in design. Walter Rendell Storey of the *New York Times* explained to his readers that Reeves, like Thomas Cole, Asher B. Durand, and other American artists before her, "first made oil sketches of historic spots along the Hudson and then developed from them a design for linens and artificial silk."[17] This collection of fabrics included patterns entitled *West Point, Newburgh, Kingston,* and *Poughkeepsie* (fig. 2.2). The latter design included a view of Franklin Delano Roosevelt's estate at Hyde Park.[18] McCutcheon's Home Furnishing Department trumpeted that these "striking new fabrics" by "Ruth Reeves, an outstanding artist and designer," were regarded by authorities as "one of the most important developments in the field of decorative prints in many years," and that her views of the Hudson conveyed "the grandeur of the river itself."[19] *Literary Digest* commended Reeve's achievement for "her effort lies in the direction of creating a national style."[20] Through her textiles, Reeves, like Sheeler, Force, and other American modernists of the time, was attempting to define an American identity in the visual arts.

In the process of creating designs, Reeves, like many New York artists, was a frequent patron of the picture collection at the New York Public Library (NYPL) where she encountered Romana Javitz, the head of this division.[21] Established soon after the library's central building opened in 1911, by 1914

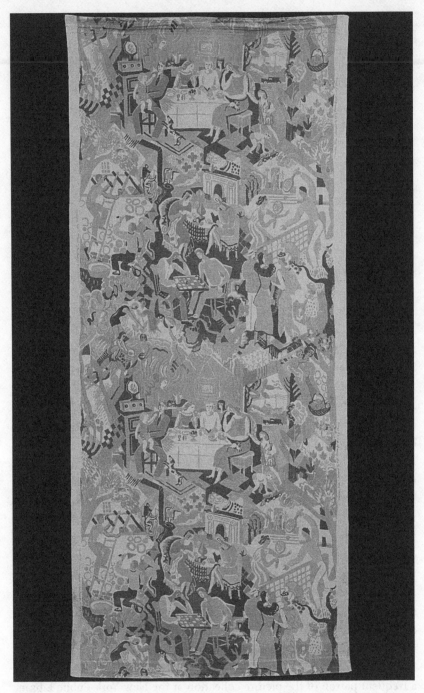

FIGURE 2.1. Ruth Reeves, *American Scene*, 1930, textile. Produced by W. & J. Sloane. While portraying American life, Reeves's designs demonstrate the training in abstraction that she received from Fernand Léger. Courtesy the Yale University Art Gallery, New Haven, CT, The John P. Axelrod Collection, B.A. 1968, 1995.49.7.

FIGURE 2.2. Ruth Reeves, *Overlooking Kingston* (section), 1934, textile. Produced by James McCutcheon & Company. This view of the Hudson River is one pattern in a series of toiles inspired by nineteenth-century American landscape painting. Courtesy Helen Louise Allen Textile Collection, School of Human Ecology, University of Wisconsin–Madison, P.R. US. 0059.

the picture collection maintained 17,991 images available for patrons to borrow. These images, initially salvaged from materials in the process of being discarded, supported the efforts of the city's movie and theater designers, advertising agencies, publishing companies, fashion designers, and other artistic professions.[22] The NYPL's picture collection was inspired by comparable predecessors that John Cotton Dana, the progressive and innovative library and museum administrator, had established at the public libraries in Denver, Colorado, and Newark, New Jersey.[23]

Born in Russia to Polish parents, Javitz grew up comfortably in the Bronx and Manhattan's Upper West Side. She began working part-time at the NYPL while studying painting at the Art Students League in 1919. After transferring from the Children's Room to the Picture Collection in 1924, Javitz was appointed head of the enterprise in 1929 on Ellen Perkins's retirement from the position.[24] In 1925, while working at the Picture Collection, Javitz traveled through Italy, Austria, Poland, Germany, France, and England, visiting libraries and learning how continental picture collections were organized. She later wrote,

> I was especially interested in how these foreign governments perpetuated in pictures changing customs and costumes of their own people. Everywhere I went I found that the record of folk arts [was] exceedingly rich and well preserved and that the governments had been interested in subsidizing this recording and documentation. . . . It seemed shameful to me then that we had not developed pride enough in our own past to record the appearance of what the people wore, the details of their kitchens, their tools, their houses.[25]

As a result of these travels and her experiences working in the picture collection, Javitz envisioned an encyclopedic visual resource that documented America's material culture. Based on her familiarity with government-subsidized European publications recording peasant costumes and her respect for the natural history catalogues produced by institutions like Charles Adams's New York State Museum, the librarian dreamed of, in her own words, "making available, without selective basis, all of the pictorial documentation we could gather and organize that the public may draw on the past to familiarize themselves with our national heritage."[26] Javitz built her picture collection documenting American life in New York City at the same time that Adams in Albany was working to expand the historical holdings in the state's museum.

Javitz understood her vocation of picture librarian as contributing to national uplift. Sharing a progressive vision with Laura Bragg, Javitz sought to serve what she called "the public," who in her account came from "suburb, tenement, studio, and factory" and included porters, teenage boys, subway riders, sharecroppers, and Vermont farmers. By educating the breadth of the population, she sought to unlock what she referred to as the "art potential of the people." In doing so, she envisioned elevating the United States beyond its fascination with the dross of commercial art designed to serve industry and free enterprise. She hoped that, through art, the nation could "show ourselves and the world that all of our effort is not materialistic alone, that we too have faith in those things that transcend barter and sale."[27]

Javitz and Reeves developed complementary visions of an encyclopedic pictorial reference source documenting American objects that could be used to foster and cultivate a worthy distinctive national culture; however, they perceived the project's benefits from opposite sides of the reference desk. As a librarian, Javitz sought to provide improved services to the widest possible range of patrons.[28] Phyllis Crawford, who was one of the earliest employees of the Index of American Design, recalled that Javitz initially described the project to her as "a series of books or portfolios . . . of American arts, exclusive of the fine arts, well-documented, valuable for stage and movie designers, illustrators of historical books, novelists and historians, and incidentally inspirational for commercial designers."[29] As librarians, Javitz and Crawford desired encyclopedic coverage of the entire field of American material culture.

Reeves, on the other hand, always conceived of the index, in her own words, as "an art rather than a research project."[30] Crawford said of Reeves that she "never lost the textile designer's viewpoint" and stressed the value of the undertaking for "designers."[31] Reeves looked on the index as a collection of carefully executed renderings of objects that she considered beautiful. In 1964, Crawford remembered that drawings of certain objects, like ornate Bennington pottery, were rejected because the subject matter was considered "ugly."[32]

FEDERAL SUPPORT

When Roosevelt's administration inaugurated the Federal Art Project in 1935, Reeves and Javitz perceived in the New Deal's underwriting of artistic activities an opportunity to create their visual catalogue of distinctively American objects. Reeves and Javitz proposed the Index of American Design to Frances M. Pollak, the director of art projects for the Emergency Relief Bureau in New York City, and Carl K. Tranum, a senior project supervisor in the same New York office of the Works Progress Administration.[33] Pollak and Tranum approved the idea because it would employ artists who were in need of relief while fulfilling the cultural purposes Reeves and Javitz envisioned.[34] In consultation with Javitz and Reeves, Pollak established an initial office to implement the project in the late months of 1935, just as

Shaker Handicrafts was preparing to open at the Whitney. Among their preliminary steps, Pollak and Javitz lured Crawford, who held a library science degree from the University of Illinois, from her job at the H. W. Wilson Company, a publisher that specialized in managing data for libraries. Javitz insisted that someone with library experience was required to ensure that the index's visual information was retrievable.[35]

With their experimental local office in place in New York City, Pollak, the emergency relief administrator, and Reeves, who like Andrews was underemployed as a result of the Depression, pitched the project to the national office of the Federal Art Project in Washington, DC.[36] Javitz's responsibilities at the NYPL kept her from further pursuing the undertaking as it progressed through the bureaucracy.

HOLGER CAHILL AND AMERICAN "FOLK ART"

In Washington, Pollak and Reeves encountered Holger Cahill, the newly appointed director of the Federal Art Project, who was a uniquely sympathetic and supportive patron because of his previous activities as a writer, curator, and art impresario. Born of Icelandic parents, Cahill had grown up in the Midwest in humble circumstances, eventually entering an orphanage in Winnipeg, Manitoba. After a transient youth working a variety of jobs, including crewing on a steamship to China, Cahill arrived in New York City in the early years of the twentieth century.[37] In Manhattan, he worked as a journalist, took classes at both Columbia University and the New School for Social Research, and became personally acquainted with the city's writers and artists, including John Sloan, Stuart Davis, Charles Sheeler, and Willem de Kooning.

In 1922, Cahill traveled to Sweden on behalf of the Swedish American News Exchange to document developments in craft production. While in Europe, he toured Skansen, the influential outdoor folk museum near Stockholm, and, like Javitz, was impressed by how Europeans preserved and documented their native material traditions. He recognized that there were few similar efforts within the United States.[38]

Upon his return, Cahill soon became intimate with a group of New York modernists who, like Juliana Force, were in the process of reconceptualizing America's artistic traditions. Edith Halpert, who was married to the painter Samuel Halpert, was the leader in this enterprise and promoted a form of cultural nationalism.[39] Halpert primarily advocated for the modern, twentieth-century art produced around her, but she began to perceive American antiques as forming the foundation for a vital and living national artistic tradition.[40]

Halpert was first exposed to this association at Hamilton Easter Field's artist colony in Ogunquit, Maine, on the coast north of Portsmouth, New Hampshire, where she spent the summers of 1926 and 1927.[41] In Ogunquit, Field, partly informed by the Dada concept of "found art," decorated the buildings he rented as artist's studios with shop signs, decoys, weathervanes, hooked rugs, and other artifacts that he termed "Americana."[42] Field's collecting and decorating practices influenced many of his guests. The artist William Zorach later remembered, "All of us were picking up early American furniture and antiques. Not only were they more beautiful than the regular manufactured products, but they were much cheaper. . . . Hunting antiques was great sport and lots of excitement."[43]

As these modernists scoured the countryside outside New York City looking for artifacts that met their aesthetic criteria, they also found themselves drawn to Shaker materials. The artist Dorothy Varian, who rented a cabin in Field's Ogunquit compound in 1923, told art historian Wanda Corn that she remembered a trip in which Bernard Karfiol, Robert Laurent, and Yasuo Kuniyoshi visited a Quaker village and "had to hire a truck to bring back their early American treasures."[44] Canterbury Shaker Village in New Hampshire, Sabbathday Lake Shaker Village in Maine, and the Shaker village at Alfred, Maine, were all easily accessible from Ogunquit, and a photograph documents Varian, Kuniyoshi, and Robert Laurent bathing in Shaker Pond in Alfred.[45] Since individuals often conflate the Quakers and the Shakers, the artists likely were acquiring Shaker artifacts on this trip. Whether or not Karfiol, Laurent, and Kuniyoshi actually visited a Shaker village, New York's circle of modernist painters and their patrons became aware of the sect's material culture during the 1920s.

Sheeler, in particular, as mentioned previously, collected Shaker materials in the 1920s in his attempts to document what he envisioned as an American tradition in design that stood in contrast to Europe. He claimed, "The Shaker communities, in the period of their greatest creative activity, have given us abundant evidence of their profound understanding of utilitarian design in their architecture and crafts."[46] Sheeler decorated his living place with Shaker objects and included them in his work. His *Americana* from 1931, currently owned by the Metropolitan Museum of Art, for example, prominently includes an oval Shaker box in its lower left corner among the other antiques the artist gathered in his residence in South Salem, New York (fig. 2.3).[47] The artist returned repeatedly to Shaker objects and buildings for inspiration throughout his career.

Working in ways that complemented Gertrude Vanderbilt Whitney and Juliana Force's efforts, Edith Halpert commercialized the link between modern American art and American antiques that this circle of artists and collectors had forged while transmitting their understanding of a national style to a broader audience.[48] A consummate saleswoman, promoter, and entrepreneur, in 1926 she opened a shop, named "The Downtown Gallery," on West 13th Street in Manhattan. In this location, she sold both Americana that she gathered outside the city and the works of modern American painters including Sheeler, Davis, Pop Hart, Max Weber, and both Zorach and his wife, Marguerite Thompson Zorach. In 1928, Paul Marchand noted in the journal *Creative Art* that "Mrs. Halpert opened her Downtown Gallery as an antique shop, with modern art as a side line."[49] In Halpert's view, however, this commentator misunderstood the endeavor. The sale of antiques made it possible for her to support and nurture American art. She described the sale of folk art as "taking in washing" to "pay the overhead for the living American artist."[50] In selling folk art in the same suite of rooms with modernist American art, Halpert elevated both genres and posited a link between the two.

By the late 1920s, Halpert and her husband, Sam, separated, with him moving to Detroit in 1929. Ultimately, Halpert and Holger Cahill became intimate friends, with Cahill also gaining a financial stake in the Downtown Gallery.[51] The art historian Diane Tepfer writes, "As collaborators Halpert and Cahill complemented each other; he gravitated toward writing while Halpert was more energetic and excelled at organizing and promoting."[52] Together, they actively developed both the value of American art and the idea that there was an American aesthetic which stood in opposition to the elevated, aristocratic traditions of Europe.

Halpert sought a variety of clients to support her enterprise. Abby Aldrich Rockefeller, wife of the industrialist John D. Rockefeller, was the most prominent customer of the Downtown Gallery. A founder of New

FIGURE 2.3. Charles Sheeler, *Americana*, 1931, oil on canvas, 121.9 x 91.4 cm (48 x 35 in.). In this work, Sheeler attempted to express what he envisioned as an American tradition in design. Courtesy Metropolitan Museum of Art, The Edith and Milton Lowenthal Collection, Bequest of Edith Abrahamson Lowenthal, 1991 (1992.24.8). Image copyright © The Metropolitan Museum of Art. Image source: Art Resource, NY.

York's Museum of Modern Art, Rockefeller originally purchased modern works but later bought hundreds of folk paintings, sculptures, quilts, pottery, and other works of art. On their purchasing expeditions throughout New York and New England to gather works for Mrs. Rockefeller, Halpert and Cahill expanded their knowledge of American material culture and became acquainted with the variety of the region's artistic traditions.[53]

While collaborating in this business venture with Halpert, Cahill was employed as a curator and administrator at the Newark Museum.[54] During this period, he was profoundly influenced by John Cotton Dana, the museum's director. Like Laura Bragg, Dana had a background in public libraries and envisioned an expanded role for museums in American society. He had thus founded the Newark Museum to serve the residents of that city just as the Charleston Museum served citizens in South Carolina's Lowcountry.[55] In 1928, Dana mounted an exhibition of well-made, inexpensive items at the Newark Museum under a sign proclaiming, "Beauty has no relation to price, rarity, or age."[56] Under Dana's influence, Cahill developed a philosophy that valued artistic production by and for a wide swath of American society, rather than valuing only masterpieces created by and for elites, thus laying the groundwork for him to appreciate Shaker crafts.[57] Cahill called Dana "one of the truly great men of our time" and claimed that he had the vision to see "that in a democracy such as ours art should not be a luxury product of a minor order intended for the select few." Rather, Cahill explained, Dana understood that "art *should be,* and *could be* interwoven with the very stuff and texture of our national life."[58]

While at the Newark Museum, Cahill curated two seminal folk art exhibitions, *American Primitives* of 1930 and *American Folk Sculpture* of 1931. Cahill also organized *The Art of the Common Man in America, 1750–1900* for the Museum of Modern Art in 1932. In mounting these shows, Cahill drew on the collection that he and Halpert had assembled for Rockefeller and the holdings of his acquaintances in the art world. In these exhibitions, and in the writings and catalogues that accompanied them, Cahill, like Schnakenberg and Force, posited that the products of preindustrial artisans and untrained artists were expressions of a unique national American spirit.[59] In producing these events, Cahill was participating in a movement that historian Warren Sussman has argued characterized American culture in the 1930s to "define America as a culture and to create the pattern of a way of life worth understanding."[60] Cahill, like Javitz, who similarly had been influenced by Dana, was part of a sweeping effort among the nation's intelligentsia to record and understand the lives and values of the American people.

With his background as a dealer in folk art and an advocate for the idea of an American aesthetic, Cahill was receptive to Reeves and Pollak when in 1936 they proposed creating a pictorial resource documenting American material culture. In the context of an international resurgence of nationalism, the Index of American Design would validate and illuminate the continuity in American products that Halpert, Force, Sheeler, and Cahill posited. In promoting the index, Henry G. Alsberg, the director of the WPA's Federal Writers' Project, explained, "The Index of American Design will give our manufacturers, industrial designers, and students the opportunity to learn what America has done in industrial art and encourage them to carry on the development."[61] Similarly, a statement of purpose for the Index of American Design dated September 15, 1937, echoes John Cotton Dana's philosophy while combining the contributions of Reeves, Javitz, and Cahill. This statement asserts, "Typical examples of an indigenous American character will be made available for study. It is hoped that such a collection will stimulate the artist, designer, and manufacturer of articles of everyday use to build upon our American tradition, and that it will offer an opportunity to the student, teacher, research worker, and the general public to familiarize themselves with this important phase of the American culture pattern."[62]

Under Cahill's leadership, the Index of American Design was established as a federal program in which artists throughout the country were employed to create watercolor plates illustrating American objects. Cahill established a national office in Washington, DC, to administer the index, and in January 1936, he hired Ruth Reeves as its national supervisor.

To find the raw material out of which the Index of American Design would be created, Reeves, Cahill, and their associates, including Nina Collier, who previously had served as an arts administrator for the Federal Emergency Relief Administration, sought out museum curators, antique dealers, and collectors of Americana.[63] Cahill specifically hoped to record and document items that previously had not been photographed and which were located outside the collections of major institutions such as the Metropolitan Museum of Art or Boston's Museum of Fine Arts.[64] The national office sent Reeves on the road to locate local collections of folk and decorative arts.

THE INDEX AND SHAKER DESIGN

Almost from its inception, Index of American Design administrators planned to highlight Shaker materials. This interest in Shaker objects partly was driven by aesthetics. In a memo written from Massachusetts on February 18, 1936, Collier reported back to the central office in Washington, "The Shaker field . . . seems to me to be extremely interesting. The exquisite simplicity of the furniture for example and the treatment of detail, the table legs, the slender chair crests and the use of plain surfaces is all very inspiring to the modern designer."[65] In this epistle, Collier was communicating to federal bureaucrats in the national capital the promotional understanding of Shaker materials that had been codified four months earlier in conjunction with the Whitney's *Shaker Handicrafts* show.

The index's administrators also immediately recognized that Shaker objects could be used to illustrate what they believed to be the American utilitarian aesthetic. Reeves asserted, "This Shaker material emphasizes and 'points the way' more clearly to what, to my mind, has always been the crux of the whole project, i.e., the depiction of the arts of America's common man."[66] These New Deal administrators thus were also making an intellectual leap in claiming that the material remains of this small religious sect, largely located in the northeast quadrant of the country, could be used to represent the national character.

Interest in Shaker materials, however, also was driven by expediency. Employees of the index felt pressure from the beginning to generate a finished product. As early as February 1936, Reeves was instructed by her superiors to publish an initial portfolio of drawings within six months. In consultation with Cahill and other administrators, she concluded that this initial publication would focus on Shaker furniture. "It seems to me," she wrote in a memo to Cahill, "that the most unique and valuable portfolio, and the simplest to gather together and publish in this short time would be the portfolio on Shaker furniture."[67] In producing this inaugural publication, Reeves assumed that she could draw on the expertise and collections of Faith and Edward Deming Andrews, Charles Sheeler, and Rita Romilly Benson, a former Broadway actress, *bon vivant,* and follower of the Armenian mystic Gurdjieff.[68] Benson, according to Reeves, had worked with Juliana Force in gathering her personal Shaker collection. Concerning Sheeler, Reeves noted, "His Shaker things are very beautiful indeed and . . . Sheeler is a fine ally for the Index to have."[69]

Reeves originally envisioned the Shaker portfolio to be a cooperative effort crossing the bureaucratic barriers between the Federal Art Project's New England office, which had its headquarters in Boston, and the New York office, administered from Manhattan. The two most easily accessible Shaker villages, Hancock, outside Pittsfield, Massachusetts, and Mount Lebanon in the town of New Lebanon, New York, straddled the border between the two states, thus necessitating bureaucratic cooperation.[70] In April, Reeves drafted a proposal for a Shaker portfolio that would include photographs of Shaker furniture within Shaker buildings; renderings of Shaker furniture, textiles, and costumes; and photographs of tools, stoves, baskets, and what she termed the "minor arts." This proposal also called for the portfolio to include the gift drawings the Whitney Museum had introduced to the public.[71]

The greatest logistical problem relating to the Shaker portfolio that Reeves and her colleagues faced was that the Shaker villages and private collections of artifacts were located at significant distances from administrative centers and from the urban areas where the project's artists resided. This geographical dilemma was overcome both by sending photographers and artists on daytrips to western Massachusetts and by transporting items from the Andrewses' collections to the Museum of Fine Arts in Boston where they were stored and recorded.[72] Understandably, Faith and Ted Andrews, who were still economically insecure, desired a role in the undertaking, and the WPA placed them on the payroll as associate research workers with the understanding that together they would work a total of ninety-six hours per month.[73]

Although initially the Andrewses had been enthusiastic supporters of the index, by May 1936 friction developed between the dealers and WPA administrators. The couple, who had benefited from the personal attention of Adams, Bragg, and Force, were unaccustomed to functioning within a bureaucracy. In a letter from Reeves to Cahill dated May 7, 1936, she indicated that the Andrewses required tender treatment if the index wished to use their materials and gain cooperation.[74] Throughout the next months, while Reeves became increasingly passionate about the value of documenting

Shaker objects, she also was required to invest expanding effort in managing, placating, and devising ways to work around the Andrewses.[75]

During these months, the index hired as an editorial consultant Constance Rourke, a cultural historian and critic who played a prominent role in the 1930s quest to define American culture and had written a laudatory and insightful review of the catalogue accompanying Cahill's folk art show at the Museum of Modern Art in New York.[76] Rourke, who also was an intimate of Sheeler and would author the first monograph on him, became a full-time employee of the index, was given the title of editor, and became enmeshed in the creation of the Shaker portfolio.[77]

Eventually Reeves moved to Pittsfield for the summer to serve as an intermediary between the Andrewses and the index's various watercolor artists, painters, and photographers. In Reeves's words, this was necessary because "the Andrews [sic] very early in the game refused to play ball" with the Boston office.[78] Reeves later reported to Cahill, "On this job I am appreciating and cashing in on the lessons I learned wangling textiles off the backs of Guatemalan Indians for five, solid months. . . . I have trod as softly as if the Andrews were Maya Indians."[79] During this summer, Alfred H. Smith, who specialized in drawing furniture, created watercolor plates of Shaker materials, as did Elizabeth Moutal, who demonstrated an expertise with textiles; Lawrence Foster; Irving Smith; John Kelleher; Victor Muollo; and Anne Ger, among others (figs. 2.4–2.7).[80] Throughout her time in western Massachusetts, Reeves worked with these artists and with Faith and Ted Andrews to choose which pieces should be documented. She also made decisions about how they would be represented. The artists drew on the Andrewses' collection of furniture and costumes but recorded items on location in the Shaker village in New Lebanon, New York, too, and from the holdings of private collectors including William Lassiter, who had secured long-term employment as curator at the New York State Museum (figs. 2.8–2.9).

Noel Vincentini and George Herlick, employed by the Federal Art Project as photographers in New York City, were reassigned to Pittsfield to create documentary photographs.[81] Because the WPA was designed to offer relief to the underemployed, index officials chose Vincentini and Herlick over Winter and Sheeler, even though the latter two photographers were recommended by the Andrewses.[82] Shooting both on the property of the Shaker villages and inside the Andrewses' houses, which the collectors and dealers had filled with Shaker furniture, Vincentini and Herlick produced

FIGURE 2.4. Alfred H. Smith, *Built-In Cupboard and Drawer,* ca. 1937, watercolor and graphite on paperboard, 27.9 x 21 cm (11 x 8¼ in.). Artists for the Index of American Design recorded Shaker material culture on site within Shaker villages. Drawn from the original located in the North Family compound, Mount Lebanon Shaker Village, New Lebanon, NY. Courtesy Index of American Design, National Gallery of Art, Washington, DC, 1943.8.16807.

FIGURE 2.5. Elizabeth Moutal, *Shaker Knitting-Needle Case*, 1936, watercolor over graphite on paperboard, 37.7 x 26.1 cm (14¹³⁄₁₆ x 10¼ in.). The Index of American Design recorded Shaker textiles as well as furniture. Drawn from the original in the collection of Faith and Edward Deming Andrews. Courtesy Index of American Design, National Gallery of Art, Washington, DC, 1943.8.13664.

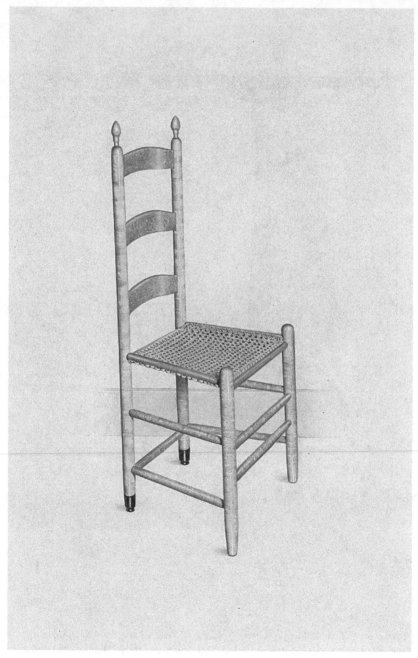

FIGURE 2.6. John W. Kelleher, *Shaker Tilting Chair*, ca. 1937, watercolor and graphite on paper, 30.5 x 25.5 cm (12 x 10¹⁄₁₆ in.). Artists from the Index of American Design often focused on simple and functional examples of Shaker furniture. Drawn from the original located in the North Family compound, Mount Lebanon Shaker Village, New Lebanon, NY. Courtesy Index of American Design, National Gallery of Art, Washington, DC, 1943.8.17149.

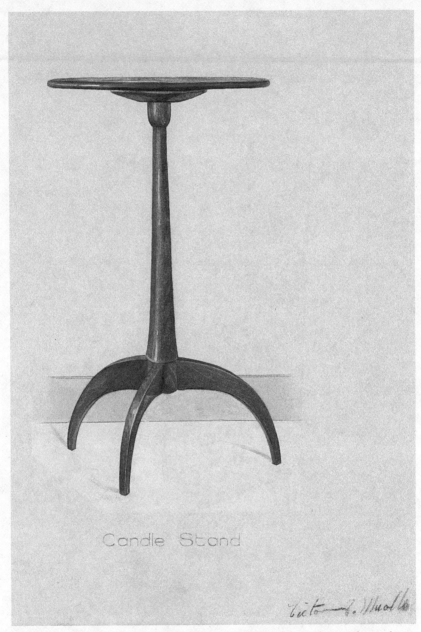

Candle Stand

FIGURE 2.7. Victor F. Muollo, *Candle Stand*, 1936, watercolor, graphite, and gouache on paperboard, 27.8 x 22.9 cm (10^{15}/$_{16}$ x 9 in.). This compelling image of design reduced to its geometric basics is the result of Muollo's skill as an artist but also represents the Andrewses' taste in selecting the candlestand for their collection and the agency of the administrators of the Index of American Design in choosing it to be recorded. Drawn from the original in the collection of Faith and Edward Deming Andrews. Courtesy Index of American Design, National Gallery of Art, Washington, DC, 1943.8.13601.

FIGURE 2.8. Unknown artist, *Shaker Woman's Costume,* 1935, watercolor and graphite on paper, 40.4 x 30.6 cm (15⅞ x 12¹⁄₁₆ in.). WPA artists recorded Shaker clothing. Drawn from the original in the collection of Faith and Edward Deming Andrews. Courtesy Index of American Design, National Gallery of Art, Washington, DC, 1943.8.17106.

FIGURE 2.9. Unknown artist, *Shaker Man's Costume*, 1936, watercolor, graphite, and pen on paper, 41.3 x 26.5 cm (16¼ x 10⁷⁄₁₆ in.). The Index of American Design's guidelines called for recording the appearance of clothing from the front and the rear. Drawn from the original in the collection of Faith and Edward Deming Andrews. Courtesy Index of American Design, National Gallery of Art, Washington, DC, 1943.8.17078.

appealing compositions that showcased the living Shakers themselves as well as the architecture and material culture of their sect.[83] These photographs, reflecting the tenor of other cultural products of the 1930s, portrayed the Shaker villages as refuges from the problems associated with the nation's industrial economic collapse and as portals to a simpler, cleaner, less problem-ridden era.[84] Reeves was pleased by what she called the "literary" quality of the photographs and reported that the Andrewses "practically swooned over them."[85]

The Vincentini and Herlick images of Shaker material culture, featuring pure geometric forms and planes within empty spaces, drew on the modernist canon created by Sheeler, Strand, and others.[86] Their image of the Great Stone Barn of the North Family of the Mount Lebanon village, for example, truncates the ends of the building to emphasize the plane of the roof and the form of the wall pierced by rhythmically placed windows (fig. 2.10). A fence with parallel rails slashes across the middle ground of the picture frame, while the sky glows luminously in the background. This image is reminiscent of Sheeler's images of Pennsylvania barns of the 1910s and Strand's photographs published in *Time in New England*.[87]

Vincentini and Herlick's photograph of wooden forms in the machine shop at the Church Family in the Mount Lebanon village also fits squarely within the modernist visual vocabulary (fig. 2.11). The circular objects accent the rectilinearity of their surroundings, and the sinuous sculptural mass in the lower left corner of the composition is both echoed and set off from the wall by its shadow. This image is more strongly reminiscent of Man Ray than Sheeler or Strand, but it still speaks to a self-consciousness on the part of the photographers.

In some cases, however, their images resemble Winter's work so closely that they must be described as derivative. Their photograph of a rocking chair, sewing table, and door taken in a building at the Church Family in Hancock, Massachusetts, for example, could easily be mistaken for part of Winter's oeuvre (fig. 2.12). In fact, it closely resembles a composition that Winter created using a rocking chair and sewing table subsequently published as plate 14 of *Shaker Furniture* (fig. 2.13). In each, the rocking chair is on the left side of the frame arranged at the same angle to the camera lens; both even include a book displayed casually on the tabletop.

Similarly, Vincentini and Herlick's image of a table and dining chairs in the Ministry Dining Room of the Brick Dwelling of the Church Family in

FIGURE 2.10. Noel Vincentini and George Herlick, "Great Stone Barn, North Facade with Roof and Cupola, North Family, Mount Lebanon (V-167)," 1936. Vincentini and Herlick's Shaker images featuring pure geometric forms and planes drew on the modernist photographic canon created by Charles Sheeler, Paul Strand, and others. Courtesy National Gallery of Art, Washington, DC, Gallery Archives, RG44D9, Records of the Index of American Design, Original Project (WPA) Images—Vincentini Shaker Villages.

FIGURE 2.11. Noel Vincentini and George Herlick, "Machine Shop, Wooden Casting Patterns, Church Family, Mount Lebanon, New York (V-48)," 1936. This image of the inside of a Shaker workspace is a modernist investigation of geometric forms. Courtesy National Gallery of Art, Washington, DC, Gallery Archives, RG44D9, Records of the Index of American Design, Original Project (WPA) Images—Vincentini Shaker Villages.

FIGURE 2.12. Noel Vincentini and George Herlick, "Shaker Sewing Table and Chair, Han-cock, Ma. (V-171)," 1936. This photograph could easily be mistaken for part of William F. Winter, Jr.'s oeuvre. Courtesy National Gallery of Art, Washington, DC, Gallery Archives, RG44D9, Records of the Index of American Design, Original Project (WPA) Images— Vincentini Shaker Villages.

Hancock, Massachusetts, resembles Winter's image entitled "Shaker Aus-terity" when it was first enlisted to publicize the Whitney's *Shaker Handi-crafts* show (figs. 2.14, 1.32). In both compositions, a trestle table is arranged in the corner of a room and chairs with woven seats are placed symmet-rically around it. Horizontal peg rails define the upper areas of the walls

FIGURE 2.13. William F. Winter, Jr., "Workstand, with Brethren's Rocker and Pipe-Rack," ca. 1935. This work is very similar to figure 2.14 by the WPA photographers. Reproduced in Andrews and Andrews, *Shaker Furniture*, plate 14. Courtesy Winterthur Library: The Edward Deming Andrews Memorial Shaker Collection, SA 558b.

while in both cases, the number of chairs on each side of the table reflects the fenestration on the far wall. Winter's image, however, is framed more elegantly than Vincentini and Herlick's in that he has eliminated the plane of the ceiling while the WPA photographers' composition is disrupted by the distraction of a pipe running just below the ceiling.

Multiple explanations are possible for the similarity of these images. Vincentini and Herlick may simply have been familiar with Winter's work and sought to emulate it. More charitably, it may be suggested that the Shaker materials called out for this sort of treatment by skilled photographers

FIGURE 2.14. Noel Vincentini and George Herlick, "Brick Dwelling, Ministry Dining Room, Church Family, Hancock, Massachusetts (V-36)," 1936. Edward Deming Andrews may have created arrangements of furniture for both Winter and the index's photographers. Courtesy National Gallery of Art, Washington, DC, Gallery Archives, RG44D9, Records of the Index of American Design, Original Project (WPA) Images—Vincentini Shaker Villages.

working in the 1930s. Ted Andrews, finally, may have observed Winter at work and arranged materials for Vincentini and Herlick to emulate his style. These familiar compositions thus may reflect the collector's and dealer's eyes as much as they do the talent of the WPA's photographers.

The index photographs of the Shaker villages' inhabitants resemble contemporaneous Farm Security Administration photographs that ennobled and celebrated America's "common people" (figs. 2.15–2.16). The Shakers, like their furniture, appear timeless. They are surrounded by the material

FIGURE 2.15. Noel Vincentini and George Herlick, "Sister Sarah, Dormitory Entrance, New Lebanon, NY (V-22)," 1936. WPA photographs of Shakers and Shaker villages resemble Farm Security Administration documentary images from approximately the same time. Courtesy National Gallery of Art, Washington, DC, Gallery Archives, RG44D9, Records of the Index of American Design, Original Project (WPA) Images—Vincentini Shaker Villages.

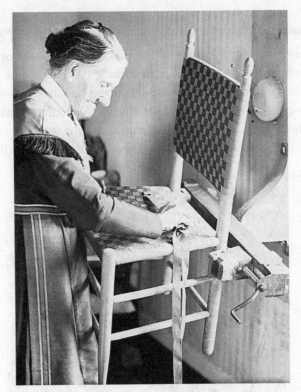

FIGURE 2.16. Noel Vincentini and George Herlick, "Sister Sarah Braiding a Chair at Shaker Colony at Hancock, Mass. (V32)," 1936. The Shakers, like their furniture, were portrayed as being timeless and as representing dignity, inner strength, and self-reliance. Courtesy National Gallery of Art, Washington, DC, Gallery Archives, RG44D9, Records of the Index of American Design, Original Project (WPA) Images—Vincentini Shaker Villages.

evidence of their sect's communal history while also apparently supported by dignity, inner strength, and self-reliance.[88]

Vincentini and Herlick's photographs of the Andrewses' house portray the clean, simple lines of the furniture and indicate how the pieces could be used in a twentieth-century home (figs. 2.17–2.18). The photograph of the Andrewses' dining room includes a trestle table as well as the same sideboard from Canterbury that they had exhibited at both the Berkshire and Whitney Museums. This view strikingly approximates the vignette

FIGURE 2.17. Noel Vincentini and George Herlick, "Dining Room of Shaker Furniture, Home of E. D. Andrews, Pittsfield, MA (V-118)," 1936. This sideboard had been included in the exhibition at the Berkshire Museum as indicated in figure 1.24. Courtesy National Gallery of Art, Washington, DC, Gallery Archives, RG44D9, Records of the Index of American Design, Original Project (WPA) Images—Vincentini Shaker Villages.

illustrating a Shaker dining room that the collectors had installed in the Berkshire Museum's gallery in 1932 (fig. 1.24). This photograph also reveals that the Andrewses had become so enamored of the Shaker aesthetic that they had installed Shaker peg boards in their own dining room, just as they had in the galleries. These images of the collectors' dwelling imply that the Shakers' virtues of simplicity and order could be imported into one's home along with their furniture, thus counteracting the societal and economic chaos of Depression-ravaged America.

Ruth Reeves also arranged to borrow the artist Yvonne Twining from the Federal Art Project's easel painting initiative to create oil paintings of Shaker subjects for inclusion in the published Shaker portfolio as context for objects documented in the watercolor plates.[89] Reeves described Twining as "a charming person and a very good artist . . . for this particular

FIGURE 2.18. Noel Vincentini and George Herlick, "Guest Room, Shaker Furniture in Home of E. D. Andrews, Pittsfield, MA (V-91)," 1936. Photographs of the interior of the Andrewses' house indicate how Shaker furniture could be used in a twentieth-century home. Courtesy National Gallery of Art, Washington, DC, Gallery Archives, RG44D9, Records of the Index of American Design, Original Project (WPA) Images—Vincentini Shaker Villages.

job."[90] The daughter of a cosmopolitan, artistic family, Twining had settled in her teens with her mother in South Egremont, Massachusetts, a town in the Berkshires not distant from Pittsfield and Hancock Shaker Village. She trained as an artist at the National Academy of Design and, like Reeves and

Javitz, at the Art Students League in New York City. In the 1930s, she developed what art historian Sharon Long Baerny termed a "hard-edged Regionalist style."[91] Although Twining's paintings were exhibited in New York City, she resided in Massachusetts because of the politics of artist support within the Federal Art Project.[92] The government defined her as a resident of Massachusetts, and thus the WPA could only employ her as an artist in that state. While working for the Federal Art Project, she produced views of familiar landscapes including Boston, New York City, and western Massachusetts.[93] A critic for the *Christian Science Monitor* said of Twining that she had "portrayed a number of handsome scenes of Western Massachusetts in which the beauty and delights of rustic life are clearly indicated."[94]

The Andrewses, who had requested unsuccessfully that Holger Cahill attempt to secure Grant Wood instead of Twining because of his facility with rural Americans and nationalist themes, arranged for space to be allocated as a painting studio within the Hancock Shaker Village.[95] Twining's painting, entitled *Shakeress at Her Loom,* differed stylistically from her other compositions (fig. 2.19).[96] Rather than a landscape, this interior scene depicts a young woman weaving. The artist has attentively filled the scene with objects that are identifiably of Shaker provenance, including built-in cabinets, a basket, a distinctive cloth apron, and even an oval wooden box peeking out from behind a half-opened cupboard door. With its handwoven textiles and plain wooden furnishings, Twining's interior scene resembles Sheeler's *Americana.* An American genre painting, this scene, like Sheeler's, is located outside of chronology. Nothing anchors it in time; the young woman could be toiling at her loom in either 1836 or 1936. As an illustration for the Shaker portfolio, this work elevated disparate objects into an iconic, timeless composition, suggesting an unbroken American tradition. The beauty of the subject's surroundings, and of her implied pious values, was meant to be transcendent. This hard-working, self-abnegating figure, like Vincentini and Herlick's photographs of Sister Sarah Collins manufacturing Shaker chairs, spoke of the heroic functionalism that twentieth-century modernists projected on the Shakers and which they hoped by association distinguished America's exceptional national identity. Upon its completion, this painting was exhibited by the Andrewses to their Pittsfield friends, creating a stir.[97]

Twining also produced a graphite-on-paper sketch of the Hancock Shaker Village, now in the collection of the Hood Museum at Dartmouth College, which may have been intended for inclusion in the Shaker portfolio

FIGURE 2.19. Yvonne Twining, *Shakeress at Her Loom*, 1936, oil on canvas, 66 x 50.8 cm (26 x 20 in.). An American genre painting, this image, like Sheeler's *Americana,* portrays a moment located outside of chronology. Courtesy David Martin and Dominic Zambito, Seattle, WA.

to provide a broader context for the documentary drawings (fig. 2.20). As a landscape, this work is more representative of the artist's larger oeuvre, yet it also complements *Shakeress at Her Loom.* While the easel painting portrays a Shaker interior, the sketch shows the outside of the buildings. The Shakeress, a female, is involved in manufacturing, while the primary figure portrayed amid the village's buildings is male and holds an agricultural implement. The sketch includes two children, even though no young people resided in Hancock Shaker Village in the 1930s. However, the composition is as timeless as the easel painting. Once again, there is nothing inherent in

FIGURE 2.20. Yvonne Twining, *Hancock Shaker Village*, 1936. Graphite on semi-transparent wove paper, 43.8 x 52.7 cm (17.2 x 20.7 in.). Probably intended for inclusion in the Index of American Design's Shaker portfolio to provide a broader context for the documentary drawings, this sketch complements *Shakeress at Her Loom*. Courtesy Hood Museum of Art, Dartmouth: Gift of Trevor Fairbrother and John T. Kirk, 2011.63.5.

the work to indicate whether the four figures inhabiting the Shaker dooryard are meant to represent Americans of the antebellum period or of the Great Depression. This lovely, quiet work presents an idyllic vision of individuals within a serene, well-maintained communal compound.

CONFLICT IN PITTSFIELD

Relations between the staff of the Index of American Design and Faith and Ted Andrews were strained throughout the summer of 1936 by a number of issues. The Andrewses repeatedly expressed concern that the artists were not doing justice to the beauty of the Shaker artifacts.[98] The couple, who believed themselves to be the only experts regarding Shaker history and material culture, also resented, by their own account, that they were denied "full authority" and felt constrained by having to answer to "absentee overlords" in Washington.[99] In July, Reeves reported to Richard C. Morrison, the coordinator of the Index of American Design within Massachusetts, that "the Andrews feel fettered where anyone suggests they work to a coherent editorial plan."[100] The couple also begrudged Charles Sheeler and Constance Rourke, whom they perceived as threats to their standing.[101]

Interpersonal politics were complicated further by the Andrewses having received money from Juliana Force to support their study of Shaker furniture, which Yale University Press was soon to publish.[102] Thus, throughout the summer, the Andrewses had conflicting allegiances between work for the federal government in support of the index's Shaker portfolio and their desire to have their own book reach press first, thus becoming the defining statement concerning Shaker furniture. As they had since they first met Adams, the Andrewses continued to seek the most advantageous deal and cooperated with the index to accrue what benefits were available, while simultaneously pursuing their own objectives. The Andrewses' book, illustrated with William Winter's photographs (many of which had been seen previously in relation to the Whitney exhibition), was published in 1937 as *Shaker Furniture: The Craftsmanship of an American Communal Sect.*[103]

A fraught situation was aggravated when photographer Noel Vincentini established a sexual relationship with one of the Andrewses' female relatives. The Andrewses disapproved of the New York photographer's behavior, and according to Morrison, they "made quite a stir about it, and kicked all the rest of the artists out of their house."[104] Reeves wrote in frustration to Cahill, "I can control a few things for you up here but I can't control people's private lives and the way in which their conduct can stymie a project. I will, somehow, I suppose, find a way out because a really fine and definative [sic] Shaker portfolio . . . is so nearly complete that I won't let even this, the worst blow, lick me."[105]

While Reeves attempted to keep a lid on a simmering pot in Pittsfield, artists and photographers from the index were concurrently documenting Shaker materials elsewhere. Morrison accompanied a photographer to take pictures of Canterbury Shaker Village in New Hampshire.[106] Alfred Smith, whose drawings index administrators particularly admired, and Howard Weld, who was part of the project's Connecticut office, recorded Sheeler's collection in watercolor (fig. 2.21).[107] John H. Davis, an artist associated with the index's Maine office, visited the Shaker village at Sabbathday Lake and produced drawings of furniture and domestic goods.[108] Constance Rourke searched for materials in Ohio and Kentucky that might be added, with the assistance of Adele Brandeis, Kentucky's state director of the index.[109]

FIGURE 2.21. Alfred H. Smith, *Shaker Kitchen Piece with Tray,* 1936, watercolor and graphite on paperboard, 27.8 x 22.9 cm (10¹⁵⁄₁₆ x 9 in.). Alfred Smith recorded materials from Charles Sheeler's personal collection, including this cabinet. Courtesy Index of American Design, National Gallery of Art, Washington, DC, 1943.8.13651.

In the Bluegrass State, artists were particularly active in Harrodsburg, near the Shaker Village at Pleasant Hill.[110] Lon Cronk and George V. Vezolles produced drawings of Shaker objects in private collections, including some owned by James L. Isenberg, a local booster and promoter of heritage tourism (figs. 2.22–2.23). [111] Eventually, all the photographs and drawings were

FIGURE 2.22. Lon Cronk, *Shaker Candle Table,* ca. 1937, watercolor and graphite on paperboard, 25.8 x 20.8 cm (10¹³⁄₁₆ x 8³⁄₁₆ in.). Constance Rourke worked with Adele Brandeis to find Shaker materials in Kentucky for artists like Cronk to record. Courtesy Index of American Design, National Gallery of Art, Washington, DC, 1943.8.17199.

sent to Washington where the index's staff, including Adolph Glassgold, catalogued and reviewed them.

The relationship between the Andrewses and the Index of American Design ended badly in the fall of 1936 with recriminations on both sides.[112]

FIGURE 2.23. George V. Vezolles, *Shaker Tin Safe*, ca. 1939, watercolor, graphite, and colored pencil on paperboard, 41 x 30.9 cm (16⅛ x 12³⁄₁₆ in.). George Vezolles recorded this food safe from the Shaker village at South Union in western Kentucky. Courtesy Index of American Design, National Gallery of Art, Washington, DC, 1943.8.10465.

Although resentments had festered for months, the final break occurred when Rita Romilly Benson, on a visit to Pittsfield, inadvertently let the Andrewses know that Alfred Smith had been recording Sheeler's collection. The Andrewses experienced this as an affront.[113] On September 12, 1936,

Morrison informed the Andrewses that "all progress on the Shaker portfolio has been stopped" because of "a lack of smooth cooperation."[114] In a letter to Constance Rourke on October 1, 1936, Glassgold reported that Cahill and he had decided to "present our two 'Shakers' with a furlough." He explained that he believed the hiatus would only be temporary because he was "satisfied that the Andrews are not ones to let a good contact slip from their fingers."[115]

Cahill terminated the couple's employment four days later.[116] Glassgold's assessment was flawed, however; the proud and jealous couple subsequently harbored resentment against Cahill for decades, writing afterward that the split had been caused by "ignorance, indifference, or carelessness" on the part of federal officials.[117] Rourke summed up the situation from the WPA's perspective by stating, "It is evident that the dissociation of the Index from the Andrews is a clear gain."[118]

Work continued on the Shaker portfolio after the break with the Andrewses. Rourke, in particular, persisted in trying to make the idea into a reality, even after Ruth Reeves left the index's employment to pursue other projects related to revitalizing American craft traditions, including working with the Southern Highlanders, Inc., to improve traditional Appalachian weaving patterns.[119] In August 1937, Glassgold reported to Cahill that in preparation for the Shaker portfolio, he had in hand sixty-five images of furniture, eighty-three of textiles, and ten miscellaneous other drawings, all from New England. Artists in Kentucky and Ohio were at work documenting Shaker materials in those states.[120]

THE LEGACY OF THE SHAKER PORTFOLIO

The federal government never published the Shaker portfolio that Reeves and Cahill had envisioned, but the drawings and photographs the index created became canonical in spite of this setback. Ultimately, the Shaker images served the purpose that Reeves and Javitz had originally conceived; they became visual resources for Americans who were interested in the sect and in American decorative arts and material culture. These sources, however, also carried their creators' imprint. They expressed the conflation of modernism and American nationalism that permeated the Index of American Design's administration from its inception. The Andrewses had culled items from the Shaker villages that they believed were most saleable to collectors attracted to the tenets of modernism. Sheeler, likewise, had gathered pieces that harmonized with his own aesthetic. Vincentini and Herlick created appealing black-and-white photographs composed of plain architecture, simple material culture, and the Shakers themselves. Reeves and the other index administrators therefore had chosen items to be recorded that best served their objective of illustrating a particular American tradition in the decorative arts.

The images produced also are noteworthy for what they failed to record. At the end of the nineteenth century, craftsmen in the Shaker villages, including Emmory Brooks of Groveland, New York; Henry Green of Alfred, Maine; Thomas Fisher of Enfield, Connecticut; Delmer Wilson of Sabbathday Lake, Maine, and others, produced ornamented furniture influenced by the Gothic revival and other Victorian design movements.[121] For example, one of Brooks's beds with ornate, turned finials appears in William Winter's 1930 photograph of Eldress Anna Case's room in the South Family compound of the Watervliet, New York, Shaker village (fig. 2.24).[122] Index staff members chose not to portray these ornamented examples of Shaker craftsmanship.

The administrators of the Index of American Design also did not share Charles Adams's interest in the economic and industrial life of the Shakers. Reeves and her cohort sought items that could serve as design sources for home furnishings and thus focused on furniture and textiles. They were not interested in recording for posterity herb presses, printing presses, trip hammers, milk-condensing equipment, and other machines. A few tape looms, spinning wheels, and other examples of tools related to textiles were recorded, but objects used in manufacturing were largely overlooked.

The index's visual record similarly did not include examples of the sect's woven poplar "fancy goods." Manufactured in the late nineteenth and early twentieth centuries by the sisters of Mount Lebanon, New York; Hancock, Massachusetts; Canterbury and Enfield, New Hampshire; and Sabbathday Lake and Alfred, Maine, poplar sewing boxes were lined with satin, edged with white kid leather, and decorated with shoe buttons and colored ribbons.[123] Textile historian Beverly Gordon has argued that, although these items have been undervalued in scholarship, from 1860 well into the twentieth century they comprised the backbone of a larger trade in fancywork among the Shakers forming the most numerous, most broadly distributed, and best known of the community's products (fig. 2.25).[124] These fussy

FIGURE 2.24. William F. Winter, Jr., "Dwelling Room of Sister Anna Case," 1930. This interior image from the South Family Dwelling House in the Watervliet Shaker Village shows a variety of objects that were not recorded by the Index of American Design including a bed with ornamental finials produced by Emmory Brooks (1807–1891) as well as chromolithographs, patterned wallpaper, ornate oriental rugs, patterned linoleum, and a highly decorated cast-iron stove. Courtesy Library of Congress, Prints & Photographs Division, Historic American Buildings Survey (HABS NY, 1-COL, 14—6).

Victorian objects did not embody the clean modernist aesthetic that the WPA's decision-makers valued and thus were marginalized.[125] Likewise, although framed lithographs, colorful decorated linoleum floorcloths, Victorian wallpaper, patterned carpets, and ornamental furniture, like those seen in Winter's photographs of Eldress Anna Case's room in Watervliet and the South Family eldress's room of Mount Lebanon, permeated Shaker villages in the 1930s, these details were carefully omitted from the index photographers' viewfinders (figs. 2.24, 2.26).[126]

The Index of American Design thus created a strictly edited visual representation of the Shakers through their material culture. Items that supported a presentation of the sect as epitomizing an American vernacular tradition of unadorned functionalism were deemed beautiful and celebrated. Those Shaker objects and spaces that undercut this portrayal and

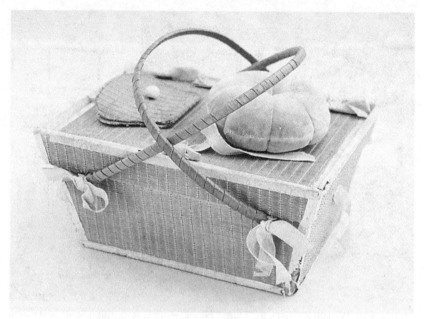

FIGURE 2.25. Shaker poplar "fancywork" sewing basket, ca. 1915–1925, 16 x 11 x 7 cm (6⅛ x 4½ x 2¾ in.). Although poplar fancywork was arguably the most broadly distributed Shaker product in the late nineteenth century, it was ignored by the Index of American Design. Courtesy Collection Hancock Shaker Village, Pittsfield, MA, 1962.308.002.

indicated an impetus within the community toward ornamentation or decoration were consistently excluded.

In the succeeding decades, the index's Shaker images were exhibited extensively in a broad range of venues across the nation and eagerly embraced by aesthetes who understood them as documenting a native American modernism. Most immediately, in September and October 1936, drawings were installed at the Museum of Modern Art in New York in an exhibition entitled *New Horizons in American Art,* curated by Dorothy C. Miller, who also had worked at the Newark Museum under John Cotton Dana and would subsequently wed Cahill.[127] The press expressed great interest in the images of Shaker items included in this show.[128] William Germain Dooley, art critic for the *Boston Evening Transcript,* happily celebrated the perceived link between Shaker materials and modernism fostered by index administrators. Dooley wrote, "Shaker culture is one rich artistic vein uncovered in New Horizons in American Art, the exhibition which

FIGURE 2.26. William F. Winter, Jr., "Eldress Room," summer 1930. This interior image from the South Family Dwelling House in New Lebanon, New York, with its hanging framed pictures, colorful floorcloth, ornamental side table, and piles of paper contrasts markedly from Vincentini and Herlick's spare and uncluttered interiors seen in figures 2.12 and 2.14. Courtesy Library of Congress, Prints & Photographs Division, Historic American Buildings Survey (HABS NY, 11-NELEB.V, 17—6).

has opened at the Museum of Modern Art. . . . Superb craftsmen, these unworldly, ascetic, God-loving people produced hand-made textiles and furniture whose simple forms and functional economy make them the first modern design in America."[129] Similarly, a writer for the *Berkshire Eagle* in Pittsfield, Massachusetts, noted, "Today those who seem to spend their time making up the longest words possible to describe simple processes, call it 'functionalism'—and functionalism has come in these modern times to be, if not a synonym, at least a correlative, of beauty. So what the simple Shakers conceived out of their un-worldly hearts and with their patient hands, has become a new school of design, a school considered highly 'modern,' and worth the consideration of students of such things."[130] The *New York Herald Tribune* published a photographic feature entitled "The Art of the American Shakers," illustrated with seven images by Vincentini and Herlick.[131] These articles appearing in popular journals indicate that the images produced by the Index of American Design buttressed what was becoming a canonical understanding of the Shakers that had been first articulated in connection with the Berkshire Museum's exhibition.

The Fogg Art Museum at Harvard University in Cambridge, Massachusetts, exhibited the index's Shaker drawings in January and February 1937 and complemented its presentation with a catalogue containing an introduction written by Constance Rourke.[132] A year later, in January 1938, the photographs were displayed at the Federal Art Gallery in Boston.[133] They also were seen in New York the next spring in an exhibition held at that city's Federal Art Gallery on 57th Street.[134]

Shaker materials were included in an exhibition of several hundred index watercolors mounted in the R. H. Macy & Company department store at Herald Square in Manhattan in the summer of 1938.[135] This exhibition also traveled to other high-end stores in the nation's urban centers. The advertisement for its installation at Marshall Fields in Chicago enticed visitors to come see Shaker furniture described as "astonishingly modern in its simplicity."[136] In Los Angeles, the works were shown on the fifth floor of Bullocks in March and April 1938.[137] Through the auspices of this federal agency, an understanding of this regional sect as representing autochthonous modernism spread beyond Massachusetts and New York to the entire nation.

An extensive exhibition of drawings and photographs of Shaker materials from the Index of American Design was mounted at the Metropolitan Museum of Art in the spring of 1943 in the midst of World War II. In announcing the installation in the *New York Times,* Walter Rendell Storey tutored his readers in the conflation of nationalism and modernism that curators and critics had assigned to Shaker crafts. He wrote, "In simplicity of form and economical methods of construction, this furniture, farm and household equipment come closer to a truly American expression than many other furnishings of their day. . . . Most of the pieces anticipate the dictum of the modern designer, that furniture perfectly adapted to use does not need ornamentation; it will achieve a natural beauty of its own."[138] To illustrate the spare elegance of Shaker furniture, Storey's article was accompanied by a Vincentini and Herlick photograph.

A feature article published in the *Metropolitan Museum of Art Bulletin* addressed this exhibition of Shaker material from the Index of American Design. Entitled "Hands to Work and Hearts to God," this piece was written by Benjamin Knotts, who served as the supervisor of the Index of American Design at the National Gallery of Art in Washington, DC, where the index's plates had found an institutional home. Watercolors of items that Sheeler and the Andrewses owned were reproduced along with a Vincentini photograph of the round Shaker barn in Hancock. However, Knotts moved beyond the beauty of the Shaker objects to make a larger point. Writing in the midst of the war, the author engaged these images to build on Franklin Roosevelt's famous "Four Freedoms" speech of 1941 in which the president identified the ideals for which America should fight.[139] "Two fundamental principles of our democracy," Knotts observed, "freedom of religion and freedom of speech—made it possible for the Shakers to live their way of life in America."[140] Knotts thus used Shaker architecture and material culture to illustrate the advantages of democracy over totalitarianism.

Exhibition of the index's Shaker images continued unabated in the postwar period. In January 1947, they were shown at the Ohio State Museum in Columbus.[141] When the Shaker Village of Pleasant Hill in Mercer County, Kentucky, opened to the public as a heritage tourism site in 1961, its inaugural exhibition was an installation of Index of American Design drawings and photographs of Shaker artifacts and architecture.[142] At the Philadelphia Museum of Art's major Shaker exhibition mounted in the spring of 1962, the curators featured the Vincentini and Herlick photographs from 1936.[143] In that same year, Hancock Shaker Village in western Massachusetts exhibited thirty-three watercolors and six photographs from the Index of American Design.[144]

Because they were readily available, these images became standard representations of Shaker furniture. They were reproduced in museum exhibition catalogues but also in the popular and scholarly press.[145] The influential critic and art historian Elizabeth McCausland drew on these works to accompany her article "The Shaker Legacy," published in the *Magazine of Art* in 1944.[146] In March 1945, the editors of *House and Garden* published a special issue of their magazine dedicated to what they called a "modern" style that was "the indigenous outcome of an American past" and claimed that "Shaker design is a native tradition with a future."[147] This issue, which suggests that "Shaker design, modeled by specific needs and created according to particular beliefs, is as aesthetically apt today as its pared-down functionalism was practical and right for the 'Believers,'" is bursting with reproductions of watercolors created under the auspices of the Index of American Design.[148] On occasion, Ted and Faith Andrews even used index images to illustrate their publications. For example, they included the Vincentini and

Herlick photographs of Sister Sarah Collins and Sister Lillian Barlow making chairs in their *Fruits of the Shaker Tree of Life,* although one image was unaccompanied by a credit line and the other was misattributed to William Winter.[149]

A design for a living room by the award-winning Swiss expatriate designer Herbert Matter from 1946 indicates how fully Americans conflated the ideas of modern design and Shakerism (fig. 2.27). Published in the magazine *Junior Bazaar* this bright room includes geometric wall decorations, a piece of sculpture, a Calderesque mobile, furniture derived from Mies van der Rohe and Charles and Ray Eames, and other hallmarks of cutting-edge mid-twentieth-century modernism. There are no visual references in the design that speak directly to Shaker material culture. Unlike Sheeler's *Americana,* Matter's design does not include a Shaker bandbox or a trestle table. The room does not hold a ladder-backed rocking chair. Nonetheless, the magazine's editors accompanied the design with a caption that read, "Here is a completely modern room . . . that we feel is thoroughly

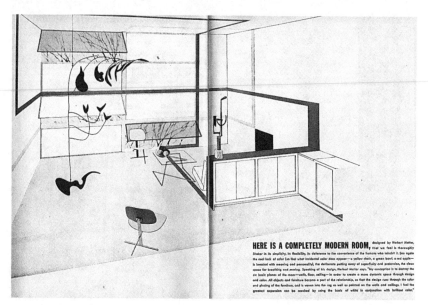

HERE IS A COMPLETELY MODERN ROOM, designed by Herbert Matter, that we feel is thoroughly Shaker in its simplicity, in its flexibility, in its deference to the convenience of the humans who inhabit it. See again the cool lack of color (so that what incidental color does appear—a yellow chair, a green bowl, a red apple—is invested with meaning and personality), the deliberate putting away of superfluity and pretension, the clean space for breathing and moving. Speaking of his design, Herbert Matter says, "My conception is to destroy the six basic planes of the room—walls, floor, ceiling—in order to create a more dynamic space through design and color. All objects and furniture become a part of the relationship, so that the design runs through the color and placing of the furniture, and is woven into the rug as well as painted on the walls and ceilings. I feel the greatest expansion can be reached by using the basis of white in conjunction with brilliant color."

FIGURE 2.27. Herbert Matter, "Living Room Design," *Junior Bazaar,* January 1946. The editors characterized this interior design by a European modernist as being "thoroughly Shaker." Courtesy Jordan Matter and the Winterthur Library: The Edward Deming Andrews Memorial Shaker Collection, No. 679.

Shaker in its simplicity, its flexibility, its deference to the convenience of the humans who inhabit it." Moreover, in the opinion of the editor, Matter's design resembled Shaker interiors because it demonstrated a "deliberate putting away of superfluity and pretension" and provided a "clean space for breathing and moving." In the minds of the American tastemakers who edited this magazine, modernism and Shaker design had been completely and thoroughly conflated.

ADAPTATIONS OF SHAKER DESIGN

The index's images of Shaker objects ultimately served the purpose that Reeves and Javitz had envisioned for them: they inspired American designers of both furniture and fashion.[150] In November 1937, the Herman Miller Company of Zeeland, Michigan, debuted a line of Shaker-inspired furniture designed by Freda Diamond (figs. 2.28–2.29).[151] A graduate of the

FIGURE 2.28. Dining room suite of Shaker-inspired furniture designed by Freda Diamond, 1937. Journalists hailed Diamond's designs as being simultaneously modern and traditional. Courtesy Freda Diamond Collection, Archives Center, National Museum of American History, Smithsonian Institution, Washington, DC.

Cooper-Hewitt School of Design for Women, Diamond, along with designer Russel Wright and others, advocated a nationalist aesthetic emphasizing casual living, "good taste," and better design in home furnishings.[152]

Available at department stores including Wanamaker's in New York and the J. W. Robinson Company in Los Angeles, Diamond's furniture was marketed to consumers as simultaneously contemporary and traditional while exemplifying American sincerity and lack of pretension.[153] A brochure for the line claimed, "A room furnished with the new 'Shaker' can seem as modern as the last tick of the clock at the same time that it breathes an air of quaintness."[154] Another promotional catalogue for the furniture asserted that Diamond's designs were "faithful in expression of the craft details and form of the early Shaker pieces, which have a brightness and lightness of design expressive of serene and otherworldly happiness."[155]

Interior design writers in the periodical press actively promoted Diamond's Shaker-inspired designs. Margaret White authored an article for *Better Homes and Gardens* entitled "You'd Swear They Were Modern."[156] In

Watervliet Dressing Table. From a deaconess' desk, which is divided into three sections, the writing top lowered to rest between the drawers.

Watervliet Stool. Designed from a Shaker swivel stool common to Shaker shops.

Watervliet Bedside Table. Design taken from a bread-cutting table, without which no Shaker home was complete.

Watervliet Bed. Shape of head and foot boards from the backboard of a Shaker pine washstand.

FIGURE 2.29. Page from the Herman Miller Furniture Company's *We Present Shaker Furniture* promoting furniture designed by Freda Diamond. As new products derived from historical precedents, Diamond's furniture, although criticized by purists, embodied the vision of the founders of the Index of American Design. Courtesy Freda Diamond Collection, Archives Center, National Museum of American History, Smithsonian Institution, Washington, DC.

the *Atlanta Constitution,* Elizabeth McRae Boykin claimed that "Shaker Furniture in Modern Settings Is Naively Sophisticated."[157] Lenore Kent, a home economics expert, writing in the *Washington Post* asserted, "Diamond . . . with great ingenuity and imagination adapted the type of construction used by the Shakers to modern-day needs. The result is a knockout. Shaker furniture combines tradition with a functionalism that is as modern as the latest newspaper. Bridging the gap between yesterday and today, it solves the home furnisher's problem of 'going modern' in a conservative way."[158]

Linking Diamond's designs to the Index of American Design was central to marketing this furniture. In promotional literature, the manufacturer noted that Diamond had found inspiration in the materials created through the Federal Art Project. An article in the *New York Sun* amplified this assertion with a secondary headline explaining, "Source Material for the Designs, Developed by Freda Diamond, Were Unearthed by WPA Federal Art Project."[159] Mildred Holzhauer, a WPA official charged with accompanying a national traveling exhibit of index artwork, proudly used Diamond's designs to illustrate the program's success to a reporter from the *Los Angeles Times.*[160]

Although home decorating columnists and trade magazines celebrated Diamond's achievement, others found her designs lacking in respect for the originals.[161] Homer Eaton Keyes, the editor of *Antiques Magazine,* referred to the pieces as Diamond's "deformed progeny" and opined that they looked "like hell."[162] Edward Deming Andrews denounced the furniture, writing, "Words cannot describe the vulgarity of the results of [Diamond's] inspiration."[163] Adolph Glassgold, within the offices of the index, was equally harsh. Having apparently lost sight of the project's initial concept that designers should derive new products from earlier sources, he wrote, "The thing smells to high heaven for its putrid design adaptation. I've rarely seen such rank and tasteless re-vamping."[164]

Whether Diamond's designs are judged inspired or inappropriately derivative, they indicate that by 1937 the material culture of the Shakers had achieved a new semiotic meaning. No longer were the group's chairs and case pieces simply the extraneous used furniture of a constricting religious sect; their material culture had entered the canon of American art. Shaker furniture had come to symbolize a native national modernism, recognized and celebrated across the continent as a viable source for American design.

Other American furniture designers followed Diamond by similarly drawing on Shaker precedents.[165]

In 1951, Paul McCobb created a set of furnishings, entitled "The Predictor Group," manufactured by the O'Hearn Manufacturing Company of
Gardner, Massachusetts.[166] A painter and department store display designer
before he opened his own design firm in 1945, McCobb had a number
of objects included in the Museum of Modern Art's *Good Design* exhibitions. Throughout the 1950s, he created unified furniture systems while
popularizing modular case pieces and the use of movable storage units as
room dividers.[167] He specifically designed his furniture for mass production, broad marketing, and a moderate price point, but he also sought to
develop a native American style of furnishings to contrast with European
influences.[168]

McCobb's Shaker-inspired Predictor Group was retailed through
Bloomingdale's in New York, W. & J. Sloane's in New York, and Maison
Blanche in New Orleans, as well as in other department stores (fig. 2.30).[169]
His suite of designs included a drop-leaf dining table and chairs, a desk,
coffee table, round table, love seat, end table, breakfront cabinet, and
lounge chair. Each piece featured aspects identifiable as being drawn from
Shaker precedents as documented in the Index of American Design. Three
drawers, for example, hung below the desk's writing surface, just as drawers often were attached to Shaker worktables and candlestands. McCobb's
breakfront, with its monumental vertical facade subdivided into drawers
and cubbyholes, is most obviously derived from a specific Shaker tradition,
although Gloria Bernhard, writing in the *Boston Traveler,* described it as
having a Mondrian-like division of space.[170] As Bernard's description indicates, throughout the suite McCobb melded Shaker design with a midcentury modern aesthetic.

Design journalists welcomed the novelty of McCobb's designs almost as
enthusiastically as their predecessors thirteen years earlier had celebrated
Diamond's furniture. Once again, they marveled at how chairs, tables, and
bureaus could be simultaneously both traditional and contemporary. The
Milwaukee Journal reported that "McCobb has turned to Early American sources for inspiration . . . yet the group is definitely modern, without frills and fussiness."[171] In Peoria, Illinois's *Sunday Journal-Star,* Elizabeth
Hillyer noted that the Predictor Group was an "important example of a
new style, a style that is contemporary, and yet a contemporary that has a

look belonging to our country's tradition."[172] A writer for the *Boston Evening American* claimed McCobb's furniture grouping "points out the furnishing direction of tomorrow with clean, simple lines, livable lines that fit the neat simple home plan" while "dramatic enough for the American personality"

FIGURE 2.30. Bloomingdale's advertisement for Paul McCobb's Predictor Group line of furniture, *New York Times*, October 28, 1951. McCobb's Predictor suite, like Diamond's furniture, merged modernism with Shaker design.

and "established as adaptable to the jet-propelled tomorrow."[173] In the *New York Times*, Betty Pepis indicated that she understood the importance of the Shaker legacy, even if she was unclear regarding the group's geographic location. She wrote that while McCobb's suite was "unquestionably modern, many of the design motifs which distinguish this group . . . are derived from the Shakers, those Pennsylvanians respected for their integrity of design."[174]

Subsequently, the Drexel Furniture Company of Drexel, North Carolina, offered a competing set of Shaker-inspired midcentury modern furniture.[175] The firm's Declaration line of furniture, introduced in 1958, was designed to be affordable and included approximately fifty different pieces that could be used throughout a residence.[176] The line was characterized by its use of walnut and walnut veneer, inlays of rosewood, and round porcelain drawer pulls.[177] Tables, chairs, beds, desks, and chest pieces were all offered in multiple variations. Concerning the variety of forms available, one journalist noted, "There's every piece one could want under a chandelier" (fig. 2.31).[178]

Kipp Stewart and Stewart MacDougall, who designed the Declaration line for Drexel, were southern Californians; Stewart was from Hollywood, and MacDougall hailed from Pasadena.[179] After serving in the Navy during World War II, they enrolled at Los Angeles's Chouinard Art Institute, which

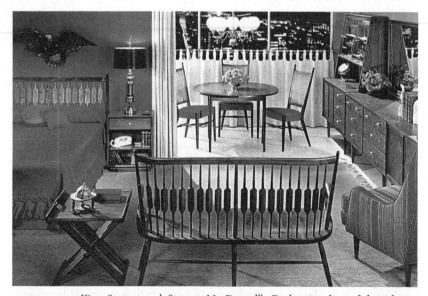

FIGURE 2.31. Kipp Stewart and Stewart MacDougall's Declaration line of furnishings, designed for North Carolina's Drexel Furniture Company. Photo collection of the author.

subsequently was integrated into the California Institute of the Arts. After both studying and teaching at Chouinard, Stewart and MacDougall worked in the architectural and engineering offices of Victor Gruen, the Viennese expatriate designer best known for his shopping malls. Each had his work included in the Museum of Modern Art's *Good Design* shows. The Californians formed a partnership in 1954 to create furniture as well as both commercial and residential interiors and exteriors. A leather and wood sling chair by MacDougall was included in an exhibition of American design that the Museum of Modern Art toured through Europe.[180]

Stewart and MacDougall's Declaration line was marketed as being inspired by the Shakers. An advertisement by Abraham & Straus in the *New York Times* observed that the Shakers were "noted as some of the finest designer craftsmen in American history" and that "Drexel's new Shaker-inspired furniture group" featured "direct lines, combining superb woods with simple beauty."[181] An image by the California photographer Dale Healy published to accompany a profile of the designers that also served to announce the introduction of the line even placed the Drexel chairs within a spare, geometric, black-and-white homage to William Winter's photographic compositions.

Drexel's furniture, however, appears to be more related to Diamond's and McCobb's derivative designs than to any actual Shaker objects. While the chest pieces are minimalist, rectilinear, and reminiscent of the sect's storage furniture, the seating furniture lacks any identifiable Shaker references such as horizontal back-slats or seats of woven tape. Just as McCobb's movable storage pieces could be used as room dividers, a Bloomingdale's advertisement illustrated Declaration cabinets serving to divide a dining room from a study.[182] Abraham & Straus affirmed the connection to these precedents by creating, on the sixth floor of their Brooklyn store, a sales space in which the new furniture was displayed among "masterpieces of modern designers" including McCobb, Diamond, George Nelson, Charles Eames, George Nakashima, Florence Knoll, and others.

Drexel's marketing reaffirmed the trope that Shaker design represented both modernism and a national tradition. Advertisements asserted that Declaration by Drexel was "as American as the Declaration of Independence . . . as modern as the space age."[183] Using coded patriotic language redolent of the Cold War, Drexel asserted that this furniture offered "a new frontier in American living" and "freedom from look alike rooms."

Advertising copy urged consumers to "assert [their] own American good taste with Declaration by Drexel."[184] Designed by Californians, manufactured in North Carolina, and marketed from Texas to Minnesota and Boston to California, the Declaration furniture line indicates that by the end of the 1950s, Shaker fever had spread to become more than a local or regional ailment.

While inspired by Shaker design, Declaration furniture was also "enhanced by modern ingenuity" to meet contemporary functions.[185] The doors featured magnetic latches, and many of the cupboards included interior electric lights. Some chest pieces had holes in the exterior back wall through which wires for radios and record players could be threaded. Other cabinets included racks for storing record albums hidden behind old-fashioned cupboard doors.[186] Drexel even collaborated with Motorola to offer Declaration hi-fi stereo cabinets and television consoles, which featured sliding tambour doors to conceal the electronic controls.[187] The latter item, designed to accent American living rooms, was advertised as being "as modern as tomorrow . . . but with the remembered past of Shaker Simplicity."[188]

Declaration by Drexel was successful, sold broadly, and stayed in production for most of a decade. In 1963, the firm reported that the line had exceeded $40 million in retail sales.[189] Declaration also received the imprimatur of the U.S. government as representing the finest in American design. The State Department's Office of the U.S. Commissioner General for the Brussels Exposition selected signature forms to be shown in the American Pavilion at the 1958 World's Fair in Brussels, a pivotal location for the international cultural Cold War.[190] The organizers of the American pavilion also displayed a Shaker tilting chair as an example of American indigenous ingenuity that preceded the modern designs of Eames, Eero Saarinen, and others.[191] The Drexel Declaration furniture was then subsequently exhibited at the 1959 U.S. trade fair in Moscow, the site of Richard Nixon and Nikita Khrushchev's famous "kitchen debate" concerning American industrial and material prowess.[192]

Notably, none of the journalists and other commentators on the Predictor or Declaration lines mentioned celibacy, religious faith, or communal ownership of property in relation to the sect. Rather they used the Shakers' identity as supposedly early American modernists to promote American exceptionalism, cultural pride, and national identity. As writers of the 1950s and early 1960s conflated Shakerism with modern design, they largely lost track of the theological source of the sect's supposed functionalism.

FASHION

Fashion designers also found inspiration in the images produced by the Index of American Design. In 1939, department stores attempted to capitalize on the public's newfound acquaintance with the Shakers. In January 1939, for example, Wanamaker's in New York City advertised women's dresses, suits, and accessories inspired by "Shaker Simplicity." The copywriter asserted that the store's designers were resurrecting the eighteenth-century Sabbathday dresses of these devout Americans. "The plain simple functionalism and austere spirit," this marketer continued, "smash straight into the core of *today's* silhouette—*the fitted bodice and the rhythmic skirt.*" This extraordinary advertising copy was accompanied by line drawings of women wearing pumps, knee-length pleated skirts, and a variety of fitted tops and jackets augmented with the era's padded, broad shoulders (fig. 2.32). To the twenty-first-century eye, the advertisement's drawings have little in common with the modest Shaker costumes recorded by the Index of American Design. However, the copy continued, "Come see our dazzling collection of pious exciting clothes." This conflicted wardrobe, in sensible natural colors, was meant to be "uncarnal" but alluring, sober but without "one whiff of quaintness."[193] In presenting these goods to customers, Wanamaker's also proudly noted its role as tastemaker in bringing Diamond's Shaker furniture to the market.

Washington's Woodward & Lothrop also attempted in the spring of 1939 to profit from the taste for Shaker materials being created by the index's drawings. On March 1 in the *Washington Post,* they offered their customers "Modern Shaker" neckwear frills described as "dainty, adorably feminine collars with a story" (fig. 2.33). Inspired by the sect's simplicity and functionalism, the store's designers had created "thoroughly 1939 neckwear" featuring frothy panels, fichus, high round collars of organdy, and plain-cut pique collars. Interested customers could find these in aisle 15 on the first floor of the firm's store located on the block bounded by 10th, 11th, F, and G Streets in the nation's capital.[194]

Pearl Levy Alexander, a New York designer, similarly participated in this enthusiasm for appropriating the Shaker identity. Working for her firm André, a design service that provided sketches to American clothing

Shaker Simplicity

The Shakers were a sober celibate little sect that settled in New Lebanon, New York, over 150 years ago. Wanamaker's resurrects the 18th Century Sabbath Day dress of these highly-sensitive, highly-religious Americans—finds in it an untapped source of inspiration for 1939 fashions! The plain simple functionalism and austere spirit smash straight into the core of *today's silhouette—the fitted bodice and the full rhythmic shirt.* Come see our dazzling collection of pious exciting clothes! Bonnets that cape down the back. A basque-line bodice that V's in a keen plumb line through the midriff, inching off the waist. Such uncarnal little fichu-jackets. In luscious soft hand-carded woolens. In smooth plain serges like the serges in the brethren's trousers. In silks and cottons as fine as those the Shaker-sisters wove. No fuss. No feathers. Not one whiff of quaintness. Shaker-fine workmanship. Tiny tucks and gussets (and a few 1939 zippers) that give an alluring body line. A few "this is strictly business" buttons. Colors like those the Shakers crushed from vegetables and the neighboring hardhack trees. *Earth colors!* Plum like fruit of Lebanon orchards. Yellow-green like figs on the bough. Pure black of undersoil of lush green Shaker meadows. Red of Shaker earth-clay pipes. You'll recall that it was Wanamaker's that unearthed Shaker furniture. It was Wanamaker's that opened Shaker House with a whole line of sharp smart functional furniture in the Shaker tradition. Now Wanamaker's brings you fresh startling Shaker-inspired, Shaker-quality clothes.

John Wanamaker

FIGURE 2.32. Wanamaker's advertisement for Shaker-inspired womenswear. Fashion designers also drew on the Index of American Design to market Shaker-themed items to the public. *New York Times,* January 19, 1939.

March 1, 1939 -

WOODWARD & LOTHROP

10TH 11TH F AND G STREETS   PHONE DISTRICT 5300

FIGURE 2.33. Woodward & Lothrop advertisement for Shaker-inspired womens-wear. By 1939, Shaker was synonymous with "modern" and carried overtones of nationalism and rectitude. *Washington Post*, March 1, 1939.

"Modern Shaker" Neckwear Frills

—dainty, adorably feminine collars with a story

Behind these exquisitely dainty little collar-frills "hangs a tale." Once there was a religious sect—early American, they were—who imposed isolation upon themselves. From that isolation sprung a native philosophy, founded on the principles of simplicity, functionalism—and a high standard of fine workmanship. Recently there has been a revival of interest in their history, their simple style. From this interest came the inspiration for this thoroughly 1939 neckwear: frothy panels, fichus, high round collars of organdy, plain-cut pique collars. Sketched $1.95

Others, $1 to $2.95

NECKWEAR—AISLE 15—FIRST FLOOR

manufacturers, in 1939 Alexander produced an image of a knee-length Shaker coat with wide shoulders, a pleated skirt, and a waste cinched by a wide leather belt and collars and cuffs of white pique (fig. 2.34).[195] A conical hat with a wide brim and a hat band with a prominent buckle completed the ensemble. Alexander's outfit is neither simple nor unornamented and has little in common with the clothing worn by members of the sect. The hat seems to refer to visual comic stereotypes of Puritans or Quakers more than it speaks to actual Shaker headwear. A designer with access to the drawings of the index and more interest in authenticity than Alexander might have accessorized a Shaker outfit with a close-fitting bonnet rather than a hat with a crown, brim, and buckle.

In 1946, the editors of *Junior Bazaar,* a spinoff of *Harper's Bazaar* aimed at a young audience, dedicated a cover feature to modest but fashionable clothing presented within a Shaker context. Appearing soon after *House and Garden*'s extensive Shaker issue, this feature may have sought to build on the larger publication's momentum. In pictures by fashion photographers Genevieve Naylor and Leslie Gill, models wearing fashions by Nantucket Natural and Wyner, and hats by Betmar and Lily Daché, posed among iconic Shaker antiques, including a cast-iron stove and tall case pieces, within the Andrewses' summer house in Richmond, Massachusetts, which they had dubbed Shaker Farm (figs. 2.35–2.36).[196] Like Wanamaker's Shaker fashions of 1939, the dresses in this postwar spread featured full skirts hemmed at the knee, belted waists, and contrasting collars and cuffs. Text, ornamented with motifs drawn from the sect's inspirational drawings, averred that the modern fashions portrayed in the magazine demonstrated "Shaker simplicity without Shaker severity."[197] Photograph captions informed readers that the dresses, skirts, hats, and accessories were available at stores including Woodward & Lothrop; Saks Fifth Avenue; Julius Garfinkel in Washington; J. P. Allen in Atlanta; Harzfeld's in Kansas City, Missouri; Bonwit Teller in Philadelphia; and other such fine retail establishments across the country.

No matter how outrageous or incongruous it may appear presently to dress ingenues and debutantes coyly in the trappings of a sect that eschewed sex and matrimony, or to simulate the style of religious piety in the pursuit of marketing luxury goods, these fashions from the 1930s and 1940s indicate how fully Shaker fever had permeated American popular culture. "Shaker" had become a recognizable, and valuable, marketing term with

GG824

DESIGNED BY
Pearl Levy Alexander

"SHAKER COAT

WHITE PIQUE
SHAKER COLLAR
WIDE LEATHER
BELT

André
570.? Avenue
N.Y. City
La 4 46 .?
7/13/39

FIGURE 2.34. Pearl Levy Alexander, "Shaker Coat" for André, 1939. Alexander's Shaker coat is neither simple nor unornamented, while the hat that completes the outfit seems to refer to early twentieth-century comic stereotypes of Puritans and Quakers. Courtesy Photo by André (Firm) © Wallach Division Picture Collection, The New York Public Library.

FIGURE 2.35. Genevieve Naylor, "Here Is engaging Shaker Simplicity," 1945. This coy model was photographed in Faith and Edward Deming Andrews's summer house, which they called "Shaker Farm." Published in *Junior Bazaar*, January 1946. Courtesy Winterthur Library: The Edward Deming Andrews Memorial Shaker Collection, no. 679.

overtones of nationalism and rectitude that could be applied broadly to consumer products.

The transition in how Americans understood Shaker objects was not an accident nor was it the result of Faith and Edward Deming Andrews

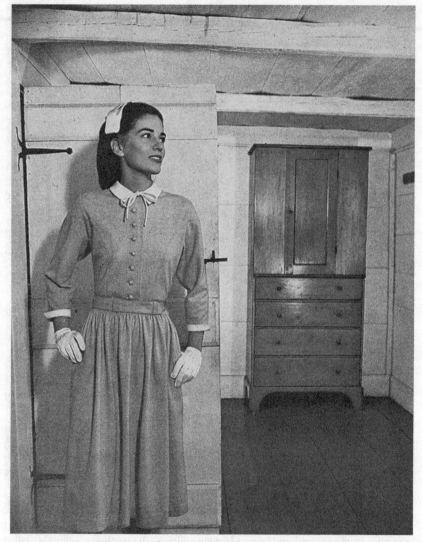

FIGURE 2.36. Genevieve Naylor, "By the Cupboard," 1945. The Andrewses' case piece added authenticity to clothing that was meant to embody "Shaker simplicity without Shaker severity." Published in *Junior Bazaar*, January 1946. Courtesy Winterthur Library: The Edward Deming Andrews Memorial Shaker Collection, no. 679.

working on their own. Rather, it was the result of the efforts of a cohort of individuals from the world of art and design, including Ruth Reeves, Romana Javitz, Holger Cahill, Constance Rourke, Charles Sheeler, Noel Vincentini, George Herlick, Yvonne Twining, and Dorothy Miller, among others. These administrators, curators, writers, artists, and photographers, in addition to the Andrewses, actively promoted Shaker material culture to the American public. They made choices that influenced how this sect's material culture was presented in the multitude of exhibitions and publications that drew on the Index of American Design. This coterie of tastemakers decided which pieces were the best examples worthy of reproduction, while also determining what other objects were undeserving of consideration. By making these evaluations, they created a canon that editors, journalists, and the public subsequently embraced. An agenda, both aesthetic and political, that conflated Shaker design and modernism to promote an exceptionalist American cultural nationalism informed the cohort's decisions. Shaker furniture was valuable to them precisely because of its ability to be used as evidence of a distinctive American style, which they believed separated the United States from other nations. Because of this agenda, the pieces they valued most, collected, and recorded were those that best supported this argument. Other objects of Shaker material culture, like woven poplar fancywork sewing boxes or Emmory Brooks's ornamented beds, did not buttress this contention and were marginalized and excluded.

In subsequent years, preservation organizations continued to reify this constructed understanding of Shaker material culture and embraced a celebration of Shaker material culture as traditional indigenous modernism when restoring compounds such as Hancock Shaker Village and Pleasant Hill in Kentucky. The same vision was manifested in installing Shaker period rooms in Delaware's Winterthur Museum, New York City's Metropolitan Museum of Art, the Philadelphia Museum of Art, and in the American Museum in Bath, England.[198] Through such public physical representations, and the continuing stream of popular publications celebrating a "naively sophisticated" Shaker style, this Depression-era, nationalist manipulation of Shaker material culture continues to inform how the American public perceives this autochthonous religious sect.[199]

CHAPTER 3
"USING MATERIAL FROM OUR OWN HISTORY IN THE ARTS"

••••••••••••••••••••••

Performing the Shakers, 1930–1950

As the previous chapters demonstrate, museums, including the New York State Museum, the Berkshire Museum, the Whitney Museum, and others, shaped popular understanding of the Shakers and Shaker culture by collecting Shaker artifacts and crafting exhibits celebrating them. Museum curators and directors promoted Shaker design as an autochthonous American modernism. This construct was supported by images fashioned by photographers William Winter, Noel Vincentini, and George Herlick, and was promoted by antique dealers like Faith and Edward Deming Andrews and Edith Halpert, government bureaucrats including Holger Cahill of the New Deal's Index of American Design, museum directors Charles Adams and Laura Bragg, and designers such as Ruth Reeves and Freda Diamond.

This strain of enthusiasm for the Shakers, which started in the 1920s and continued throughout the period of this study, was predominantly visual. Moreover, these promoters shaped their image of the Shakers in such a manner that the believers themselves were essentially invisible. Museums, authors, and dealers portrayed the sect in an almost archeological fashion through the objects that they had left behind, such as buildings, chairs, and other furnishings. Mid-twentieth-century photographers mostly did not aim their viewfinders at the actual physical bodies of Shaker men and

138

women. Clean Shaker spaces were more elegant when presented unpolluted by the mundane reality of people.

Simultaneously, however, another group of individuals promoted an alternative, but related, strain of Shaker fever. This cohort specifically enlisted the human body to interpret the Shakers through dance and theater and was predominantly uninterested in Shaker architecture or antiques. Drawing on American traditions of pageantry and civic performance, and influenced by a blossoming interest in American folk music, these individuals directed dancers and actors who were not members of the sect to perform Shaker dances, dramas, and rituals on public stages. Clothing, as theatrical costume, is notable as the only aspect of Shaker material culture that concerned these individuals.

While a diverse group of enthusiasts, including men and women, Christians and Jews, old-line American WASPs and recent immigrants, sparked the twentieth-century understanding of Shaker design, the group responsible for codifying the theatrical performance of Shakerism in the 1930s and 1940s was remarkably homogenous. Doris Humphrey, Miriam Cramer, Marguerite Melcher, and Clarice Carr were all educated women who were either Congregationalist or Unitarian, and thus inheritors of the liberal Protestant tradition derived from New England Calvinism. As agents of early twentieth-century reform, these women also were drawn to the Shakers' utopianism and rejection of the status quo, whether expressed as militarism, individualism, religious bigotry, or mistrust of dancing.

Educated women who came of age in the first half of the twentieth century, like Laura Bragg and Juliana Force, these Shaker enthusiasts benefited from the first-wave feminism of the Progressive era but were still limited by proscribed gender roles. While expanding their activities outside the domestic sphere, they created professional identities and status in the traditionally feminine pursuits of arts and teaching, rather than in their era's normative masculine realms of business, politics, or the law. Humphrey, Cramer, Melcher, and Carr all drew on skills derived from their education as middle-class Protestant women to introduce the American people to Shaker history and culture. Simultaneously, they enhanced their status in the public realm as dancers, researchers, writers, and experts. These women can be understood as functioning as a group because they evaluated each other's work, corresponded, and in some instances developed significant long-lasting friendships.

Linked by shared ethnicity, religion, and class, these women also were connected by geography. Cramer, Melcher, and Carr all became enamored with the Shakers because they each lived near a Shaker community that had failed by the early twentieth century.[1] Cramer grew up and was educated in and around Cleveland, Ohio, near what had been the North Union Shaker Village, while Melcher and Carr both had ties to Enfield, New Hampshire, the rural community that was home to the Shakers' village referred to as "Chosen Vale." In studying the history of their local Shaker communities and conveying that story to the world, these women fulfilled traditional female roles of conservators of tradition and curators of local memory.

From their distinct beginnings, all four women sought to convert their interest in the Shakers into success in New York City, which at the time was the center of American theater, dance, and music; three of them succeeded. Humphrey became an internationally recognized modern dancer in part because of her *Dance of the Chosen*, first performed at Hunter College in New York. Melcher's *Rose in the Wilderness* was presented by the Abbe Practical Workshop off Broadway on the West Side, with Carr serving as a musical consultant, while Cramer aspired without success to have her *More Love, Brother* produced on Broadway.

This chapter examines the two-decade period bracketed by the first performance of Doris Humphrey's *Dance of the Chosen* in 1930 and the production of Marguerite Melcher's *Rose in the Wilderness*, directed in 1949 by Gloria Monty, who would go on to produce the television soap opera *General Hospital*. During this time, the performances depicting the Shakers transformed from abstract artistic representations loosely inspired by the sect with little direct correlation to historical reality into relatively accurate reconstructions of the past based on extensive research in archives and printed sources. Throughout the period, these productions aspired to professional standards and, at times, achieved public acclaim. In the process, audiences had their understanding of this unique American religious sect shaped by performers pretending to be adherents. Further, because of these productions, the American reading public was exposed to the concept of the Shakers due to articles promoting and reviewing these works in periodicals ranging from the *Claremont Daily Eagle* of Claremont, New Hampshire, and the *Christian Century* to the *New York Times* and *Vanity Fair*. Moreover, this coterie of educated, middle-class, Protestant women created a standard for how performances interpreting the sect would be staged in subsequent decades.

DORIS HUMPHREY AND THE SHAKERS

In January 1933, *Vanity Fair* magazine announced that J. P. McEvoy's revue entitled *Americana* and presented at New York City's Shubert Theatre on 44th Street west of Broadway featured Doris Humphrey's dancers performing a piece based on the religious ceremonies of the Shakers, a group that the publication's editors characterized as a "strange, fanatic sect which flourished in Massachusetts in 1774, whose members believed that the body could be shaken free from sin."[2] The magazine's designer accompanied this announcement with a striking photograph by Edward Steichen. The photographer used Humphrey's troupe, in dark costumes with contrasting white caps, to create a powerful diagonal composition in which figures simultaneously stretch toward the upper left corner of the frame while gazing rapturously toward the top right. Creative lighting and repetitive patterns of body parts highlighted against shadows and dark clothing lend a haunting visual character to Steichen's publicity photograph.[3]

Humphrey originally presented her Shaker-inspired dance composition under the title *Dance of the Chosen* at Hunter College in New York City on November 12, 1930.[4] This work opened with a dozen dancers evenly divided between men and women. Both genders wore somber costumes that Pauline Lawrence designed, and knelt facing a single woman, understood to be an eldress, who sat on a bench at the rear of the stage. Divided by gender with women on the left and men on the right, the dancers rocked back and forth with increasing intensity until they rose to their feet and formed lines facing each other with the leader taking a position between the two columns. The group then reformed into two rotating crosses with the dancers' arms intertwining but never touching. The performers trembled, jogged, reached out toward each other, and jumped into the air to simultaneously express sexual longing and religious ecstasy.[5] As excitement built, the eldress made several leaps. The other dancers joined her until the entire company made a final leap releasing tension, joy, and energy. Writing in 1949, the dance critic Margaret Lloyd said of Humphrey's choreography,

> The design of *The Shakers* was wrought of small quiverings and tremblings that increased to violent shakings and twistings of the whole body; of running half-falls, the forward or backward thrust of the supporting leg keeping the body in a constant state of off-balance, never lost; of single wild jumps into the air. Brief ebbs in the action, allowing for the descent of the Holy Spirit, replenished the communicants for an even more vigorous declamation of

fiery faith, expressed partially in words. At the end, the men kneeling on one side, women on the other, encircled the leader, their vibrating palms held in ecstasy.[6]

Originally performed without musical accompaniment, the only auditory features of the work were the sound of the dancers' feet on the wooden stage along with occasional chanting and exclamations. At the peak of tension, the female leader of the dancers cried out, "Ye shall be free when ye are shaken free of sin!" When the dance was performed in Brooklyn in the summer of 1933, the musical accompaniment included a drum, an accordion, and a female chorus trained by Hall Johnson, a choirmaster and arranger famous for his work with traditional African American musical forms.[7] By the time the work was reprised in McEvoy's *Americana*, the dancers were accompanied by the sound of a drum beating.[8] The performance built, peaked, and subsided in less than ten minutes.[9]

While Steichen's photograph published in *Vanity Fair* used composition to indicate movement, other early pictures of the choreography are more static. Soichi Sunami, a Japanese-born photographer whose images of New York dance companies appeared regularly in the press in the 1920s, created a series recording the piece's early performances. These works document the blocking of the dance and indicate the barren starkness of the set design (fig. 3.1). Sunami's exposures also demonstrate that Lawrence's costumes, while gesturing toward American religious garb through contrasting fabric color and wimples for the women, did not attempt to accurately reproduce Shaker clothing. The men's wide-brimmed hats more closely resembled the stylized headgear of the Quaker icon used to market oatmeal and other cereals in the early twentieth century than any haberdashery that Shaker brethren actually wore. In 1943, Elizabeth K. Dale of Columbus, Ohio, an amateur Shaker enthusiast familiar with the Shakers from her childhood in Pittsfield, Massachusetts, called to Humphrey's attention what she perceived as shortcomings in the details of the dancers' wardrobe. She wrote, "Can you tell me about the Shaker men's costumes? They didn't seem to be like any I recall seeing—although the spirit of them, as well as of the women's costumes, was harmonious with what I recall."[10]

An uncredited image appearing in the *Literary Digest* for October 1932 and titled by the editors "A Bit of Americana in the Dance" also helps to demonstrate the dance as it was staged as part of J. P. McEvoy's *Americana* (fig. 3.2).[11] This photograph portrays Doris Humphrey's dancers kneeling

FIGURE 3.1. Soichi Sunami, "The Humphrey Weidman Group in *The Shakers.*" Sunami's photograph of an early production of Doris Humphrey's *The Shakers* illustrates the arrangement of the dancers early in the piece but also exhibits the abstract nature of the production's design and costumes. Courtesy Jerome Robbins Dance Division, The New York Public Library for the Performing Arts, Astor, Lenox and Tilden Foundations.

(in their dark costumes with white accents) while gazing fixedly up at their leader, who points heavenward. The dancers' bare feet contrast with the supposed modesty of the sect's dark dresses and covered heads, yet the work's triangular composition effectively conveys the dance's engagement with the tension existing between physicality and spirituality.

In the decades since its initial performance, aficionados have identified *Dance of the Chosen,* otherwise known as *The Shakers,* as a canonical work of American modern dance.[12] At its genesis in 1931, John Martin, the dance critic for the *New York Times,* declared that the work was "of excellent stuff" and "of striking originality both in subject and in treatment."[13] Conceived soon after Humphrey and her colleague Charles Weidman broke with the Denishawn School run by Ruth St. Denis and Ted Shawn, the work premiered at a moment when Humphrey, Martha Graham, Agnes de Mille,

FIGURE 3.2. Unidentified photographer, "A Bit of Americana in the Dance," 1932. Published in *Literary Digest*, October 29, 1932, 17. This image, which dates from when *The Shakers* was incorporated into a revue entitled *Americana* in 1932, utilizes a triangular composition and a pointing hand to emphasize the relationship of the group to God. Courtesy Boston Athenæum.

and Helen Becker, who performed under the name Tamiris, were transforming American dance by rejecting historical precedents and exploring new techniques.[14] Celebrating the successes of these choreographers, Martin declared, "American dance has come of age!"[15] Similarly, in reviewing McEvoy's 1932 *Americana*, Brooks Atkinson asserted that the show "set a pioneer's standard with its choreography."[16]

Edward Cushing, writing in the *Brooklyn Daily Eagle*, voiced a minority opinion in criticizing the work. In February 1931, Cushing characterized *The Shakers* as "an overlong folk study," which he believed should be "shortened and sharpened and intensified, or dropped altogether."[17] Three years later, an unnamed critic writing in the same paper disagreed. This commentator asserted, "This dance, representing the religious and ecstatic frenzy of that curious American sect, is about as exciting a work as the present day dance has to offer. It gives a true spiritual catharsis, which is the highest aim of any art."[18]

Subsequent critics and scholars have tended to agree with Martin in marking this moment as a turning point in American dance.[19] *The Shakers* was popular from the moment it was first performed and remained part of Humphrey's repertoire until she died in 1958.[20] More than fifty years after her death, it is probably the most frequently performed piece of her choreography, staged in Germany and even in Taiwan with the dancers' utterances translated into Chinese.[21]

Although the work portrays a group from the American past, Humphrey herself classified the work as part of a modern oeuvre. In this argument, the dance's American source material helped to define it as modern, just as American imagery worked to identify the paintings of Stuart Davis and Gerald Murphy as modern in the visual arts.[22] In leaving the Denishawn School with Weidman, Humphrey sought a more authentic national identity as a dancer. She complained that with her former troupe, she had learned to dance as the Japanese, the Chinese, the Spanish, and other exotic groups moved. As a choreographer, she wished to discover how she as a contemporary American should dance. Similarly, in 1933, John Martin declared, "The dancers of the world may gather in solemn conclave and declare officially that there is no American dance, but there will be and is an American dance none the less."[23] Humphrey hoped to be able to break free from traditional European and Asian dance forms to invent a modern American approach to dance in which motion derived from feeling. In the words of dance scholar Barbara Hausler, Humphrey was developing "a unique language of movement with which to communicate her experiences as an artist living in twentieth-century America."[24]

Humphrey's work was also modern, however, in that she abstracted her source material. Humphrey's particular strain of Shaker fever was based on the Shaker practice of worship through movement, which contrasted starkly with many American denominations' prohibitions against dance because of a fear of licentiousness.[25] At the time, religion similarly fascinated many of the figures in American modern dance. Martha Graham investigated the figure of the Virgin Mary in her 1931 piece *Primitive Mysteries.* Ted Shawn had earlier represented Native American religious practices with *Dagger Dance* in 1914 and *Xochitl* in 1921. He returned to this subject matter in 1934 with *Ponca Indian Dance.*[26] Humphrey revisited the relationship between dance and religion by staging the nocturnal rites of a fictionalized cult of Bahaman nature worshippers for Hall Johnson's 1933 *Run, Little Chillun,* with the African American subject matter indicated by the use of dialect in its title.[27]

Although inspired by dance as worship, Humphrey did not intend *The Shakers* to be understood as a faithful recreation of the sect's liturgical practices. At first, the title of the work did not even identify the figures in the dance as Shakers; she simply called them "the chosen." In composing her work, Humphrey did not learn traditional Shaker dances from members of the faith. Rather, she used lithographs and other images as visual sources to explore the intersection between dance and American religion. In a letter from late September 1930, she told her family about her undertaking, noting, "I'm interested in doing a danced [sic] based on religious cults—the general thesis being Shakerism—They did a dance you know with definite formations and gestures and music. The subject is fascinating to read about—but it is chiefly important as a starting point for the composition. The subject is never the point—you know—I agree with Roger Fry who insists that Cézanne's apples are as important as Raphael's Madonnas."[28] As an artist, Humphrey was not constrained to represent her source material literally. Like Paul Cézanne, as a modernist she claimed the authority to use her art to express the way the world appeared to her, rather than slavishly attempting to reproduce reality. Her dance was meant to be an enlightening, creative artistic construct, not an ethnographic examination.

DORIS HUMPHREY, MARY WOOD HINMAN, AND FOLK DANCE

Although Humphrey and her New York admirers construed *The Shakers* as novel and modern, the work's identity is more complicated. An examination of Humphrey's career trajectory indicates that her seemingly revolutionary choreography was actually strongly rooted in the earlier Progressive reform movements of pageantry and physical education. To fully understand the genesis of this celebrated work requires recognizing that earlier in her career, before coming to New York, Humphrey had been shaped by these movements both as a student and as a professional. Rather than a *sui generis* modernist work conceived in New York City in the 1930s, Humphrey's performance of Shaker-inspired choreography was the direct result of her training with Mary Wood Hinman at the Francis W. Parker School in Chicago at the turn of the century.

Born in 1895 in Oak Park, Illinois, Humphrey was the child of educated parents who belonged to the liberal Protestant Congregationalist Church and had interests in the arts. Her mother, Julia Ellen Wells, held degrees from Mount Holyoke and the Boston Conservatory of Music. Horace Buckingham Humphrey was a graduate of Beloit College, had pursued a career in journalism, was an amateur photographer, and managed a hotel catering to theater professionals.[29]

When noted educational reformer Francis W. Parker opened a school in Chicago's affluent North Side in 1901, the Humphreys enrolled their daughter in this progressive institution.[30] John Dewey, the Chicago-based educational philosopher, called Parker "more nearly than any other one person . . . the father of the progressive educational movement."[31] Like other Progressives, Parker disapproved of the transformations in American society wrought by industrial capitalism and the dogged pursuit of self-interest. In response, he sought to use education to effect social change, foster democracy, and contribute to spiritual and intellectual growth.[32] Anita McCormick Blaine, daughter and heir of manufacturer Cyrus McCormick, underwrote Parker's vision by contributing half the school's budget and providing scholarships to one-third of its students.[33]

In this dynamic environment, students created and performed theatrical presentations, known within the institution as "exercises," comprising an important aspect of the school's pedagogy.[34] The subjects of the student programs were wide-ranging, from patriotic celebrations of Washington's birthday, Lincoln's birthday, and Memorial Day, to explorations of other cultures, including the Jewish festival of Sukkot and the classical feast of Dionysus, to presentations of laboratory experiments and mathematical concepts.[35] Parker and his followers believed that planning and presenting exercises provided students with active, integrated involvement in the learning process. One graduate enthusiastically supported this pedagogy by asserting, "The morning exercises give splendid training for public speaking, encourage latent talent, develop self-confidence, poise, co-operative spirit, tolerance, and breadth of view."[36]

Further, school leaders promoted role-playing to encourage students to expand their awareness of the human condition and to identify more fully with others. Martha Fleming, who worked to develop the program of presentations at the school, explained (using the hierarchical language of the time) that through dancing, imitation, impersonations, and dramatic plays, "the child may consciously link himself with the past of the race, with the primitive peoples still living, and at the same time learn to know and express himself."[37] Students frequently used costumes, music, and dance to expand their empathy with individuals different from themselves because of time, place, or culture. Humphrey's choreographed representation of the Shakers thus had direct roots in the educational practices of her Progressive school.

Moreover, at the Francis W. Parker School, Humphrey became a protégé of Mary Wood Hinman, a contemporary and competitor of the folk dance pioneer Elizabeth Burchenal, who taught at the school from 1906 to 1919.[38] Raised in the prosperous North Shore Chicago suburb of Kenilworth, without formal training Hinman had established herself as a dance teacher by working with neighborhood children. She coached the students at the University of Chicago in their presentation of the first Blackfriars Show in 1898 and professionally provided private instruction. At about the same time, Jane Addams offered Hinman the opportunity to teach at Hull House, the influential settlement house for the education, assimilation, and uplift of the city's immigrant population. Influenced by the educational philosophies of John Dewey, who was moving in the same Chicago circles, at Hull House Hinman developed an educational program in gymnastics, folk dance, and social dance for students to follow from kindergarten through graduation from high school.[39]

Hinman also established her own Hinman School of Gymnastics and Folk Dancing in Hyde Park as early as 1904. According to dance scholar Selma Landon Odom, the two-year program at this school "offered folk, English country, ballroom, and interpretive dancing; pantomime, ballet, and clogging; pedagogy (with practice teaching), pageantry (or practical stage production), and 'Books,' a course on dance history, folk customs, the 'new art,' civic responsibility, and women's position in the modern world."[40] While teaching, Hinman continued to educate herself, studying Scandinavian dance at the Royal College at Nääs, Sweden, and by collecting dances in England where she established a long-term professional relationship with the folklorist Cecil Sharp. Eventually, the omnivorous Hinman would travel to record music and dance in Russia, France, Sicily, Switzerland, Germany, Hungary, the Middle East, Latin America, and the American Southwest.[41]

Based on her experiences in the field and classroom, Hinman published numerous books and articles that shaped the developing field of American dance pedagogy. At this time, Progressive reformers led by Luther Halsey Gulick were actively promoting the teaching of folk dancing in settlement houses, on playgrounds, and in public schools.[42] In New York City, Gulick hired Burchenal, a graduate of Dudley Sargent's Normal School of Physical Training and an acquaintance of Cecil Sharp, to promote dancing through the city's public schools athletic league.[43] By 1910, seventeen cities, including New York, Baltimore, Pittsburgh, and Chicago, had instituted programs to teach schoolchildren folk dancing.[44] Advocates believed that dancing was physically beneficial but also ameliorated cultural differences and worked to create a new American identity conflating the traditional cultures of the nation's immigrants. Gulick illustrated his manifesto, *The Healthful Art of Dancing*, published in 1910 by Doubleday, Page, with images of dancing children supplied by both Hinman and Burchenal.[45]

While a student at the Parker School, Humphrey began assisting Hinman in teaching at her school. In 1912, Humphrey, still a teenager, gave private lessons at the studio while also performing as a dancer at Hull House and other venues. As an instructor at the school she staged a work she choreographed entitled *Greek Sacrificial Dance*, set to Franz Schubert's *Moment Musical*.[46] After graduating from the Parker School, Humphrey continued to teach and eventually also received a diploma from Hinman's school, which at times was characterized as a normal school.[47]

As a normal school, Hinman's classes were meant to prepare young women for new careers teaching dance in the public schools and in civic playgrounds, and in producing the civic pageants that had become popular at the time and in which Hinman played an active role.[48] Civic pageantry, as produced by intellectual reformers, welded Progressivism with antimodernism to create a story of local community development that could provide residents with an understanding of how the past related to the often-threatening future.[49]

Hinman's school was part of a larger educational movement to train women in the interdisciplinary skills required for pageant production. The 1917 brochure for the Hinman School of Gymnastic and Folk Dancing note a class in pageantry, which included "practical work in stage setting, costuming (the dyeing and making of costumes), and the giving of a pageant written and prepared by the students."[50] As dance scholar Naima Prevots has documented, curricula similar to that offered by Hinman in Chicago were also adopted before 1925 by Columbia University, Dartmouth College, the University of California at Los Angeles (UCLA), the University of California at Berkeley, the University of Wisconsin, Pennsylvania State College, and the University of Southern California.[51]

Hinman's classes in pageantry fit into the curriculum of her school as dance often played a prominent role in these community productions. In their pageant instruction manual entitled *Community Drama and Pageantry,* published by Yale University Press in 1916, Mary Porter Beegle and Jack Randall Crawford suggested that dance could be divided into three classifications: "Plot dances" furthered the narrative of the work. "Illustrative dances" educated the audience about a group or a culture. In the words of the authors, "this form of dance may be used either to depict the manners and customs of a particular period or nationality, or as a symbolic dance to enhance the poetic value of a scene."[52] Finally, "dance interludes" presented larger allegorical or symbolic themes within pageants and often personified abstract ideas such as progress or science.

Having received diplomas from both the Parker School and Hinman's school, Humphrey followed her mentor's path and became a professional dance instructor, giving classes in both children's and ballroom dancing. Her teaching was motivated in part by family financial reversals. Humphrey's career trajectory was boosted when Hinman published dances composed by the younger woman in her five-volume *magnum opus* entitled *Gymnastics and Folk Dancing,* including *Greek Sacrificial Dance.*[53] As a dancing instructor, Humphrey spent one summer teaching at the Outdoor Players Camp in Peterborough, New Hampshire, where she expanded her repertoire by learning English traditional sword dancing.[54] However, she quickly grew frustrated and restive.

In 1917, Humphrey, with Hinman's encouragement, abandoned teaching to study at the newly created Denishawn School in Los Angeles led by Ruth St. Denis and Ted Shawn.[55] For the next decade, she toured the United States and the world with this influential dance troupe, which pleased vaudeville audiences while developing modernist choreographic aspirations. St. Denis incorporated scarves, draperies, and decorative costumes into her dances to create Orientalist pictorial fantasies that supposedly drew on Egyptian and Hindu motion to illustrate exotic philosophies and cultures while featuring girls in apparently risqué outfits. Shawn brought other strands of romanticism to the group, including Native American, Aztec, and Hungarian themes.[56]

With her background at the Parker School and in pageantry, Humphrey found a comfortable professional position in the Denishawn troupe, making a living doing what she had been trained to do since entering school. In 1918, the Denishawn dancers were photographed wearing classical robes that would have been equally fitting for Humphrey's *Greek Sacrificial Dance* or for an exercise on Cicero at the Parker School.

Humphrey's *The Shakers* manifested the lessons she had learned at the Parker School, with Hinman, and as a dancer with Denishawn. Rather than being a modernist break from traditional dance, it was conceptually linked to Humphrey's Progressive education, experience in folk dance and pageantry, and St. Denis's performance practices. Humphrey used impressionistic costumes to remove the dance from the temporal reality of the theater. Imaginative lighting and simple curtains set off the costumes to good advantage but were not difficult to create.[57] As with an "illustrative dance" from a pageant, she educated the audience about a particular cultural group through dance. Like an "exercise" from the Francis W. Parker School, the work simultaneously enlightened and educated those who watched it.

However, unlike her mentor Mary Wood Hinman, Doris Humphrey was interested in creating choreography rather than in collecting dances from ethnic or religious groups. While apparently educational, Humphrey's *The Shakers* bore little relation to actual Shaker practices. It was not derived from fieldwork or from written sources. As Humphrey noted in her letter to her family, the Shakers were not the point of the work; rather, the piece was a meditation on religion expressed through dance.

BARBARA MORGAN AND MODERNIST PHOTOGRAPHY

In 1938, while Shaker fever was raging due to the influence of the Index of American Design, Barbara Morgan photographed Humphrey's troupe performing *The Shakers*. Two of Morgan's images have become iconic representations of Humphrey's choreography and, over the last eight decades, have influenced how the Shaker sect has been viewed. The first portrays Humphrey, wearing a white bonnet and collar, encircled by four female and three male dancers all of whom gaze rapturously skyward while bending backward at the knees, waist, and neck (fig. 3.3). Eight pairs of extended white hands seem to float weightlessly at the ends of sixteen sleeves, which blend into the dark tones of the stage setting. As the central figure, Humphrey obstructs our view of one of the other female dancers. This hidden figure's arms seem to extend out of Humphrey's shoulders, giving the leader a supernatural appearance while her skirt floats around her waist like a disc,

FIGURE 3.3. Barbara Morgan, "Doris Humphrey SHAKERS (Humphrey-Weidman Group)," 1938. Barbara Morgan's photograph of Humphrey's dancers emphasizes geometric form and composition. Courtesy Barbara Morgan Wight Gallery Collection, Library Special Collections, Charles E. Young Research Library, UCLA.

echoing the circular brims of the male dancers' dark hats. With their arms outstretched and their necks bent backward, the dancers appear as though they could be suspended from above, like marionettes on invisible cords.

Morgan's second image of the dance portrays Beatrice Seckler performing a spectacular leap while two other female dancers gaze up at her from kneeling positions with hands folded in prayer (fig. 3.4). The female dancers' gaze, along with Seckler's outstretched right hand, form a strong diagonal through the composition, as with Steichen's earlier work, yet the composition is divided into alternating dark and light vertical rectangles of drapery. The soles of Seckler's feet, extended out improbably straight, run parallel to these verticals while her arms stretch out like the wings of a soaring bird. The dancers' costumes form simple geometric shapes: Seckler's skirt falls as a half-circle, her colleagues' kerchiefs make triangles.

FIGURE 3.4. Barbara Morgan, "Doris Humphrey SHAKERS (Bea Seckler Solo)," 1938. Courtesy Barbara Morgan Wight Gallery Collection, Library Special Collections, Charles E. Young Research Library, UCLA.

Morgan, a modernist photographer with roots in painting, created abstract compositions based on Humphrey's work. Just as Humphrey claimed that her dance would use Shaker worship as a starting point but did not seek to represent it accurately, so Morgan drew on Humphrey's three-dimensional choreography as inspiration to produce compelling graphic arrangements in two-dimensional black and white. As photographic historian Peter C. Bunnell has written about Morgan's entire oeuvre of dance photography, "The photographs, each of which is expressive of an aspect of a particular dance, primarily reflect the beauty of themselves as pictures."[58] Throughout her career, working in a variety of media, Morgan, like William F. Winter, was committed to modernist design and graphic experimentation. As photographic historian Curtis L. Carter argues, she believed in "subordination of realism to the spirit, the idea, and the emotion."[59]

When Morgan created these images of Humphrey's troupe, she was the leading photographer of choreography in the United States and possibly the world. Writing of Morgan's images, the critic Elizabeth McCausland asserted, "Without question, these are the best photographs of the dance today."[60] Born in Kansas in 1900, Morgan, whose birth name was Johnson, grew up in California and attended UCLA from 1919 to 1923. After graduating, she joined the UCLA faculty where she taught design, woodcut, and painting. She produced both paintings and woodblock prints, showing them in galleries, museums, and libraries throughout the state.[61] In 1925, she married Willard D. Morgan, a photographer who moved the couple to New York City to pursue a career in photojournalism.[62]

In New York, Barbara Morgan explored photography as a medium for creative expression.[63] Just as Charles Sheeler earned money photographing works of art for Albert Barnes, John Quinn, and Walter and Louise Arensberg, Morgan photographed Barnes's idiosyncratic collection of African art.[64] In creating images of fertility sculptures from Sudan and masks from the Ivory Coast, Morgan learned the importance of lighting.[65] She embraced the modernist photographic aesthetic developing in New York City at the time that also influenced William Winter.

Morgan had long been interested in dance and worked with Bertha Wardell, a dance instructor at UCLA who had been trained by Isadora Duncan, to present dancers as the subject of life drawing classes. Morgan later explained that Wardell had assisted her to "understand rhythm and body mechanics for use in painting."[66] Morgan's interests in dance and photography meshed in New York when Julien Bryan, the director of the International Film Festival, introduced her to Martha Graham. Graham and Morgan found shared interests and established a friendship that extended for sixty years. Morgan almost immediately conceived of producing a book of photographs of Graham and her choreography.

Together, Morgan and Graham developed a method for creating dance photographs. Although earlier she had worked with a Leica camera, for her images of the dance Morgan switched to a Speed Graphic camera that produced a 4-x-5-inch negative. Working in studios that she maintained for the purpose, Morgan removed dancers from the spaces in which they usually performed.[67] These alternative venues allowed Morgan to exactly manage the lighting she required.

As she became more expert in dance photography, Morgan used her knowledge of Graham and her choreography to manage every aspect of her images. Morgan wrote, "Previsualization is the first essential of dance photography. The ecstatic gesture happens swiftly, and is gone. Unless the photographer previsions, in order to fuse dance action, light and space simultaneously, there can be no significant dance picture."[68] She thus generated conditions in which she made compositions in black and white in a two-dimensional medium that referred to dances performed before audiences but which, in many ways, were distinct from the theatrical form. To explain her undertaking, Morgan described herself as a "kinetic light-sculptor."[69] She wrote, "I think of the bodies in their space as a series of convex and concave forms in rhythmic motion. I send light upon these forms, making patterns of light tones, middle tones, and dark tones; over *convex* heads, backs, breasts, thighs, bent knees; and *concave* eye sockets, undercut jaws, armpits, knee recesses, etc. The full emotion of the design is in the sum of the parts."[70]

Having started by working with Martha Graham, Morgan moved on to photographing the leading figures in American dance. Between 1936 and 1940, she cooperated with more than forty dancers and choreographers.[71] Her images, beyond documenting bravura dance performances, play with the polarities of light and dark, of straight and curved, of horizontal and vertical, of flesh and fabric. Within the artistic milieu in which Morgan functioned, these dichotomies would have been understood to resonate with other, more philosophical dualities including body and soul, good and evil, and sin and salvation.

Morgan's images of dancers captured mid-motion were distinct from the work of other dance photographers who had preceded her, including Soichi Sunami, the White Studio, Albert Witzel, and even Edward Steichen. Compared to Morgan's intensely kinetic figures, Ruth St. Denis and her Denishawn dancers seem practically wooden in photographs by Witzel and the White Studio.[72] While conceived as abstract compositions, Morgan's images also were meant to convey the dynamism and energy of modern dance.[73] Capturing dancers in mid-air became a hallmark of her style, as seen in the image of Bea Seckler as well as in "Martha Graham Celebration (Trio)" of 1937 and "Martha Graham El Penitente (Erick Hawkins Solo, "El Flagellante)" of 1940. Art critic and commentator Elizabeth McCausland noted the links among modern dance, modern art, and the new style of dance photography. She wrote, "The modern dance is like modern painting and modern sculpture, clean, with crisp edges, of rigid and muscular materials. The photographs of the modern dance must be likewise, with

great definition of values, not flowing draperies, with forms solidly modeled in light, but not swept by theatrical or stagey spotlights."[74] McCausland
used similar language about clear lines and rigid materials when celebrating the Shaker legacy in architecture and the decorative arts in 1944.[75] She
thus articulated the period's aesthetics, which found abstract beauty in
both stark nineteenth-century Shaker furniture and in Morgan's carefully
orchestrated geometric dance photographs.

Morgan's images were creatively composed and matched so beautifully
the American modernist aesthetics of the 1930s and 1940s that they were
hailed as triumphs from the moment that they came out of her developing baths. In January 1939, Columbia University's Department of Fine Arts
exhibited the photographs. Subsequently, Morgan sent them on a tour of
colleges and universities.[76] Writing in *The New Masses* in January 1939, Elizabeth Noble characterized Morgan's photographs of Graham, Humphrey,
and the other dancers as "a revelation."[77] Similarly, in October 1940, John
Martin, the *New York Times*'s dance critic, called Morgan's work "stunning"
when it was included in a show at the Museum of Modern Art (MOMA).[78]

In 1945, MOMA, in cooperation with the Inter-American Office of the
National Gallery of Art, prepared an exhibition of Morgan's photographs,
including images of *The Shakers,* which they entitled *Modern American
Dance.* This exhibition, mounted in the museum's Auditorium Gallery,
was part of a program that also featured shows by the influential geometric
painter Piet Mondrian and the modernist photographer Paul Strand.[79]

Although this exhibition opened initially at MOMA, it was designed
primarily as an early example of Cold War diplomacy (fig. 3.5). Spanish-
language and Portuguese versions of the show were prepared to travel to
Cuba, Brazil, and other countries in Latin and South America.[80] Funded by
the State Department, the Inter-American Office was charged with "admin-
istering, maintaining, and expanding a program of artistic exchange with
the other American Republics."[81] Carrying a decidedly jingoistic subtext in
the context of the end of World War II, *Modern American Dance* was meant
to declare the United States simultaneously a global leader in choreography
and photography.

Morgan's images of Humphrey's *The Shakers* featured prominently in the
publicity for the photographic exhibition. On April 1, 1945, the *New York
Times* published the image of Humphrey seemingly with four arms while
surrounded by dancers.[82] Later that week, the *New York World-Telegram*

FIGURE 3.5. Soichi Sunami, "Installation View of the Exhibition, *Modern American Dance*," 1945. This installation photograph by Morgan's colleague and competitor Soichi Sunami from 1945 documents the inclusion (at lower left) of Morgan's image of *The Shakers* in *Modern American Dance* at the Museum of Modern Art. Note also the modernist furniture being used in the gallery. Courtesy The Museum of Modern Art, New York, NY, USA. Digital Image © The Museum of Modern Art / Licensed by SCALA / Art Resource, NY.

reproduced Morgan's image of Bea Seckler completing her astounding leap while garbed in pseudo-Shaker garments.[83] Commenting on the latter photograph, the accompanying caption reductively informed readers, "The dance stems from 19th century ritual of New England sect."

While this explanatory statement may have seemed to make sense to the *New York World-Telegram*'s readers, almost no aspect of it is wholly correct. In this case, the Shakers functioned more as a symbolic trope than as an actual historic group. Although the Shakers had villages in New England, the group was headquartered for most of its existence in New York State and contained believers from as far west as Ohio and as far south as Georgia.

The group both predated and existed after the nineteenth century. Seckler's dance did not "stem" from that of the Shakers but rather was loosely inspired by it.

The inclusion of Barbara Morgan's photographs based on Doris Humphrey's *Shakers* within the traveling exhibition is compelling. These images were used to promote American exceptionalism and progress in the arts internationally in a program the State Department funded at a moment when the United States and Soviet Union were vying for global dominance.[84] The images, however, are modernist photographic compositions derived from a choreographic appropriation of the worship services of a small, unique American religious sect. Humphrey's representation of the Shakers, in turn, was shaped by her Progressive education, which promoted dance as physical education for women, theatricals as modes of cultural expression, and pageants as tools of assimilation and national identity.

The bonnets that Humphrey and Seckler wear, as well as their outstretched arms and legs, are surely signifiers, as they were reproduced repeatedly in books, magazines, and newspapers. Exactly what meaning they carried is difficult to discern. In Humphrey's choreography, and in Morgan's representation of that dance, the Shakers served as disassociated icons of American modernism. Rooted in a romantically unspecified American past (sketched breezily as nineteenth-century New England), the group was used by both choreographer and photographer to explore issues of national identity in terms of the dichotomies of energy and restraint, tradition and innovation, community and individuality, asceticism and sexuality.

MIRIAM CRAMER AND MORE LOVE, BROTHER

While Doris Humphrey's *The Shakers* did not claim to be an accurate representation of Shaker dance and worship, it influenced many theatrical presentations that followed. Miriam Cramer's 1945 production entitled *More Love, Brother* was among the earliest of these. Born in 1905, Cramer was the daughter of John, an investment banker and Miriam, a respected sculptor, devoted Unitarian, and leader in Cleveland, Ohio's art community.[85] The younger Cramer attended the Hathaway Brown School, a female preparatory academy located in Shaker Heights, a suburb of Cleveland, and took dancing lessons from Eleanor T. Flinn, a local instructor.[86] As a teen, Cramer drew positive notices for her dance performances and had a photographic portrait of her as a dancer published in the *Cleveland Plain Dealer.*[87] She attended Flora Stone Mather College, the women's educational institution associated with Western Reserve University, where she was active in dramatics, graduating in 1928. Subsequently, she took roles in local theatrical productions, and like Hinman and Humphrey, established her own school of dance.[88] Cramer also taught dancing at Cleveland's Laurel School, Western Reserve University, the Akron YWCA, the Cain Park Theater, and local settlement houses, including Merrick House.[89]

Cramer continued her dance education under Eleanor Frampton, who arrived to found a department of modern dance at the Cleveland Institute of Music in 1931. Frampton was a colleague of Humphrey and Weidman in the Denishawn dancers and had performed as part of the Humphrey-Weidman Troupe in New York City. She also had attended Wellesley College, earned a B.A. in physical education from the University of Nebraska, and conducted her own schools in California and Nebraska.[90] Although the Institute of Music originally planned that Humphrey and Weidman would supervise instruction within the new department, Frampton quickly made the program her own. She did, however, frequently host her former colleagues in Cleveland in the 1930s and 1940s.[91]

Cramer was Frampton's student in the late 1930s and thus became acquainted with her instructor's famous friends and their methods. In 1936, she was part of the ensemble that presented a composition Frampton choreographed based on a poem by Walt Whitman. This twenty-minute work, entitled *The Road before Us,* which told a tale of an American pioneer, was set to music by the local composer Lionel Nowak and represented a movement of the 1930s to create art around American national themes.[92] In June 1937, the *Cleveland Plain Dealer* published a photograph of Cramer participating in a modern dance class at the Cleveland Institute of Music with Weidman acting as a "guest teacher."[93]

From a young age, Cramer also found satisfaction and praise as a writer. In 1924, as part of a YWCA Christmas celebration, she debuted a new lullaby in which she had composed words for Antonin Dvorak's *New World Symphony.*[94] While at Flora Stone Mather College, she contributed to student publications and subsequently had poems published in the *Cleveland Plain Dealer.*[95]

In 1944, Western Reserve University provided Cramer with a grant to create a play on a Shaker theme. Her funding paid for her to conduct research at the Western Reserve Historical Society and to produce a play in cooperation with the university's dramatic and music departments.[96] Under the direction of Barclay Leatham, Western Reserve's Department of Drama and Theatre endeavored to produce new and experimental theater.[97] Cramer's grant formed part of a larger push by the university to focus on "the Great Lakes Region," with a special emphasis on the region's songs, history, folkways, and political and economic struggles.[98] Cramer reported, "Since the university has 'endowed' me with a fellowship this year so I can write a play on the Shakers, I am having a whirl digging into the marvelous collection of manuscripts preserved at the Western Reserve Historical Society."[99] In doing so, she followed both Humphrey and her teacher Eleanor Frampton in creating a work that both drew on and spoke to the American experience.

The Shakers were of local interest since a Shaker village had been located just outside of Cleveland for much of the nineteenth century in the area that would become Cramer's hometown of Shaker Heights. As she noted, she conducted research in the extensive Shaker manuscript collections held by the Western Reserve Historical Society. Her interest, however, was amplified by her close association with modern dance through settlement houses, Frampton, and Weidman. In approximately 1940, she arranged Shaker dances for a worship scene representing the community's past in a production at Cleveland's Merrick House.[100] She later reported, "The dances . . . are what led me to a study of the interesting people. I am a dancer and choreographer, and as such have always been looking for native folk material. It was the Shaker music and dance that opened up the bigger picture to me, and drove me on to doing the play."[101] Although Cramer does not mention it specifically, her understanding of Shaker dance likely was shaped by Humphrey's choreography. In fact, Cramer may have attended Humphrey and Weidman's performance of *The Shakers* that Frampton had sponsored in Cleveland as recently as October 1941.[102]

In April 1945, Cramer's three-act play, entitled *More Love, Brother,* premiered at the university's Eldred Theater.[103] The title was drawn from a Shaker mode of greeting.[104] Fifteen Western Reserve University students performed in the play. Cramer, whom newspaper notices described variously as an "assistant professor of dramatic arts" and as a "graduate student at Western Reserve University," oversaw its choreography.[105] The production included Shaker songs performed a cappella and in unison by the cast based on music Cramer found in the Western Reserve Historical Society's collections.[106]

More Love, Brother, which one critic called a "literately written folk drama dug out of Greater Cleveland's own soil," explored the tensions inherent in a hierarchical religious organization in which members attempt to lead celibate lives.[107] The production, which at times incorporated text lifted directly out of nineteenth-century Shaker sources, revolves around three pairs of men and women. Eldress Lydia and Elder Matthew are portrayed sympathetically as leaders of the community who have consistently placed the common good above their own desires. Eldress Abigail and Elder Richard, in contrast, enjoy the benefits of living in the community without having fully embraced the sect's ideals. Abigail follows Shakerism because it protects her from having to address difficult existential questions while Richard is an intolerant enforcer of orthodoxy. Sister Thankful and Brother Freeman, who are respectively eighteen and twenty years of age, find their devotion to life within the village tested by their growing romantic love for each other as well as by the questionable leadership demonstrated by Abigail and Richard. Mercy Elkins, a medium who presents supposedly divinely inspired messages but who is manipulated by Richard for his own selfish ends, articulates in trance the latent conflict among these characters.[108]

Scenes representing liturgical dance both within the Shaker meetinghouse and in an outdoor grove punctuated the drama. The latter piece of choreography focused on the sexual attraction suppressed by the young couple and condemned by older community members. Unlike in Humphrey's earlier work, the ritual dances and Shaker songs integrated into *More Love, Brother* were derived from Cramer's scholarly research.[109]

More Love, Brother expressed Cramer's admiration for the Shakers. She understood love as the essence of Shakerism. She later explained to a group of Unitarian women that the Shakers loved God: "They could think of no better way of attesting that love," she said, "than loving all that he had created. They loved one another, and—highly important—they loved themselves. They loved their neighbor and their enemy."[110] For Cramer, the Shaker tenets of purity, love, peace, justice, holiness, goodness, and truth were sound principles that created ideal communities which failed due to human frailty. The Shaker religion challenged its believers to focus their lives on their faith and thus put aside romantic attachments, personal goals, and selfish motives.[111] Cramer hoped that this story of love and sacrifice set in the past would speak to the American generation fighting World War II.

Although the production only ran for one weekend in April, Glenn Pullen, the local theatrical critic, wrote a positive review. "By deftly weaving quaint, melodic songs as well as curious folk dances into the action," he commented, "[Cramer] has made it a frequently engaging saga." He also indicated that since "her heart belongs to the terpsichorean arts," Cramer's work was at its best during the dance sequences, which he believed, choosing the wrong *grand dame* of modern dance, would remind his readers of "Agnes De Mille's choreography." Pullen's review culminated by claiming, "What Miriam Anne Cramer actually has in 'More Love, Brother' is the framework for a unique folk musical show, on the order of 'Oklahoma.' Translated into colloquial terms, with more earthy conflicts in drama and more musical pageantry, I think it would have a good chance of reaching Broadway."[112] Lois Wohlgemuth, writing in the *Cleveland Press*, was less generous with her praise. She opined that the first act was "talky" and that what narrative there was in the production did not start in earnest until the second act. Most damningly, she indicated, "There is no real action in the play at all, for the author's main purpose seems to be to give an insight into the lives of the communistic devout Shakers."[113]

Unsatisfied with the short run of her production at the Eldred Theater, Cramer sought other outlets for the play. Scripts and information about the production were mailed to both coasts. Paramount Studios was supposedly interested in the property, as were the William Morris Agency and Arthur Hopkins, a New York theatrical impresario.[114] On a local level, Cramer worked to have *More Love, Brother* added to the schedule of the Cain Park Theater, a municipally owned amphitheater in Cleveland Heights where she taught dancing.[115] She succeeded in persuading the venue to include her work in the summer schedule, which also featured productions of sophisticated Broadway comedies, musicals, a Gilbert and Sullivan operetta, and a puppet show.[116]

At the Cain Park Theater, Sydney H. Spayde, who came to Cleveland from the Civic Play House in Kalamazoo, Michigan, produced and directed *More Love, Brother*. Spayde gave the show what the *Plain Dealer* called a "much more pretentious production" than it had received at the Eldred. He expanded the chorus of Shaker maidens, as well as including a larger population of male believers. Further, Cramer explained, "Some of the historical material has been dropped to lighten dialogue. . . . The speeches now run shorter and crisper."[117]

As produced at Cain Park in August 1945, *More Love, Brother* was a three-act play with a cast of thirty-one that included both professionals and undergraduates from Western Reserve University.[118] Cramer continued to supervise the dancing and arranged more Shaker music that she harvested from the archives. The production's program included lyrics for two Shaker songs: "More Love," which spoke of the ties binding the Shaker community, and "Warring Song," which urged believers to employ a spiritual bow and arrow to battle the Devil.

Photographs produced to publicize the show emphasized Cramer's narrative exploring romantic tension within the sect and the issue of religious authority. One image of an awkwardly staged tableau portrays village elders working to separate Brother Freeman from his love interest, Sister Thankful (fig. 3.6). Another composition depicting a dance sequence in which the actors sang "Shoot the Devil," a Shaker song Cramer found at the

FIGURE 3.6. Probably by Geoffrey Landesman, "Dramatic Scene from 'More Love, Brother,'" 1945. This woodenly staged scene from one of Miriam Cramer's dances portrays members of the Shaker community working to separate two young people who have become tempted by romantic love. The actors are identified as Shakers by their bonnets and dark, broad-brimmed hats. Courtesy City of Cleveland Heights.

Western Reserve Historical Society, portrays two members of the community expressing mixed emotions concerning Sister Mercy's receiving gifts of the spirit (fig. 3.7).[119] Unlike Barbara Morgan, the creator of these photographs was more interested in capturing facial expressions and dramatic

FIGURE 3.7. Geoffrey Landesman, "'Shoot the Devil' Dance Sequence from 'More Love, Brother,'" 1945. This staged promotional photograph has more in common with nineteenth-century history paintings than it does with Barbara Morgan's modernist compositions. Courtesy City of Cleveland Heights.

gestures than in creating negative spaces and patterns of light and dark. These staged, pictorial photographs by Geoffrey Landesman are reminiscent of nineteenth-century American history paintings by artists such as Emanuel Leutze or Christian Schussele in that they seek to convey an entire narrative by freezing a single dramatic moment. Elaborate costumes serve as visual tools by which the artists convey their subjects' characters and motivations.

Sets designed by Vern Adix and Harold C. Mantz portrayed locations in and around the North Union, Ohio, Shaker village including the office of the elders, the meeting room within a dwelling house, the dwelling house kitchen, and an open-air sacred grove (figs. 3.8–3.10).[120] In creating the

FIGURE 3.8. R. Marvin Wilson, "Scene from 'More Love, Brother,'" 1945. This photograph documents Miriam Cramer's choreography representing the Shakers' ecstatic dance. The dancers' upstretched arms are reminiscent of gestures in Doris Humphrey's *Dance of the Chosen*. Courtesy City of Cleveland Heights.

FIGURE 3.9. R. Marvin Wilson, "Scene from 'More Love, Brother,'" 1945. Note that Vern Adix and Harold C. Mantz's scenic design for the kitchen includes a large cabinet, pegs on the walls to hang items, and a Shaker stove, all objects that were becoming iconic representations of the sect's life. However, the prop chairs seem to be standard American Windsor chairs, rather than Shaker ladder-back chairs. Courtesy City of Cleveland Heights.

FIGURE 3.10. R. Marvin Wilson, "Scene from 'More Love, Brother,'" 1945. This scene, set in an outdoor, open-air worship space, emphasizes Shaker separation of the genders and thus both celibacy and gender equality. Courtesy City of Cleveland Heights.

kitchen, the set designers incorporated a large vertical cupboard, a short rectangular iron stove, and pegboards on the walls, all artifacts that curators and collectors associated ichnographically with the sect. Students of the decorative arts will note that the chairs in this image are standard American Windsor chairs, rather than typical Shaker ladder-back seating furniture. This lapse in realism is an indication that, for these Shaker productions, costuming was more important than other aspects of Shaker material culture. However, it also may have been the result of the fact that these chairs are three-dimensional props, rather than simply painted two-dimensional scenic details, and Shaker reproduction furniture was not yet easily or cheaply available in the marketplace.

The reprised *More Love, Brother* was even more enthusiastically received than the earlier run of the play. William F. McDermott, the theater critic for the *Cleveland Plain Dealer,* called it "a folk study of the manners and customs of the Shaker community" and judged it "an original and exceptionally interesting example of the use of community resources in the making of a play." In passing, McDermott noted that the Shakers "were communists but not Marxists. . . . They believed in spiritualism [and] thought that God was both male and female. . . . Yet they were good farmers and successful salesmen of herbs and garden seeds."[121]

Glenn Pullen reported in the same paper, "What I saw is a great improvement over [Cramer's] original opus. . . . Miss Cramer amplified its most dramatic scenes, lightening the episodic, simple saga with many flashes of imagination and color." As he had in April, Pullen particularly liked the dance scenes, which may have continued to be influenced by Humphrey. He reported, "When a score of quaintly-garbed elders and eldresses suddenly break into a frenzied prayer-meeting dance, shaking their hips and hands ecstatically to drive the devil out of a poor sinner, these scenes have a tremendous theatrical impact." A devoted local booster, Pullen again asserted that Cramer's play could be transformed into a Broadway musical.[122]

Pullen took his enthusiasm to a national audience by publishing a review in *Variety*. Writing in a snappy, show-biz style, Pullen proclaimed,

New, rewritten . . . straw-hatter contains far more theatrical life . . . She paints a rather persuasive panorama of the Shakers whose credo was the antithesis of the Mormons' code . . . Fanatically stern advocates of celibacy, humility, and godliness, they paradoxically liked to sing and dance while they worked . . . Colorful ritual dances . . . combine all the rhythmic characteristics of jitterbug hoofing and the old-time shimmy. Sometimes the ecstatic dances follow a primitive pattern . . .

Pullen's *Variety* review concludes by asserting, "Quaint background is curiously fascinating, while the stylized story fairly shouts for more Shaker music and frenzied dancing."[123]

Pullen's astounding review, written for the entertainment industry, and McDermott's more analytic response for the local paper, together express much of what captured the public's attention about the Shakers at this time.[124] For these critics, Cramer's play allowed an exploration of the dialectics troubling American society at the end of World War II. As Americans, the Shakers were puritanical and religious, but they also were driven to ecstatic dancing. They were repressive and colorful, American and primitive, spiritual but economically productive, old-fashioned but able to accept a feminine godhead.

Pullen's predictions that *More Love, Brother* might make it to Broadway never came to fruition, and Miriam Cramer never wrote another play. Her career as a playwright ended when in 1946 she married Sidney Andorn, a Cleveland radio personality, at the First Unitarian Church in Shaker Heights.[125] For years, however, Cramer continued to be viewed as an expert on the Shakers and participated in activities around Cleveland celebrating and memorializing the group.[126]

MARGUERITE FELLOWS MELCHER AND THE SHAKER ADVENTURE

Broadway and Hollywood may have passed over *More Love, Brother* at least in part because the waters had been fouled by another theatrical property. Marguerite Fellows Melcher, the wife of Frederic G. Melcher, longtime editor of *Publisher's Weekly* and president and chairman of R. R. Bowker, the influential publishing and bibliographic firm, had been attempting for a decade to get a Shaker play produced in New York or made into a Hollywood film.[127]

Marguerite Fellows was born in Boston in 1879 to a New England family. Her father was from Weathersfield, Vermont, and her mother grew up in Enfield Center, New Hampshire, adjacent to the Enfield Shaker Village. Her great-aunt Zelinda Smith and great-uncle Elias Smith, her grandmother's sister and brother, were members of the sect and resided in the Shaker compound.[128] While attending Newton High School in Newton, Massachusetts, Fellows spent summers in Enfield and thus became familiar with the Shakers, their religion, and their customs. She graduated from Smith College in 1901 before marrying Frederic Melcher in 1910.[129] The couple settled in Montclair, New Jersey, when her husband was hired in 1918 by *Publisher's Weekly,* an influential trade publication headquartered in New York City.[130] Unitarians and progressive Democrats, Frederic and Marguerite Melcher were educated, liberal WASP reformers.[131] Within the publishing industry, Frederic sought to improve children's literature and thus was a cofounder in 1919 of Children's Book Week and in 1922 established the Newberry Medal for excellence in children's books. Later, in 1937, he supplemented this award with the Caldecott Medal for outstanding children's book illustrations.[132] Marguerite Melcher spent most of her adult life as a wife, mother, and grandmother but also consistently worked with words, serving as a translator, poet, playwright, and author.[133]

In the 1930s, she wrote her first play dealing with Shaker themes while also having other works produced by the Smith College Theatre Workshop and the Unity Players, an amateur theatrical group associated with Montclair's Unity Unitarian Church.[134] Entitled *Steps unto Heaven,* with an alternate title of *The World Is Good,* Melcher's one-act play was created for the centenary celebration of the Union Church at Enfield Center, New Hampshire, and produced in that location on August 11, 1936. The play was thus produced in the summer following the Whitney Museum's influential Shaker exhibition in New York City, at the same time that artists were recording Shaker objects for the Index of American Design, and three years after Humphrey's *The Shakers* was performed on Broadway.[135]

The drama centers on conflict between Jim Eastman, a man portrayed as a drunkard and unfit father, and Ellen Eldridge, his sister-in-law who has joined the Shaker community because of the pain she saw her sister endure in her unhappy marriage. Celia Eastman, the man's daughter, feels that in order to escape her father's control she must choose between a husband selected by him or her aunt's trajectory of joining the celibate communitarian sect. The play's conflict is resolved by the girl following neither path and instead taking a position keeping house for the local protestant minister and his elderly mother until she can secure an alternative option.

Melcher's *Steps unto Heaven* portrays the Shaker community negatively as an asylum into which weak individuals escaped when they were not strong enough to manage life in the outside world. Characters in the work repeatedly emphasize that the Shaker community offered only the appearance of safety from the sins of the world. The minister advises the girl, "Real safety comes from within. You have to be safe in your own mind and spirit before you can be safe in the world." Similarly, Nathan Fifield, a trustee of the church, asserts, "This is our world. Our lives are a part of the world's life. The evil in the world is our responsibility." Melcher portrayed the protagonist's possible withdrawal from the world by joining the sect as jettisoning responsibility and failing to fully engage with her surroundings. In contrast, the village church was depicted as a force for good in a challenging world. Melcher had Fifield proclaim, "The Shaker faith is doomed by its very perfection. . . . This church is a living faith, rooted in an imperfect world and growing as the world grows, keeping always a little ahead. When the Shaker faith is no more, when the Shakers are scattered and gone, this church will still be standing, still living, still a needed part of the living world to which it belongs."[136]

Set in New Hampshire in 1836, *Steps unto Heaven* purports to be a representation of the role of Shakerism within an American community. However, as it was performed in churches in both New Hampshire and New Jersey in the decade before World War II, it also can be read as a condemnation of American isolationism in a time of international political crisis and an assertion of the importance of liberal Protestantism within American life.

In the year of the performance of this Shaker-themed drama, the cosmopolitan Melchers circulated to their friends and acquaintances a Christmas card with a poem Marguerite presumably penned. This Christmas poem, which commented on Soviet dialectical materialism, Nazi intolerance, and the violence of the Spanish Civil War, resonates with themes also expressed in *Steps unto Heaven*:

> Lord Jesus owns no place to pray
> In Russian Soviet
> The Nazarene is turned away
> Where Nazi hate is met
> And if to Spain his footsteps stray
> He finds no peace as yet.
> How blest is America today
> That we are free to bid him stay.[137]

In this short Christmas poem, the Melchers asserted the importance that freedom of religion played in the United States, in which "we are free to bid [Christ] stay." In this way, the United States, they claimed, was distinctly different from the atheist Soviet Union, hatred-filled Germany, and Spain torn by Civil War.

Steps unto Heaven also explores the tension between security and adventure within human life, a theme that Melcher would develop more fully in other works. Every individual, she believed, craved these two concepts. "People have to have *some* security," she explained, "or they would wear themselves out; they have to have some adventure, or the security would go stale on their hands; would become too stupid and uninteresting to endure. The proportion of these two elements in a person's life make life what it is."[138] For Fifield and for the minister, joining the Shakers would mean that Celia was giving up life's adventure for the Shaker's economic security.

While *Steps unto Heaven* was being performed, Melcher worked to develop a script for a larger Shaker production she entitled *Rose in the Wilderness*, drawing the name from a Shaker song that her mother had sung.[139] This work played on Melcher's interest in the dialectic between security and adventure by contrasting Caleb, a Shaker workman, with Pletus, a prophet and religious leader within the community. Caleb, a true believer, works ardently to create a utopia free from poverty or war. Pletus, in contrast, takes advantage of the community's assets by falsifying religious gifts and cheating on his vows of celibacy. In Melcher's play, Caleb is murdered, and without his guidance the community fails. The epilogue depicts aged Shakers living in a village that is falling down around them while they sell off spinning wheels to make ends meet. *Rose in the Wilderness* sought to convey that, while in the twentieth century Shaker villages appeared to be unchanging havens within a transforming world, in the nineteenth century they were places in which individuals confronted existential human dilemmas.

Melcher's *Rose in the Wilderness* was inspired by the actual history of the Shaker community in Enfield, New Hampshire. Caleb Dyer, a trustee and pillar of the community, was murdered by Thomas Weir in 1863 in a conflict over custody of Weir's daughters, who had been placed with the Shakers while their father served as a volunteer in the Civil War. Following Dyer's death, the Enfield Shaker Village failed to regain the prosperity it had experienced under his leadership.

Melcher circulated her work broadly among New York's theatrical community, hoping that the fashion for the Shakers created by museum exhibits and images of Shaker furniture would help it to gain traction. "I wonder if you have happened to notice the attention that the Shakers are getting from many sources right now," she wrote to a New York insider in 1939, citing Freda Diamond's furniture being shown at Wanamaker's and including two advertisements clipped from a newspaper.[140]

The entertainment industry provided only discouragement. Audrey Wood of the Century Play Company candidly informed her "I am sincerely doubtful that this subject matter will hold up in a commercial vehicle today."[141] Alexander L. Crosby similarly advised, "I doubt if the play is meant for Broadway, and the fault is with the potential audience.... I suppose that the proper commercial strategy would be to provide swing music."[142] Oscar Hammerstein II sent Melcher what was probably a standard rejection. He wrote, "I found your play, ROSE IN THE WILDERNESS, very well written but it is not suitable for my purposes at this time."[143] Doris Frankel of Audrey Wood Play Broker and Author's Representative similarly indicated that the work lacked a love story and a conventional plot line. However, she offered the suggestion that Melcher try the material in another medium, commenting, "Have you ever thought of doing a novel?"[144]

Joseph A. Brandt, an ambitious young scholar and former journalist who had recently taken the helm of the Princeton University Press, subsequently solicited Melcher, based on her experience in writing the play, her family connections, and her familiarity with the topic, to draft a book about the Shakers for a series he was creating to celebrate those Americans who resisted conformity and uniformity.[145] In December 1938, Brandt, who had a reputation for courting unconventional, nonacademic authors and landing his books on the lists of the Book-of-the-Month Club, explained his vision for the series in a letter to Melcher.[146] He wrote,

> As I view the philosophic purpose of The American Peoples series, it is this: The history of the United States has been toward uniformity, toward conformity. Essentially, our history is an imperial one, just like that of most other great nations, except we are so close to the Indian, for instance, that we do not think of our ruthless conquest of his as imperialistic. Perhaps it will add to our understanding of our country if we now look at the peoples who did not wholly conform. Equally interesting are those Americans like the Shakers who resisted the wave of uniformity. If this approach to the series is sound—and I think it is—then there is certainly room and need for your own book.[147]

Brandt's interest in documenting nonconforming Americans in the late 1930s must be understood in the context of the growth of fascism in Europe and the expansion of Hitler's National Socialist Party in Germany in particular. In this series, Brandt sought to use the Shakers to differentiate America from Europe by arguing that the United States had groups of nonconformists who would not participate in a totalitarian state. Sinclair Lewis similarly used a curmudgeonly Vermont Yankee newspaper editor as the bulwark against American fascism in his It Can't Happen Here of 1935.[148]

Brandt, who sought to make his series appeal to a popular audience while also working to define America's national identity, urged Melcher to create a study that would be primarily literary and interpretive rather than strictly scholarly.[149] He hoped the manuscript would "reflect the qualities of these people which caused them to withdraw from the all-absorbing American culture."[150] In conducting research for her book, Melcher drew on published works by Shakers and enthusiasts including Edward Deming Andrews, collections at the New York Public Library and Dartmouth College, and contacts in Enfield and other locations with Shaker villages.[151]

Published by Princeton University Press in 1941, *The Shaker Adventure* was an easily digested sweeping history of the sect that argued the Shakers had achieved a balance between security and adventure. Economic security provided by communal effort, she claimed, allowed spiritual and religious adventures.[152] The work also differed from other publications of the time concerning the Shakers in that it paid little attention to the sect's architecture and material culture.

Melcher identified closely with the Shakers; she portrayed them as forbears to the Progressives and to the reforming Roosevelt administration that was currently in power. The critical view of the sect expressed in *Steps unto Heaven* is absent from *The Shaker Adventure*. In explaining the creation of the sect, the author asserted that it was rooted in revolt "against smugness and bigotry in religion, revolt against social and economic evils, revolt against the uglier side of human nature."[153] This description of the sources for Shakerism is broad enough that it also could characterize the motivation behind muckraking photographs by Jacob Riis and Lewis Hine or the output of the photographers working for the New Deal's Farm Security Administration.

As a strategy to ameliorate these problems, Melcher claimed, the Shakers engineered a society without economic insecurity or income inequality.[154] "One of the intangible legacies the Shakers left to the world," she claimed, "is their demonstration that it is possible for man to create the environment and the way of life he wants, *if he wants it enough*. Man *can* choose. In a world of defeatism, this is a cheering thought."[155]

As an active Unitarian, Melcher also identified with the Shaker's religious beliefs. Although she gave an extensive accounting of Shaker religious practices in the heart of her study, in her conclusion she described the sect in a simplistic manner that could be applied to the tenets of her own twentieth-century liberal Protestant denomination. She asserted, "Their theology was on the deistic, non-trinitarian, humanistic side in the midst of churches that still held to the old Jonathan Edwards ideas of theism, the Trinity and predestination."[156]

Melcher's book bore the intellectual imprint of Brandt, the man who had commissioned it. The conclusion echoed Brandt's words about non-conformists and their role in American society. She wrote, "In future days of humanity, it may appear that the small, unpopular groups which stood deliberately aside, kept steadfastly apart from the course of normal, organized churches and political and economic systems, were the groups which contributed most in the long run to the mental and spiritual side of human progress. They are the experimenters, the adventurers."[157] If Melcher earlier made it sound as though the Shakers were the precursors of the Progressives and the New Deal, here she identified them as a component of American nonconformist dissent that included the Plymouth Colony's Separatists, Pennsylvania's Ephrata, and Brigham Young's Church of Latter-Day Saints. This "come-outer" impulse, in which believers abandon established practices to found their own communities, brought the Shakers to America in the 1770s and would make the sect appealing to participants in the countercultures of the latter half of the twentieth century.[158]

Although not scholarly, Melcher's thoughtful, engaging study filled a void in the literature. It was broadly reviewed and well received.[159] Writing for the *American Historical Review,* Watt Stewart of the New York State College for Teachers wrote, "In this work, excellent as to format and composition, Mrs. Melcher has made a fine contribution to the history of the social experiments of the nineteenth century."[160] In the *New York Times,* Herbert Gorman noted, "Mrs. Melcher has told the story of the Shakers with distinction and constant currents of interest."[161] In the *Christian Century,* in a largely positive review W. E. Garrison suggested, however, that Melcher lacked critical distance. "Mrs. Melcher's admirable and moving account," the reviewer wrote, "is wholly sympathetic. Shakerism is part of her own family tradition and she is for it as against all critics in the days of controversy."[162] Similarly, writing in the *American Sociological Review,* Allan W. Eister of the Friends' Central School in Philadelphia observed, "The author, evidently a lay historian, conveys an unmistakably sympathetic respect for the simplicity of Shaker living."[163]

Members of the Shaker sect also greeted *The Shaker Adventure* enthusiastically. In a letter to Princeton University Press, Sister A. Rosetta Stephens, a Shaker from Mount Lebanon, New York, wrote, "It is not only delightfully written, with a keen understanding of the hopes and aims of the Shakers, but very authentic as to detail."[164] Prudence A. Stickney, a trustee of the Sabbathday Lake Shakers, expressed her admiration for the book in a letter to Melcher of April 1941. She explained, "I feel you are a real friend, and I am writing to tell you how much we all appreciate your book, 'Shaker Adventure.' It is the best I have ever read, and so true. You realize as no one else has, their early persecutions and struggles to plant this gospel."[165] The sisters in Canterbury, New Hampshire, paid the book the highest possible honor by selling it to the village's visitors. Sister Mary A. McCoy informed Melcher, "Your book, 'The Shaker Adventure' has been read by all the members of our family. We advocate and recommend it to our daily visitors; many are deeply interested, and are buying them from us. Sister Josephine has already sold 18 of the books and has ordered more this last week."[166]

Other sufferers from Shaker fever similarly respected Melcher's contribution. Miriam Cramer called it "one of the 'special' books in my library."[167] Even Edward Deming Andrews, never one to be effusive about others' work concerning the Shakers, grudgingly complimented Melcher. "On the whole," he wrote, "I think you have done very well, especially in your selection and characterization of figures representing the dominant forces in the movement."[168]

Melcher's *The Shaker Adventure,* although written by a layman and lacking both critical distance and historiographical awareness, entranced readers with its literary style and positive vision of the believers. It served for decades as a standard source on the sect. In the 1960s, Melcher secured the copyright to the work from Princeton University Press and had it republished by the Press of Western Reserve University, currently Case Western Reserve University, in Cleveland. Subsequently the Shaker Museum and Library in Old Chatham, New York, kept it in print. More than seventy years later, Americans can still purchase new copies of Melcher's study, which sought to define America by its nonconformists in the years leading up to World War II.

CLARICE CARR AND THE ENFIELD SHAKER SINGERS

While Marguerite Melcher was attempting to get *Rose in the Wilderness* produced and simultaneously writing *The Shaker Adventure,* another woman from Enfield, New Hampshire's small community was also conducting research into the Shaker's musical heritage and working to ensure its preservation and celebration. In the 1940s, Clarice Jennings Carr organized a group of local women into the Enfield Shaker Singers, who performed Shaker songs in costume for regional and national audiences. As Carr was not a dancer, like Doris Humphrey or Miriam Cramer, or a playwright, like Marguerite Melcher, the Enfield Shaker Singers' performances centered around music.

Comparable to the other figures in this chapter, Clarice Carr was an educated white woman from a liberal Protestant background. Born in New Hampshire in October 1905 to parents from the Granite State, Clarice Jennings graduated from High School in East Hardwick, Vermont, and enrolled in the fall of 1923 in Mount Holyoke College, the same women's school Humphrey's mother attended.[169] At the time, she told the school that she was interested in music, English literature, and basketball.[170] Majoring in French and minoring in music, she graduated in the class of 1927.[171] After spending a summer studying in Colorado, Jennings responded to a request from the superintendent of schools in Enfield, New Hampshire, to teach music and French. She had never before heard of Enfield but was pleased to secure employment. Within two years, the young teacher had married Fred Parker Carr, an Enfield resident, a veteran of the Spanish American War, and an attorney with a degree from Boston University's School of Law.[172] William Miller of the Congregational Church in East Hardwick, Vermont, officiated at the nuptial ceremony. Soon after their marriage, Clarice Carr withdrew from teaching and devoted herself to raising two sons, giving private piano lessons, and participating in the life of the community through the PTA, the local woman's club, and her church.

On arriving in Enfield in 1927, Jennings was entranced by the Shaker village that stood empty along the western bank of Mascoma Lake. The Shakers had only recently moved out of the village to consolidate into the Canterbury Shaker Village and had sold the Enfield property to the Missionaries of Our Lady of La Salette, a francophone Catholic brotherhood.[173] As a musician, the young teacher was particularly interested in the manner in which the sect interwove song and dance into their worship.[174] Soon established as a permanent resident of Enfield, Jennings became something of an expert on the Enfield Shaker community through research at Dartmouth College and at the state library in Concord.[175] In 1942, *Yankee Magazine*, a magazine dedicated to a regional identity in opposition to Roosevelt's nationalism, published a short literary piece she wrote set in the Enfield Shaker village. Clarice Jennings Carr's work revolved around the moral lessons learned from a team of oxen falling through the ice on a wintry frozen lake.[176]

In 1946, cultural boosters approached Carr concerning the possibility of presenting material related to the Shakers at a statewide folk festival scheduled to take place in May in Manchester, New Hampshire.[177] To fulfill this request, she recruited a group of friends, all of whom were either schoolteachers or former schoolteachers, to perform Shaker songs and dances. Before finalizing plans, Carr wrote to the Shaker Central Ministry in Canterbury, New Hampshire, to seek their approval for the undertaking.[178] In May 1946, Ruth Dennis, Ann Tarney, Phyllis Goodwin, and Dorothy Sanborn performed as the Shaker Singers in Manchester under Carr's direction.[179] Sponsored by the New Hampshire Recreation Council, the New Hampshire Folk Festival featured sea chanteys, lumberjack songs, South American folk songs, African American spirituals, and dances identified as Greek, Finnish, Swiss, Hungarian, Czech, Russian, French, Italian, and Bavarian, along with music performed by the Shaker Singers. Sunday evening culminated with dancing led by Ralph Page, the influential contra dance caller from Nelson, New Hampshire.

Carr's Shaker Singers wore pseudo-Shaker costumes to add verisimilitude to their performances (fig. 3.11). These costumes were ankle-length

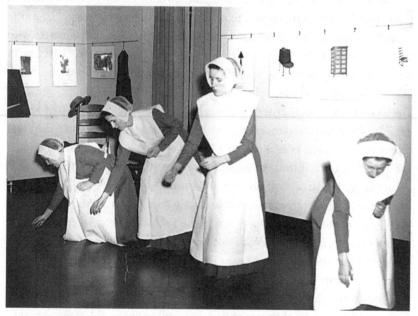

FIGURE 3.11. M. Milne, "Enfield Shaker Singers Performing at the Manchester Historic Association," October 1949. The Enfield Shaker Singers performed in costumes that, although not necessarily historically accurate, emphasized piety and distanced them from American popular culture of the 1940s. Note the images from the Index of American Design on display, which provide a context for the performance. Courtesy Manchester Historic Association, Manchester, NH.

dresses with long sleeves of dark or drab material overlaid with white aprons and bibs. The singers also wore white bonnets that framed their faces. Although these costumes were not scrupulously accurate reproductions of Shaker garments, they were closer approximations than the garb that Doris Humphrey's dancers wore and were crafted by women who lived in a community that had personal experience with the sect. Whatever their accuracy, the costumes distanced the Shaker Singers from the American culture of the 1940s that celebrated Betty Grable's legs and embraced the pinup art of Alberto Vargas while emphasizing the piety, humility, and modesty of Shaker women. Carr's Shaker Singers did not include male participants but instead focused on female performance, a practice emphasizing the gendered enthusiasm for Shaker music and dance that was consistent with Humphrey's and Cramer's experiences of Shaker fever.

In creating the Shaker Singers, Carr likely was influenced by the pageant tradition at Mount Holyoke, which, as with many American colleges for women, had been instituted in the nineteenth century.[180] As a student, Carr would have been exposed to, and with her espoused interest in music probably participated in, an annual college pageant that culminated with the crowning of the May Queen. This annual tradition was a legacy of the Progressive-era conception of dance and performance in which Mary Wood Hinman trained Doris Humphrey. Committees at Mount Holyoke created costumes and scenery while faculty from the Department of Physical Education trained dancers for the performance. Drawing on a different theme or story each year (including Pocahontas, the Pied Piper, Heidi, and the Aeneid), during this era Mount Holyoke students performed outside before an audience of as many as two thousand spectators.[181]

Carr's Shaker Singers made such a strong impression in Manchester that they were invited to participate again the following year when the newly founded New Hampshire Folk Festival Federation held its second annual festival in Peterborough on May 31 and June 1, 1947.[182] Peterborough was a logical community for this event because of its ongoing involvement with folk music and dance, including being the location where Humphrey was first introduced to English sword dancing. Following on the trajectory set a half-century earlier by reformers and playground activists such as Hinman, Elizabeth Burchenal, and Luther Gulick, the New Hampshire Folk Festival sought to create bonds within the state by sustaining folk traditions while simultaneously educating the public about diverse traditions. A greeting printed at the top of the event's program set the tone by asserting, "May we all grow in appreciation and understanding of one another's cultural traditions as we share and learn more of our rich folk heritage at this Festival."[183] The festival was part of what one enthusiast of the time called "a widespread interest in folk expressions, which has now burst into blossom, stimulated by a growing spirit of nationalism."[184] In this context, Shaker music was seen simply as one aspect of the Granite State's rich, multicultural patrimony. Just as Marguerite Melcher had celebrated the Shakers as representing American freedom of religion in 1936 in the context of the growth of European fascism, in the earliest days of the Cold War folk festival organizers celebrated American ethnic diversity as a contrast to the perceived forced conformity of the Soviet Union.[185] Because of their successes in Manchester and Peterborough, organizers of larger folk festivals invited the Shaker Singers to participate in their events. In November 1947, the women from Enfield traveled to Boston to perform "Early Work and Worship Songs" in the Fourth Annual New England Folk Festival held that year at the Boston YWCA.[186] Ralph Page, the influential New Hampshire square and contra dance impresario, served as master of ceremonies for this event, which featured multicultural groups from Vermont, New Hampshire, and Massachusetts including a troupe from Harvard College performing Irish dances.

Subsequently, Carr's group, now called the Enfield Shaker Singers, received an invitation to perform at the 14th Annual National Folk Festival held in St. Louis.[187] Sarah Gertrude Knott, the festival's guiding spirit, explained that the purpose of the festival was "to bring a cross section of the most representative folk treasures together on one festival program, to see what the story would tell of our people and our country."[188] The Enfield Shaker Singers were the first group from New Hampshire to be invited to perform there.[189] Carr said of her singers who would attend the festival, "Their voices are light and uncultivated. I think they are good. They love the songs."[190] Carr worked diligently within the town of Enfield to secure donations to finance the trip to St. Louis.

The festival's program clarified for the audience that "these singers are not Shakers, but learned the songs from some of the last Shakers at New Hampshire's other community in East Canterbury, and from elderly neighbors of the Enfield community, people 'of the world' who can well recall the songs that they often heard sung at Shaker meetings."[191] In this context, Carr and Knott wished to emphasize that the Shaker Singers, while not Shakers themselves, were presenting an accurate performance of this American sect, rather than simply an artistic representation. Although Carr consistently made it clear that her performers were not members of the faith, at least one St. Louis newspaper editor was unclear about the distinction and headlined an article "Shakers to Sing at Folk Festival."[192]

When Knott again invited the Enfield Shaker Singers to the National Folk Festival in 1950, the Voice of America recorded the music portions of the event so that it could be broadcast internationally to educate the world about American culture.[193] Transmitting American folk music to Europe, of course, was part of the same Cold War propaganda effort that sent to Latin America Barbara Morgan's image of Beatrice Seckler leaping into the air while garbed as a Shaker. In both cases, the sect's heritage comprised one aspect of the message concerning the nation's greatness and its fitness to be the leader of the free world. In a letter thanking Clarice Carr for making the trip to St. Louis, Sarah Knott noted that the Enfield Shaker Singers had brought "a few minutes of simple, religious fervor and sincerity" to the program.[194]

SHAKERS OFF-BROADWAY

As denizens of Enfield, which boasted a population of 1,690 residents in 1940, Marguerite Melcher and Clarice Carr inevitably met and, because of their shared interest in the Shakers, became friends.[195] In late 1948, when Melcher convinced New York's Abbe Practical Workshop, an experimental theater group run by Robert O'Byrne and Gloria Monty on the city's far west side, to produce her *Rose in the Wilderness*, she called on Carr to serve as a consultant and manage the music for the production.[196] The former schoolteacher from rural New Hampshire was thrilled to be involved with the New York theater world. Melcher also convinced Doris Humphrey to contribute choreography to the culmination of the third act, which, like Cramer's *More Love, Brother*, presented a set piece of a Shaker worship service complete with ecstatic dancing and chanted singing.

Gloria Monty, who would go on to produce the soap opera and pop sensation *General Hospital* in the late twentieth century, directed Melcher's play.[197] Monty had previously acted at the Cleveland Playhouse in Cleveland so she may have been willing to give Melcher's work a chance after other producers turned it down because she was aware of Cramer's success at the Cain Park Theater. The off-Broadway show ran for only two nights,

January 5 and 6, 1949. Reviews of the production were mixed. Robert Garland of the *New York Journal American* wrote patronizingly, "Under Gloria Monty's schoolmistressy guidance, the Abbe Practical Workshoppers give a sincere unslovenly performance."[198] Vernon Rice in the *New York Post* also was dismissive, writing, "'Rose in the Wilderness' is not without its shortcomings, but it has honesty and integrity in its writing and in its production."[199] Murray Gross in the *New York Star* said, "That Miss Melcher knows her subject and treats it with loving respect is readily apparent. She has courageously treated a difficult problem—how to maintain one's religious faith while facing the realities of everyday living. Her drama is an intermittently interesting tale, honestly written and provocative in content."[200] Similarly, in the *New York Telegram,* William Hawkins asserted, "There is a ceremonial formality about much of the action throughout the play, and this is accompanied by music based upon the actual hymns of the sect. These themes have a fascinating indigenous quality as the melodies take unusual intervals to create a mood of melancholy self-righteousness."[201] *Variety* judged the play "a little thin and perhaps occasionally contrived for Broadway, but . . . superior fare for strawhats, little theatres, and community groups."[202]

Writing in the *New York Times,* Brooks Atkinson offered the kindest review, calling the play "a contribution to American dramatic literature." He observed further that it "was a play of considerable intellectual and religious integrity that penetrates deep into the nature of faith." He indicated that Melcher offered "an austere and resolute inquiry into the souls of some very earnest people." Finally, he complemented the production's "fanatical unearthly dance," saying that it "preserves the plainness of Shaker manners and catches the silent passion of the Shaker spirit." Ultimately, he concluded, "This dance is a trifle too good for the rest of the production."[203]

In contrast, Estella Weeks, a researcher at the Library of Congress and acquaintance of both Melcher and Carr, was offended at the showcasing of Humphrey's choreography as representing the Shaker tradition. In a letter to Erwin O Christensen, the curator of the Index of American Design at the National Gallery of Art, Weeks complained that the dance, "though labelled a 'could-be Shaker' dance by one reviewer was very wide of anything ever described by the Shakers themselves, or by worldly observers of their dance. . . . It *was* more Humphrey than Shaker."[204]

Clarice Carr traveled to New York to see Melcher's play produced. She subsequently wrote to congratulate her friend on her success, as did a number of Melcher's associates and acquaintances.[205] Jerome Count, who ran the Shaker Village Work Camp in New Lebanon, New York, and who is discussed at some length in chapter 5, was "very much impressed" by the performance.[206] Charles C. Adams, by this time the former director of the New York State Museum and one of the earliest collectors of Shaker materials, wrote,

> It was indeed a great pleasure to attend your play "Rose in the Wilderness." . . .
> I am in hearty sympathy with using material from our own history in the arts
> instead of remote material. I feel also that it is not necessary to follow literally
> every phase of history. You have based your play on the Shakers, and have
> made one that will help the present generations to visualize something of
> their life and time. The essentials of Shaker life are there—so it seems to me—
> and the actors did well their part.[207]

Nancy Larrick, an author, critic, and specialist in children's literature with a graduate degree from Columbia University, compared *Rose in the Wilderness* to *Oklahoma,* just as critics had linked Cramer's *More Love, Brother* to Rodgers and Hammerstein's smash hit from six years earlier. Drawing on her larger vision of American arts, Larrick wrote, "The play was particularly interesting to me as another example of our present day development of the folk opera to combine serious thought with a study of folkways by means of words, music and choreography. Porgy and Bess also did it beautifully. Oklahoma and Finian's Rainbow approached it on the lighter side."[208]

Variety's assessment that *Rose in the Wilderness* would be good fare for students and "strawhats" proved faulty. The work has never subsequently been staged, even though Melcher once again placed the script in the hands of an agent following the premier hoping that good reviews would assist in selling it.[209] However, the production did introduce Clarice Carr to Doris Humphrey, and the Enfield Shaker Singers subsequently performed with Humphrey's dancers at venues including the Eighth American Dance Festival, sponsored by Connecticut College and held in New London, Connecticut.[210]

PERFORMING THE SHAKERS

Although neither *Rose in the Wilderness* nor *More Love, Brother* became a box-office smash to compete with *Oklahoma,* the women responsible for performing Shakerism on stage in the years between 1930 and 1950 had a lasting impact on how Americans and the world at large understood the Shakers. Melcher's *The Shaker Adventure* is still in print seven decades after it was published. Humphrey's *The Shakers* continues to be performed around the globe. Barbara Morgan's images of Humphrey and of Beatrice Seckler inspire new generations of choreographers and designers who stage Humphrey's abstraction of Shaker worship.

While these cultural products from the middle of the twentieth century continue to shape the public's perception, the cultural context in which they were produced has been lost and with it their full meanings. None of these works is a simple gift; none of them is purely what it appears to be. *Dance of the Chosen* may be a canonical work of American modern dance, but it also is a transitional piece by an ambitious choreographer emerging from her training in pageantry and folk dance while seeking a modern form of dance identifiable as American. Barbara Morgan's photographs document Humphrey's creativity, yet they also are compositions in their own right, shaped by the modernist photographic canon and distributed internationally to serve national diplomatic purposes as the United States asserted its authority as leader of the free world. Melcher's *Shaker Adventure* is more than a book about the Shaker experience. It is a literary historical study written by a frustrated playwright who contemplated spirituality and materialism while celebrating the virtue of nonconformity just as the United States was battling fascism. The songs Clarice Carr revived from the archives and performed at the National Folk Festival are examples of Shaker music, but they are also midcentury celebrations of nationalistic multiculturalism presented as a Cold War counterpoint to forced Soviet orthodoxy. These Shaker songs simultaneously served as vehicles by which an educated, middle-class woman from a small rural New Hampshire town transcended her local surroundings, thus gaining status as a national performer. Created by Protestant, educated American women with reformist impulses, these works situated a small, eccentric regional religious sect as worthy of national attention and representative of larger cultural values and aspirations.

Although these productions never threatened to outpace *Oklahoma*, they set the stage and created expectations for the next wave of Shaker plays and pageants produced between 1950 and 1965, which are examined in chapter 5. Rather than being created with aspirations for Broadway, this subsequent group of Shaker-inspired productions were generated in the context of an expanding American historic preservation movement and were presented either within historic Shaker villages—including South Union, Kentucky; Hancock, Massachusetts; and Mount Lebanon, New York—or as part of efforts to preserve these compounds. In these productions, actors and enthusiasts sang and danced in Shaker garb as an avenue to preserve the spaces believers had previously sanctified for their own use. The performances in these spaces, however, were shaped and informed by the contributions of Humphrey, Cramer, Melcher, and Carr.

CHAPTER 4
INSTITUTING A SHAKER MUSEUM

....

The Shaker Museum at Old Chatham
and the Yale University Art Gallery

B y the middle of the 1940s, many Americans had become cognizant of the
Shakers and their material culture through museum exhibitions, drawings and images created by the Works Progress Administration, and features
in the periodical press. Collectors and enthusiasts had acquired an appreciation for Shaker heritage and asserted that the sect's achievements reflected
positively on the nation and that its history should be known more broadly.
Although Charles C. Adams had ensured that the New York State Museum
in Albany owned a large collection of Shaker materials, the curious could
find sources of information scarce. With a responsibility to interpret the
natural and cultural history of a large state, at any one time the museum
could only afford space to display a small fraction of its Shaker materials.
Visitors to Shaker settlements found them either closed and repurposed or
inhabited by elderly residents who desired the economic benefits of visitors
while simultaneously resenting the intrusive presence of tourists.

Between the end of World War II and 1960, two groups of individuals
attempted to establish institutions to permanently exhibit Shaker materials and interpret the sect's history. Each planned to create an organization,
established on a privately accumulated collection, that would interpret the
Shakers to the public and provide access to material created by the sect.
Beyond this shared mission and the similarity of the collections inherent in

being drawn from the Shakers' legacy, the history of these two attempts to establish permanent Shaker museums are distinctly divergent. John S. Williams, a stockbroker with a summer residence in Columbia County, New York, founded the Shaker Museum at Old Chatham, an institution with a successor that exists into the present. In contrast, Yale University, with its great wealth and extensive intellectual and professional expertise, miscarried in its attempt to make the Yale University Art Gallery an internationally recognized center for the preservation and study of the Shaker heritage. Analysis of these two undertakings provide insight into how distinct groups of scholars and administrators understood the history and legacy of the sect.

JOHN S. WILLIAMS AND THE SHAKER MUSEUM AT OLD CHATHAM

The Shaker Museum at Old Chatham, chartered by New York State in 1950, was the first institution founded specifically to collect and interpret the material heritage of the Shakers. Based on a collection accumulated by a single wealthy individual, the Shaker Museum can be understood as reflecting the antimodernist impulse that motivated Henry Ford to establish Greenfield Village in Michigan and which led to the establishment of similar institutions including the Shelburne Museum in Vermont and Old Sturbridge Village in central Massachusetts. In each case, an American's economic ability and insatiable appetite for gathering material artifacts resulted in the establishment of an institution dedicated to heritage interpretation.

John Stanton Williams was born into a prosperous and socially prominent New York mercantile family.[1] He was named after his grandfather, who in the middle decades of the nineteenth century used his connections in the ship-chandlery business to establish Williams & Guion, a successful shipping firm known for promoting the transition from sail to steam.[2] Upon his death, the elder John Williams was a member of the New York City Chamber of Commerce, Produce Exchange, Shipmaster's Association, and other commercial and financial organizations. Blair S. Williams, one of five sons of the patriarch and father of the museum founder, pursued a career on Wall Street after attending a private school in the city. As a stockbroker, he was a partner in a succession of influential firms including Dominick & Williams; Williams, Nicholas & Moran; Rhoades, Williams, & Company; and the eponymous Blair S. Williams & Company.[3] As befit a man of his time and position, Blair Williams served on the governing committee of the New York Stock Exchange and was a member of the Union Club, the St. Nicholas Society, and the Century Association. He contributed to the intellectual life of the city by serving on the board of the Heye Foundation's Museum of the American Indian, a position he assumed in 1930.[4] He also married into another of New York's oldest and most influential families, wedding Elsie Schuyler Lefferts in 1899.[5]

Their son, born in 1901 and also named John Stanton Williams, attended the Pomfret School, a private boarding school in Connecticut, and Princeton University, graduating in the class of 1924.[6] Upon leaving college, he was welcomed into his father's firm, rising to the position of partner.[7] Within a year of graduation, Williams held a seat on the New York Stock Exchange. He subsequently formed his own brokerage partnership named Williams & Southgate, which in 1941 merged into the investment banking firm of Graham, Parsons & Company.[8]

In 1935, Williams, who resided in Hewlett, on the western end of Long Island, purchased an eighteenth-century farmhouse and its surrounding acreage, in Columbia County, New York, near the Massachusetts state line west of Pittsfield. Williams hired the New York City architectural firm of Polhemus & Coffin to transform the property into a country estate suitable for a man of his stature, featuring a modern kitchen and bathrooms, recreation rooms, closets, and facilities for servants.[9] Polhemus & Coffin, who were experienced in designing country houses in a variety of styles in Connecticut; New Jersey; Newport, Rhode Island; other areas of New York State; and on Long Island, provided Williams with a Colonial Revival confection, completed in 1936 and featuring a two-story symmetrical Georgian five-bay main block with a service wing.[10] Williams christened his rural retreat "Good Hope Farm," commenced raising Aberdeen Angus cattle, and became active in the local Republican Party.[11]

In Columbia County, Williams undertook the genteel pastime of collecting antique agricultural equipment.[12] Like many in the first half of the twentieth century, the gentleman farmer in his Colonial Revival retreat became concerned that American life was changing and material traces of the past were vanishing.[13] The stockbroker pursued his new avocation with Roger Williams, a slightly older Columbia County native who had attended the U.S. Naval Academy and became wealthy as the vice president and director of the Newport News Shipbuilding and Dry Dock Company in Virginia.[14]

In his search for obsolete farm implements in the countryside surrounding his pastoral sanctuary, John Williams inevitably found his way to the barns of the Shaker villages of New Lebanon, New York, and Hancock, Massachusetts, each located less than twenty miles to the east. Notably, Williams, who spent time in the Berkshires and in New York City, succumbed to Shaker fever and began collecting the sect's materials soon after their cultural import was established by the early shows at the Berkshire Museum in Pittsfield and the Whitney Museum in Manhattan. Unlike Faith and Edward Deming Andrews, who bought the Shakers' unwanted objects with an eye toward resale, Williams had the economic means to acquire artifacts simply for the satisfaction of owning them. Rather than focusing on domestic goods that had value in the expanding antiques market, like Charles Adams at the New York State Museum, the stockbroker was drawn to materials related to the sect's economic activities. From farm implements, Williams turned to various categories of tools, and from there to an encyclopedic gathering of Shaker material culture.[15] Over the ensuing decades, his interest in the Shakers spread beyond those villages closest to him, until Williams was gathering materials omnivorously from all the settlements. He also pursued objects that were not of interest to other connoisseurs, including washing machines, fire engines, and even a belt-driven seven-ton double trip-hammer from the Mount Lebanon blacksmith shop.[16] Williams claimed the latter item in the 1940s when Shakers were clearing out a building so that the property could be transferred to the Darrow School.[17]

As Williams visited the declining Shaker villages (with money in his wallet), he developed relationships with the residents. Sister Emma Neale, who lived at various times in New Lebanon and Hancock, assisted Williams in acquiring the materials he desired. He claimed that over the years, he got to know Neale as well as "a thirty-five year old neophyte might know an eighty year old lady."[18] Ricardo Belden, a Hancock Shaker, also had repeated interactions with Williams. Subsequently, the collector became close to Eldress Emma King, the sect's presiding leader.[19] In 1954, King wrote from the Shaker village in Canterbury, New Hampshire, "Mr. Williams is always welcome to visit us. We may not have all he would like but we will do our best for him each time he comes." She continued, "We feel there is mutual friendship between Old Chatham and East Canterbury."[20]

Like many elites of his time, following the precedents set by Henry Ford and John D. Rockefeller, in the decade between 1940 and 1950 Williams sought to transform his collection into a museum. Because of his social class, Williams was familiar with museums and understood their operations and governance. He joined his father on the board of the Museum of the American Indian, eventually serving as its chairman.[21] Similarly, his friend Roger Williams served as president of the Board of Trustees of the Mariners' Museum in Newport News, Virginia.[22] As early as 1940, John Williams mounted what he termed a "preserved and restored" Shaker blacksmith shop on his estate in Columbia County. Neale and Belden attended the private opening of the installation. Later, the collector would install part of his collection in an historic building at the crossroads that defined the community of Old Chatham.

THE SHAKER MUSEUM FOUNDATION

In 1950, Williams established the Shaker Museum Foundation to facilitate making his now voluminous collection available to the public. On July 21 of that year, he received a provisional charter for the museum from the New York State Board of Regents.[23] He recruited fifteen local residents to serve on the board of the new organization, including both local civic leaders and wealthy New Yorkers with country houses in the region.[24] Roger Williams, who had initially introduced John Williams to the joys of old agricultural equipment, became one of the first board members. Zelina Brunschwig, of the prestigious textile firm Brunschwig & Fils, also owned property in Columbia County and joined the board.[25] The New York art dealer Mortimer Brandt similarly became a trustee.[26]

As part of his efforts to develop the museum, Williams hired Hamilton Phelps Clawson as the institution's curator.[27] Clawson, born in 1892, was the son of John Lewis Clawson, a millionaire banker and merchant from Buffalo who collected Elizabethan antiquarian books.[28] As a youth, the curator, who went by Phelps, attended the Hill School in Pottstown, Pennsylvania, and Yale University. Upon graduation, he pursued a career as a poet, served as an aviator in the U.S. Air Corps during the First World War, led the life of a *bon vivant*, and made national headlines by marrying and quickly divorcing a Russian-born actress.[29]

Following his disastrous marriage, Clawson embarked on a new career as an archeologist and Egyptologist. He traveled to Egypt with an expedition sponsored by Harvard University and the Boston Museum of Fine

Arts during which he participated in the discovery of the tomb of Queen Hetepheres, mother of Cheops, the builder of the Great Pyramid at Giza. Following his return to his hometown, he became associated with the Buffalo Society of Natural Sciences, the sponsor of the Buffalo Museum of Science.[30] In 1937, the society received a grant from the Rockefeller Foundation that allowed it to send Clawson to Copenhagen to attend the International Anthropological and Ethnological Congress and to bring museum professionals (including E. K. Burnett and George Heye of the Heye Foundation) to Buffalo to consult on how the museum should exhibit its anthropological collections.[31] As the museum's curator of anthropology, Clawson installed a "Hall of Primitive Art," displaying the material culture of "primitive cultures" from around the globe, and in 1941 published a guide to this new permanent exhibition.[32]

In his catalogue, entitled *By Their Works,* Clawson argued that with "a certain amount of knowledge and imagination," visitors can learn about entire cultures and civilizations from objects in a museum case.[33] Similarly, in an article published in the magazine *Hobbies* in 1941, the museum curator suggested that collectors could appreciate African artworks if they were "considered in the light of the social and religious life of the people who made it."[34]

"RELICS OF INVENTIVENESS"

With his archeologist's experience and museum background, Clawson assisted Williams with developing an acquisition policy, restoring those pieces that were not in pristine condition, and arranging the collection for public display.[35] Williams's dairy barn was appropriated for a museum space and galleries of Shaker objects were installed (fig. 4.1). Clawson created exhibits that showcased Shaker artifacts while simultaneously doing little to camouflage the fact that the materials were displayed in a barn. Walls were built to simulate period rooms, but the structure's rafters and roof boards were left "unashamedly exposed" according to a later director (fig. 4.2). This arrangement required visitors to exercise "the willing suspension of disbelief" while learning about the sect.[36] The museum also did not attempt to portray a particular period in Shaker history or give the impression that the organization was static. Rather, a staff person asserted that the Shakers were "still a vital, contemporary community whose members sit in late Victorian

FIGURE 4.1. The dairy barn on John Williams's "Good Hope Farm" was appropriated for the display of his Shaker collection. Courtesy Shaker Museum | Mount Lebanon, New Lebanon, NY.

FIGURE 4.2. A Shaker brother's bedroom installed in the dairy barn at the Shaker Museum at Old Chatham, ca. 1955. The exposed rafters and roof boards reminded visitors that they were actually within a repurposed barn rather than a Shaker dwelling. Courtesy Shaker Museum | Mount Lebanon, New Lebanon, NY.

rockers in front of last-year's television set, with an 1815 candlestand along-side."[37] While the museum stopped short of displaying television sets, its vignettes eschewed the minimalism of Winter's modernist photographs and more accurately included patterned carpets and ornamented ceramics used by believers at the end of the nineteenth century (fig. 4.3).

Neither Williams nor Clawson were aesthetes, thus the Shaker Museum did not particularly emphasize furniture design nor the spare simplicity of Shaker objects. Rather, the exhibits and their interpretation tended to focus on innovation, inventiveness, and ingenuity. The museum argued that the industries of this little-known religious sect helped to usher in the familiar reality of the mid-twentieth century by inventing such conveniences as washing machines, flat brooms, packaged seeds, and condensed milk.[38] Writing in the *New York Times* in 1953, Sanka Knox reported that the

FIGURE 4.3. Louis H. Frohman, "Dining Room Installation at the Shaker Museum at Old Chatham," ca. 1965. The Shaker Museum at Old Chatham displayed artifacts used by Shakers throughout history including fancy transfer-printed ceramics. Courtesy Shaker Museum | Mount Lebanon, New Lebanon, NY.

"Shaker relics" displayed by the museum "tell, first and foremost, of Shaker industriousness, their inventiveness."[39] A syndicated newspaper article about the museum from 1958 written by Inez Robb expressed the museum's interpretive slant with the headline "Shaker Museum Has Relics of Inventiveness."[40] The *Berkshire Eagle* bragged that the Shaker Museum had "given a permanent home to the numerous ingenious tools and machines used by the Shakers in producing the classic articles which fill . . . other museums."[41]

Correspondingly, in addition to the vignettes portraying Shaker living spaces, Clawson and Williams installed rooms dedicated to collections of tools, devices, and manufacturing processes. The museum eventually included spaces dedicated to a cobbler's shop, a tinsmith's shop, a carpentry shop, a blacksmith's forge, a broom-making shop, a dressmaker's room, and a room with looms for textile production, among other such displays (fig. 4.4). In a glowing promotional article in the *New York Times,* the travel writer Richard Shanor reported, "In all, there are some 14 shops

FIGURE 4.4. Corner of the Shaker Museum's Carpentry Shop with "old Shaker-made foot lathes." The Shaker Museum at Old Chatham emphasized the ingenuity of Shaker manufacturing processes. Courtesy Shaker Museum | Mount Lebanon, New Lebanon, NY.

and workrooms at Old Chatham."[42] These spaces, while demonstrating the artistry of Shaker products, also emphasized the ingenuity and pioneering quality of the Shakers' production processes. The Medicine Room, for instance, displayed the workbench on which, the museum claimed, Gail Borden perfected his invention of condensed milk.[43]

The Shaker Museum prospered even though it was only open during the summer season. The press provided good coverage, on both the local and national levels, and individuals donated Shaker items to augment those Williams collected.[44] In 1955, the board of directors purchased from Williams seven acres on which the barn and other museum outbuildings were located.[45] That same year, the state's provisional institutional charter became permanent. The number of visitors to the museum rose steadily throughout its first years. In 1958, the *Chatham Courier* reported that more than ten thousand individuals had visited the site during the summer. The local newspaper endorsed Williams's efforts to celebrate the "inventive genius" of the Shakers and called the museum "a very important factor in the cultural life of this county."[46]

As the museum prospered, Williams and Clawson also earned the approbation of the remaining Shaker sisters. Eldress Emma King, in particular, was supportive of the endeavor, which she understood as a monument to her religious organization. In 1950, the eldress wrote to Clawson, "Your description of the Museum and the work it represents was very interesting and I think you have just cause to be proud of the project. . . . Your work will live in history for future generations."[47] Five years later, she would similarly write, "I am much pleased with the progress of the Museum and interested in its success. . . . The ideals you both hold are making of the organization a wonderful memorial to the Shakers and a noteworthy exhibit to the world."[48]

In 1959, at the age of sixty-seven, Clawson retired from his position at the museum. To replace him, the board hired Robert F. W. Meader as the museum's director. Born in 1908, Meader had previously served a short tenure as the director of the Libby Museum, an institution in Wolfeboro, New Hampshire, centered on the founder's eclectic collection of natural history specimens.[49] Meader was a graduate of Brewster Academy, a boarding school in Wolfeboro, and held a bachelor's degree from Middlebury College in Vermont. He received a master's degree from the University of Pennsylvania in 1931. During the 1930s, he taught Latin and English at Brewster Academy, subsequently served as a teacher at a number of other preparatory schools throughout the northeast, and in the 1950s was an assistant professor of English and art at Susquehanna University in Selinsgrove, Pennsylvania.[50] While at Susquehanna, Meader demonstrated a range of talents that served him well at the Shaker Museum. While fulfilling his teaching obligations, he also organized art exhibits and published an article for the university's scholarly journal celebrating the beauty of churches built in New England before 1850. After that date, Meader argued, "American standards came to their absolute nadir" in all fields of art.[51]

At the Shaker Museum, Meader catalogued the collections, composed labels, organized exhibits, wrote public relations articles, and built a library collection.[52] Robert Kimball, who worked at the *Berkshire Eagle,* reported to Amy Bess Miller, the wife of the paper's editor, that Meader was "quite nice and several cuts above Clawson."[53]

As the museum's director, Meader continued and amplified the interpretive focus Williams and Clawson had established. In 1961, in an article in a promotional magazine published by the State Bank of Albany, Meader asserted that the Shakers "deserve to be known more for their extraordinary mechanical cleverness and inventiveness, and for their tremendous enterprise." He concluded, "The country, though it hardly knew the Believers, has been reaping continuously the benefits of Shaker inventions and labor-saving devices, of farming and building and furniture making."[54]

ANNUAL SHAKER FESTIVALS

In the late 1950s and throughout the 1960s, the Shaker Museum held an annual festival in early August as a significant component of its programming and funding strategy. The inaugural event in this series took place between 1 and 6 p.m. on August 4, 1956, and included a fashion show and an antique show as well as tours of the museum. Like a traditional fundraising fair or bazaar, the festival was largely organized by women of the community.[55] Helen Pitcher Christiana, the wife of a prominent Columbia County lawyer, served as the general chairman of the festival. Anna R. Alexandre, a New York socialite with a summer house in Lenox, Massachusetts, functioned as the "regional chairman for the central Berkshire region." Judith Lee Davenport Callan, the wife of the publisher of the local *Chatham Courier,* organized the fashion show.[56]

What had begun as an activity for a single afternoon over the ensuing decades stretched out over two days and was enlarged to attract individuals who may have had only a passing interest in the history of a celibate, communitarian religious sect. Antique dealers from New York, Connecticut, and Massachusetts set up booths from which to peddle their wares to wealthy vacationers.[57] By 1968, organizers bragged that more than one hundred dealers from as far away as the mid-Atlantic would participate.[58] A display of antique cars became an annual facet of the celebration: in 1962 it was organized by the Automobilists of the Hudson Valley but in 1969, the cars were coordinated by Albany Antique Auto Club.[59] Students from Jerome Count's Shaker Village Work Camp demonstrated craft activities, and eventually an art show was incorporated into the celebration.[60]

Although many features of the festival remained the same year after year, each time the organizers sought to introduce some new attraction. In 1958, the fashion show included a collection of hats designed by John Frederics and inspired by Shaker bonnets and Shaker fabrics.[61] The Albany Institute of Art cooperated with the Shaker Museum to present a show of paintings of the Hudson River School in 1967.[62] The 1968 festival included an exhibition of works by the painter Eric Sloane, celebrated for his loving portrayals of preindustrial aspects of the national landscape, while Norman Rockwell and his wife attended the 1969 carnival to sign copies of his book *Willie Was Different*.[63]

The *New York Times* annually printed photographs of the women who took leadership roles in promoting what became an annual remote summer gathering of New York society. In the festival's second year, the *Times* noted that "many New York women with summer homes in the Berkshire area are serving on the committee for the event."[64] Similarly in 1958, the editor of the *Times* ran an article with the headline "Vacationers Aid Shaker Museum in Old Chatham."[65] Esther Leeming Tuttle, a former actress from New Canaan, Connecticut, who had been educated at the Warrenton Country School in Virginia, chaired the festival in 1966.[66] The wife of Franklin B. Tuttle, the chairman and chief executive of the Atlantic Companies, an insurance conglomerate, Esther Tuttle had a country residence in Kinderhook, New York.[67] Nanette Hogan Wells Hahn, the wife of Paul Hahn, the president of the American Tobacco Company, who had a home in Canaan, New York, was for many years an active participant in the festival's success.[68] Margaret Fraser Daley, whose husband was a vice president and director of Stein,

Hall & Company, a New York–based international chemical company, had a summer retreat in East Lebanon, New York, and also regularly volunteered with the festival.[69] Following her duty as chair of the festival, Esther Tuttle joined the board of the museum and actively served the institution for twenty-five years. Jerome Count, director of the Shaker Village Work Camp, was similarly invited by Williams to join the board because of his involvement with the annual festival.

John S. Williams, the scion of an elite New York mercantile family, was a representative member of a class of wealthy New Yorkers who sought solace in the bucolic countryside of eastern New York State in the middle of the twentieth century. He sought intellectual and organizational stimulation by collecting Shaker materials and creating an institution through which he could share his interests with the public. With the assistance of Phelps Clawson and Robert Meader, eccentric prep-school–educated museum professionals who knew little about the Shakers before entering the stockbrokers' employ, Williams created an institution that continues to steward the Shaker heritage in the twenty-first century.

The museum succeeded because it provided a cultural gathering place for vacationing New Yorkers and offered its neighbors a vision of the Shakers that was not threatening. In Old Chatham, the Shakers were portrayed as ascetic and inventive entrepreneurs seeking improved means of manufacturing. Music, dancing, and celibacy were mentioned but not emphasized. Religious zeal was downplayed. The Shakers were not presented as the forbears of aesthetically progressive modern designers; rather, they were conceived as diligent, Protestant capitalists whose spiritual descendants might conceivably populate the research and development laboratories of America's postwar corporations.

Williams invested personal financial resources into his endeavor, but he also built a community of supporters for the organization through his personal networks and the annual Shaker festival. After gaining an institutional charter, he continued as the founder and guiding spirit of the institution, located directly adjacent to his summer residence, yet he welcomed the input and involvement of a wide range of individuals including Zelina Brunschwig, Jerome Count (about whom we will learn more in the next chapter), Nanette Hogan Wells Hahn, Esther Leeming Tuttle, Eric Sloane, and Norman Rockwell. What started as one man's personal obsession became a nationally recognized local cultural center focused on the history

of a religious group. Williams himself did not offer a revelatory new interpretation of the significance of the sect, but his abilities as a collector and
organizer produced an ongoing legacy.

THE ANDREWSES AND THE YALE UNIVERSITY ART GALLERY

The story of Williams and the Shaker Museum at Old Chatham stands in
sharp contrast to Faith and Edward Deming Andrews's miscarried attempt
to establish a center for Shaker studies at Yale University in exactly the same
years. Williams had the finances and the social connections to establish a
new institution wholly dedicated to Shaker history and culture. In contrast,
the Andrewses experienced great frustration negotiating with the multiva-
lent bureaucracy at Yale while attempting to establish an institution dedicated to Shaker studies under the mantle of the larger university. Although
a number of institutional dynamics initially seemed to suggest that the
university would be supportive of such an endeavor, ultimately the collectors were frustrated by a roiling administration and lack of institutional
commitment.

In the spring of 1956, representatives of Yale University, including
Charles Sawyer, the dean of the School of Fine Arts, and Lamont Moore, the
director of the Yale University Art Gallery, began conversations with Faith
and Edward Deming Andrews concerning acquiring the couple's much
admired Shaker collection.[70] The university sought to procure the couple's
holdings not because of a particular admiration for Shaker religion or communal life but because it was a high-profile collection that could be used to
expand the institution's curriculum and programming related to American
culture. Absorbing the Andrewses' Shaker collection, which offered rich
opportunities for interdisciplinary investigation, made strategic sense for
a number of divisions within the university, including the Yale University
Art Gallery and the American Studies Program. Through the generosity of
wealthy donors, including Francis Patrick Garvan and William Robertson
Coe, the university had established itself as a center for the study of American decorative arts and had developed significant collections of American material culture within the gallery while simultaneously launching a
nationally renowned American Studies Program dedicated to educating
students, fostering research into American institutions, and promoting a
Cold War vision of American democracy.

For a short while, institutional politics seemed to align to make Yale's acquisition of the Andrewses' collection propitious. The Andrewses moved to New Haven, and their collection was placed on deposit at the Art Gallery. Within less than two years, however, dynamics shifted within the bureaucracy, the Andrewses became disaffected, and the couple withdrew their gift. By 1959, the opportunity to establish a permanent Shaker museum on the Yale campus had passed.

The Andrewses' interaction with the university nevertheless provides perspectives on the study of American culture in the middle of the twentieth century and the role of the Shakers within that undertaking. Notably, this episode makes evident how Yale's educational curricula was influenced by the agendas of wealthy conservative donors and by the dynamics of the nation's military intelligence community during, and just after, World War II. For a brief moment, the acquisition of Shaker material culture by a prestigious eastern university aligned with both elite cultural nationalism and the country's expanding international interests. Thrown into the midst of this complex, institutional bureaucracy driven by multiple actors with disparate agendas, the Andrewses were unable to negotiate the outcome they desired.

AMERICAN DECORATIVE ARTS AND YALE

In the preceding decades, Yale had established itself as a nationally significant center for the study of American decorative arts. In 1930, Francis Patrick Garvan, a Yale graduate from the class of 1897, made a pivotal donation of what he referred to as "American Arts and Crafts" to Yale's Gallery of Fine Arts in the name of his wife, Mabel Brady Garvan. Before his death in 1937, the gallery's donor doubled this initial gift of five thousand items.[71] Garvan, like many elites of his generation, found in American antiques a connection to the nation's colonial, Anglo-American heritage. During a period when the country was being reshaped by immigration and income inequality based on industrialization, antique silver and old brown furniture spoke to Garvan and his cohort of stability and cultural association with the nation's founders. By giving his collections of silver, furniture, pewter, glass, prints, ceramics, and numismatics to an educational institution, Garvan hoped to use these historic items to shape the future of the United States. "The University was to become," explained art historian Everett V. Meeks soon after Garvan's death, "the agency for spreading the doctrine of innate American

culture, thereby bringing to the people, particularly the youth of the country, a knowledge of the finer things in the lives of their forbears and a new
insight into their own native inheritance."[72] Garvan's gift enriched scholarship in American material culture at Yale by providing students with access
to inspirational objects but also had a national impact since the gallery regularly loaned objects to museums and historic sites across the country.[73]

Garvan personally selected John M. Phillips to serve as the curator of
Yale's collection.[74] Phillips, who was a silver connoisseur and dealer, held
both a B.A. in Latin and history and an M.A. in English literature from
the University of Pennsylvania.[75] During the 1930s, Phillips introduced
courses on American decorative arts and architecture into the Yale curriculum, including one, mockingly dubbed "Pots and Pans" by undergraduates,
which he taught until his death.[76] When the Yale administration created
the Department of the History of Art in 1941, Phillips, with his expertise in
American decorative arts, was folded into the new unit.

During the Second World War, Phillips served in the Office of Strategic
Services, U.S. Army Intelligence, and as part of the U.S. government's Monuments, Fine Arts, and Archives program dedicated to protecting cultural
resources during wartime and recovering looted artworks.[77] This important
group of American curators and scholars has come to be referred to as the
"Monuments Men." At the end of the war, Phillips returned to his position
as curator of the Garvan Collection at Yale. Subsequently, he was appointed
director of the Yale University Art Gallery in 1948.[78]

Lamont Moore was hired to serve as the Art Gallery's associate director
in 1948 to assist Phillips with administrative duties.[79] Moore graduated from
Lafayette College in 1932 and afterward received a Carnegie Fellowship to
travel in Europe while studying art and architecture.[80] Upon his return,
he enrolled in John Cotton Dana's Apprenticeship School at the Newark
Museum, arguably the first program in the United States offering practical
training in general museum methodologies.[81] Following graduation, Moore
joined the staff of the Newark Museum, serving as supervisor of the Education Department from 1934 to 1941.[82] He later indicated his ideas about
art education were based on Dana's precepts. He believed that "works of
art were like books since they were informative and inspirational . . . and
they should be made accessible to all people."[83] Moore, thus, like Holger
Cahill and Dorothy Miller, was educated by Dana to value objects and to
view them as educational resources. His service in Newark also meant that

he was in the greater New York area in 1935 when the Whitney Museum mounted its exhibition of Shaker material.[84] In 1941, as the National Gallery of Art prepared to open in the nation's capital, Moore joined that institution as the curator of education. From 1943 to 1947, after being drafted, he also was active in the U.S. Army as one of the Monuments Men.[85] In Europe he was involved in inventorying and managing many of the most important Nazi caches of stolen masterpieces. During this time he may have encountered Phillips with whom Moore would work at Yale after serving a short term as the associate director of the American Academy at Rome. Upon Phillips's death in 1953, Moore assumed the position of director of the Yale University Art Gallery.[86] During that time he also served as the curator of the Mabel Brady Garvan Collection.[87]

In negotiating with Faith and Edward Deming Andrews to donate their renowned Shaker collection to Yale University so that it could supplement the Garvan Collection, Moore worked with Charles Sawyer, the dean of Yale's School of Fine Arts and director of the school's newly configured Division of the Arts.[88] A graduate of Phillips Andover Academy and Yale University, Sawyer had a long career in the arts, serving as the founding director of Andover's Addison Gallery and as the director of the Worcester Art Museum. Gertrude Vanderbilt Whitney and Juliana Force had attempted to hire him as the second director of the Whitney Museum, a position he declined in favor of his friend Lloyd Goodrich. Immediately following World War II, Sawyer worked with Phillips in the Office of Strategic Services in documenting and managing Europe's looted artworks, eventually moving to Washington to serve as the assistant secretary to the Commission for the Preservation of Monuments and Works of Art.[89] When he returned to Yale in 1947, he sought to introduce contemporary ideas about art and design to the institution. Sawyer had encountered the Andrewses at Laura Bragg's dinner party marking the opening of the Shaker exhibit at the Berkshire Museum when he was serving as the director of the Addison Gallery.

Through the philanthropy of Francis Garvan and the activities of the national government during World War II, the Yale University Art Gallery had thus developed into an institution with both a significant collection of American decorative arts and a staff trained in managing and protecting artifacts and works of art with national cultural resonances. The community of art scholars at Yale, including Phillips, Sawyer, and Moore, who had served with the Office of Strategic Services and the Monuments Men, acquired firsthand experience in stewarding and documenting national material patrimonies. Simultaneously, through their broader experience within the American art world, they had been exposed to installations at both the Berkshire Museum and the Whitney Museum that celebrated Shaker objects as important manifestations of America's cultural legacy.

AMERICAN STUDIES AT YALE

In their negotiations with the Andrewses, Sawyer and Moore also involved David Potter, the William Robinson Coe Professor of American Studies and the director of the Yale American Studies Program, which had been established in 1948 under the leadership of Norman Holmes Pearson to provide undergraduate and graduate students with the opportunity for interdepartmental or interdisciplinary study.[90] Pearson, who like Sawyer had graduated from Phillips Andover and Yale, was a specialist in American literature rather than art or material culture. Literary scholar Michael Holzman has argued, however, that Pearson was most important historically for the role he played as a spymaster for the Office of Strategic Services during World War II (a role that apparently continued covertly after his return to New Haven).[91]

Following the war, during the early days of the Cold War, Pearson and others at Yale came to view educating individuals about American life, institutions, and principles as a means to promote national interests. As a component of this endeavor, the university established the Yale School of American Studies for Foreign Students.[92] During a six-week summer program, students from around the world, who were required to read and speak English fluently, took courses at Yale focusing on American culture, politics, and economics.[93] In 1950, the program's forty students included individuals from Austria, Germany, Greece, Iceland, Italy, Yugoslavia, and Indochina.[94]

During their time at Yale, students in the program visited representative American sites. In 1950, among other locations, the students toured West Point, Yankee Stadium, and Standard Oil Refineries in New Jersey.[95] In August 1954, instructors from Yale took twenty secondary school teachers from France on a visit to nearby Mystic Seaport, a maritime museum on Long Island Sound, where they toured a restored whaling ship.[96]

This summer program was meant to contribute to international understanding as a means of fostering peace. However, it also aimed explicitly to introduce foreign students to the principles and institutions undergirding and energizing American democracy. Ralph Henry Gabriel, a senior historian who had long taught an undergraduate course in "American Thought and Civilization" with Stanley Williams, explained that this program was designed to extend "American cultural influence" by providing future world leaders with "an understanding of American life and culture."[97] Yale's president Charles Seymour indicated that "the aiding of young foreigners intent upon teaching careers to study in America forms a crucial phase in the defense of the free world."[98] Pearson, active in the summer program and likely recruiting intelligence agents from among its students, utilized the field of American Studies as one aspect of the United States' Cold War international propaganda campaign.[99]

While educating international students during the summer, Yale also established a program through which regularly enrolled students could pursue the interdisciplinary study of American culture during the academic year. In the 1948–1949 academic year, the university created the American Studies Program with Gabriel serving as chairman and Pearson filling the role of director of undergraduate studies.[100] Just as the summer program was meant to shape the thinking of international students, Yale's undergraduate American Studies major was concerned with preparing students, who at that time were exclusively male, for participation in the Cold War. In advocating for the program, Dean William C. DeVane explained in a letter to Seymour that American Studies at Yale could serve as "a weapon in the 'cold war'" with which to convince the world that "we have something infinitely better than Communism to offer them."[101] Seymour passed this message along to the general public in a speech to the alumni in which he requested an income of $25,000 annually to support a comprehensive program of American Studies as "the most effective method of fighting communism."[102] William Sloane Coffin, who at the time was a Yale senior on the path that would lead him into the CIA, claimed that the United States needed to formulate "a political faith around which the non-Communist world can rally."[103]

Writing in 1955, Potter explained to readers of the *Yale Alumni Magazine* that the American Studies major was meant to "give the undergraduate an adequate understanding of the incredibly complex society of which he is already a member, and of which he may in the future be a leader." "When the Free World is really only half a world," he continued, "destiny demands of him that he be prepared to defend an ancient heritage of freedom."[104]

In 1950, Yale's development office was able to use the program's nationalist agenda to secure a donation of more than $500,000 from William Robertson Coe to endow a chair and support the endeavor.[105] Born in England in 1869, Coe had made a career in insurance before marrying Mary Huttleston Rogers, the daughter of Henry Huttleston Rogers, one of the wealthiest men in the country because of his interests in Rockefeller's Standard Oil.[106] Subsequently, Coe was involved in railroads, western land speculation, and resource extraction. His wife's wealth allowed him to develop varied interests including breeding race horses, horticulture, and the history of the American West. The latter topic he believed to be particularly important because he understood it as embodying the American values of self-reliance and enterprise.[107] Later in life, Coe associated with Edward Beach Gallaher, an inventor and manufacturer who ran the Clover Manufacturing Company and who, through his publication, the *Clover Business Letter*, was an ardent, vocal critic of Roosevelt's New Deal and what he perceived to be the socialist and communist threat to the United States.[108] Like Coe, Gallaher supported Yale's American Studies Program as a way to buttress conservative values, donating $50,000 in 1950.[109]

Potter, a prominent and well-respected consensus historian, was named the first William Robertson Coe Professor of History.[110] Potter had received a B.A. at Emory University before earning his M.A. and Ph.D. at Yale, completing his doctorate in 1940 under Gabriel. Influenced by anthropologists such as Margaret Mead and sociologists including David Reisman, Potter's scholarship posited the existence of a "national character" that served as a causal force in history.[111] His scholarship thus fitted him for leadership within Yale's interdisciplinary American Studies Program and made him a good candidate for Coe's endowed chair. Potter's personality, politics, and temperament also made him a fitting aspirant for the Coe professorship. "I myself," he wrote, "am a convinced believer in the importance of free enterprise and individualism and the dangers of collectivism and statism."[112] His background and training had instilled in him tendencies toward elitism, a commitment to the standing social order, and feelings of *noblesse oblige*.[113]

Potter's most important work, *People of Plenty: Economic Abundance and the American Character*, developed out of lectures he presented in 1950 at the Charles R. Walgreen Foundation for the Study of American Institutions at the University of Chicago.[114] Funded by Charles Rudolph Walgreen, the inventor of the modern drugstore, this foundation countered what the retailer saw as un-American teachings promulgated at the University of Chicago and sought to instill in students an appreciation for the American way of life.[115] Published in 1954, Potter's interdisciplinary *People of Plenty* argued that material abundance had shaped American identity and created a shared set of values.[116] American prosperity, he wrote, had been created by "the ventures and the struggles of the pioneer, the exertions of the workman, the ingenuity of the inventor, the drive of the enterpriser, and the economic efficiency of all kinds of Americans, who shared a notorious addiction to hard work."[117] Although Potter's work engaged midcentury concerns such as the absence of community, the hazards of mass culture, and the peril of rampant materialism, his writing also claimed national identity was based on shared national experiences derived from the Protestant work ethic and supposedly common values emphasizing individualism.[118] Daniel Horowitz, an American Studies scholar, has identified in *People of Plenty* and Potter's other writings conservative positions formed in response to twentieth-century transformations in American society. Horowitz claims that Potter's "key values" included commitments "to an organic community in which people had fixed status but corporate membership; to the pride in meaningful labor performed within one's station; to skepticism about the virtues of competition and mobility that undermined a sense of place; to individuals unalienated by modernization; and to order, proportion, and belonging."[119] Many of these values could be understood to be embodied within Shaker villages.

Coe, who maintained a residence in Cody, Wyoming, also funded an American Studies Program at the University of Wyoming that taught the importance of American principles. In 1948, he made an initial donation of $10,000 and in return received an honorary doctorate in law. With Coe's support, the University of Wyoming established a summer program to educate high school teachers. Potter, whom one colleague characterized as "a conservative outraged by the New Deal," assisted in implementing the new undertaking.[120] A donation of cash and securities of approximately $785,000 that Coe made in 1954, after Gallaher's death, allowed the University of Wyoming to pursue the summer program, add an undergraduate major, establish an endowed chair, erect an American Studies building, and significantly enhance the university's library.[121]

Using Coe's money in the context of the Cold War, Wyoming's American Studies Program claimed that it was "designed as a positive and affirmative method of meeting the threat of socialism, communism, totalitarianism, and to preserve our freedom and our system of free enterprise."[122] Expressing an ideology that conflated Frederick Jackson Turner's frontier thesis with Gallaher's contempt for the growth of the welfare state, the Wyoming program according to its publicity suggested students would learn about "a free America developed from the pioneer spirit which expresses the principle that men must depend upon themselves, their own vigor and initiative and must not surrender their liberties to government."[123] George Duke Humphrey, the president of the University of Wyoming, asserted that Coe's donation would allow the Wyoming American Studies Program to serve as a "citadel of freedom and inspiration in the Rocky Mountain region," and dutifully checked the names of potential instructors with Joseph McCarthy's House Un-American Activities Committee to ensure ideological purity.[124]

Although Yale's goals for the American Studies Program largely harmonized with Coe's vision, the faculty and administration bridled at the philanthropist's desire for political tests. Alfred Whitney Griswold, the president who succeeded Seymour, and William DeVane, the dean of the college, both explained to Coe that Yale's faculty was composed of superior scholars and teachers with exceptional moral and intellectual integrity who could be trusted in their devotion to their country and their students. Potter similarly assured Coe that a Yale undergraduate, when provided with the facts, could be relied on to "stand upon his own feet and use them for himself."[125] Although William F. Buckley—who took classes in the American Studies Program, graduated from Yale, and entered the CIA—complained that the faculty was not adequately doctrinaire in upholding Coe's vision for his gift, Yale's administration refused to suspend academic freedom and allow the donor to impose controls within the classroom.[126]

With its interdisciplinary humanistic curriculum offering students the opportunity to study history, literature, visual arts, and even aspects of American folk culture, the American Studies Program at Yale proved attractive to undergraduates. In 1951, 235 students enrolled in Pearson's "Twentieth Century American Prose" course, making it the largest advanced course offered by the English Department.[127] In 1955, Potter reported that the previous year, 81 seniors received their degrees in American Studies, making it the college's third most popular major behind history and English.[128] In

1958, the program could claim 111 undergraduate majors and 14 graduate students. President Griswold, himself trained as a historian, expressed concern that American Studies was "bleeding History white."[129]

Donors find it difficult to argue with success. Although Coe's son, William Rogers Coe, continued to apply pressure on the college to have the faculty indoctrinate students into the benefits of free enterprise, the donor remained loyal. Upon his death in 1954, Coe made a bequest of $4 million to Yale, including $1,240,000 earmarked for further support of American Studies.[130]

THE COLLECTORS AND THE UNIVERSITY

With an established collection of American decorative arts, a burgeoning American Studies Program serving both undergraduates and graduates, and bank accounts full of money earmarked for promoting the exceptional nature of American culture, Yale approached Edward Deming Andrews about donating the collectors' holdings of Shaker materials. Andrews at that time was serving as dean of students and head of the history department at the Scarborough School, a private coeducational country day school in Scarborough-on-Hudson, New York, where he had been employed since the 1930s.[131] Charles Sawyer, as dean of the School of Fine Arts, made the initial contact, but Lamont Moore, director of the Art Gallery, quickly assumed responsibility for the negotiations.[132] Working with representatives from both the University Library and the American Studies Program, Moore developed a proposal for Andrews to donate Shaker books, artifacts, and artworks to the university and also take a leave of absence from the Scarborough School to work on accessioning the collection and teach about the Shakers within the American Studies Program.[133] Potter would subsequently write that he was enthusiastic about using the program's funds to support the Art Gallery's efforts to build its holdings, while also believing that the Shaker materials could provide a case study through which students might explore an American subculture in its entirety.[134] Potter was excited that Shaker materials could provide an object lesson for the interrelation of all aspects of a culture, including religion, art, music, and material culture, but he also probably was attracted to the Shakers as a predominantly white, Protestant sect that functioned without support from the state, was characterized by a sturdy internal hierarchy, and promoted a strong work ethic.

In June 1956, Andrews and the university reached an agreement that he would accept the title "Consultant in Shaker History and Culture," that he would have a two-year contract with compensation of $7,500 per year, and that he would teach within the American Studies Program. Edgar S. Furniss, Yale's longtime provost, subsequently described Andrews's salary as a "quid pro quo for the gift of the collection."[135] Based on divisions of responsibilities within the university, the Andrewses' books and manuscripts were to go to the library (as had Coe's collection of western publications) while the prints, drawings, furniture, and other realia would be held by the Art Gallery.[136] Andrews's compensation was drawn from the income on Coe's bequest.[137]

In a letter dated June 27, 1956, Lamont Moore made it clear that, as part of this arrangement, the Yale Corporation required an agreement through which Andrews would donate to the university his collection of "artifacts, prints, manuscripts, religious drawings and paintings, books, etc." In the same communication, Moore requested a "gross listing" of the number of objects of each category that were to be included in the donation. Based on this listing, the university's legal counsel could draw up a formal instrument of gift.[138]

With this agreement apparently in place, over the course of the summer of 1956 the Andrewses began the process of transitioning their household to New Haven and their collection to Yale. Rather than taking a leave of absence, Andrews resigned his position from the Scarborough School, possibly thinking that his temporary position might transform into something more permanent.[139] In August, Moore received a preliminary list of what the Andrewses planned to include in the gift. Both Moore and Ted Andrews worked to make plans with moving companies to transport holdings from the couple's residence in Yonkers and their summer home in Richmond, Massachusetts.[140] In transferring the collection to Yale, items had to be retrieved from long-term loans at the New York State Historical Association in Cooperstown and the Berkshire Museum, in Pittsfield, Massachusetts.

Both the donor and the university were eager to publicize their agreement. As the holder of a doctorate from Yale, Andrews saw the gift as contributing to the vitality of his alma mater, but even more importantly, this elite institution's desire for his collection bestowed status on him. Similarly, his appointment to the university as a consultant in Shaker history and culture cemented his ostensible standing as the recognized expert on the topic.

The university, for its part, was pleased to be able to claim a collection that had been repeatedly exhibited at prestigious institutions and which had been gathering renown for decades.

With the collector's input, the Yale News Bureau drafted a press release announcing the gift, emphasizing that "the largest privately-owned collection in the United States of Shaker furniture, literature, and other artifacts" was coming to Yale.[141] The press release struck a nationalist note by claiming an American identity for the Andrewses' Shaker materials. The news bureau staff writer quoted Moore as saying that while the collection would augment Yale's already strong decorative arts collections, it would also extend their value since "present Yale holdings in early Americana are deeply influenced by European styles whereas the Shaker crafts and arts are more indigenous." The statement indicated that Andrews, who was "an outstanding authority on the Shakers," would serve a two-year appointment on the Yale faculty as a consultant on Shaker history and culture and would participate in the American Studies Program.[142]

Newspapers and periodicals across the country picked up the story, indicating that Americans had become familiar with the idea of Shaker culture. The *New York Times* entitled its story simply "Yale Gets Art."[143] The *Cleveland Plain Dealer* put a more positive and broadminded spin on its coverage, trumpeting, "Public Gets Treasure of Shaker Heirlooms."[144] Both the *Berkshire Eagle* and the *Springfield Union* used the gift as an opportunity to highlight Faith and Ted Andrews as celebrities from the publications' home regions.[145] Even *History News,* published by the American Association for State and Local History, carried a report of the gift.[146]

The Andrewses were initially optimistic about their relationship with Yale. The spring of 1957 was marked by enthusiasm for a range of projects that the couple hoped could be pursued with the assistance of the university. "Though the most comprehensive collection of Shakeriana is now at Yale," the Andrewses wrote, "the whole situation is in a fluid state, as we see it, and can be enlarged and vitalized by work in the field."[147] Photographs by Robert J. Kelley, which document the initial installation of the Andrewses' collection at the Yale University Art Gallery and were subsequently published in the *Magazine Antiques,* are highly reminiscent of William Winter's photographs and of how the materials had been installed in galleries going back to the earliest exhibitions at the New York State Museum and the Berkshire Museum. In addition to the gallery's presentation of decorative arts, in January 1957 an exhibition of the Andrewses' Shaker materials was mounted at the school's Sterling Library.[148] The *New Haven Register* trumpeted, "Yale Library Exhibition Gives New Interesting Data on Shakers."[149]

Beyond these initial forays, Andrews pursued a number of other agendas beyond the cataloguing of the collection and teaching of classes for which he had contracted. He sought to expand the gallery's holdings by taking advantage of what he perceived to be the opportunity to acquire materials from the Shaker village in Canterbury, New Hampshire, occasioned by a shift in the sect's leadership.[150] He corresponded with Yale University Press concerning the publication of a scholarly edition of a manuscript history of the Shakers.[151] He tried to enlist the prominent architectural historian Carroll L. V. Meeks in a project to preserve Shaker architecture.[152] He met with Fenno Heath, the director of the Yale Glee Club, in an attempt to convince Heath to present a "lecture recital" featuring Shaker songs. He pitched a Shaker pageant to the university theater.[153] However, few of these proposals received positive or productive responses.

In making these overtures, the couple demonstrated a profound misapprehension of their place within the university's complex and hierarchical bureaucracy, as they had misunderstood their relationship with Holger Cahill, Ruth Reeves, and the federal power structure of the Index of American Design approximately twenty years earlier. At Yale, Andrews understood himself as the acclaimed leading scholar on the Shakers. He aspired to use the collection that the couple had accumulated over more than three decades to leverage the university's disparate financial and human resources to create a center for the study and appreciation of Shaker culture. Yale administrators, on the other hand, simply sought to employ Coe's financial contribution to the American Studies Program to augment their already-strong holdings of American decorative arts in the Garvan Collection by acquiring an assemblage that had gained iconic status through exhibition at influential and respected institutions and reproduction, in both drawings and photographs, by the Index of American Design. Andrews's temporary position teaching an undergraduate class and cataloguing the collection to facilitate its accessioning was simply meant to entice this eccentric alum into allowing his life's work to be absorbed into the university's purview.

Andrews, however, had so successfully deluded himself concerning his agreement with the university that he wrote a glowing, self-promoting article entitled "The Shakers in a New World" for the *Magazine Antiques*. In this piece of puffery, the collector promised that, in the future, students at Yale could "learn of the work and gain insight into the spirit of an inspired American folk" in a "congenial environment." The article asserted that the Yale University Art Gallery would dedicate a space so that objects could be displayed "as distinct groupings to illustrate various types of Shaker art and craft," and that another space would be installed to reproduce a Shaker meeting room with "white walls, blue peg boards, moldings, and doors, and, at one end, the benches, windows, and panel frames from the eighteenth-century church at Hancock."[154] Andrews's article also indicated that the gallery would publish a catalogue fully documenting every object, book, and broadside in the collection and would mount a series of changing exhibitions drawn from the new holdings.

Although much of 1957 was a honeymoon between the collectors and the university, the two parties sustained the good feeling by ignoring an important point of conflict. They had failed to reach consensus concerning the deed of gift through which ownership of the collection would be transferred to the university. Although drafted in the summer of 1956, by June 1957 the donors had yet to sign it, even though Andrews was collecting paychecks from Yale.[155] Furniss later recalled, "The Andrews [sic] never executed the deed of gift because they were not entirely satisfied with successive drafts of the legal document."[156] Andrews noted that the document contained "minor errors of fact."[157]

While Andrews settled into his position at Yale and envisioned that his contract would be extended, the university's political landscape shifted. Many of the Yale administrators who had found value in the Shaker materials left their positions. Moore was preoccupied with planning for his personal future, because in June 1956 he had been informed that his appointment as director of the Yale Art Gallery would come to an end in June 1957.[158] Charles Sawyer left Yale to become the second director of the University of Michigan Museum of Art in Ann Arbor.[159] David Potter stepped down as chair of American Studies, went on sabbatical, and was wooed away from New Haven by Stanford University. Edgar S. Furniss, the provost who had approved Andrews's salary, announced he was retiring at the end of the year.[160] Each of these bureaucrats, who might have eased Andrews's time on campus, were preoccupied with their own professional transitions.

The university hired Andrew Carnduff Ritchie, the director of painting and sculpture at the Museum of Modern Art, to succeed Moore as director of the Art Gallery. Although Ritchie, like Phillips and Moore, was a veteran of the Monuments and Fine Arts Section of the U.S. Army, he differed in many ways from his predecessor. A native of Scotland who had immigrated to the United States at the age of fifteen, Ritchie returned to Great Britain for graduate work after his undergraduate career at the University of Pittsburgh. He received a doctorate from the Courtauld Institute of Art at the University of London. As a noted scholar of English painting and twentieth-century sculpture, Ritchie's approach to art was less populist, more European, and more aesthetic than his predecessor's had been.[161] Where Moore had been influenced by Dana's Progressive beliefs formed in the context of a publicly funded museum meant to serve the masses, Ritchie brought to Yale experiences working at the Museum of Modern Art and the Frick Collection, valued the eye of cultivated and sophisticated connoisseurs, and enjoyed challenging public taste. Early in his tenure at the gallery, Ritchie made news by acquiring modern paintings and sculpture by Pablo Picasso, Jacob Epstein, and David Smith.[162] In the *Times* of London, Ritchie's obituary noted that he had "delighted in the chance of siting a major Seated Figure by Henry Moore in the context of first-rate modern architecture at a time when such a conjunction was still a novelty."[163]

Early in his administration, Ritchie decided to reduce the amount of space in the gallery dedicated to Shaker materials. He believed that the gallery's limited space could be better used for other purposes and held that much of the Andrewses' collection was unsuited for display in an art gallery.[164] The new director did not share the American Studies approach to material culture that had been cultivated by Potter, Sawyer, and Moore and which had justified the wholesale acquisition of the Andrewses' collection. In early September 1957, Ritchie suggested to Ted Andrews that, since the paperwork had never been formally completed, the extent of the gift might be curtailed. In a more formal meeting called for September 12, 1957, Ritchie explained to the donors that there was only space to display a few objects, that the gallery had inadequate "dead storage" to house the entire collection, and that he would not commit to a permanent Shaker installation. He also explained to them that in looking at the institution's files, he found no legal papers committing the university to any of the couple's dearly held expectations.[165]

The Andrewses, who had kept their options open by refusing to sign the deed of gift with the university, found that this tactic had misfired. The gallery's new director saw no value in their extensive and supposedly comprehensive collection, much less in allowing them to continue to collect in the name of the university using gallery funds. Rather, Ritchie asked the affronted collectors to draft a new agreement that would bring to the university a much smaller and selective group of objects.

For the remainder of the academic year, the aggrieved Andrewses pled their case to anyone who might listen to them. The Yale bureaucracy treated them politely and fairly but did not challenge Ritchie's authority concerning space and policy within the Art Gallery. Potter assured them that he felt "quite badly about the way matters have developed."[166] Furniss, in the final days before his retirement, indicated to them that the "outcome is disappointing to all of us who were parties to the original negotiations" but also echoed Ritchie's assessment that "there is no way of evading the fact that we can not provide the requisite housing."[167] Eventually, the couple conferred with Gabriel; Pearson, who had taken over as the head of American Studies; Norman S. Buck, who had succeeded Furniss as provost; and Reuben Holden, the secretary of the university.[168] None offered what the couple considered satisfaction.

Ultimately, with their dream for a center of Shaker study unrealized, the Andrewses decided that if the university did not want everything that they had to offer, they would not donate anything. Mario De Pillis has noted, "In early 1958, the Andrewses withdrew their gift, causing great pain and embarrassment to all involved."[169] They embarked on the arduous process of retrieving books and manuscripts, which had already been accessioned and catalogued, from the University Library.[170] As they removed their beloved objects from the Yale University Art Gallery, the collectors began making overtures to the Smithsonian, Williams College, and other institutions concerning accepting the collection.[171]

Although Ritchie ultimately rejected the Andrewses' collection as unworthy of accession into the holdings of the Yale University Art Gallery, this failed attempt to house what the Andrewses claimed was the preeminent Shaker collection at a prestigious eastern university is useful for illustrating the status the sect and its material culture had gained by the middle of the 1950s. In soliciting the collection, David Potter, an academically trained historian participating in the American Studies movement sustained by Cold War nationalism, found common cause with Lamont Moore, a museum administrator infused with John Cotton Dana's belief in the educational and inspirational qualities of objects. Both were sustained by patterns of academic philanthropy from businessmen including Francis Garvan and William Coe, who supported educating undergraduates about American Anglo-Saxon exceptionalism as a means of warding off the threats of immigration and communism. The Shaker materials collected by Faith and Edward Deming Andrews were appealing to these individuals because they had gained cultural cachet through their association with the Index of American Design and the Whitney Museum, among other institutions, but also because they represented a native, Protestant religious and decorative art tradition. During the Cold War, Shaker materials could be used to represent an American culture that was simultaneously material and spiritual.

Ted Andrews's failure to establish a center for the study of Shaker culture at Yale stands in stark contrast to John Williams's successful founding of the Shaker Museum at Old Chatham. Whereas Andrews wished to harness the immense intellectual and economic capital of the world-renowned university to lend status to his collection and his endeavors to explicate the Shaker sect, Williams simply used his own financial resources to create an institution and then drew on his interpersonal relations with both locals and wealthy New Yorkers vacationing in Columbia County to perpetuate the organization he had created. Although the two figures were active in the same years and lived in close proximity, because of their different backgrounds and visions their interactions were limited and they did not develop a friendship.

Andrews, who was never fully financially secure, hoped that he could perpetuate his work in spreading knowledge of the Shakers by placing his collections securely within an established institution. With missionary zeal, he hoped that Yale would take over the responsibility he felt for continuing to spread Mother Ann's gospel in the modern world. Unfortunately, the fragile alliance of university administrators that made this goal appear feasible evaporated while he attempted to strengthen his position on campus. Ultimately, Ted Andrews misunderstood his tenuous place within the university hierarchy, as he did repeatedly throughout his life, and both insulted and came to resent those whose good favor he required to pursue his vision.

In contrast, Williams, the stockbroker, maintained no grand reforming vision for American society. Rather, he understood the Shakers as ethical, innovative entrepreneurs who had helped to shape modern American society, but, as a successful Republican businessman, his interests were antiquarian rather than evangelical. His museum sought to celebrate the past, not disrupt the status quo. Because his museum was nonthreatening, Williams attracted wealthy benefactors to the property for annual festivals during which they supported the museum by purchasing antiques, admiring old cars, and participating in fashion shows. Although critics might fault John Williams, Phelps Clawson, and Robert Meader for presenting an interpretation of the Shakers that did not adequately engage the sect's theology, to do so would be to undervalue their success in stewarding the Shaker material legacy into the future.

CHAPTER 5
"REAL AMERICANA"

....

Shaker Pageants, Adapted Sites, Folk Music,
and Heritage Tourism

In the 1930s and 1940s, Doris Humphrey, Miriam Cramer, Marguerite Melcher, and Clarice Carr drew on Shaker history and culture to fashion theatrical works for sophisticated urban audiences. Although rooted in the geographic backgrounds of their creators, *Dance of the Chosen; More Love, Brother;* and *Rose in the Wilderness* were meant to be performed in theaters untethered from specific localities. Each creator hoped that her work would be performed in New York City. The Shaker figures represented in these works were positioned as part of a larger, abstract American identity, just as the characters in Rodgers and Hammerstein's *Oklahoma* were meant to speak to the broader American mythos rather than simply to the specifics of the former Indian Territory, or the dancers in Martha Graham's *Appalachian Spring* represented more than just the people of the eastern mountains. While Melcher, Cramer, and Humphrey's works investigated, and frequently celebrated, Shaker culture, they were not directly linked to the preservation of Shaker landscapes or material culture.

After 1950, increasing numbers of Americans, many of them teenagers and college students, dressed as Shakers, sang the sect's music, and performed its dances. While inspired, as Carr was, by the burgeoning folk music revival, the new Shaker productions also were linked to movements to preserve or restore particular Shaker villages and were motivated, in part, by a

desire to profit from the growing heritage tourism economy through contributions and ticket revenues or by selling recordings and other souvenirs.

Between 1950 and 1965, costumed Shaker musical productions were performed in association with former Shaker villages in New Lebanon, New
York; Hancock, Massachusetts; and South Union, Kentucky. Jerome Count,
a left-leaning retired attorney from New York City, harnessed teenage passion and a countercultural ethos to establish himself as an entrepreneur and
impresario in New Lebanon. Across the state line in Massachusetts, Edward
Deming Andrews, the Shaker pundit and inveterate self-promoter, cooperated, at least for a time, with faculty and staff from Smith College to create
a production associated with the Hancock Shaker Village. In South Union,
local residents worked with faculty and students from Western Kentucky
State College to create a pageant that they hoped would simultaneously preserve the memory of the local Shakers and stimulate the region's economy.
In each of these endeavors, individuals functioned under the assumption,
at least partly correct, that Americans would pay to see people dressed as
Shakers sing and dance. Each production also worked to establish legitimacy as an interpretation of Shaker heritage while facing resistance from
the few remaining Shakers living in New Hampshire and Maine who feared
their religious beliefs and practices were being incorrectly represented and
possibly ridiculed.

While promoters in each location met with varied levels of success, they
all created performances that changed how both audiences and the performers themselves thought about the Shakers. They also fashioned cultural
products, including choral arrangements, publications, and sound recordings, which have lived on beyond the context of their creation. In these
locations, musical activities resulted in the production of phonographic
records of nonbelievers singing Shaker hymns, thus allowing a broad audience to experience Shaker music in their own homes while gaining a fuller
understanding of, and appreciation for, the sect's beliefs. Building on the
efforts of the liberal, Protestant, female interpreters of the Shakers who
came before them, the impresarios associated with these three locations
marshaled American twentieth-century antimodernist nostalgia and curiosity about the country's folk culture to move Shaker music and dance from
a marginal, nearly forgotten position to recognition as a subcategory of the
nation's musical heritage, with its own recordings, literature, and choral
compositions.

JEROME COUNT, WORK CAMPS, AND LEFTIST ACTIVISM

In the years immediately following the end of World War II, Jerome and Sybil Count sought to establish a camp for teenagers in the countryside surrounding New York City. At the time, the South Family of the Mount Lebanon Shaker Village was closing down, with its residents relocating to the Hancock Shaker Village, situated to the east on the other side of the border between New York and Massachusetts.[1] The sect's central ministry sold the vacant property to Harry Burley, Walter Wilson, and Harry Dilson, all of neighboring Chatham, New York. The new owners hoped to build on the region's identity as a summer resort to promote dance festivals on the property while also holding classes in furniture making. The *Berkshire Eagle* reported that Doris Humphrey would direct the dance program in its first year.[2]

These new owners, however, failed to establish the proposed dance festival and thus resold the compound to the Counts.[3] The property included a dwelling house, workshops, barns, and other outbuildings. On this campus, they established an educational institution that, because of its location, they named the Shaker Village Work Camp (fig. 5.1).[4]

A retired attorney from New York City, Count had led a high-powered, prominent career, serving frequently as an advocate for liberal causes.[5] At the beginning of the Great Depression, he had worked with John Haynes Holmes, the outspoken reforming pacifist pastor of the Unitarian Community Church of New York, located at 34th Street and Park Avenue, to ameliorate suffering in the city.[6] Count served as the chairman of the church's Social Justice Committee.[7] He also worked for many years as an officer of a cooperative summer retreat for adults located in Crafts, New York, operated by the Homestead Foundation, a nonprofit organization affiliated with Holmes's church.[8]

As the Roosevelt administration attempted to rebuild the nation's shattered economy, Count served as counsel for the Public Committee on Power Utilities and Labor and the Brotherhood of Utility Employees, receiving widespread attention for representing the union in grievances against the Brooklyn Edison Company related to labor policies and rates.[9] He argued for cooperation between consumers and workers in pressuring the government to regulate utilities.[10] Similarly, in 1934 he was one of two hundred signatories on a letter to Franklin Roosevelt urging him to strengthen the National Recovery Administration and experiment with cooperative

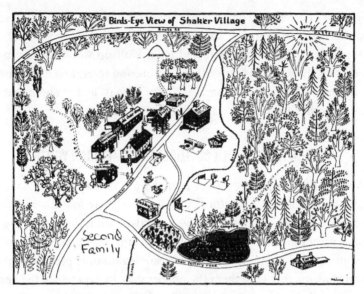

FIGURE 5.1. Heine, "Birds-Eye View of Shaker Village," ca. 1950. The Shaker Village Work Camp used the compound of the New Lebanon South Family to educate teenagers. Playing fields, campfires, and trails typical of American summer camps, were complemented by a poultry house and garden where campers learned to grow their own food. Reproduced in *Shaker Music Lives Again* (Pittsfield, MA: Shaker Village Work Camp, 1952). Collection of the author.

control of key industries.[11] From 1939 to 1941, Count served as chairman of the Committee on Civil Rights of the Non-Sectarian Anti-Nazi League, a primarily Jewish group that advocated for a boycott of German goods while endeavoring to stifle domestic support for Hitler's National Socialist administration.[12]

During the Second World War, Count served the nation as an attorney within the Office of Price Administration, District of New York. Various records indicate that he held the position of rationing attorney and of price attorney within this agency.[13] In 1945, his expertise was recognized by the Association of the Bar of the City of New York when he was appointed as an auxiliary member of that group's standing committee on administrative law.[14]

Sybil A. Wolfson Count, Jerome's spouse, was a professional educator and camp counselor. Born Sylvia Wolfson in 1913 in New York City to Jewish immigrants from Russia, she held both B.S. and M.A. degrees from New York University.[15] From 1936 to 1941, she taught school in Milford, Connecticut, where her father ran a cigar- and newsstand, serving as the supervisor of health and physical education for junior high and high school students.[16] For five years she was the waterfront director of a summer camp in Massachusetts. Between 1942 and 1944, Wolfson worked as a program director for the Red Cross, organizing leisure and recreational activities for service men overseas.[17] She married Count in 1945, and at about that time apparently changed her name to Sybil.[18]

WORK CAMPS, FOLK CULTURE, AND AMERICAN YOUTH

Following the war, Jerome Count retired from the law and became what an associate called an educator "by inclination."[19] He found a role for his educational proclivities and his wife's expertise within the developing field of work camps for American youth. Starting after World War I, liberal religious groups and Progressive educators founded summer programs for high school students that gave them the opportunity to experience the benefits of labor while simultaneously providing them with the chance to participate in establishing and maintaining rules for their own behavior.[20] Writing in the *Clearing House,* a journal for junior and senior high schools, Louise Evans of the American Youth Commission called work camps "perhaps the most important educational development of the depression."[21]

The American Friends Service Committee, an agency of the Society of Friends (Quakers), was a leader in this left-leaning movement. Beginning in 1934, the Friends created camps in which students could address the problems of modern American life while developing their character.[22] The committee located camps where students worked to alleviate economic distress while learning to interact with members of the community as well as other campers. "Barriers of race, class and cultural differences," a promotional pamphlet from 1941 suggested, "tend to disappear in the fellowship of hard physical labor."[23]

The Associated Junior Work Camps, a nonprofit organization associated with the Progressive Education Association and based in New Haven, Connecticut, also assumed a national role in promoting this summer educational movement. Recognizing the value of the experiences offered by the New Deal's Civilian Conservation Corps for young men from distressed families, the Associated Junior Work Camps established programs for young people from "comfortable" families who had never experienced manual labor. Reformers were concerned that an extended adolescence created by child labor laws, mandatory school attendance, and parental coddling was creating a generation of incompetent and irresponsible middle-class teenagers. "Boys and girls of the age that now buys comic books or squeal over Sinatra for self-expression and excitement," explained Harriet Eager Davis in *Parents' Magazine*, in previous generations "were already sailing the high seas, fighting Indians, driving the covered wagons and helping to make homes in the wilderness."[24] In an article about work camps in 1953, the *New York Times* quoted a mother as saying, "I frankly cringe at the thought of nearly grown individuals, full of physical and intellectual energy, lolling aimlessly about for two or three months each summer."[25] Hugh B. Masters of Michigan's W. K. Kellogg Foundation expressed the problem succinctly. He wrote, "By the time a young person reaches adolescence he needs to have opportunities to make the transition into adulthood readily and efficiently." [26]

Organizers believed that allowing campers to participate in camp government taught responsibility and prepared young people for adult democratic citizenship.[27] The American Friends Service Committee emphasized that their campers would "cooperate in simple group living."[28] Moreover, Masters noted, physical work was required if a large group was to live together comfortably and safely. "All the camp routine," he wrote, "becomes an educational experience for the campers, including such duties as cleaning the dining-room, making the beds, taking care of the horses, and performing other tasks that contribute significantly to the growth and development of modern youth." Although labor formed the primary activity at work camps, evening programming frequently drew on Progressive educational models to include folk dancing, music, and theatricals. The cultural critic Marjorie Garber notes, "The word *work* in 'work camp' signified a solidarity with labor on the part of the affluent, progressive middle class."[29]

Because of his liberal activities and association with the utilities union, Jerome Count likely was aware of Camp Woodland in Phoenicia, New York, which was supported in part by New York City's left-wing Drug Store Union local 1199.[30] Founded in 1940 by Norman Studer, a former graduate student of John Dewey at Columbia University and at the time a teacher at the progressive Elisabeth Irwin High School in Manhattan, Camp Woodland embraced the work camp program.[31] Children from five to fifteen toiled to support the camp by maintaining buildings and trails, preparing and serving meals, managing a post office and library, and taking care of animals.[32]

Studer, however, also worked consciously to integrate the culture of the Catskills into the curriculum of the camp because he believed that students would benefit from understanding the life and culture of common people. The camp sought to promote cooperative action that brought people together across generations, class divides, and divisions between urban and rural identity.[33] Studer worked to provide opportunities in which young campers drawn from urban backgrounds would learn at the feet of older, rural residents of the Catskills. George Van Kleek, a local caller, led weekly square dances. Older campers created a museum of folk culture.[34] Herbert Haufrecht, the camp's musical director, instituted in 1941 a program in which students collected the region's folk songs.[35] Historian Paul Mishler has argued that Studer was attempting to create a "historically grounded vision of the possibilities of life in the United States drawing upon urban radicalism and rural traditionalism."[36]

Every summer the camp hosted the Catskills Folk Festival, which drew artisans, storytellers, dancers, and singers including mainstays of the folk music revival like Pete Seeger, who also taught with Studer at the Downtown Community School in Manhattan.[37] Frequently, the festival featured a chorus composed of as many as one hundred campers, with orchestral accompaniment, performing a choral piece based on local history and incorporating folk melodies. With music created by composers including Haufrecht and Norman Cazden, a musicologist and composer who had trained with Charles Seeger and worked with Doris Humphrey, these works explored topics including Sojourner Truth's struggle for racial and gender equity; an eighteenth-century antirent war that had occurred in Delaware County, New York; and the creation of the New York City reservoirs.[38] B. A. Botkin, the influential folklorist who had worked at the Library of Congress's Archive of American Folk Song and the New Deal's Federal Writers' Project, attended the festival and consulted with Studer in 1944.[39] Because of Studer's politics and what his staff was teaching at Camp Woodland, during the second red scare he was called to testify before the infamous House Committee on Un-American Activities.[40]

SHAKER VILLAGE WORK CAMP

When Count established his camp at the South Family of the New Lebanon Shaker Village, he reproduced Studer's educational program while making changes required by the location in a former Utopian enclave rather than a rural area inhabited by farmers and loggers. The first year he drew approximately fifty teenagers from thirty-seven schools in ten states, including California.[41] Campers at Count's Shaker Village Work Camp were expected to devote three hours in the morning to work for the good of the camp but then after lunch had the opportunity to participate in a two-hour workshop in some aspect of creative or folk art, including photography, painting, sculpture, folk dancing, folk music, or instrumental or choral music. In the late afternoon, campers could participate in athletics or recreational activities including swimming, boating, baseball, tennis, archery, bicycling, and horseback riding. Teenagers at the camp received guidance from the adult staff, but the founders emphasized personal responsibility and self-control. A brochure for the camp explained to the parents of potential attendees:

> Teenagers who come to Shaker village are expected to carry out their obligations to the community, including the morning work projects and afternoon workshops. In return for the freedom which villagers have, they are expected to respect the rights and feelings of others and to be ready and willing to learn the techniques of group living, self-discipline, and self-government. They are expected to aspire to sound work habits, mature thinking, and attitudes of competence in whatever they undertake.[42]

In another pamphlet, the Counts quoted John Dewey's "The School and Society" to explain the necessity for adolescents to participate in meaningful work.[43] The Counts emphasized manual labor and creative endeavors equally, and expected all campers to participate in both.[44] In a self-published pamphlet entitled *When Your Adolescent Resists Work and Study*, Count explained that "the term work refers to both manual and intellectual work," and "it is the author's premise that work is not only a source of earning a living, but should provide a means of continuous development of the individual through the satisfaction derived from effectively contributing his work to useful ends."[45]

Although the camp program was meant to instill ethics, discipline, and proper behavior into campers, religion was notably absent. The Counts' weekly schedule did not include time for church services, prayer, or even meditation. At the time, conversely, many work camps were run by religious organizations, such as the Society of Friends or the World Council of Churches, and faith formed a central component of the experience.[46] Unlike even the Boy Scout camps of the time, the Shaker Village Work Camp did not ask attendees to believe in God. In establishing their training ground, the Counts went beyond the "nonsectarian" label of the Anti-Nazi League to create an essentially agnostic institution.[47] Ironically, the Counts located their secular camp on property formerly owned by a religious community and ultimately came to embrace and celebrate many of the sect's tenets.

When the Counts purchased the New Lebanon property in 1946, the couple knew little about the Shakers, their history, or their culture.[48] However, the Counts undertook to educate themselves. As an attorney, Jerome was practiced in the process of "discovery." In December 1946, one of Count's associates, who identified herself only as "Mrs. P.," compiled a bibliography for him at the New York Public Library on Fifth Avenue.[49] Based on this document, Count dispatched letters requesting materials from the Federation of Arts, Brentano's Booksellers, and the New York State Museum.[50] Count even sought information from the Diamond Crystal Salt Company, because at the time they marketed table salt under a Shaker brand. Count wrote, "I have recently acquired a parcel of Shaker property in Mt. Lebanon, Massachusetts [sic], and am very interested in information concerning the Shaker people. It was brought to my attention that your product has a picture of a Shaker woman on the box. Would you please let me know the history of this trademark and send me any written literature you have on the subject."[51] In response, B. W. Cleland, the firm's advertising manager, informed Count that they actually knew very little about "the Shaker cult" and that the image of the Shaker girl was simply meant to assure consumers that their salt "shakes or pours easily."[52]

Mrs. P. also brought to Count's attention that Estella Weeks, a researcher at the Library of Congress, had earlier mounted an exhibition there that drew materials from a number of sources, including photographs of Shaker architecture from the Index of American Design.[53] Count sent a letter to Weeks asking for her assistance. "I understand," he wrote, "that several years ago you sponsored an exhibition on the Shakers which was very inclusive and we would like as much information on these people's backgrounds as possible."[54]

The same day, Count wrote to the National Gallery of Art, explaining, "Shaker Village Work Camp is a new organization beginning this year and we understand that you have photographs relating to the Shakers. Would you please advise us how we can obtain these for use at our camp."[55] In response, Erwin O. Christensen provided photographs of Shaker buildings, furniture, and textiles; color slides; and duplicate copies of the watercolors made for the Index of American Design.[56] The images that Christensen shipped to Count thus exactly fulfilled the mission envisioned by Ruth Reeves, Romana Javitz, and Holger Cahill: they educated the American public about its national heritage.

The Counts quickly became cognizant of the fact that the mission of their camp harmonized with Shaker ideas about the dignity of labor and the importance of individuals functioning within a community. Count's involvement with the Unitarian Church, and specifically with John Haynes Holmes's cooperative, pacifist, and activist version of Unitarianism, made him open to Shaker beliefs and practices, just as it had influenced Marguerite Melcher and Miriam Cramer.[57] "[The Shakers] raised communal industry and housekeeping to the level of highly developed arts," Count wrote. "Their communal organizations resulted in almost self-sufficient economic groups, basically agricultural, but leading to all types of industry and creative crafts."[58] Where other promoters of the Shakers, including Miriam Cramer, had celebrated the Shakers in spite of their communism, Count endorsed them because of it. Jerome and Sybil Count embraced the stewardship of their property and promoted an appreciation of the Shaker heritage.[59]

The Counts also soon recognized that their location could prove valuable in advertising their camp to parents and differentiating it from Camp Woodland and other work camps, even though the program they offered was remarkably similar. Writing in the *New York Times Magazine* in 1949, Mary Roche reported, "Work at camp consists of restoring the old buildings, reconstructing the old looms and broom-makers, weaving, preserving and making other products according to the old Shaker formulas. In the course of helping to set up a small museum of Shaker products, the children also do historical research. Meanwhile they live in close intimacy with Shaker architecture and Shaker furniture."[60] In this remarkable example of reformist environmental determinism, Shaker design was believed to have the power to improve teenagers simply through its presence. Over the two decades during which they operated the camp, the Counts used the Shaker mystique to get their program featured in periodicals including *Sports Illustrated, Seventeen, Parents' Magazine, The Yorker,* and *Classmate.*[61]

Because folk music, singing, and dancing would form an aspect of the camp's activities, Jerome and Sybil Count hired Margot Mayo for the camp staff. Mayo was a folklorist, educator, and promoter of square dancing who lived in New York City.[62] An avowed communist, she taught in private schools (including the Walden School on the Upper West Side), led a group called the American Square Dance Group based on East 13th Street, and was the author of a book of square dance instructions designed to empower groups to provide their own informal and inexpensive recreation.[63] In many ways she filled the role for her generation in New York City that Mary Wood Hinman had earlier played in Chicago. Mayo also was acquainted with Studer and his camp, having participated in a 1946 folklore meeting that he organized at which Botkin and Pete Seeger were on the program.[64] As a folklorist, Mayo had participated with Robert Stuart "Stu" Jamieson in trips to Kentucky and Tennessee to record fiddlers and banjo players for the Library of Congress's Archive of Folk Song.[65] Mayo wrote of her responsibilities at the Counts' camp: "I have a folklore workshop which is devoted to learning dances (American and foreign), songs, tall tales and so on. Folklore research projects are carried on in a separate group. Last summer, teenage youngsters did research in Folk Song in American History, Shape-Note Hymns, Jazz and Its Origins, Shaker Lore, and the transcribing of Shaker music into modern music notation. . . . Folklore has a definite influence in all the camp life."[66]

Mayo, in turn, brought with her associates from the New York City folk music scene including Jamieson, square dance caller Johnny O'Leary, and Harold Aks.[67] Participation in the Walden School, a private progressive day school founded by Margaret Naumburg, a student of John Dewey, linked many of the camp's staff and students.[68] Aks had been trained in choral conducting at the Julliard School of Music, taught at the Walden School, and led an organization in the city called the American Folk Group.[69] Robert C. Opdahl, who played piano for square dances, followed his college housemate Jamieson to the camp.[70] Subsequently, Tony Saletan, a New York–born, Boston-based folk singer educated at the Walden School and Harvard College, served on the staff at Count's camp and, having discovered the song "Michael Row the Boat Ashore" in a nineteenth-century collection of African American songs in his alma mater's Widener Library, taught it to Pete Seeger when he visited the property.[71]

Just as Haufrecht and Cazden had researched and recorded the folk music of the Catskills, Mayo and her colleagues turned their attention to Shaker music. Brother Ricardo Belden, an elderly Shaker who lived in the

Hancock Shaker Village and who had spent much of his life as a member of the sect, acted as a tutor and enthusiastic supporter.[72] For the young folklorists, he explained tempo, demonstrated dance patterns, and indicated which songs were appropriate for various occasions (fig. 5.2).[73] Besides

FIGURE 5.2. Brother Ricardo Belden demonstrating Shaker dance steps at the Shaker Village Work Camp, ca. 1950. Courtesy Collection of Hancock Shaker Village, Pittsfield, MA, 1986–1048.

singing for the campers and staff, Belden also provided the Counts with nine manuscript Shaker hymnals from which the campers and staff could learn.[74] The staff likewise benefited from microfilm that Count purchased from the Library of Congress which included six hundred manuscript pages of Shaker songs compiled in the 1840s by Russell Haskell in Enfield, Connecticut.[75] Margot Mayo was also familiar with Isaac Newton Young's 1843 *A Short Abridgement of Rules of Music,* which was available at the New York Public Library's Research Division, and which explained the Shaker system of music notation.[76]

Beyond music, other activities within the camp explored Shaker culture. During the first two years, campers made confections based on Shaker recipes and began to sew costumes.[77] Subsequently, the camp borrowed Shaker broom-making machinery from the New York State Museum so that the teenagers could make brooms and set up looms to weave Shaker-inspired fabrics (fig. 5.3). By 1960, the camp had established a metalworking shop producing reproductions of antique tinware and a pottery shop in which participants produced ashtrays, vases, and jugs that they decorated with symbolic designs drawn from Shaker spirit drawings.[78]

The camp drew teenagers from around the country, including California and Ohio, but more than half of the participants came from in and around New York City.[79] Because many parents were close enough that they could visit for a day, the summer season culminated with an event in August in which the teenagers presented their accomplishments to parents, visitors, and the general public.[80] Staff and residents mounted exhibits of photography, ceramics, drawings, paintings, and weavings. In 1948, participants performed choral music by classical composers, modern dance, instrumental classical music, madrigals, and square dances. The event also featured a public interview with Ricardo Belden concerning his life as a Shaker.[81] By 1952, the camp had converted the Shakers' chair shop into a theater with a seating capacity of four hundred, and during the open house this facility housed performances of modern dance, madrigals, a small chorus, and the all-camp chorus. A square dance, to music performed by the camp orchestra, was held in the barn.[82] During the open houses, campers staffed a store that sold goods produced at the camp both to parents and to tourists who had been drawn to the site by advertisements.

As the camp prospered and the staff's capacity for managing performances increased, in the summer of 1949 Count contacted Miriam Cramer

FIGURE 5.3. A teenager weaving Shaker textile patterns on a loom at the Shaker Village Work Camp. Photograph by Orlando of Three Lions. Although the resemblance is probably coincidental, this image echoes Yvonne Twining's painting *Shakeress at Her Loom* of two decades earlier. Image from *Classmate* 61, no. 30 (July 25, 1954): 1. Collection of the author.

about the possibility of receiving a script of *More Love, Brother*. She referred him to her agent in New York City.[83]

Count's staff did not require Cramer's script, however, because they had Belden to assist them in planning a public performance. In 1950, as part of parents' weekend, the camp presented a reenactment of a Shaker worship service. Aks, Mayo, O'Leary, and Jamieson arranged the music and dance.[84] Belden personally tutored the students in their movements (fig. 5.4).

FIGURE 5.4. Brother Ricardo Belden tutoring the students of the Shaker Village Work Camp in Shaker dance. Belden, who worked repairing clocks, was often photographed wearing these denim work clothes. Note the romantic painting of a peasant in folk costume in the background. Courtesy Collection of Hancock Shaker Village, Pittsfield, MA, 1988–3116.

Because Count had come to respect the sect and wanted to maintain good relations with their leadership, the camp requested and received permission to hold the performance from the eldresses of the nearby Hancock Shaker Village. Eldress Fanny Estabrook attended the event along with Belden.[85] Marguerite Melcher and her husband also were present at the campers' performance. She gushed in a letter to Count,

> My husband and I had a wonderful time at your "Open House" and enjoyed every minute of it. We are both impressed with the spirit of the campers: their zest and excited interest in all the projects. It seems to me that real enthusiasm for life is the best gift any adult can give to any adolescent. And you have certainly given them that. . . . The folk-dancing was very exciting. And of course the Shaker dances were the high-spot. But we do think the man who handled the singing was exceptionally good.[86]

From this moment, performances of Shaker music and dance became an important component of the Shaker Village Work Camp program (fig. 5.5).

FIGURE 5.5. Dancing at an open house at the Shaker Village Work Camp, ca. 1954. Ricardo Belden looks on from the steps. Courtesy Shaker Museum | Mount Lebanon, New Lebanon, NY.

Each year until the enterprise closed in 1970 after Count's death, teenagers who attended the camp learned Shaker songs and dances and performed them for a range of appreciative audiences.[87]

In 1952, the camp produced and distributed a 12-inch 78 rpm recording of twelve Shaker songs performed by a "Teen-Age Choral Group" conducted by Harold Aks.[88] This disc, which is the earliest recorded performance of Shaker music, included "Simple Gifts," a tune that had previously been appropriated by Aaron Copland for his *Appalachian Spring* (composed to accompany a Martha Graham dance performance), and had thus entered the American musical canon. The record's title, *Shaker Folk Songs,* is indicative of the camp's close connection to the larger ongoing populist reclaiming of American folk culture, as spearheaded by individuals including B. A. Botkin and Alan Lomax. The promotional brochure similarly indicates the creators' awareness of the work of Botkin and other folklorists by asserting, "The creation of the large wealth of Shaker music was a true folk process."[89] In writing about the music on the recording, Bert Sonnenfeld, a camp staff member, presented a romantic vision in which this "folk idiom" was the natural aural manifestation of a utopian existence. "The music of the Shakers," he claimed, "was essentially joyful music created of a confident sense of piety and of the joyful life, where all members of a community shared equally in the work and responsibilities."[90]

The songs on the recording could alternatively have been identified as Shaker religious songs or Shaker ecclesiastical music; by calling them folk songs, the camp staff and administration chose to situate them within a particular ideological conception of the vernacular culture of the United States. At the same time, however, this secular, almost atheistic camp was disseminating music of decidedly Christian content, even if it was a distinctly unorthodox version of the faith. Nonetheless, the campers recorded on this disc performed songs addressing salvation, "followers of the Lamb," and Emmanuel, as well as the virtues of "Mother's Love."[91] By labeling these works as "folk songs," Count and his employees made these expressions of faith more palatable to their nonsectarian public, including both those who purchased the record and the parents of varying religious backgrounds who entrusted their children to the camp for six weeks at a time.

In 1954, Count commissioned Jacob Druckman to compose a cantata based on themes in Shaker music. Druckman, who subsequently won a Pulitzer Prize in 1972, had been a student of Aaron Copland's at the Berkshire Music Festival and was a master's candidate at the Juilliard School.[92] Druckman spent summers at the Berkshire Music Center at Tanglewood in Stockbridge, Massachusetts, and was a friend and colleague of David Conviser, another Julliard student who succeeded Harold Aks as music director at the Shaker Village Work Camp.[93] Druckman thus was a frequent visitor at the Shaker Village Work Camp and brought musicians from Tanglewood to perform for the teenagers.[94]

Druckman conducted research for his cantata at the Library of Congress, attended rehearsals of the choral group at the camp, and took advice from Ricardo Belden. He produced a piece that drew on seven Shaker songs, none of which appeared on the camp's previous recording. Although the piece was entitled *The Simple Gifts,* it did not include the melody that Copland had made famous.[95] The work was written for the camp's chorus of 125 voices and was debuted at the camp under the direction of Conviser, who subsequently had a long career as the music director of a synagogue in Miami, Florida. The camp produced and distributed a 78 rpm recording of the premiere performance, claiming that the work was "an expression of the Work Camp's interest in using material which is indigenous to the historic site now occupied by the teen-age project."[96] The brochure for the recording of Druckman's cantata claimed that it was "the first work for choral use inspired by Shaker songs."[97] Roger Hall, a scholar of Shaker music, notes that the performance of Druckman's cantata captured in the original recording was "not so good, especially the solo parts."[98]

The music world, however, respected the quality of Druckman's work and recognized its potential for promoting liberal social change. In October 1956, Elaine Brown, the director of Singing City, an interracial, interfaith chorus with a nonviolent social action agenda based in Philadelphia, wrote to Count requesting twenty copies of the composition.[99]

Aks also subsequently published, with the Edward B. Marks Music Corporation, a suite for mixed chorus and piano entitled "Three Shaker Songs." This piece included two songs ("Come to Zion, Sin-sick Souls" and "O, the Beautiful Treasure") that appeared on the 1952 record, and one ("O Brethren, Will You Receive") that did not. Although conceived as a suite, the songs were each also published individually.[100] While Druckman's cantata is lengthy and designed specifically for large numbers of voices, Aks's arrangements are brief and unpretentious. Although it is unclear what audience he had in mind for this work, the suite would be accessible for amateur groups. In creating this composition, Aks, a liberal who frequently conducted Brooklyn's Interracial Fellowship Choir during worship services, expanded the repertoire of liturgical music available to church choirs.[101] Building on his experience at Count's camp, Aks for the first time made Shaker songs available in modern arrangements that could be performed within mainstream houses of worship alongside more standard Protestant hymns associated, for example, with Isaac Watts or the evangelicalism of the Second Great Awakening.

In 1956, Count's organization also published a book of Shaker songs meant for a less sophisticated audience. Entitled *Songs of the Shakers,* this publication claimed that its "research, planning, illustration and printing" were done by teenagers at the Shaker Village Work Camp. The songs were represented by lyrics accompanied by simple melodies conveyed by hand-drawn staffs and notes. Reproduced as mimeographs on inexpensive paper, the pages were bound with plastic rings between white cardboard covers.

Both covers and a cardboard frontispiece were decorated with illustrations silk-screened in two colors that combined with the white ground to produce abstract, modernist, three-color compositions.[102]

A graphic design in red and grey graced the cover, which also bore the book's title, showing eight abstracted male and female figures in suits, bonnets, and long dresses facing each other (fig. 5.6). The modernist cover, with

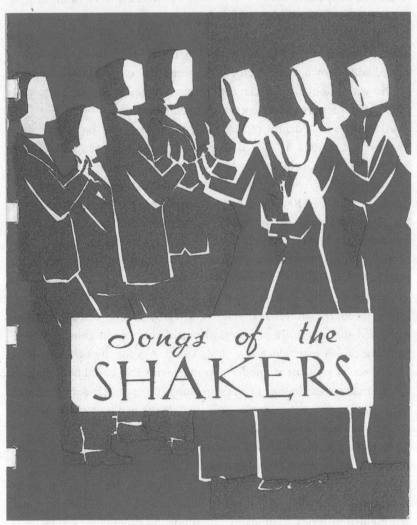

FIGURE 5.6. Artist unknown, *Songs of the Shakers*, 1956, paint on cardboard. Cover of a mimeographed songbook produced by the Shaker Village Work Camp. Courtesy Shaker Museum | Mount Lebanon, New Lebanon, NY.

its rhythmic repetition of dancing figures with raised hands, may have been inspired by an engraving entitled *Shaker Worship—The Dance* that served as an illustration for Charles Nordhoff's *The Communistic Societies of the United States,* published by Harper and Brothers in 1875 (fig. 5.7).[103] This image of dancing Shakers, based on earlier satirical images, had been employed on the camp's 1952 brochure marketing the *Shaker Folk Songs* record.[104]

The frontispiece illustration is a composition in blue, black, and white showing abstracted Shaker sisters and brethren dancing in an energetic intertwined fashion (fig. 5.8). Where the cover image is composed of straight lines and angles, the figures in the frontispiece are characterized by sinuous curves. They also seem to be organized on the dance floor in concentric circles rather than the opposing lines of Nordhoff's engraving. This image was probably inspired by a wood engraving by Joseph Becker of Shakers dancing in a circle at New Lebanon published in *Frank Leslie's*

SHAKER WORSHIP.—THE DANCE.

FIGURE 5.7. Artist unknown, *Shaker Worship—The Dance*, from Charles Nordhoff, *The Communistic Societies of the United States* (New York: Harper and Brothers, 1875), 144. Courtesy © British Library Board / Robana / Art Resource, NY.

FIGURE 5.8. Artist unknown, untitled, 1956, paint on cardboard. Illustrated page from a mimeographed songbook produced by the Shaker Village Work Camp. Courtesy Shaker Museum | Mount Lebanon, New Lebanon, NY.

Illustrated Newspaper in 1873 and which was subsequently broadly republished, including in Faith and Edward Deming Andrews's *The People Called Shakers* (fig. 5.9). In both the illustration from the camp's songbook and the original wood engraving, a circle of male Shakers in long coats and

FIGURE 5.9. Joseph Becker, *New York State the Shakers of New Lebanon—Religious Exercises in the Meeting-House,* 1873, wood engraving. Published in *Frank Leslie's Illustrated Newspaper,* November 1, 1873, 124. Courtesy © 2020 Stock Sales WGBH / Scala / Art Resource, NY.

pants with their arms and legs arrayed in a variety of gestures surrounds female Shakers in dresses and bonnets facing in an opposing direction. As with the image on the book's front cover, the figures in this work have been abstracted and their faces left blank, allowing the dancing figures to be interpreted ambiguously as worshipping believers from the nineteenth century or as teenage reenactors demonstrating, for their parents and others, what they have learned over the summer.

A three-color modernist composition similarly graces the back cover of the book, portraying in green, rust, and white three Shaker sisters seated on a long bench with their mouths open, presumably in song (fig. 5.10). All three are identified as Shakers by their long dresses with shawls or yokes draped over their shoulders and chests. The middle sister knits while singing; her Shaker identity is further reinforced by the oval carrier in which her ball of yarn rests. This charming image, which indicates that Shaker music was not used exclusively in worship but also formed a part of the sect's day-to-day lives, is signed T. Kowal, probably indicating a graphically oriented teenage camper.

FIGURE 5.10. T. Kowal, untitled, 1956, paint on cardboard. Rear cover of a mimeographed songbook produced by the Shaker Village Work Camp. Courtesy Shaker Museum | Mount Lebanon, New Lebanon, NY.

Revenues from the sale of this book, like that of other camp products, was designated to a scholarship fund meant to help students offset the camp's attendance fees. *Songs of the Shakers* was popular enough that within a few years, the camp had exhausted the entire run. In August 1962, Count regretfully informed Deedy Hall of the Shaker Museum at South Union, Kentucky, that he was unable to fulfill her request for several dozen of the songbooks.[105]

PERFORMANCES AT THE SHAKER MUSEUM

After the Counts had owned the property in New Lebanon for most of a decade and the Shaker Village Work Camp had become an established institution, in July 1955 John S. Williams and the board of the Shaker Museum at Old Chatham, New York, invited Jerome Count to join their organization, which had been formalized in 1950.[106] Within months, Count was placed on a committee, headed by Helen Pitcher Christiana and composed largely of wealthy New Yorkers who summered in the Berkshires, to organize a festival to benefit the museum during the summer of 1956.[107] The one-day festival was planned to include tours of the museum, an antiques show and sale, a fashion show, and sales of items produced in the remaining Shaker villages of Hancock; Canterbury, New Hampshire; and Sabbathday Lake, Maine.[108] In April 1956, Williams informed his fellow trustees that "Jerome Count has very kindly offered to have his whole camp of 150 trained voices serve as a choir, singing Shaker music. The camp is also prepared to produce an exhibit of Shaker dancing in costume."[109]

A photograph taken at the festival shows a group of approximately twenty dancers in costumes meant to identify them as Shakers arranged on a grassy site outside the barn that held the Shaker Museum's collections (fig. 5.11). The girls wear bonnets, shawls, and long dresses while the boys wear dark pants and vests, white shirts, and old-fashioned ribbon ties. Ricardo Belden and Jerome Count stand between the dancers and a relaxed summer audience in straw hats and short sleeves and separated from the dancers by a rope. An additional group of young people in light colored shirts and darker skirts and pants, presumably a nondancing choir, stands between the dancers and the barn. This astounding photograph depicts children from New York City and across the country, trained at a left-wing camp run by a Unitarian and a Jew to love work, think creatively, and live cooperatively, dressed as members of a celibate, communitarian sect and performing to entertain socialites and summer tourists at a museum founded and supported by a WASP New York investment broker at his country estate.

FIGURE 5.11. Villagers from the Shaker Village Work Camp perform in costume at a benefit festival for the Shaker Museum at Old Chatham, New York. Jerome Count stands with his hand in his hip pocket to the far right of the image. Brother Ricardo Belden wears a cap and stands with his back to the camera. Courtesy Shaker Museum | Mount Lebanon, New Lebanon, NY.

The museum's "Shaker Festival" was such a success that Williams decided within two weeks that it should become an annual event. He wrote to Count, "A somewhat belated letter to thank you and so many at the Shaker Work Camp for all that you did for the museum benefit. The singing and dancing was greatly appreciated, and I am sure drew many people. I want to state right now, however, that next year we must have a proper platform, and proper loud-speaking facilities ready for you. An effort like yours deserves more effort from us."[110] The next year, the *Berkshire Eagle* featured a performance by the campers in the headline of their article publicizing the museum's festival.[111] A photograph from a later festival, possibly the one held in 1957, shows a larger group of campers performing in more sophisticated costumes on a stage prepared for their use (fig. 5.12).

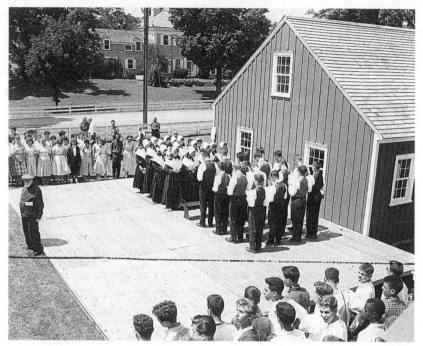

FIGURE 5.12. Teenagers from the Shaker Village Work Camp perform at the Shaker Museum at Old Chatham. Ricardo Belden again signals his approval by his presence. One of the two gentlemen conferring by the fence in the background may be Jerome Count. Courtesy Shaker Museum | Mount Lebanon, New Lebanon, NY.

Subsequent festivals included increased involvement from the teenagers at the camp. They installed booths in which they demonstrated spinning, weaving, broom-making, and the production of pegs for Shaker-style peg-boards.[112] Items produced at the camp were likely also sold at the festival, as they were at the camp's open houses, with proceeds going toward a scholarship fund for teenagers who could not afford to pay the full tuition.[113] These funds offset student costs but also augmented the Counts' income. In August 1960, Williams wrote to Count about that year's event. "Speaking on behalf of your fellow trustees," he indicated, "I know that the ritual service adds a great deal to the Festival. Those that saw it were fully appreciative and I have spoken to many who regretted exceedingly that they missed the performance. . . . [Also thanks for] in particular the work done in the Textile House and most particularly to those who worked in the broom shop."[114]

Although Count and Williams maintained cordial relations, not everyone at the Shaker Museum approved of the teenagers from the Shaker Village Work Camp. Erin Beisel, an employee at the museum, found them disreputable and even warned Miriam Cramer Andorn against sending her daughter to the camp. "The S. W. group put on our Shaker songs, dances during the Festival and do a good job," she wrote, "but—Let me just say that they are New York *City* teenagers and oh dear, *to me,* typical Greenwich Village, and close resemblance to Beatniks. . . . Let me suggest that before you ever do make any arrangements, you look into it more—or best of all pay them a visit."[115]

As the camp continued, the Counts and their staff became increasingly sophisticated about their representations of the Shakers. Drawing on Index of American Design watercolors, the weavers at the camp sought to create replicas and adaptations of historic Shaker textiles.[116] Ellen Count, the daughter of the owners and a student of art and design, studied Shaker clothing as a way to garb the camp's performers and in hopes of producing a publication on the topic.[117] The staff at the National Gallery to assist her lent the camp renderings of capes, kerchiefs, cloaks, men's coats, and other textiles.

The sweet, somewhat feminine adolescent watercolors that Ellen Count produced in the 1950s for the camp's Shaker Costume Research File are obviously influenced by the aesthetics of the federally funded WPA project (figs. 5.13–5.18). Count's image of a Shaker woman in a long brown dress with a linen kerchief is reminiscent of an anonymous Index of American Design drawing of a Shaker woman's costume drawn from the collection of Faith and Edward Deming Andrews that is in the collection of the National Gallery (figs. 5.15, 2.8). Both works even have a rear view of the figure sketched in pencil to the right of the main figure. Count's image of a Shaker man's long coat similarly includes a smaller sketch of the rear and harmonizes with a representation of a Shaker man's costume owned by the Andrewses and created for the index (figs. 5.17, 2.9). Although Count was inspired by the items produced by WPA artists, her paintings are not mere copies. These drawings may be representations of clothing in the collection of Shaker material culture that her parents were actively accumulating.[118] A catalogue of Shaker artifacts at the camp includes listings of Shaker bonnets, dresses, capes, and kerchiefs.[119]

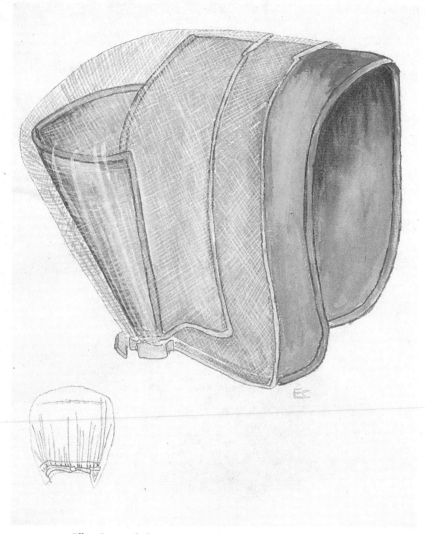

FIGURE 5.13. Ellen Count, *Shaker Bonnet,* ca. 1955, watercolor and pencil on paper. Courtesy Shaker Museum | Mount Lebanon, New Lebanon, NY.

In 1958, Jerome Count contracted with Moses Asch of Folkways Records to release an LP of Shaker songs performed by his campers.[120] Folkways was an obvious commercial partner since the label had built a reputation in the 1950s for producing educational recordings of American folk music

FIGURE 5.14. Ellen Count, *Shaker Cloak*, ca. 1955, watercolor and pencil on paper. Courtesy Shaker Museum | Mount Lebanon, New Lebanon, NY.

performed by Woody Guthrie, Huddie Ledbetter, and Pete Seeger, among others.[121] Asch was eager to add Shaker music to the recorded encyclopedia of sound that he was producing through his record label.[122] Folkways' contract stipulated that the record would be released in September 1958 and

FIGURE 5.15. Ellen Count, *Shaker Women's Costume*, ca. 1955, watercolor and pencil on paper. Courtesy Shaker Museum | Mount Lebanon, New Lebanon, NY.

that Count would receive a fifty dollar payment for conducting research and writing liner notes, fifty dollars as an advance on royalties, and thirty cents in royalties on each album sold subsequently.[123] Count also hoped to be able to turn a profit by buying the records from Asch at half of the retail

FIGURE 5.16. Ellen Count, *Shaker Women's Costume*, ca. 1955, watercolor and pencil on paper. Courtesy Shaker Museum | Mount Lebanon, New Lebanon, NY.

price and then selling them in the camp store.[124] In the text he developed for the planned album's liner notes, Count claimed that Shaker songs were "the simple offering of a simple people" and explained that the recordings had been produced at the Shaker Village Work Camp as "a contribution to American history and culture."[125]

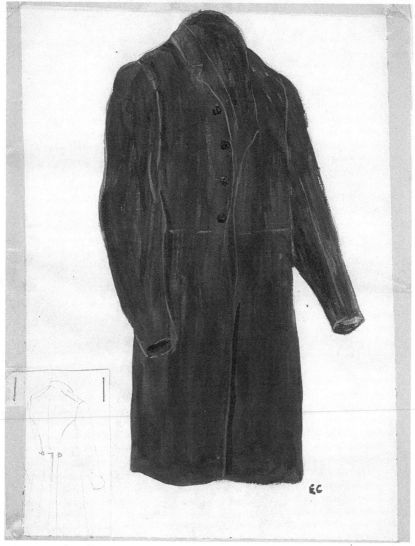

FIGURE 5.17. Ellen Count, *Shaker Men's Coat*, ca. 1955, watercolor and pencil on paper. Courtesy Shaker Museum | Mount Lebanon, New Lebanon, NY.

Despite Asch's promises, the record did not materialize as suggested. Asch blamed the delay on a negative business cycle produced by transitions in the record business caused by the technological demands of stereo and high-fidelity recordings.[126] Over the course of almost two years, Count became increasingly distraught concerning Asch's failure to honor

FIGURE 5.18. Ellen Count, *Shaker Men's Coat,* ca. 1955, watercolor and pencil on paper. Courtesy Shaker Museum | Mount Lebanon, New Lebanon, NY.

his contract and indicated a concern for competition from another "ambitious researcher."[127] Ultimately, in March 1960, Count decided that he could not wait longer and asked Asch for the return of the camp's tape so that he could pursue alternative strategies.[128]

The Shaker Village Work Camp's relationship with the Shakers was also changing at about this time. Ricardo Belden died in December 1958 at the age of eighty-nine.[129] Eldress Fannie Estabrook similarly passed away less than two years later in September 1960.[130] With these local collaborators and participants gone, the Counts found that the Shakers in Canterbury and Sabbathday Lake disapproved of their performances of the sect's worship services. John Williams wrote to Count in January 1962 to explain that the teenagers' performance would be dropped from the festival in the coming summer. He stated,

> On a recent visit to Canterbury I discovered to my great surprise that there existed a very deep and strong feeling against our having the Shaker service performed. I find not the slightest criticism against you and your good works. I have done my best to explain that everything has been done in an authentic and dignified manner but Robert [Meader] tells me the opposition still exists and also exists in Maine. Therefore, in planning the Festival for this year I have come to the reluctant conclusion we will have to give up the service.[131]

Williams sought a position that would satisfy the Shakers while maintaining cordial relations with Count and his camp. In this same letter, he indicated that he hoped that the teenagers from the camp might continue to be willing to assist in interpreting textile and craft traditions.

Count did not let the disapproval of the Shaker central ministry deter his organization from continuing to represent and interpret the sect. Students continued to learn Shaker songs and dances and perform them at the camp's open house. In 1962, the camp created a new edition of *Songs of the Shakers* featuring a cover silk-screened in five colors and a plastic binding that ran the entire length of the spine (fig. 5.19).[132] Produced by Gerald Marks, a staff member, and William Epstein, a camper, the new songbook, Count claimed, was "far superior" to the first edition in that it included more songs, had a better quality of printing, and offered an improved binding.[133]

In 1962, Count issued through Shaker Village Work Group the recording he had hoped Folkways would press and distribute. A 10-inch disc, it was entitled *14 Shaker Folk Songs* and featured recordings of campers that had been made over the years, including some from performances at the Shaker Museum festivals.[134] One side of the record was devoted to an interview

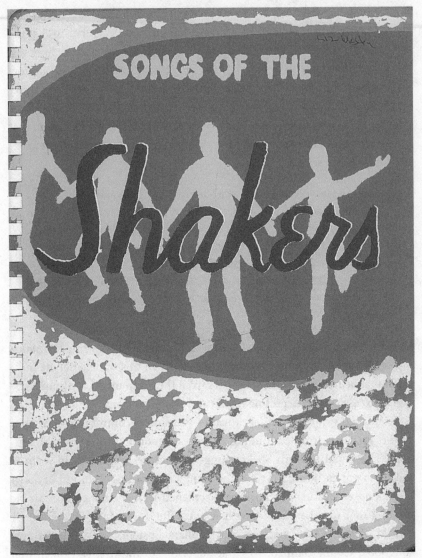

FIGURE 5.19. Unknown artist, *Songs of the Shakers*, 1962, paint on cardboard. Cover of the second edition of the songbook produced by the Shaker Village Work Camp. This cover, silk-screened in five colors, lacks the modernist graphic representation of the sect that characterized the earlier edition. Courtesy Shaker Museum | Mount Lebanon, New Lebanon, NY.

between Jerome Count and Ricardo Belden.[135] This interview once again demonstrated the camp's special standing and legitimacy in performing Shaker music by indicating that they had been tutored and authorized by a member of the sect.

In 1966, Tony Saletan, the folk singer, brought national exposure to the students of the Shaker Village Work Camp. Saletan had secured a job working for WGBH, Boston's educational television station. As part of his duties, he hosted a series of specials meant for use in classrooms in which he played folk music while visiting heritage sites including Plimoth Plantation, the U.S.S. *Constitution*, Old Sturbridge Village, the Saugus Iron Works, Fort Ticonderoga, Mystic Seaport, and the Paul Revere House. These programs, which harmonized with the interdisciplinary progressive educational practices of the work camps while also echoing the nationalist agenda of Yale's American Studies curriculum, were then distributed nationally through National Educational Television, a precursor to PBS, as part of a series entitled *What's New*.[136] In this series' program devoted to the Shakers, Saletan visited the Sabbathday Lake Shaker Village in Maine and spoke with Sister Mildred Barker, who would later become that community's spiritual leader. The show then transitioned to film of Shaker Village Work Camp teenagers dressed as Shakers and performing Shaker music.[137] In the midst of their performance, some campers simulated "the gift of shaking" by rolling uncontrollably on the floor.[138] The show returned to a sense of serenity by concluding with Saletan singing "Simple Gifts."

Barker, who had a longstanding distrust of media interest in the sect, was horrified by the program and particularly by the teenagers' performance.[139] She wrote to Helen Upton, a collector of Shaker artifacts,

> The program on the whole would have been quite good except that at the end the Shaker Work Group put on a Shaker dance and it was very disturbing to say the least. I was so upset that I couldn't sleep and haven't quite gotten over the whole thing. . . . I had no idea that they were intending to put on the dance or I would have had nothing to do with it and would have gone to any length to have it spopped [*sic*]. It was ridiculous and I have written both Mr. Count and Mrs. Miller and the TV station protesting it being carried over the school networks as an educational program for children between the ages of 10 and 12 years. I have had so many letters written me about it by people who know us and what we are and are as disturbed as I am.[140]

Individuals within the community of Shaker enthusiasts found it frustrating that the ladies in Maine and New Hampshire sought to suppress this vital aspect of the Shaker heritage. Robert Meader, director of Williams's Shaker Museum at Old Chatham, characterized their objections as "violent and almost psychopathic." In a letter to Brother Thomas Whitaker, a

Benedictine monk who was a Shaker enthusiast because he resided within what had been the Shaker village in South Union, Kentucky, Meader explained the sisters' stance concerning the teenagers from the work camp performing Shaker dance and music. He wrote, "They resolutely refuse to see the point of presenting them, even if inadequately, as a record of a folkway now gone. They prefer to leave it embalmed, which infuriates me, but there is nothing we can do. I hope they will let us have a choir to sing the songs—without dances! They're so damned peculiar at times there is no predicting what they will do."[141]

Whether Mildred Barker approved of the teenagers' reenactment or not, their performance on a nationally syndicated show on National Educational Television marked the pinnacle of a remarkable twenty-year trajectory during which Jerome and Sybil Count employed a Shaker site and Shaker cultural materials to educate teenagers about work, creativity, self-reliance, cooperation, and self-government. At its peak, the camp had enrolled 210 students and employed a staff of 50. Following Jerome Count's death in 1968, in 1970 Sybil Count sold the former Shaker property to an investment group associated with educators who sought to continue the camp's operation.[142]

Having known nothing about the Shaker faith when they purchased the camp property in New Lebanon, by harnessing the energy of their students and staff, the Counts became significant, if unrecognized, interpreters of the Shaker heritage. Between their acquisition of the South Village in 1947 and Jerome Count's death in 1968, the couple was responsible for making available the first audio recording of Shaker songs, the first choral arrangements of Shaker music, and a multitude of live performances of seemingly accurate representations of Shaker song and dance in New Lebanon, at the Shaker Museum, and on national television. Jerome Count's educational philosophy, business acumen, and ability to hire talented individuals made it possible for Ricardo Belden to teach young people his beloved songs, for Margot Mayo to conduct research in Shaker manuscripts, for Johnny O'Leary to arrange Shaker dances, for Harold Aks and David Conviser to conduct choral concerts of Shaker music, for Jacob Druckman to compose a cantata inspired by Shaker music, and for Tony Saletan to introduce Americans to these marginalized aspects of their musical heritage. Possibly as importantly, the Counts and their staff imbued a large group of left-leaning, energetic, and creative young people from New York City and across the country with a love of Shaker history and culture. In the second decade of the twenty-first century, many of these former teenagers have fond memories of their summers at the Shaker village and an enduring love for the Shaker heritage.

EDWARD DEMING ANDREWS AND SHAKER PAGEANTS

While the teenagers of the Shaker Village Work Camp were performing Shaker music and dance at the former Shaker village in New Lebanon and at the Shaker Museum at Old Chatham, Ted Andrews was working to present his own theatrical presentation based on the Shakers. Andrews envisioned a production, which, like Miriam Cramer's *More Love, Brother* and Marguerite Melcher's *Rose in the Wilderness*, would tell a story while also featuring music and dance. In the 1950s, Andrews toyed with a number of titles for his work including "Children of the Free Woman," "The Blue Cloak," "The Shakers Shaken," and, drawing on the words of a Shaker hymn, "Come Life, Shaker Life." His fragmentary scripts and scenarios for these productions are variously labeled "A Shaker Folk-Play," "A Shaker Folk Opera (In Three Acts, with Prologue)," an "American Opera," and a "Folk Play, with Music."[143]

Andrews, who at the time had a temporary appointment at Yale so that he could catalogue the collections of books and artifacts he had promised to the university, sought to enlist support for his production from leading lights in the world of performing arts. He wrote to Lincoln Kirstein of the City Center in New York; Frederic Cohen, the director of the Opera Theater at the Julliard School of Music; Ernest Bacon at the School of Music, Syracuse University; Rosaria Mazzeo and Boris Goldovsky of the Boston Symphony Orchestra; John W. Gassner of the Yale Drama School; and the Pulitzer Prize–winning playwright Thornton Wilder, among others.[144] Wilder was Andrews's most enthusiastic correspondent. He assured Andrews that his project was "wonderfully attractive" and contained "elements more varied and of richer significance than I had imagined." However, Wilder also warned Andrews to put "as little emphasis on spoken dialogue as possible" and rather to have the play "danced, or sung, or mimed to narration." Wilder further worried that the themes inherent were inadequate to "fill an entire evening."[145] Douglas Moore, an important American composer on the faculty of Columbia University who worked with American folk themes, similarly informed Andrews that he did not believe the Shakers presented promising material for an opera but suggested that a ballet might be the best form in which to present the sect's culture, since the "dancing is so vivid and interesting." Moore recommended that Andrews contact choreographer Agnes de Mille.[146]

Rather than communicating with de Mille, Andrews used the insights provided by Wilder to attempt to interest Doris Humphrey in the production. "We believe," he wrote, "and Mr. Wilder agrees—that the play (with its religious overtones, its dramatic conflict between the spirit and the flesh, its native American quality, its use of original costumes, music, dance, and setting, etc.) has unique possibilities as theatre."[147] Humphrey, who had been presenting the Shakers on stage for more than two decades at that point, did not need Andrews to convince her. She responded, "As you know, I have a very deep interest in all Shaker matters, and am very glad to hear you have a play ready." As a realist, however, Humphrey informed Andrews that she was solidly booked with engagements for the immediate future and that his real challenge was putting money together to fund the production and pay composers and choreographers. "These people," she wrote, "are very busy and notoriously poor. They might be interested but would not be able to spare time from more earning-a-living matters."[148]

Humphrey suggested that rather than attempting to find funding for a commercial production, Andrews might have better luck seeking support from educational sources. She indicated that he might attempt to get a grant from the Ford Foundation because it continued to have traces of Henry Ford's interest in "old-time" America. She went on to suggest that the most promising route would be to garner interest from a college art festival, suggesting the University of Illinois and Brandeis University as possible patrons.

Andrews received Humphrey's letter enthusiastically and asked her again if she would be willing to take a leadership role in the undertaking. He embraced her suggestions about the Ford Foundation and Brandeis University, and flattered her that he believed she was the only artist who could do justice to the material. In doing so, he minimized her financial concerns. "Once we have an experienced director and choreographer," he wrote, "we are confident that the money can be found."[149]

In a subsequent letter, Humphrey continued to attempt to educate Andrews about the realities of theatrical productions. "You might have quite a search for friends, & by the way you'll have to have a realistic budget before you know what to ask for. & you'll need expert advice about that," she wrote. She also warned that the administrators at Brandeis might already have scheduled their performances for next spring, so Andrews should line up his funding before thinking about scheduling performances.[150]

When Andrews shared Humphrey's correspondence with his longtime friend Catherine White, who lived on Manhattan's Upper East Side, she urged him not to be discouraged. White told him that she was elated by the choreographer's honesty and understanding of the business of arts administration. White also embraced the idea of seeking out Brandeis University as a patron. "Brandeis," she wrote, "does have oceans of money and endless sources for more. All the Jewish money in the country. It is anxious for recognition; it is rushing in where academic angels fear to tread."[151]

ROBERT PARKS AND THE SMITH COLLEGE "SHAKER FESTIVAL"

As the relationship between Andrews and Yale University unraveled, he seems to have temporarily set aside his dream of staging a Shaker folk opera. In 1960, however, a different New England educational institution provided him with the opportunity to mount a Shaker musical production. Andrews saw his vision take material form not at Yale or at Brandeis but at Smith College.

In 1960, Robert O. Parks, who had served as the director of the Smith College Art Museum since 1955, arranged to mount a two-part exhibit on the campus in Northampton, Massachusetts.[152] This exhibit, which was on view from January 4 to January 25, 1961, combined a traveling show of Shaker inspirational gift drawings with an installation called *The Work of Shaker Hands*, which included photographs by William Winter, artifacts from the Andrewses' collection, Index of American Design photographs from the National Gallery of Art, and Charles Sheeler's 1956 *On a Shaker Theme*. Lent by Stephen and Sybil Stone, Sheeler's painting draws on the artist's ongoing love of the sect's architecture to create a colorful abstract composition that could be compared to Stuart Davis's midcentury experiments with landscapes (fig. 5.20).[153] The exhibition of the Andrewses' Shaker gift drawings was organized by the Smith College Museum of Art and traveled to eight academic museums throughout New England during the 1960–1961 academic year.[154]

FIGURE 5.20. Charles Sheeler, *On a Shaker Theme*, 1956, oil on canvas, 58.42 x 73.98 cm (23 x 29⅛ in.). Courtesy Museum of Fine Arts, Boston. Gift of the Stephen and Sybil Stone Foundation. 1972.61. Photograph © 2020 Museum of Fine Arts, Boston, MA.

Photographs of the exhibition as it was mounted in Northampton show a simple installation of canonical Shaker furniture, including a trestle table and bench, chest pieces, ladder-back chairs, and candlestands, interspersed with Shaker clothing displayed on mannequins and baskets hanging from pegboards. The works are shown on plain linoleum floors offset by walls painted in a light hue. The name of the exhibit is spelled out in a simple modern sans-serif font centered above a tall secretary. Shaker tinware is displayed in a glass-front case, while framed photographs and drawings are suspended from a ceiling molding (figs. 5.21–5.22). The objects displayed in this exhibition, and the ideas conveyed by them, had changed little since the Whitney's *Shaker Handicrafts* exhibit a quarter century earlier.

Parks, who also served on the newly formed board of Shaker Community, Inc., the nonprofit corporation established to preserve and restore the Hancock Shaker Village, was assisted in presenting the Shaker exhibition by Dorothy Canning Miller of the Museum of Modern Art, who had been

FIGURE 5.21. Mannequins wearing Shaker clothing in *The Work of Shaker Hands*, Smith College Museum of Art exhibition, January 4–25, 1961. Note the trustees desk owned by Faith and Edward Deming Andrews and the framed portrait photograph of Sister Sadie Neale by William F. Winter, Jr., which were also exhibited at the Whitney Museum of American Art. Courtesy 52. Departments, College Archives, Smith College, Northampton, MA.

FIGURE 5.22. Mannequin wearing Shaker clothing in *The Work of Shaker Hands*, Smith College Museum of Art exhibition, January 4–25, 1961. Note the inspired drawings hanging on the wall and the tinware in the display case. Courtesy 52. Departments, College Archives, Smith College, Northampton, MA.

interested in the Shakers since the 1930s. Miller was also a Smith graduate of the class of 1925 and a member of the Smith College Museum of Art's visiting committee.[155] Amy Bess Miller, the president of Shaker Community, Inc., also assisted in mounting the exhibit at the college. Parks, Dorothy Miller, and Amy Bess Miller all viewed the Smith show as an opportunity to generate enthusiasm and support for the new preservation endeavor that they planned would eventually receive the Andrewses' collection.[156] In a letter to a potential funding source, Parks explained, "Our long-range plan is to help call attention to the major Shaker communities . . . at Hancock and New Lebanon on the Massachusetts–New York line. We are helping to investigate ways to ensure the preservation, restoration, and conservation of these communities as national monuments."[157]

Influenced by the Cold War enthusiasm for the American Studies movement, which sought to understand artworks and artifacts within their broader cultural context, and supported by the Smith College program in American Studies, Parks planned an interdisciplinary series of events to accompany the exhibition. In March 1960, he explained to Dorothy Miller, "When we exhibit the Shaker drawings here members of our Religion, History, Art and Government departments will conduct some kind of symposium on American communitarian societies."[158] As Parks ultimately arranged it, this symposium, which was held on Saturday, January 7, 1961, was opened by a lecture by Ted Andrews entitled "The People Called Shakers." Andrews's presentation was followed by a symposium addressing "Communitarianism in America," which brought together an interdisciplinary panel including Daniel Aaron, a professor of English at Smith who also served as the college's director of American Studies; Mario De Pillis, an instructor in history at the University of Massachusetts; Robert Gessert, an assistant professor of religion at Smith; Gertrude Huntington, a sociology scholar who was married to a member of the Smith faculty; Cecelia M. Kenyon and Oliver W. Larkin, both professors of art at Smith; and Arthur Mann, an associate professor of history at Smith.[159] An article in the Smith College newspaper promoting a weekend of events in conjunction with the exhibition, which came to be called "Shaker Studies at Smith," made explicit the event's connection to American Studies by quoting David Potter, the Coe Professor of American History at Yale who had led that school's influential American Studies Program. Potter, this article asserted, had claimed, "This [Shaker] culture represented a deliberate alternative to the prevailing

American culture, and therefore it offers a perspective upon American culture at large."[160]

Andrews viewed Parks's programming as the opportunity he had been seeking for years to present a Shaker pageant and thus to reassert his authority within Shaker music. In March 1960, Andrews proposed to Parks "a joint concert, using women's as well as men's voices, might be a possibility for the projected symposium at Smith—with a selection of the best songs from the 170 plus which I transcribed for my unpublished study."[161] Parks built on Andrews's proposal, but in doing so created a dynamic which eventually led to conflict between the two. Just as Andrews first embraced the Index of American Design because it brought attention and resources to his collection but eventually came to resent Cahill's authority, the collector embraced Parks because of his position in the Smith College Art Museum but grew to begrudge the director's prerogative.

Parks drew on Smith College's musical and theatrical expertise to stage a musical "Shaker Festival," which took place on Sunday, January 8, 1961, the day following Andrews's lecture and the symposium on American communitarianism. This musical event, held in Smith's John M. Greene Hall, was composed of three sections: a costumed restaging of a Shaker worship service, a choral presentation featuring New England music popular during the years that Shakerism assumed its form, and an orchestral performance of Aaron Copland's *Appalachian Spring*, because of its adaptation of Shaker motifs. During the recreated Shaker worship service, the students performed fifteen Shaker songs including "Come Life, Shaker Life," "Who Will Bow and Bend Like a Willow," "Ine Vine Violet," "O I Love Mother," and "Simple Gifts." All five of these had previously been recorded and disseminated by the Shaker Village Work Camp's choir.[162] Surprisingly, this evening of Shaker-themed music did not include either Druckman's *The Simple Gifts* or Aks's "Three Shaker Songs," although residents of the Berkshires (like the Andrewses or Amy Bess Miller) might have been cognizant of these works composed more than half a decade earlier. Faith and Ted Andrews possibly did not desire these works to be more broadly disseminated because of their jealous protection of their authority as Shaker experts. Copland's work, on the other hand, had already become so well-known that it would have been a glaring omission if not included.

Iva Dee Hiatt, who would later be described as the "presiding genius of choral music" at the college, taught Shaker hymns and songs to the Smith

Glee Club and Choir. Hiatt, a native of Indiana, had been trained at the University of California and taught at the San Francisco Conservatory of Music before joining the Smith faculty in 1948.[163] In presenting Shaker music, the Smith students cooperated with the male Glee Club from nearby Amherst College under the direction of J. Heywood Alexander, a Princeton graduate who subsequently had a long career as a performer and musicologist.[164]

Edith Burnett, an associate professor of theater and director of the theater department's dance program, trained both Smith and Amherst students to perform dances inspired by Shaker worship. Like Doris Humphrey and Miriam Cramer, Burnett had performed in pageants and taught private dancing lessons before joining the Smith faculty in 1924 as a physical education instructor. For decades before her retirement in 1962, Burnett, an aficionado of modern dance, choreographed and staged dance performances on the Smith campus. Her 1988 obituary in the *Smith Alumnae Quarterly*, however, claimed that she took particular pride in her work in staging the Shaker performance.[165]

As the campus prepared for the Shaker Festival, Burnett, like others before her, turned her attention to Shaker theatrical costumes. In November 1960, Parks corresponded with Andrews about this issue. "Edith Burnett," the museum director wrote, "would like to have the girls make their own costumes and wonders whether you and Faith would be willing to have the costume material that you are selecting for our exhibition sent up soon to serve as patterns." Burnett was particularly interested in seeing a lawn bonnet, a scarf, and the material out of which skirts and dresses were made.[166] The costumes worn by Burnett's dancers, thus, resembled the clothing from the Andrewses' collection put on display in the museum's galleries.

Copland's *Appalachian Spring* was performed by a combined Smith Amherst Orchestra under the direction of Marion DeRonde, an associate professor in the Smith Department of Music. Beyond being an accomplished musician, DeRonde was Burnett's longtime companion and domestic partner.[167] Members of the Smith College community, which has a noteworthy history of varying gender identities and domestic relationships, may have been drawn to the Shakers' rejection of standard Protestant family structures and definitions of sexuality.

Because Parks hoped to gain national recognition both for the Smith College of Art and for the effort to preserve Hancock Shaker Village, he arranged for Bill Randle of radio station WERE in Cleveland to make audio recordings of Andrews's lecture, the symposium, and the concert. Randle, a jazz disc jockey, record producer, polymath, and early promoter of Elvis Presley and rock music more generally, had a broad interest in recording and disseminating American folk and popular culture.[168] In 1957, for example, Randle taped ten hours of interviews and performances by the blues performer Big Bill Broonzy and released these materials as a five LP boxed set through the Verve record label.[169] Randle subsequently earned a doctorate in American Studies from Western Reserve University in 1966.[170] Smith College's Shaker Festival was attractive to Randle because, as we have seen, for geographic reasons residents of Cleveland had a particular interest in the sect's heritage. Like other enthusiasts of his generation, Randle found in Shakerism a possible solution to the racial strife, alienation, and social breakdown of American society. Echoing Miriam Cramer, Randle wrote in 1961, "In a world that has not yet learned to live in harmony, in a society where individuals have not yet learned to live together in a stable fashion in even the smallest family units, much less large and complex human aggregates, we have something to learn from the example of the Shakers."[171]

Photographs by Northampton's Arlene Studio of the Shaker Festival are reminiscent of similar images of Doris Humphrey's *Dance of the Chosen;* Miriam Cramer's *More Love, Brother;* Clarice Carr's Enfield Shaker Singers; and the Shaker Village Work Camp's dance performances (figs. 5.23–5.25). Although documentary evidence that Edith Burnett was directly influenced by these previous stagings of Shaker dance has yet to surface, the similarities are striking. One photograph shows lines of women in long dresses and bonnets separated from lines of men by a single figure, presumably marked as a religious elder by his dark calf-length coat. This arrangement, likely taken before the start of the dancing, echoes the opening of Humphrey's *Dance of the Chosen* of 1934 as recorded by Soichi Sunami and the beginning of the outside worship service in Cramer's 1945 production. At another point in the performance, a line of women in Shaker garb kneel in humility during a solo performance in a manner reminiscent of a promotional photograph of the Enfield Shaker Singers performing at the 1946 New Hampshire Folk Festival. One image shows lines of dancers with the male participants holding their hands at waist height with palms up, just as Ricardo Belden had tutored the Shaker Village Work Camp's dancers. The Smith and Amherst students in this image are of the right generation that they might have had previous experiences with Shaker music and dance at

FIGURE 5.23. Arlene Studio, Northampton, Massachusetts, "Theater Students Directed by Edith Burnett, Performing as Part of a Shaker Festival at Smith College," January 8, 1961. Women from Smith dressed as Shakers in long dresses, scarves, and bonnets face toward men from Amherst College wearing pants and vests. As in the staging of Doris Humphrey's *Dance of the Chosen* and the grove scene of Miriam Cramer's *More Love, Brother,* a single religious authority separates the genders. Courtesy 52. Departments, College Archives, Smith College, Northampton, MA.

the work camp. In each of these images, the modernist decorative framing of the windows above the dancers' heads are sympathetic to the abstract compositions of quadrilaterals that William Winter arranged in his stark photographs of Shaker interiors in the 1920s.

According to all accounts the Shaker Festival was a success. Parks claimed that 475 individuals attended Andrews's lecture, 600 were present at the symposium, and about 1,500 watched the musical performance, with attendees coming from every New England state, New York, New Jersey, Delaware, Pennsylvania, and Ohio.[172] *The Sophian,* the Smith campus newspaper, reported, "The choirs and dancers were well coordinated. The singers' tone quality was good and pitch exact. Solos were ably performed."[173] Margaret Rollins, who was married to Carl Rollins, a renowned typographer employed by Yale University, informed Marguerite Melcher that she

FIGURE 5.24. Arlene Studio, Northampton, Massachusetts, "Theater Students Directed by Edith Burnett, Performing as Part of a Shaker Festival at Smith College," January 8, 1961. Non-Shakers seek to interpret Shaker worship through dance. Some of these college students may have attended Jerome Count's Shaker Village Work Camp. Courtesy 52. Departments, College Archives, Smith College, Northampton, MA.

thought "the festival on Sunday evening was absolutely superb."[174] The *Smith Alumnae Quarterly* reported that the recreation of the Shaker worship service was "unexpectedly moving, as male and female voices sang the simple hymns, and the costumed groups marched, wheeled, went through stylized motions of sowing, digging, sawing; scattered blessings and whirled in ecstacy [sic]." The concert as a whole, the *Alumnae Quarterly* concluded, "was an outstanding performance, and again profoundly moving when voices joined the orchestra in a climax of tuneful worship."[175] Thomas C. Mendenhall, the president of Smith, was so pleased with the event that he wrote Parks two congratulatory letters in the first week following.[176]

Faith and Ted Andrews were extremely pleased by the event too. Faith told Deedy Hall of the Shaker Museum at South Union, Kentucky, that "the Smith Festival was a most exciting event—the theatre people did an outstanding job."[177] Ted immediately expressed his satisfaction with the

FIGURE 5.25. Arlene Studio, Northampton, Massachusetts, "Theater Students Directed by Edith Burnett, Performing as Part of a Shaker Festival at Smith College," January 8, 1961. Smith students dressed as Shakers attempt to express the sect's spiritual love. Courtesy 52. Departments, College Archives, Smith College, Northampton, MA.

production while writing in a self-serving and flattering fashion to Edith Burnett. He wrote,

> Our gratitude for what you accomplished at the festival on Sunday evening is impossible to express adequately. Suffice it to say that the "Shaker Meeting" exceeded our greatest expectations, demonstrating as it did—for the first time—the inherent beauty of the Shaker mode of worship and its exciting dramatic possibilities. It was an inspired achievement, and one so unique

and precious that it *must* be made available, in this or expanded form, to a wider audience. Please extend our thanks to Miss Hiatt, Miss De Ronde and all others who made the festival one of the most memorable experiences in all the years of our work in the Shaker field.[178]

The Andrewses thus congratulated their collaborators but simultaneously reasserted their authority, claimed the success as their own, and pretended that the productions overseen by Miriam Cramer, Marguerite Melcher, and Jerome Count's staff had never occurred. Notably, Parks, who brought everyone together and made the evening possible, is missing from the enumerated list of individuals to whom the Andrewses wished their thanks to be extended.

Drawing on his newly formed contacts within the Smith College Departments of Music and Theatre, Ted Andrews enthusiastically worked to use the success of the Shaker Festival to leverage the production of a larger "symphonic drama." Within a week, Andrews had written to Hugh Ross of the Manhattan School of Music to inquire as to whether the Tanglewood Festival would be interested in restaging the "Shaker Meeting" the next summer.[179] At the same time, Edith Burnett informed Andrews, "You have stimulated a great deal of excitement in other members of the faculty. Vincent Brann, whom you met at the Parks' and Edward [*sic*] London, a new composer in the Music Department feel that your collected material should be used in the form of a historical outdoor pageant and given at Hancock! I have not heard any of Mr. London's works but do know he is very interested in composing for ballets and operas."[180] Vincent Brann, Edwin London, and Edith Burnett cooperated with Andrews for the next few years in attempting to create a musical Shaker production.[181]

While Andrews cultivated members of the Smith faculty who could assist him to make his vision of a Shaker pageant a reality, he found himself at odds with Robert Parks concerning the tapes Bill Randle had made of the Shaker weekend at Smith. While Andrews had been focused on turning the Hancock Village into a museum and preparing the "Shaker Studies at Smith" weekend, Randle had been cooperating with the Shaker ministry and its associate, Charles "Bud" Thompson, to record the sisters in Canterbury, New Hampshire, and Sabbathday Lake, Maine, talking about their lives, presenting information about Shaker history, and singing Shaker songs.[182] With the assistance of Thompson in Canterbury and Theodore Johnson in Sabbathday Lake, Randle recorded Marguerite Frost, Bertha Lindsay,

Miriam Wall, Mildred Barker, Emma King, Aida Elam, Lillian Phelps, and Frances Carr, among others.[183] Working with the Press of Western Reserve University, Randle used these tapes to produce a boxed set of long-playing records entitled *The Shaker Legacy,* released in a limited edition of 250.[184] Marketed as a nonprofit project comprising part of "The American Culture Series," Randle's boxed set sold well enough to make him believe he could release a subsequent album.

On March 7, 1961, Parks wrote to Andrews informing him of Randle's interest in providing distribution for the successful program the art museum had presented two months earlier. Parks assured Andrews that Randle's company, Cleveland Broadcasting, Inc., sought to produce the records as a public service to libraries, schools, and colleges, and that the records would be packaged with a bibliography, illustrations, interpretive materials, and full credits. Parks also assured Andrews that he had already received approval from Herbert Heston, the college's director of development and public relations, and Donald Sheehan, a history professor who served as assistant to President Thomas Mendenhall.[185] Parks concluded his note by saying, "I see no reason the firm should not be authorized to proceed with its plan. . . . I hope you will give your consent to go ahead."[186]

Andrews, predictably, refused to cooperate. He saw Randle's distribution of records as competition. He also claimed that he could not assent to allowing these tapes to follow a previous recording since he did not know "the quality of the other" set. Andrews asserted that since he had been working with Burnett, DeRonde, Brann, and London to transform the Smith "Shaker Meeting" into a symphonic drama that would serve as part of Hancock's broad educational plan, he did not think it was wise to allow Cleveland Broadcasting to distribute the tapes that Parks had authorized.[187]

Parks understood Andrews's lack of willingness to cooperate in the project as selfishness and egotism and told him so. In a letter dated April 4, 1961, the museum director warned Andrews frankly, "Your reputation will not be enhanced if jealousy becomes an attribute of it." Parks explained that Randle was educated, intelligent, and wealthy. The museum director assured Andrews that Randle had the means and background to produce a product that would reflect well on everyone involved, enhance Andrews's further ventures, and "give Smith the recognition that might be regarded as its due." Parks pointed out to Andrews that he had been only one member of a team of approximately three hundred people who had been involved in producing "Shaker Studies at Smith."

Parks went on to scold Andrews for attempting to control all Shaker scholarship while simultaneously bemoaning the fact more younger people were not interested in Shaker history and theology. "You must realize, Ted," he wrote, "that you have no monopoly on this material as such. Any serious student can easily obtain it at, say Sabbathday Lake." He urged Andrews to be more open and to nurture and cooperate with younger scholars in the field of Shaker studies, rather than standing in their way and guarding his intellectual territory.[188] Parks's assessment of the situation apparently was not unfounded, since at approximately the same time Julia Neal of Bowling Green, Kentucky, noted, "The Andrews [*sic*] . . . are jealous (especially Mrs. A.) of anyone else who gets a foot in the Shaker door."[189]

Andrews was affronted by Parks's bluntness and sought support from other members of the small community surrounding the nascent effort to preserve Hancock Shaker Village. Mario De Pillis, another member of the board of Shaker Community, Inc., was horrified by the accusations leveled at Andrews and accused the museum director of self-aggrandizement and cowardice.[190]

Andrews thus found himself once again in a difficult position created by overlapping interests and differing agendas. The breakdown of relations between Andrews and Parks was reminiscent of the parting of the ways that had taken place more than two decades earlier between the collector and Holger Cahill and the Index of American Design. Andrews had desired Smith College's status and influence in promoting both the Hancock Shaker Village project and his attempt to stage a Shaker symphonic opera. Thus, he had welcomed Parks onto the board of Shaker Community, Inc., and had taken advantage of the museum's institutional resources in mounting and publicizing an exhibition and festival. Yet, at the same time, Andrews wanted to maintain his status as the preeminent interpreter of the Shakers and retain control over the Shaker-inspired materials that he had produced cooperatively with others. The conflict with Parks left Andrews with two alternatives, neither of which he found palatable. He could give over control of the festival's tapes, which he believed could undermine his creation of a Shaker musical play, or he could further alienate and offend a board member of the newly established museum that was offering him a high-profile position, an income, and an institutional foundation for further exploiting the Shaker heritage.

Andrews was spared from having to choose between these alternatives by an unexpected event. On April 14, Robert Parks was arrested with a seventeen-year-old male high school student from Amherst in the parking lot of a roadside restaurant in Hadley, Massachusetts. Parks had apparently picked up the young man while the latter was hitchhiking. The two were charged with committing unnatural acts and arraigned in the district court.[191] Parks's arrest appeared on the front page of the *Springfield Daily News*, the largest paper in the region, and his arraignment was reported in the Sunday edition of the *Springfield Republican* under the headline, "Smith Professor Pleads Innocent in Morals Case."[192] Documents in his personal archive at Winterthur suggest that Andrews used a typewriter and carbon paper to make transcriptions of a damning article to distribute to board members of the Shaker Community, Inc.[193]

Because Smith College had been rocked by a scandal concerning male professors owning and distributing gay erotic literature earlier in the academic year, the school's administration immediately placed the museum director on leave. Mendenhall informed Parks and his wife that unless he tendered his resignation to the trustees, under the school's faculty code Parks would be obliged to publicly defend himself against the state's charges before the Faculty Committee on Tenure and Promotion. To avoid further disgrace, both personally and for his wife, Parks chose to resign. Mendenhall reported to the visiting committee of the college's art museum that he had accepted this resignation "with very sincere regret for there is no question but that he had been an energetic, effective, and imaginative Director, and, as you all well know, we shall be lucky to find his equal."[194] Similarly, on April 19, Amy Bess Miller accepted Parks's resignation from the board of the Hancock Shaker Village but asserted that he "has been most helpful from the very start of our project and the Smith weekend gave us an impetus which would otherwise have been hard to produce."[195] Margaret Rollins wrote to Marguerite Melcher, "I am sorry for everybody concerned—including Tom Mendenhall. He (Bob Parks) has real ability, but I had become aware that he was an unstable personality."[196] Parks resumed his career, distant from homophobic persecution, as the curator of the Ringling Museum of Art in Sarasota, Florida.[197]

With Parks removed from his positions at Smith and at Hancock, no one in Massachusetts had any motivation to allow Randle to reproduce the tapes. Brann and Burnett corresponded with Randle and with the Western Reserve University Press to inform them of their unwillingness to allow the tapes to be used. Brann hoped that with this conclusion, Randle would destroy his copy of the recording.[198]

Yet, the tapes circulated within private circles. Vincent Brann used his position within Smith's Language Lab and Recording Studio to duplicate them.[199] Someone, possibly Bill Randle, provided a copy of the tape to Sister Mildred Barker of the Shaker village at Sabbathday Lake, Maine. In April 1961, she reported to Julia Neal of Kentucky that she had played the tape during a visit to Canterbury. "These songs were old Shaker songs," she wrote, "and we thought they were done with great reverence. In fact, for singers who do not know the old Shaker music, very well done indeed."[200] Barker's admiration of this performance indicates an inconsistency in Shaker reactions to performances of Shaker music, and in that of Barker herself, since this letter was written within a year of John Williams's informing Jerome Count that the Shaker Museum would no longer support musical performances because of the disapproval of Sabbathday Lake and Canterbury.

Although Andrews's resistance meant that Randle was not able to release recordings of the Smith Shaker Festival, this music eventually became available to the public. In 1975, Vincent Tortora, a filmmaker who had produced a documentary entitled *The Shakers in America,* approached Moses Asch of Folkways with a second proposal for a record of Shaker music.[201] Since he had not otherwise acquired a recording of Shaker music since Count had withdrawn his proposal in 1960, Asch used this opportunity to issue an album entitled simply *Music of the Shakers.* It included all fourteen Shaker songs performed during the festival; credited Burnett, Hiatt, and Brann for their roles; and included extensive, although relatively uninspired, liner notes.[202] Brann had an attorney write to Asch to complain that his name was used incorrectly on the packaging without his permission and inquired about how Tortora had acquired the master tapes, but this did not cause Folkways to recall the recording.[203] Since it was against Asch's principles to let an album go out of print, this record has been publicly available continuously since 1976. Currently, the recordings that Andrews refused to let Parks distribute are easily available without cost through Spotify, the internet music streaming service.

A "SYMPHONIC DRAMA" AT HANCOCK

After Robert Parks decamped from Massachusetts to his new job in Florida, Vincent Brann, Edwin London, Edith Burnett, and Ted Andrews continued discussing how to transform the Smith College pageant into a formal "symphonic drama." Without Parks to provide institutional support through the

Smith College Museum of Art, the group turned its attention to the newly formed Shaker Community, Inc., as a likely sponsor for their production. While desiring the benefits of being associated with Amy Bess Miller's museum, Andrews and his colleagues simultaneously hoped that the theatrical production would have a certain amount of autonomy. Brann suggested to Andrews, "I see no reason why this whole operation can't be operated as a related, tangent part of the Shaker Community, Inc., but under a quite separate subsidiary staff."[204] Brann envisioned an organization entitled "Shaker Productions," which would produce a pageant for the museum but would have its own general manager, business manager, artistic director, and professional staff. He believed that a Shaker drama presented in an outdoor theater would provide a national reputation for the preserved Shaker village. Brann was cognizant that the Shaker Village Work Camp was presenting performances of Shaker music and dance, but he hoped to produce a sweeping, spectacular professional theatrical production that would overshadow the efforts of the campers.[205]

Brann thought that his group could create a tourist product that would complement and compete with the numerous summer outdoor theater productions inspired by the Pulitzer Prize–winning playwright Paul Green of the University of North Carolina and established throughout the Southeast and lower Midwest.[206] Brann was motivated particularly by *The Lost Colony*, produced at Manteo, North Carolina; *Unto These Hills*, performed in Cherokee, North Carolina; and *Horn in the West*, based in Boone, North Carolina.[207] Green, a reforming populist southerner, sought to use outdoor theater to express the majesty of American history as lived by the unrecognized rank and file of the nation including settlers, Revolutionary War soldiers, Appalachian mountaineers, and Native Americans.

At the University of North Carolina, Green had been influenced by a community of scholars interested in shaping folklore into a national culture. This circle included the sociologist Howard W. Odum, best known for his collections of African American songs published in the 1920s, and Frederick Koch, who had been recruited to North Carolina to cultivate cultural programs throughout the state. Koch had previously run the Dakota Playmakers, an innovative program at the University of North Dakota in which students wrote one-act plays and performed them throughout the state.[208] In Chapel Hill, Koch formed the Carolina Playmakers, a "theatre of cooperative folk arts" that aimed to assist young playwrights to translate the traditions and folkways of common people into original dramatic forms.[209] During the New Deal, the Federal Theatre Project named Koch the regional advisor for the Southeast and supported his efforts to create a "native drama."[210] Under the influence of Odum and Koch and in the context of the New Deal's nationalist populism, Green collected folklore and incorporated it into productions meant to mirror America back to itself.[211] The project shared by Koch and Green was not unlike the Index of American Design's efforts to educate the public about national traditions in material culture.

In 1949, Green explained that what he termed "Symphonic Drama" should become a national art form because "our richness of tradition, our imaginative folk life, our boundless enthusiasm and health, our singing and dancing and poetry, our lifted hearts and active feet and hands, even our multitudinous mechanical and machine means for self-expression" were "too outpouring for the confines of the usual professional and killingly expensive Broadway play and stage."[212] Similarly, the playwright and drama critic John Gassner claimed the "outdoor theatre movement is patently a peoples theatre in a profoundly American sense."[213] While Green and his cohort claimed to have created something new, they had, of course, been influenced by the earlier generations of pageants and pageantry that had shaped Mary Wood Hinman and Doris Humphrey.[214]

Although exploring and celebrating the history and heritage of particular locations, Green's dramas, and those of his followers, benefited from the nation's growing mobility. With increasing numbers of Americans owning automobiles and roads continually improving, first through the Good Roads Movement and subsequently by the Eisenhower administration's support of the highway system, summer outdoor dramas could draw audience members from hundreds of miles. As car-crazy Americans struck out to explore their nation, outdoor theater productions assisted them in educating themselves concerning regional history and culture, whether it be the first English settlement of North America at *The Lost Colony* in North Carolina or the creation of American popular music in the *Stephen Foster Story* in Bardstown, Kentucky.[215]

With the enthusiastic backing of Faith and Ted Andrews, Brann produced for the Board of Trustees of Amy Bess Miller's Shaker Community an ambitious proposal for an outdoor Shaker pageant. This pitch, which also bore the names of Burnett and London, argued that a spectacular outdoor drama would require a significant investment by the board but that it could create an enduring revenue stream while simultaneously raising public awareness of the Shakers and the preserved village. Brann envisioned a pageant in two acts, presented at night in an outdoor amphitheater, which would recount the entire story of the sect, from its origins in England to its settlement in New York State and expansion to Kentucky, to its decline and the efforts of preservationists to "keep the Shaker ideal alive forever."[216] This show would be produced year after year, thus reducing production costs as scenery and costuming could be reused annually. Music and dance, he suggested, would be used throughout to emphasize the contrast between the believers and the outside world.

The proposed production would have required approximately twenty actors, at least thirty-two additional singers and dancers, and an orchestra of fifteen. Following the pattern set by other summer outdoor productions, Brann envisioned hiring college students who could be employed for a "modest living wage."[217] By hiring students, the nonprofit could keep expenses down by avoiding professional unionized actors and musicians. Brann believed that the performers' wages could be reduced even further if the museum built a dormitory and dining hall in which the performers could live and take their meals.

To house the performance, Brann proposed building an amphitheater seating approximately one thousand on the Shaker village's property. The projected complex surrounding the auditorium would also include dressing rooms and other backstage facilities, a box office, concession stands, and roofed areas where the audience could seek shelter in inclement weather.[218] After scouting the territory in the spring of 1961, Brann had identified a "very good site" on a "secluded hillside, hemmed in by other hills and sufficiently removed from highway noise to make it a possible spot for theatrical production, yet not too far distant to make it inaccessible for patrons."[219] Brann suggested that Harry E. Davis could come up from Chapel Hill, or some other engineer could be employed, to provide technical advice concerning equipping and rigging the amphitheater. Davis, who had made a national reputation for himself as the director of Unto These Hills in Cherokee, North Carolina, was the chairman of the Department of Dramatic Art at the University of North Carolina.[220] Although Brann estimated that constructing the theater might cost $100,000 to $125,000, he was optimistic that this money could be raised from foundations and private philanthropists.[221] He also suggested that the organizers might be able to arrange a "student work camp" that could build the theater in the first year and possibly serve as the production staff subsequently.[222] Brann obviously recognized the benefits of Jerome Count's operation on the other side of the state border.

Ted Andrews, who by this point had assumed the position of curator of Shaker Community, presented Brann's proposal to the board at a meeting in December 1961. At that time, Amy Bess Miller appointed a committee, chaired by Catherine White, the Andrewses' friend, to report on the proposal. Even before the scheme was submitted, White, who supported the concept of a pageant, had informed Brann that Miller had reservations about a musical production since such an undertaking had the potential to divert funds from the preservation of the Hancock property, which formed the corporation's core mission.[223]

Because Miller understood the committee chair's emotional connection to the project, in February she sent White a letter gently reminding her that her committee was made up of only members of the board and that the group's charge was "to report but not to act." Miller urged White, in preparation for the next board meeting, to create a report that would include "facts and figures, ways and means, the feasibility and practicability of accepting the proposal." This report, she counseled, should also consider how the production would fit into a summer cultural market already saturated with musical performances and theatrical productions. In concluding the letter, Miller revealed her own opinion, stating, "I feel there is so much already engaged in, outlined and started to do in connection with this restoration that our batting average will not be seriously depleted if we just stick to our last as it were."[224]

Upon receiving Miller's epistle, White, who was an enthusiast rather than a business consultant, resigned from the Committee to Report on the Pageant Proposal. In a letter to Margaret Rollins, whose husband was on the Hancock board, Miller explained that she regretted the resignation but that White obviously had misunderstood the purpose of the committee. Miller further opined that the challenge of creating a report that would withstand scrutiny by businesspeople and residents of Berkshire County was probably "just a little bit beyond her." As a diplomatic leader and skilled consensus builder, Miller assured Rollins, "I think it is a good idea but has been presented too early."[225] She suggested that the idea of a drama would more suitably be discussed in 1963 or 1964. In a letter accepting White's resignation from the committee, Miller firmly reinforced her earlier point about the necessity of thorough research before embarking on a theatrical undertaking. She then firmly defended her leadership of the fledgling institution. "My vision is not grounded, nor my horizons narrowed," Miller wrote, "but my sights are still firmly fixed on the importance of the preservation of the spirit of the Village and as always practical aspects have to be considered."[226] Without a chairman, the Committee on the Pageant Proposal failed to provide a report when the board met on March 24, 1962.[227]

Having not been informed of White's resignation and not fully aware of the level of Miller's resistance, Brann optimistically continued to hope that Shaker Community, or at least the committee interested in the pageant, would support the endeavor. On March 28, 1962, with the approach of the conclusion of the academic year, Brann wrote to Andrews in hope that the proposed symphonic drama might provide some income, even "a modest token sum to help piece out a long summer." In exchange for a stipend, Brann suggested, he could work with London to flesh out how the music and the text of the production could be integrated. Alternatively, if there was support for the endeavor, he suggested he could participate in planning sessions related to the construction of the amphitheater.[228] In reply, Andrews informed him that he had recently suggested to the board that a strategic plan might include "a less ambitious project, modeled perhaps on the Smith festival, using the skills at Smith and utilizing some local talent."[229] Andrews did not mention to Brann that by this time, his relationship with Miller and Shaker Community had begun to sour because of what the president of the corporation subsequently described as "work[ing] against this organization . . . while on our payroll."[230]

In the ensuing months, Miller worked bureaucratically to put to rest Andrews's lavish dream of a Shaker theatrical presentation. Following White's resignation, Miller reconstituted the pageant committee. In this new configuration, it continued to include the Andrewses, Catherine White, and Margaret Rollins. However, Miller secured a new chairman in Frank O. Spinney, the professional director of Old Sturbridge Village, and placed on the committee Wilbur H. Glover, the museum veteran Miller had recently hired to be the director of Hancock Shaker Village, and Charles R. Crimmin, a prominent local Unitarian attorney.[231] As seasoned nonprofit administrators, Spinney and Glover were well aware of an organization's inability to commit to unfunded expenditures. Similarly, Crimmin, who had extensive experience as an auditor as well as a fundraiser within his church, would have understood the financial realities of Brann's vision.

Unsurprisingly, at the end of July, this committee decided to recommend to the board not to actively pursue Brann's proposal. The committee's report stated in part that "the ambitious pageant proposed by Mr. Brann was beyond the financial resources of Shaker Community in the foreseeable future." Further, the committee decided that they would similarly not recommend a less ambitious theatrical production be presented in the next two years but suggested that if Brann wished, he could submit to them completed outlines or scripts "in the hope that a presentation would be possible at some time." In closing, the committee noted that "the attitude of the Shakers themselves on the use of their music and dance forms" might serve as a limitation on what sorts of programs it would be political to present in the future and that their desires should be taken into consideration.[232]

As a result of the pageant committee's findings, Miller initiated a conversation on the subject of presenting Shaker music and dance among herself, Glover, and Shaker eldresses Emma King and Gertrude Soule. In this dialogue, King explained that they had asked John Williams of the Shaker Museum at Old Chatham to discontinue the Shaker Village Work Camp's performances because she had "become convinced that it was impossible to recover the true spirit and authentic forms of the dance," and thus representations led to "ridicule by the performances, since modern audiences could have no understanding of the conditions which led the leaders to introduce the dance as a form of worship." When questioned by Glover, the Shaker leader further elaborated that it might be possible to present Shaker songs acceptably in a concert format, but that some contemporary performances became unsuitably "jazzy."[233]

Although Brann unrealistically believed that Glover and Miller were "leaving the door open" and that Andrews might still work on "finding angels" to fund the production, the combination of financial realities and the disapproval of the Shakers brought the curtain down on Andrews's long dream of producing a Shaker "folk play" at Hancock.[234] The one-night production at Robert Parks's Shaker Festival at Smith College, recorded for posterity by Bill Randle, was the closest he would come to realizing his ambition. Miriam Cramer, Marguerite Melcher, and Clarice Carr had been slightly more successful: each had created pieces presented to multiple audiences. Yet none of the performances of these three resulted in recordings.

The Smith pageant, directly against Andrews's intent, ultimately was distributed as a commercial recording. Jerome Count, however, outpaced all of his contemporaries. By harnessing willing teenage enthusiasm, Count successfully presented performances of Shaker music and dance for decades and also produced, pressed, and distributed his own recordings.

SHAKERTOWN REVISITED AND THE SHAKER MUSEUM AT SOUTH UNION

While the board of Amy Bess Miller's Shaker Community, Inc., decided that staging a pageant would detract from the institution's mission to preserve the Hancock Shaker Village, the Shaker Museum at South Union, located in Logan County, near Bowling Green, Kentucky, used a musical drama to build its profile and institutional capacity. First staged in 1962, the museum's *Shakertown Revisited* ran annually until 1991 and generated both money and enthusiasm for purchasing and preserving the local Shaker village, which had closed in 1922 when the last few residents dispersed.[235]

Two friends, Deedy Price Hall and Julia Neal, who grew up in Auburn, Kentucky, near the South Union Shaker Village, founded and gave shape to the Shaker Museum at South Union.[236] In the 1930s, Hall, with her husband, Curry, purchased property and a building that previously had been owned by the Shakers as part of their grove of sugar maples. She started collecting Shaker materials seeking to furnish a room, but her collection grew with purchases and gifts from her local friends. She gathered broadly, acquiring furniture, clothing, manuscripts, farm tools, and tableware, among other things. Eventually her holdings outgrew her house.[237]

In 1960, Hall moved her collection out of her residence and established a Shaker Museum. Her husband had previously acquired a church structure that had been vacated by the Auburn Christian Church to use as part of his tobacco farm, but Hall appropriated this building to hold her collection. She decorated the interior of the church to resemble the inside of a Shaker building with white walls, blue woodwork, and brown windows. In this space, she installed furniture to represent an adult retiring (or bed) room, a child's room, a dining room, and a kitchen.[238] Writing about the museum after it opened to the public, Marion Porter, a contributor to the *Louisville Courier-Journal*, noted that "her [Hall's] generosity makes it appear she had been affected by the Shaker share-the-wealth idea."[239]

Although she owned the building and the collection, Hall drew on volunteers and local residents to support her endeavor. She explained to one reporter, "Of course the collection is a private one, and as of now we're footing all the bills ourselves. However, several civic leaders here have offered to help any way they can, and it might turn out to be a community project. We may eventually incorporate the museum."[240] Hall involved the community in a variety of ways, including enlisting Eloise Hadden, a home economics teacher at Auburn High School, to create Shaker costumes for her volunteer guides, eight of whom were present on the museum's opening day.[241] By the end of the first summer season, representatives from the local Rotary Club, Chamber of Commerce, PTA, Ministerial Association, and American Legion volunteered to serve on the new museum's board. Granville Clark, an attorney from the nearby village of Russellville, drew up incorporation papers pro bono, and local businesses including the Auburn Roller Mills and Auburn Mills, Inc., provided in-kind donations of services.[242]

In creating the Shaker Museum at Auburn, Hall sought to celebrate and commemorate the sect, but she and her colleagues, like James Isenberg in Harrodsburg twenty-five years earlier, also sought to create an attraction that would contribute to Auburn's identity and economy. Jane Morningstar of the *Park City Daily News* claimed that the museum contributed to "community promotion."[243] From the first day it opened, the Shaker Museum sought coverage in periodicals ranging from the *Automobile Bulletin,* published by the American Automobile Association, to the *Louisville Courier-Journal.* Local businessmen were willing to support the museum and serve on its board because they understood that visitors would buy gasoline, eat in restaurants, and possibly stay at local hotels and motels. In 1960, Virginia Hutcheson, the secretary of the Shaker Museum, explained to Brown Lee Yates, a public relations officer for the Commonwealth of Kentucky, "Although the relics are privately owned by Mrs. Curry Hall and the building which will be the home of the Shaker relics is owned by Mr. Curry Hall, the project is a community one and has the backing of the ROTARY CLUB, CHAMBER OF COMMERCE, and other organizations. We feel that the SHAKER MUSUEM will be an added attract for Auburn and Logan County as well as Warren, Simpson, and other surrounding counties."[244] In 1961 Wilson W. Wyatt, Kentucky's lieutenant governor, invited Hall, because of her activities with the Shaker Museum, to serve on the newly formed

Kentucky Development Council, which was charged with fostering the state's economic progress.[245]

Deedy Hall's childhood friend Julia Neal was her closest ally in founding the Shaker Museum. Like Hall, Neal was a native of Auburn, Kentucky, and had known the last Shakers before the village closed. She earned an associate's degree from Bethel Women's College in Hopkinsville, Kentucky, and subsequently a B.S. and M.A. from Western Kentucky State Teacher's College (later Western Kentucky State College, now Western Kentucky University).[246] While an undergraduate, in 1926, Neal penned an article entitled "Shakertown of Long, Long Ago" for the *College Heights Herald*, the campus newspaper. "The buildings, surrounded by weeds and uncut grass, and some of them in bad repair," she wrote, "fail to reflect the glory that was once theirs. Thus a visit to the Shakertown of today brings only heartache and the realization that for us 'there has passed away a glory from the earth.'"[247] At a young age, Neal had found in the Shakers a theme to which she would return for the rest of her life. Just as Marguerite Melcher's summers with family in Enfield, New Hampshire, had set her on the path to interpret the Shakers to the world, Neal's childhood in Auburn motivated her to speak, write, and organize on behalf of the Shaker heritage.

After receiving her master's degree, Neal worked as a temporary faculty member in the English Department at Western Kentucky State Teacher's College. At the conclusion of her employment, her mentor Gordon Wilson wrote of her, "Miss Neal is a woman of fine culture, she has traveled extensively, and is widely read. I wish it were possible for us to keep her in our department."[248] Neal then served as the dean of residence at the Kingswood School for Girls in Cranbrook, Michigan, while taking graduate summer courses in American literature and culture at the University of Michigan that were offered to augment the university's interdisciplinary undergraduate American Studies curriculum.[249] In 1940, she submitted a paper on Shakerism as part of a course on American religion using primary source material drawn from Shaker journals on deposit at her Kentucky alma mater.[250] Based on the quality of this paper, Roy W. Cowden enrolled Neal in Michigan's graduate writing program, since the university did not yet offer a formal graduate degree in American culture.[251] Neal spent a year on the campus of the University of Michigan, serving as a dormitory assistant, taking classes, and writing a history of the South Union Shaker community.[252] In 1945, her work, which she entitled "By Their Fruits," was awarded a prestigious six hundred dollar Avery Hopwood Award by the University of Michigan as the year's best extended essay.[253] Because of this recognition, a representative of the University of North Carolina Press solicited her manuscript. North Carolina published *By Their Fruits: The Story of Shakerism in South Union, Kentucky* in 1947.[254]

By Their Fruits was both more detailed and less ambitious than Melcher's *The Shaker Adventure,* published six years earlier. Where Melcher had attempted to explain the entire Shaker movement, Neal used manuscript sources to focus tightly on the history of a single community. W. Francis English of the University of Missouri praised Neal's book for being "an interesting story of one of the smallest and least known" of the nation's communal societies.[255] Writing in the *Annals of the American Academy of Political and Social Science,* R. E. E. Harkness commended Neal for having "given an excellent portrayal from authentic sources" of one of the Shaker villages but also noted that Neal was overly credulous and had missed the "social significance of the rise of the Shakers."[256] Adele Brandeis, who was familiar with the Shakers from her service as an administrator in the Kentucky office of the Index of American Design, was kinder in the *Louisville Courier-Journal.* Brandeis used her review as an opportunity to articulate a nostalgic postwar antimodernism concerning the sect. She wrote, "The lives of the believers were full and varied and it seems strange to think that people of whom we have such a vivid picture should be practically as extinct as the dodo. They came to functionalism too early, a personal functionalism, and there is no place for such people in this mechanized world. To read this book is to raise the question again: How far backward does progress take us?"[257]

In 1946, Neal left Michigan to take a teaching position as an associate professor of English at Florence State University in Alabama. Throughout this time, she maintained contact with her childhood friend Deedy Hall. In 1960, Neal returned to Auburn to assist in opening the new museum. That same summer, she received a four hundred dollar grant from the Southern Fellowship Fund, which allowed the two, along with Hall's mother, to travel north to meet with William Lassiter at the New York State Museum; visit with Faith and Edward Deming Andrews at their house in Richmond, Massachusetts; attend the Shaker Festival at the Shaker Museum at Old Chatham; and tour the Shaker villages at Hancock and New Lebanon.[258] They also visited the Sabbathday Lake Village in Maine, where they met with Sister Eleanor Peacock, and the village in Canterbury, New

Hampshire, where they met Eldress Emma King, Bud Thompson, and the remaining sisters.[259]

As early as April 1960, before the museum was even open, Hall suggested to a reporter that she and her friends might start an annual "Shaker Festival" so that visitors from across the country could come to Auburn to get a better understanding of the Shakers and spend money in local businesses.[260] After her trip north with Julia Neal, during which they had a chance to see Count's Shaker Village Work Camp teenagers perform and talk with Faith and Edward Deming Andrews about the Smith College Shaker Festival and their ideas for a "symphonic drama," Hall added a pageant to her plans. Just as Miriam Cramer had drawn on the resources of Western Reserve University and Andrews had tapped Smith College's talent, Hall and Neal reached out to Western Kentucky State College to implement their vision.

Russell H. Miller, the school's director of speech and dramatics within the English Department, worked with Neal to adapt her *By Their Fruits* into a script for a musical pageant entitled *Shakertown Revisited*.[261] Miller, who held bachelor's and master's degrees from the University of Mississippi, had taught at the Bowling Green Business University starting in 1934 and spent six years as director and producer of the Bowling Green Players Guild. After the United States entered World War II, Miller enrolled in the army in 1942. While in the service, he directed shows for the military in West Africa. With a return to peace, he joined the English Department at Western Kentucky State College in 1947. Subsequently, he took a leave of absence to pursue a doctorate in education at Columbia University's Teacher's College.[262] As his doctoral thesis, under the sponsorship of Magdalene Kramer of the Department of Teaching Speech, Miller wrote a symphonic drama in the mode of Paul Green entitled *Giants Lie Sleeping* about the cave region of western Kentucky's Green River Valley.[263] One of Miller's colleagues described him as a complex personality who could quickly put together a successful show by delegating authority but took his work seriously and demanded complete allegiance.[264]

Miller's script for *Shakertown Revisited* tells the story of the South Union Shakers in two acts divided into four scenes each. Between scenes, a narrator advances the plot using text and ideas drawn from Melcher's study, exploring how the Shaker community balanced the conflict between security and adventure. The first act opens with Mother Ann Lee imprisoned for her beliefs. After being released from jail, she anoints missionaries to travel to the American Southwest, meaning Kentucky and Tennessee, to gather new believers. Subsequent scenes show the Shakers espousing their principles, dancing in worship, converting Kentuckians, and welcoming Andrew Jackson and James Monroe to their prosperous village (fig. 5.26). Following the intermission, the Civil War intrudes on the Shaker village with both Union and Confederate soldiers encroaching on the Shakers' paradise (fig. 5.27). After the war, the Shakers are tested by their own carnality, by the Ku Klux Klan's threatening them for their tenets and burning a building, and by increased technology and consumerism. Miller used pianos, phonographs, cars, and telephones to represent the corroding effects of modern American society. The final scene dramatizes the closing of the village and the auction of the property.[265] The *College Heights Herald*, the Western Kentucky State College newspaper, said of Miller's script, "'Shakertown Revisited' is real Americana. It should appeal to both Kentuckians and tourists as well."[266]

FIGURE 5.26. D. E. MacGregor, "Production Shot of *Shakertown Revisited*, Auburn, Kentucky," 1962. The first act of this Shaker pageant included a representation of the Shakers' religious dancing. Courtesy Library Collection, South Union Shaker Village, KY.

FIGURE 5.27. "Scene from *Shakertown Revisited*, Auburn, Kentucky," 1962. The second act of the pageant includes a scene in which the sect's pacifism is tested by Civil War soldiers. Note the basketball markings on the Auburn High School gymnasium floor. Courtesy Library Collection, South Union Shaker Village, KY.

Ruth Morriss, another faculty member at Western Kentucky, arranged the music. Morriss, a native of nearby Russellville, had earned a B.A. from Peabody College in Nashville. She subsequently also earned an M.A. and did postgraduate work at the University of Colorado at Boulder and at the Eastman School of Music in Rochester, New York.[267] Morriss researched and arranged both Shaker hymns and melodies and also suitable popular American music of the late nineteenth and early twentieth centuries for the production.[268]

As their plans for *Shakertown Revisited* came together, Hall and Neal wrote to the Shaker sisters whom they had met during their trip in 1960 to broach with them the idea of a theatrical production. In return, they received a noncommittal letter from Sister Bertha Lindsay that once again expressed the sisters' concerns about Old Chatham and the Shaker Village Work Camp. "I think the idea of a Shaker Pageant quite interesting,"

Lindsay wrote, "'By Their Fruits' should be fine material. I am sure that Julia will not allow anything to be ridiculed. There have been dances etc. done at Old Chatham of which we did not approve, in fact it seemed like making fun of religious zeal, so we were not too elated over any of these plays. However, if you can vouch for Mr. Miller, I surely can know Julia is sincere and will present Shakerism at its best."[269]

The production of *Shakertown Revisited* was the key event of a weekend-long Shaker Festival held from July 20–22, 1962, in the midst of an antique sale, an antique car show, an art exhibit, tours of the Shaker property, and other attractions. Neal claimed that the festival, which was remarkably similar to the annual event sponsored by the Shaker Museum at Old Chatham, was "the biggest project ever before undertaken in Auburn."[270] The pageant itself was staged in the gymnasium of the Auburn High School, under the direction of Russell Miller, with scenery mounted on turntables and painted by T. Hal Gomer. Eloise Hadden, the Auburn High School home economics teacher who had clothed the museum's guides, served as costumer and created apparel that featured what by this time had become a standard attire of dark slacks and vests for the men and long dresses for the women accented with light-colored scarves and bonnets (fig. 5.28).[271] A cast of approximately seventy was drawn from the community with students from the college's Western Summer Players taking many of the primary roles and with music presented by the Russellville Civic Chorus directed by Ruth Morriss.[272] J. Granville Clark, the board's attorney, served as the pageant's narrator in the role of Elder Logan Johns.[273]

The pageant received positive reviews. The critic for the *Park City Daily News* proudly trumpeted, "Kentucky has another successful pageant following in the footsteps of 'The Stephen Foster Story,' 'The Book of Job,' and "Wilderness Road.' . . . Many outstanding bits add up to an interesting show."[274] Cola C. Turner in the *Auburn News* claimed, "The cast of over 65 persons gave an outstanding performance."[275] After declaring the festival a "civic triumph," the reporter for Russellville's *News Democrat* elaborated by explaining, "Perhaps the finest achievement was that the dedicated Auburn sponsors had contrived to show in a truly splendid way the essential nobility, artistry, and godliness of the tiny, misunderstood Shaker sect, resurrecting the Shaker way of life not as a curiosity but as a faith."[276]

Commentators were also kind to the show in private correspondence. George M. Chinn, the director of the Kentucky Historical Society, wrote in

FIGURE 5.28. "Scene from *Shakertown Revisited*, Auburn, Kentucky," 1962. Bonnets and scarves worn by female cast members identified them as Shakers. Courtesy Library Collection, South Union Shaker Village, KY.

praise to Russell Miller. "By your genius," he observed, "you have reached the highest form of the art by weaving into the fabric of entertainment a simple but colorful pattern. This is by far the most outstanding presentation of its kind in existence and its flawless interpretation by local folks is truly remarkable. The amazing thing is that you have not deviated one particle from the recorded progress and eventual failure of the Shaker's communal effort to establish an earthly utopia."[277] In writing to Barry Bingham, publisher of the *Louisville Courier-Journal* and a supporter of the preservation at the Shaker Village of Pleasant Hill in Kentucky, Ted Andrews could barely suppress his jealousy. He opined about *Shakertown Revisited*, "Though the Pageant at Auburn may leave much to be desired, it shows what can be done with cooperation and enthusiasm. At least it was a beginning, and more than we have been able to do here pageant-wise."[278]

The Auburn pageant, however, was more than a beginning: it was a foundation. In subsequent years, the presentation of the pageant expanded. The second year the organizers presented the pageant for five nights instead of three. Of the 1963 performance one critic noted, "The Shaker dances contribute mightily to the pep of the first part of the pageant and we wished there had been more dancing and singing and less narrative conversation."[279] That second year, the organizers also mounted an exhibit of drawings and photographs of Shaker materials from the Index of American Design borrowed from the National Gallery of Art.[280] By 1965, the reputation of the festival and pageant had grown to the point that the National Association of Travel Organizations chose the Auburn Shaker Festival as one of the top ten events in the nation for the month of July 1965.[281]

In 1965, the organizers also produced a 33⅓ rpm 12-inch recording that they could sell at the pageant. Produced by Russell Miller, the recording, which did not receive distribution beyond the Shaker Festival, included Shaker music arranged by Ruth Morriss and performed by the pageants' cast as well as readings from Julia Neals's *By Their Fruits*. Although a relatively unsophisticated production, the record found an audience. Judith Brinkman, the assistant director of the Kentucky Guild of Artists and Craftsmen, informed Hall, "The record of 'Shakertown Revisited' has been played several times since we've been home."[282]

As momentum grew and the community became more ambitious, Hall and her compatriots formed a nonprofit corporation entitled "Shakertown Revisited, Inc." They soon believed their facilities were inadequate to support the vision they had of a tourist attraction with a national reputation. Hall, like Brann, imagined a building that could serve as a permanent physical home for a Shaker pageant. Unlike Brann's outdoor amphitheater, however, the building Hall proposed also would serve as a community center with a swimming pool and a library. Locker rooms, she believed, could allow changing into swimsuits while at other times serving as a dressing room for the pageant. Hall also envisioned that this structure could aid larger community purposes. Besides fulfilling local needs, the swimming pool might be attractive to potential tourists. Moreover, she explained to one potential funder, "We feel that this plan would help tie our community closer together and give us a reasonable showing in attracting a small amount of industry to help balance our local economy."[283]

Shakertown Revisited was unable to raise funds for the structure they envisioned in Auburn. In 1971, however, the group successfully leveraged a matching grant from Kentucky governor Louie B. Nunn to purchase historic Shaker buildings and five acres of property at the South Union site. Hall and Neal relocated the museum's collections into the 1824 Centre House and for years the annual pageant was mounted under a large tent on the grounds.[284] Although the Shaker Museum at South Union no longer performs Russell Miller's magnum opus, this Shaker symphonic drama created a lasting legacy in the preserved Shaker buildings that draw pilgrims from across the country. The corporation that manages and maintains the property continues to recognize its roots in community theater by maintaining the name Shakertown Revisited.

The pageant's influence also extended beyond the village and outside of Logan County. In the decades following her involvement with Miller's pageant, Morriss formed a performing group, reminiscent of Clarice Carr's Enfield Shaker Singers, which she called variously the South Union Shaker Singers, after the village where they had originated, and the Western Shaker Singers, in recognition of the school where she had served on the faculty. Under her directorship, performers from the area around Bowling Green performed Shaker music at the Shaker Museum at South Union, the Shaker Village at Pleasant Hill, the Shaker Bicentennial Celebration in Cleveland in 1974, and other venues.[285]

IMPACT

During the years between 1950 and 1965, the aspirations of those who staged performances of Shaker music and dance often exceeded their outcomes. Deedy Hall's Shakertown Revisited never built a community center in Auburn with swimming pool and auditorium. Vincent Brann was unable to convince Amy Bess Miller's Shaker Community to stage a symphonic drama in the star-lit Berkshire woods with a cast of college students and music by Edwin London. Jerome Count's recordings of his teenage campers did not achieve national distribution or popular acclaim.

Yet, their successes are more significant than their shortcomings. The Folkways album produced from the tapes of the 1960 Smith College Shaker Festival continues to be broadly and easily available. Tony Saletan's educational television program was broadcast nationally on public television stations. The Shaker Museum at South Union owns and preserves important Shaker buildings largely because the community came together in 1962 to stage Russell Miller's outdoor production. Ruth Morriss, having become familiar with Shaker music through the pageant, subsequently performed the sect's songs for audiences throughout the lower Midwest. Count produced and distributed both recordings and songbooks that disseminated Shaker melodies. Possibly more importantly, his camp introduced hundreds, if not thousands, of teenagers to Shaker music and culture and had a profound influence on many of them. Nancy McDowell, for example, who first encountered Shaker music at Count's camp in the 1950s, made these songs part of her professional identity as a musician and, in 2007, released a compact disc of new recordings of music inspired by the sect, including Druckman's *The Simple Gifts*.[286]

Although each individual, from Margot Mayo and Vincent Brann to Robert Parks and Deedy Hall, came to the idea of Shaker performances and pageants with their own motivations, by building on the foundations that Doris Humphrey, Miriam Cramer, Marguerite Melcher, and Clarice Carr laid, collectively they took Shaker music, which had been a relatively forgotten backwater of American cultural life, and reintroduced it to the national stage. Although the Shaker leaders in New Hampshire and Maine frequently disapproved, nonbelievers, wearing dresses and bonnets and dark slacks and vests, regularly performed Shaker songs and dances for enthusiastic audiences at public events, in festivals, and in pageants. At the Shaker Valley Work Camp, the Shaker Museum at Old Chatham, and the Shaker Museum in Auburn, Kentucky, these performances became annual tourist attractions that supported educational institutions, drew travelers, and contributed to local economies. By performing Shaker songs and dances and claiming a place for them within the national musical canon, the participants in these events gave a nearly moribund sect an expanded relevance within America's consciousness.

CHAPTER 6
OPENING THE VILLAGES TO THE PUBLIC, 1955–1965

·····················

I n 1962, the journalist Richard Shanor, writing in the magazine *Travel*, reported on a booming subfield of heritage tourism. "Today," he wrote, "an increasing number of visitors each year are discovering . . . the fascination of Shaker history, the beauty of Shaker craftsmanship, and the amazing number of ways Shaker hands and minds have contributed to the American heritage."[1] Shanor and the editors of *Travel* recognized the fruits of the efforts outlined in the previous chapters.

Between 1955 and 1965, the Shaker villages of Hancock, Massachusetts; Canterbury, New Hampshire; and Harrodsburg, Kentucky were made available to the public as heritage sites. As the previous chapters have indicated, these openings built on decades of growing public interest in the sect and were milestones in the reevaluation of Shaker life and culture. For the first time, institutions dedicated to interpreting Shaker material culture and architecture *in situ* formally welcomed visitors. Previously, organizations including the New York State Museum and the Shaker Museum at Old Chatham had exhibited Shaker objects in galleries removed from where Shakers lived. In contrast, Jerome Count's Shaker Village Work Camp had interpreted aspects of the Mount Lebanon Shaker Village as a byproduct of youth education. With the opening of Hancock, Canterbury, and Pleasant Hill (in Harrodsburg, Kentucky), visitors could now see the sect interpreted by public historians on sites where the faithful had labored and worshipped.

For the most part, Shakers did not play leading roles in creating these museum compounds. Rather, they paid close attention as historic preservationists, community boosters, history enthusiasts, and local elites attempted to reshape the villages to serve not the needs of the sect but those of the American touring public. At each of these sites, non-Shakers made decisions that advanced the status of the villages as didactic landscapes and tourist attractions rather than as religious communities.[2]

The people who reshaped these villages into heritage sites were in regular correspondence with each other.[3] They visited one another's sites.[4] They read and evaluated publicity in the press and learned from each other's successes and failures. However, they also functioned within their respective institutional contexts, and even though they all started with roughly the same raw material (that is to say, declining or abandoned Shaker villages), they achieved markedly different outcomes. Whereas the backers of Hancock Shaker Village in the Berkshires posited a role for Shaker architecture and material culture as part of the evolution of a modern and distinctly American aesthetic, Shakertown at Pleasant Hill outside Harrodsburg promoted the Shaker village as an agrarian retreat. Canterbury Shaker Village nurtured a personality cult that formed around the surviving Shaker sisters in residence. How site administrators understood their missions affected decisions concerning the restoration and interpretation of the villages. While the Shakers had shaped their villages in accordance with their religious beliefs, the various Shaker village administrators tailored these compounds to fit more secular agendas.

Placing the various restorations within their historic contexts helps explain how differing interpretations of the Shakers and the Shaker legacy were imposed on each site.[5] When set against the backdrop of the postwar *pax Americana* and the economic, social, and political circumstances of the 1950s and 1960s, the restorations offer insight into how some Americans, both individually and collectively, negotiated transformative events in the life of the nation, whether it was the Cold War, the red scare, the civil rights movement, or the nuclear arms race. During these years, Americans also celebrated the Civil War centennial and scored important victories for historic preservation, including the creation of the Historic Preservation Act of 1966 and the success of the National Trust for Historic Preservation following its establishment in 1949.[6] In many respects, the preservation and interpretation of Shaker villages functioned to ameliorate national anxieties associated with change.

HANCOCK SHAKER VILLAGE

The effort to preserve Hancock Shaker Village began shortly after the death in 1957 of Eldress Frances Hall, the leader of the sect's central ministry and one of the last of that community's believers. Eldress Emma B. King, a Canterbury, New Hampshire, resident and Hall's successor, decided in 1959 to close and sell Hancock Village, just as the Shaker leadership had disposed of moribund Shaker villages in the past. In July 1960, a group of preservationists headed by Amy Bess Miller, the wealthy wife of the editor of the local *Berkshire Eagle* newspaper, bought the village.[7] Robert Kimball, a member of Miller's coterie who worked at the *Berkshire Eagle* and was active in the Berkshire Art Association, claimed that he and his friends were suffering from "Shaker fever."[8] Miller, who earlier had furnished her family home with Shaker furniture because of its "simple lines, durable construction, and pleasant finish," described herself as "more than just ordinarily enthusiastic; I was totally absorbed, and spent the years from 1937 to 1959 in pursuit of Shaker history and artifacts."[9]

Miller surrounded herself with an impressive group. Unlike John Williams, who largely filled his board with wealthy friends and social connections, with the help of the Faith and Ted Andrews, Miller sought out and included experts and professionals from the museum field, academia, and the burgeoning field of historic preservation.[10] Robert O. Parks, the director of the Smith College Art Museum, was one of the founding members of the board, and S. Laine Faison, director of the Williams College Museum of Art, also was involved. Similarly, Dorothy Miller, a curator at the Museum of Modern Art in New York City, who was married to the Index of American Design's Holger Cahill and had been interested in Shaker materials since the 1930s, was eager to participate in the project. Professor David Potter, Coe Professor of American History at Yale and former chair of the university's American Studies Program, was interested in the Shakers from an American Studies perspective and had established ties to the Andrewses while they were at Yale. Carl Rollins, printer emeritus to Yale University, had similarly become acquainted with Ted Andrews during his sojourn in

New Haven and may have been interested in the Shakers because of the time he spent in a utopian community in his youth.[11] Philip Guyol, director of the New Hampshire Historical Society, and Frank Spinney, director of Old Sturbridge Village, in Sturbridge, Massachusetts, brought professional public history experience to the undertaking.[12]

The Andrewses saw in Amy Bess Miller's organization a new institutional backer that would value their collection and expertise. In their familiar pattern of flattering potential patrons and seeking support for their ongoing projects, they curried favor with the editor's wife. In November 1959, they wrote to her, "For us to give over this material and see it properly installed at Hancock would be the realization of an ideal."[13] Although Miller viewed them as longtime friends, at this late point in their careers she also recognized them as controversial figures. Bert Little, the director of the Society for the Preservation of New England Antiquities and a noted collector of American folk art, told Miller that Hancock would be the Andrewses' last chance because they were "on the outs with so many people."[14] Miller similarly recognized that some individuals within the Shaker community nursed grievances against the antique dealers. To Dorothy Miller, Amy Bess Miller described the pair as "two extremely difficult people—supper [sic] critical and suppr [sic] emotional."[15]

Miller was able to assemble an august board for her endeavor because of the popular interest in the Shakers but also because the Berkshires had long been a retreat for cosmopolitan sophisticates with interest in arts and culture.[16] Notable earlier residents included writers Herman Melville and Edith Wharton, sculptor Daniel Chester French, and diplomat Joseph Hodges Choate. Although picturesque, beautiful, and rural, the area is easily accessible from both Boston and New York. *Time* magazine described Hancock's supporters as being "made up largely of well-off summer residents of the Berkshires."[17] The new nonprofit organization complemented other institutions already established in the region dedicated to the promotion of classical music, gardening, drama, dance, and sculpture.[18]

Miller's group recognized from the beginning that its new undertaking would compete with John Williams's Shaker Museum. Early on, Donald Miller, the publisher of the *Berkshire Eagle* and Amy Bess Miller's brother-in-law, with Lawrence K. Miller, the organizer's husband, met with Robert Meader to discuss the possibility of Williams moving his institution to Hancock.[19] Williams made it clear that he was not interested in merging his institution into the new effort or relocating his collection but eventually agreed to serve on the board of the upstart institution located on the other side of the state border.[20]

Early in the process, Hancock's supporters also sought assistance for their endeavor from foundations and other organizations. Individuals not suffering from Shaker fever, however, offered little encouragement. The Rockefeller Foundation, through Blanchette Ferry Rockefeller, who herself was a collector of Shaker furniture, declined to support the new institution because Charles Fahs, the foundation's humanities expert, opined that the project required an endowment as well as continuing expenses for maintenance and staffing, and that an institution focused solely on the Shakers would prove difficult to sustain in the long term.[21] Walter Muir Whitehill, the architectural historian and nonprofit administrator best known for his service as director of the Boston Athenæum, was damning in his reaction. He characterized the effort to save the village as "an effort in antiquarian piety, engaged in preserving what is at best a footnote to American history." He continued, "The Shaker crafts are aesthetically pleasing, yet I see nothing in the Shaker way of life that has value for present or future Americans."[22] Richard Howland, the president of the National Trust for Historic Preservation, wrote that he was sorry he could offer the group only "good advice and cold comfort." Howland noted that "funds for a project that involves acquisition and restoration of so many buildings, their suitable furnishing, operation and maintenance, is beyond the scope of most privately incorporated philanthropic corporations." However, he indicated the Commonwealth of Massachusetts might be willing to offer some public support since "tourism is big business as the Chamber of Commerce boys say."[23]

In their restoration of the Hancock compound, Miller, the Andrewses, and the museum's board were guided by the conflation of Shakerism and modern design outlined in chapters 1 and 2, which the Andrewses were implicated in creating. A fundraising pamphlet written by Ted Andrews explained the project using adjectives suggestive of simplicity and balance, indicating how important visual qualities were to the group's vision. "The property will be restored," the text contends, "to give the village its traditionally neat and orderly appearance. The purity and quiet dignity of Shaker architecture . . . are among the Community's greatest assets."[24]

William Winter's photographs of the 1920s and 1930s, which by 1960 had been reproduced repeatedly and had also influenced subsequent photographers, were central to how the group believed the village should look. At approximately the same time that they were working to reshape the Hancock Shaker Village into a tourist attraction, Faith and Edward Deming Andrews wrote, "The Shaker artisans were content with their concept of what was satisfactory in form: perfect squares, oblongs, circles, arches and ovals, straight lines and gentle curves, subdued colors and durable materials. The standard was simplicity but in elevating simplicity to the plane of refinement of line and grace of form, they achieved a distinct style, complete in itself, an ultimate accomplishment so pure that the product had almost the quality of an abstraction."[25] This evocative text indicates that the Andrewses had mastered the diction of modernism and of art history, yet also demonstrates that their understanding of Shaker material culture had become abstracted from the actual historicity and corporality of the buildings, objects, and people. They became so accomplished at marketing their conception of Shaker furniture as art that their language no longer referred to the reality of the items they were discussing. They seem to be describing Winter's contrived photographic constructs, rather than the actual spaces the Shakers inhabited.

The nonprofit's administrators, including Ted Andrews who served as its curator, did what they could to reshape the compound according to their shared vision of how an ideal Shaker village should look. Linoleum flooring was taken up and walls were removed.[26] Framed portraits and lithographs were taken down from the walls. Objects manufactured in the world outside the village were banished from view. Rooms that were to be opened to the public were furnished with material from the Andrewses' collection, which had been promised to and then withdrawn from the Yale University Art Gallery. These changes perpetuated an aesthetically pleasing and artistically gratifying, albeit anachronistic and questionable, representation of the Shakers (figs. 6.1–6.2).

The Church Family's brick dwelling house, furnished with objects from the Andrewses' personal collection, was the first space opened to the public.[27] Sympathetic journalists and connoisseurs of art and architecture from across the country repeated the aesthetic judgments concerning the Shakers that they had heard from curators, commentators, and scholars over the course of the previous thirty years. In describing the Hancock project for the *New York Times* in 1961, Richard Shanor noted that the "typical Shaker living quarters . . . will show graphically why the clean, simple Shaker look

FIGURE 6.1. William F. Winter, Jr., "Dining Room, Shaker Church Family Main Dwelling House," 1931. This 1931 photograph of the dining room of the Church Family dwelling house in Hancock illustrates a space inhabited by living members of the sect and decorated with framed wall hangings and linoleum on the floor. Courtesy Library of Congress, Prints & Photographs Division, Historic American Buildings Survey (HABS MASS, 2-HANC, 4—24).

FIGURE 6.2. Church Family dwelling house, dining room interior, Hancock Shaker Village, after restoration. Public spaces at the Hancock Shaker Village were staged to resemble William Winter's spare photographic compositions. Courtesy Louis Nelson.

is so admired by modern decorators. Their craftsmen designed with function uppermost, built well and never spoiled their straight-grained maple or pine with unnecessary weight, ornament or finishes."[28] More recent scholarship, notably by Susan L. Buck, contradicts this modernist understanding by documenting the range of paints Shakers used to augment their furniture.[29]

The village's connection to modernism was further undergirded by its exhibition and eventual acquisition of Shaker objects owned by Charles Sheeler. In 1962, after they had been included in an exhibition entitled *The Shakers: Their Arts and Crafts* at the Philadelphia Museum of Art, Hancock borrowed fifteen pieces from the artist including tables, case pieces, and a swivel chair.[30] These items had the extraordinary distinction of having provenances that linked them both to the sect and to one of the iconic figures in American modern art. Moreover, some objects had the further benefit of having been recorded by the Index of American Design and included in Sheeler's paintings.

Wilbur Glover, the director of Hancock Shaker Village, and the Andrewses conferred with the artist and with Edith Halpert to plan an exhibit meant to include Shaker furniture and Sheeler's paintings.[31] This exhibition was intended to establish a relationship between Sheeler and the museum in hopes of bringing down the asking price for his collection. The show never came to fruition, however, probably because of inadequate security and environmental controls within the new museum's historic buildings.

Miller subsequently negotiated with Halpert, who had served as Sheeler's agent through much of his career, to purchase the artist's Shaker furniture. Miller found Halpert to be "a most uncozy woman" but desired the furniture, which she found to be "very fine" and possessed important associations.[32] After Sheeler's death, the museum sent his widow $10,000 in two installments for his tables, chairs, chests, and other Shaker artifacts.[33]

The Andrewses eventually built on the research that had gone into planning Hancock's abortive exhibition to mount a show of Sheeler paintings and Shaker furniture at the Albany Institute of History and Art in the spring of 1965. The Albany show featured furniture and objects from both the Shaker Museum in Old Chatham and Hancock Shaker Village, including items the latter institution had recently acquired from the painter.[34] The show also featured both Sheeler's paintings *On a Shaker Theme* (fig. 5.20) from 1956, which previously had been in Robert Parks's exhibition at the

Smith College Museum of Art in 1960, and the less abstract *Shaker Build-ings* from 1934 (fig. 6.3).[35] These works were inspired by the Church Fam-ily laundry and machine shop at Hancock Shaker Village and specifically linked the restored village with modern American painting.[36] In association with this exhibition, the Andrewses published an article entitled "Sheeler and the Shakers" in the journal *Art in America*.[37] Although mounted else-where because of security and environmental concerns, this exhibition pro-duced by the curator of Hancock Shaker Village cemented the relationship between modernism and the site.

Between 1965 and 1968, Hancock Shaker Village restored the 1826 round stone barn on the property, completing a task that had been on its agenda from the start (fig. 6.4). This project was spearheaded by the popular artist and illustrator Eric Sloane, whom one biographer called "the undisputed master of preindustrial Americana," and underwritten by Great Barrington summer residents Frederick and Carrie Regina Sperry Beinecke, philan-thropists whose wealth was derived from S. & H. Green Stamps.[38] Sloane,

FIGURE 6.3. Charles Sheeler, *Shaker Buildings*, 1934, tempera and graphite on gesso panel, 25.1 x 35.2 cm (9⅞ x 13⅞ in.). When displayed at the Albany Institute of Art and History in 1965, Sheeler's painting, inspired by the Church Family machine shop at Hancock, linked the preserved village to the American modernist tradition. Courtesy Chrysler Museum of Art, Norfolk, VA, Gift of an Anonymous Donor, 80.224.

who had studied at Yale University and the Art Students League, produced multiple portraits of the Shaker barn and included a drawing, an oil painting entitled *Round Stone Barn*, and a schematic diagram of it in his 1966 book *An Age of Barns* in which he also described round barns as "the first American 'Modern Architecture.'"[39] Hancock's historic agricultural structure formally resembled round and curved structures designed in the middle of the twentieth century by innovative American architects including Richard Neutra, Buckminster Fuller, and Frank Lloyd Wright.[40] Sloane's painting of the barn, which he completed at about this time, is reminiscent of Sheeler's work both in the manner in which the subject is composed of juxtaposed geometric forms and by its reverence for Shaker subject matter as a manifestation of praiseworthy historic American values.[41]

FIGURE 6.4. Eric Sloane, *Round Stone Barn*, ca. 1966, oil on panel, 71.2 x 61 cm (28 x 24 in.). This painting of the Hancock round barn by Eric Sloane, which appeared in Sloane's *An Age of Barns* (New York: Funk and Wagnalls, 1966), 65, is reminiscent of a Charles Sheeler painting in both its interest in geometric form and its appropriation of Shaker subject matter. Courtesy the Estate of Eric Sloane and the Gallery @ Weather Hill Farm, Collection of Drs. James and Elizabeth Mauch.

The barn restoration gained national attention and cemented the site's status as the home of modernist antecedents.[42] In *Harper's Magazine,* the influential art historian Russell Lynes repeated a familiar theme. He suggested the barn was "a characteristic model of Shaker efficiency, beautiful in its simplicity and the sophistication of its concept and structure."[43] In the *New Yorker,* the journalist Janet Malcolm went further in her admiration by writing, "The recently restored round stone barn is in itself well worth the trip. As one enters it, one has the same feeling of being in the presence of a great architect that one has on entering the Guggenheim."[44]

SHAKERTOWN AT PLEASANT HILL

Hancock Shaker Village thus served as a site through which the educated northeastern elite of Massachusetts and New York constructed a modernist and nationalist genealogy to challenge the continental aesthetics of European modernism.[45] At Shakertown at Pleasant Hill, outside Harrodsburg, Kentucky, the circumstances were different. Rather than being preserved for aesthetic and historical purposes, residents of Harrodsburg worked to preserve the Shaker village for the economic impact it could have on its surroundings.

James L. Isenberg, a third-generation American of German Jewish ancestry born in 1881, set the trajectory for how the Shaker village in Mercer County, Kentucky, would be developed and interpreted. Isenberg was a member of a cohort that historian Richard D. Starnes has identified as southern "business progressives who envisaged tourism as a valuable avenue for growth."[46] As the owner of a dry-goods emporium, Isenberg understood that tourists brought dollars into the local economy and that, once spent in the community, those dollars benefited individuals not directly involved in tourism. Between the 1910s and the early 1930s, Isenberg organized a broad range of constituencies to create Kentucky's Pioneer Memorial State Park, which drew travelers with a federally funded monument, a reconstructed settlers' stockade, and a chapel housing the log cabin in which Abraham Lincoln's parents had been married.[47] Isenberg rose to statewide prominence through his success with the park, serving on the statewide Kentucky Progress Commission, a government agency dedicated to promoting tourism, as well as being appointed director of the Kentucky State Fair by Governor Ruby Laffoon.[48]

Isenberg also organized a group he called the Shaker Association, made up of approximately fifteen local residents. This group purchased property within the former Shaker village and established an early museum of Shaker relics.[49] As a proud resident of Harrodsburg and a promoter of local history, Isenberg furthermore developed a collection of Shaker items. When artists from the Index of American Design, including Lon Cronk, William Paul Childers, and George Vezolles, ventured to Harrodsburg in 1937 and 1938, they recorded architectural features and objects that they identified as being owned by Isenberg and C. B. Sullivan, the village's primary landowner (figs. 6.5–6.6).[50]

FIGURE 6.5. William Paul Childers, *Shaker Medicine Chest*, ca. 1937, watercolor, graphite, and pen and ink on paperboard, 30.6 x 25 cm (12¹⁄₁₆ x 9¹³⁄₁₆ in.). When Childers drew this medicine chest, the Index of American Design recorded that it was owned by Isenberg and Sullivan. Courtesy the Index of American Design, National Gallery of Art, Washington, DC, 1943.8.13490.

FIGURE 6.6. Lon Cronk, *Shaker Rocking Chair*, ca. 1938, watercolor, pen and ink, and graphite on paper, 36.5 x 30.4 cm (14⅜ x 11¹⁵⁄₁₆ in.). When Cronk drew this rocking chair, the Index of American Design recorded that it was owned by Isenberg and Sullivan. Courtesy the Index of American Design, National Gallery of Art, Washington, DC, 1943.8.16630.

Onward Kentucky Movement

In 1935, James Isenberg recognized the economic potential of the Shaker legacy and established a statewide nonprofit corporation, called the "Onward Kentucky Movement," with headquarters at Harrodsburg's abandoned

Shaker village. This New Deal–era nonprofit corporation was meant to coordinate the production and sale of goods marketed under the "Shakertown Countryside Industries" brand (fig. 6.7).[51]

Isenberg hoped that the Onward Kentucky Movement would bring federal money into Kentucky, just as he had succeeded in convincing Congress to have the Department of War erect Harrodsburg's National Pioneer Monument in 1934. The new project would tap resources offered by the Department of Labor, the Federal Housing Administration, and the Public Works Administration to jumpstart the economy and create what Isenberg termed "permanent substantial recovery for Kentucky." The visionary businessman believed home industries located in Kentucky that sold in both local and national markets would benefit the people of the state because money would thus be retained rather than "going out of the community." Cooperative communities for the impoverished, such as those created by the Department of the Interior's Subsistence Homesteads Divisions and Resettlement Administration, also factored into Isenberg's plan, with the first

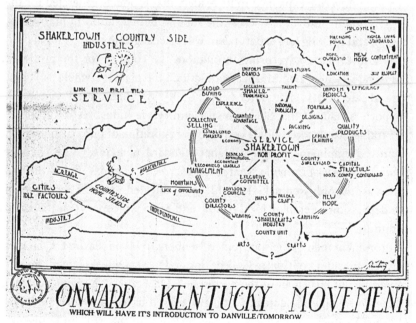

FIGURE 6.7. "Onward Kentucky Movement," 1935. This graphic illustrating the mission and function of James L. Isenberg's Shakertown Countryside Industries appeared in Danville's *Kentucky Advocate*, May 23, 1935.

such initiative to be located at the former Shaker village in Mercer County.[52] Isenberg claimed that he had federal approval to locate subsequent homesteads in Danville and Versailles, Kentucky.[53]

Under this plan, individuals across the state would produce smoked meats, textiles, needlework, canned food, and a variety of arts and crafts.[54] A "supervisory unit" located at Shakertown would distribute raw materials raised in Kentucky to trained crafts workers, assure uniform quality of the finished products, and coordinate the sale and marketing of finished goods.[55] The cost of administration would be shared among participants across the state, while the corporation would be managed by a board made up of locally selected representatives.

All products of the cooperative nonprofit were to be sold under the "Shakertown Countryside Industries" brand and carry an image of a Shaker woman in a bonnet carrying a torch with the word "L I F T" emanating like rays of light (see fig. 6.7).[56] This word was meant to convey economic uplift but also indicated cooperative activity since the word was an acronym formed from the first letters of the phrase "Link into Firm Ties."[57] The *Kentucky Advocate* explained to its readers that products generated for the corporation by individuals across the state would be "uniform in formula, design, and packing and expert talent will be engaged to gain national publicity and to place advertising throughout the country for the proposed industry."[58] Isenberg optimistically described the plan as a whole as "a better and safer way to march our people on the way to financial recovery."[59] Supporters claimed that Shakertown Countryside Industries would result in a trained labor force, home ownership, restoration of purchasing power, improved employment, and a higher standard of living.[60] The *Danville Daily Messenger* of Danville, Kentucky, described Isenberg's Shaker-themed vision as "the only Kentucky-born idea promulgated since the beginning of the depression to employ local people and restore prosperity in the small communities."[61]

Prominent men of the state joined Isenberg in his endeavor. Dr. Charles J. Turck, president of Centre College, located in Danville, assumed the role of permanent chairman of the nonprofit.[62] Dr. Frank L. McVey, president of the University of Kentucky, similarly served as a vice chairman of the Onward Kentucky Movement.[63] James Speed, a journalist from Louisville, served as another vice chairman. Speed had previously published an article in Louisville's *Herald-Post* promoting the role of the Historic American

Buildings Survey in documenting Shakertown as a site for tourist interest (fig. 6.8).[64] The Onward Kentucky board was filled out by civic leaders and men of affairs from cities throughout Kentucky, including Lexington, Versailles, Louisville, Somerset, Stanford, and Lancaster.

Onward Kentucky chose the image of a Shaker as its brand and selected Shakertown as the location of the nonprofit's headquarters because the celibate sect had a reputation for producing quality goods and because their philosophy of shared property and communal effort for the good of everyone within the society resonated with the organization's New Deal philosophy. Frances Jewell McVey, the wife of the university president, served as the organization's mouthpiece for this vision of the sect.[65] At an Onward Kentucky meeting held at the University of Kentucky, she gave a presentation entitled "Quaint Shakertown."[66] In this lecture, McVey emphasized the success of the sect's cooperative economic undertakings and the beauty of

FIGURE 6.8. Theodore Webb, "Shaker East Family Dwelling House, Shakertown, Mercer County, KY," February 1934. This Historic American Buildings Survey photograph was published in Louisville's *Herald-Post* to accompany an article by James Speed about the federal agency's efforts to document the Shaker village and how it could lead to regional heritage tourism. Courtesy Library of Congress, Prints & Photographs Division, Historic American Buildings Survey (HABS KY, 84-SHAKT, 1–1).

the remaining structures in the Shaker village outside of Harrodsburg.[67] In an earlier publication, appearing in the boosterist *Kentucky Progress Magazine,* McVey had written that "[Shaker] cattle were famous throughout the land. . . . The women . . . were excellent cooks and their preserves, jellies and pickles were as renowned as were the farm products of the men."[68] Revealing a regional bias, the author opined that the Mercer County Shakertown "lacked a certain austerity found sometimes among Shakers," perhaps "because of the topography of the land or the temperament of the people."[69] Isenberg's Onward Kentucky project, like many New Deal recovery efforts, carried with it overtones of nativism and an early twentieth-century privileging of the needs of white Protestant Americans. The group's choice of a Shaker sister as its logo thus not only spoke of cooperative action and economic development but also suggested a basis in the Weberian Protestant work ethic and in a regional, historically grounded, Anglo-American identity.

Isenberg's vison for a market of consumer goods produced in Kentucky assumed physical form in the Onward Kentucky Exposition held at the state capitol in Frankfort on June 5–7, 1936. This event, which one newspaper account called a "miniature world's fair," drew displays from the majority of the state's counties.[70] Supported by organizations ranging from the Frankfort Ministerial Association to the Lexington Board of Commerce, the exposition was buoyed by Governor Benjamin "Happy" Chandler, who declared the scheduled dates "Onward Kentucky Days."[71] The event brought together samples from across the state so organizers could find the products best suited for broad marketing and manufacturing.[72] The exhibit of "Cookery Arts," for example, included jams, jellies, fruit cake, candies, confections, pickles, relishes, farm-made sorghum, water-ground meal, lye, hominy, and beaten biscuits.[73] Rugs, quilts, and furniture were similarly displayed. The gathering culminated with the governor auctioning off the one hundred best country cured hams, raising a total of $1,321 for the organization.[74]

As a result of Isenberg's enthusiasm for Shakertown, in 1936 Daniel Mac-Hir Hutton, the editor of the *Harrodsburg Herald* and one of Isenberg's close associates in the Kentucky Pioneer Memorial Association, produced a guidebook to the Shaker village.[75] Entitled *Old Shakertown and the Shakers,* this seventy-two-page illustrated pamphlet was printed by the press of the *Harrodsburg Herald.*[76] Providing an overview of the site and illustrated with both historic photographs and nineteenth-century engravings,

Hutton's brochure went through numerous editions and remained in print for decades.

In August 1936, Isenberg was struck ill and taken to the Norton Infirmary in Louisville.[77] His obituary in the *Lexington Herald* indicated that the strain of producing the Onward Kentucky exposition had brought on his physical collapse.[78] He suffered a number of relapses, never recovered, and passed away on October 31, 1938. Without his charismatic and effective leadership, Onward Kentucky ground to a halt and the vision of Mercer County's Shakertown as an economic driver soon faded.

Shakertown "Restored"

Isenberg's efforts, however, bore fruit nearly a quarter century later when Jane Bird Hutton, the boosterist newspaper editor of the *Harrodsburg Herald* and the daughter of Isenberg's closest associate, drew Barry Bingham, the wealthy philanthropic editor of the *Louisville Courier-Journal*, into a movement to consider anew economic development strategies for Shakertown at Pleasant Hill.[79] Bingham, in turn, brought Earl Wallace, an influential petroleum executive and Wall Street financier, into the project.[80]

A self-described "history buff" who dismissed the Shakers as "misfits and eccentrics," Wallace nevertheless fell in love with Shakertown because it offered "an oasis" of peace from the transformations Kentucky was undergoing in the middle of the twentieth century.[81] Under Wallace's leadership, a nonprofit organization was formed in 1961 composed of many of the state's most prominent families. In 1963, the group secured an economic development loan from the U.S. Department of Commerce to help them transform the Shaker village into an economic engine for the region.[82]

Although the Shakers themselves had exploited industrial technologies, Wallace envisioned a preindustrial, premodern village. He hired James Cogar, who previously had worked at Colonial Williamsburg, the nation's leading purveyor of picturesque history, to implement that vision.[83] Besides having significant experience at Williamsburg, Cogar was a Kentucky native and held a B.A. from the University of Kentucky and an M.A. from Harvard University.[84] Cogar, in turn, brought in Peter A. G. Brown, director of preservation services for Colonial Williamsburg, to confer on how to configure the site to realize its maximum potential as a tourist attraction.[85]

Wallace and Cogar's plan, which was implemented beginning in 1965, focused on erasing late nineteenth- and early twentieth-century modifications from the landscape. Utility lines were buried, Victorian porches were removed, and missing architectural elements were replaced. Guest rooms, conference facilities, and simple craft shops were created within an Arcadian setting.[86] Just as John D. and Abby Aldrich Rockefeller maintained Basset Hall as a residence at Colonial Williamsburg, Bingham and his wife established an abode in a renovated building on the property at Pleasant Hill.

Wallace and Cogar reshaped Pleasant Hill into a bucolic landscape undisturbed by the strife, conflict, and technological transformations of postwar America. Even though the Shakers were technological innovators, the site's twentieth-century stewards chose not to restore or interpret the village's water-powered fulling and sawmills. According to Cogar, Pleasant Hill would be attractive for conferences because large organizations demanded a quiet place away from the rush and noise of metropolitan areas for study and reflection.[87] The fact that the Shakers had not relied on slave labor to support their agricultural endeavors allowed Shakertown at Pleasant Hill to celebrate Kentucky's antebellum, preindustrial society without broaching the fractious issue of slavery in the midst of a national debate over segregation.[88]

Following James Isenberg's lead in understanding heritage tourism as a springboard for economic development, many Mercer County residents, including Hutton, saw a direct connection between the work at Pleasant Hill and efforts to enrich the region.[89] In 1961, the *Lexington Leader* noted, "Kentucky's Shakertown can easily become as famous as Virginia's Williamsburg, Ford's Dearborn Village and the comparatively few other restorations of this kind. The successful preservation and operation of Shakertown will bring to Lexington and other central Kentucky cities many, many times the amount of money they invest in this campaign."[90] Similarly, that same year the Kentucky Travel Council chairman Alex Chamberlain endorsed the Shakertown project "both for its economic advantages to the Commonwealth as a major tourist attraction and as an important cultural agency of the region."[91] In response to the news that the Shakertown restoration had received a government Economic Development Administration loan, the *Harrodsburg Herald* predicted that the village would develop into a "tourist attraction that will pull in at least 150,000 people a year and provide jobs for more than 280 people."[92]

Although Pleasant Hill was successful as a tourist attraction, some critics believed that its research and interpretation lacked intellectual rigor. In

1964, for example, Robert F. W. Meader, the director of the Shaker Museum at Old Chatham, New York, wrote, "Pleasant Hill seems to be a gung-ho for the fast buck and the superficialities. They are plowing ahead at a great rate without either researching what they are doing or being interested in doing so. . . . I have little use for Cogar, and find that use decreasing. He's just a shallow tourist-maniac, for my money, interested in the externals and without much of an idea what to look for."[93] Meader's comments may reflect professional enmity, but they also highlight the endemic concern for balancing historical research and interpretation with commercial exploitation of a village that is both a historic site and a tourist attraction.

CANTERBURY SHAKER VILLAGE

Whereas the preservationists at Hancock and Pleasant Hill created museums from moribund Shaker villages, in Canterbury, New Hampshire, a museum was established while Shakers still inhabited the village. The surviving Shaker sisters became a central attraction of the site. Motivated in part by economic necessity and also because they had seen John Williams's success in educating the public about the history of their sect, the eleven remaining Shaker sisters actively welcomed visitors to the village beginning in the 1950s.[94] In 1964, Bertha Lindsay bragged to Julia Neal that Canterbury had welcomed more than three thousand visitors from thirty-eight states and twenty-eight countries.[95]

Charles "Bud" Thompson, a non-Shaker in the sisters' employ, played a central role in opening the village to the public. A folk singer from the Boston neighborhood of Roslindale, Thompson was enamored of Shaker music as it had come to be popularized by the Shaker Village Work Camp and others. He arrived in Canterbury in the late 1950s seeking new songs.[96] The Shakers befriended Thompson and hired him as a factotum and man of general purposes.[97] He lived in the village with his wife and family and helped the Shaker sisters maintain the facility, escorted them to business meetings, drove them to church, and performed other tasks.[98] Over time, Thompson acquired authority and responsibility until he was called, at various times, the village's curator and director of interpretation, among other honorifics.[99]

In 1960, Thompson established a museum of Shaker objects in the village's meetinghouse.[100] Next to items created in the village, he displayed artifacts that had been brought to Canterbury as other villages folded. In describing the installation in 1961, the *New Hampshire Sunday News* reported, "Hundreds of items, representative of Shaker life in years long past, have been gathered from many of the former villages. They are on display daily, except Sunday and Monday."[101]

Although the Canterbury Shakers had allowed visitors to the village since the first half of the nineteenth century, Thompson's museum marked a turning point in the life and history of the community. With Thompson's help, the residents of Canterbury grew increasingly aware of the village's potential as a tourist attraction. The Shaker sisters themselves, particularly Marguerite Frost, Lillian Phelps, Aida Elam, and Bertha Lindsay, worked with Thompson by incorporating tours into their communal work. By 1966, the Shakers were reporting approximately four thousand visitors annually.[102]

For many visitors to Canterbury, the surviving Shakers were more of an attraction than the museum or the village itself. These women, however, were not representative of the sect's historical mainstreams. Although they practiced celibacy and lived communally, their lives differed in many respects from those of their institutional predecessors. Notably, they lived in a village that was much more homogenous in terms of age and gender than most previous Shaker settlements had been. They were no longer engaged in large-scale agriculture or manufacturing. They had even stopped performing the sect's characteristic dances during worship. Alex Ghiselin, writing in the *Boston Globe*, appraised the situation by concluding that the village was "not yet the museum it will become, but no longer a community, really."[103]

Yet, in the eyes of many of their admirers, these last residents epitomized the Shaker experience (fig. 6.9).[104] The sisters became central to the interpretation of Canterbury Shaker Village, and a cult of personality quickly formed around them. Repeat visitors to the site curried favor with their beloved Shakers, who on occasion gave spiritual and personal guidance. Regular visitors competed with each other to see who could gain greatest access to the private spaces of the dwelling house.[105]

For the Shaker sisters themselves, the role of the village—and their roles within the village—remained largely unchanged. Canterbury was their home first and a tourist attraction second, even after the establishment of Thompson's museum. It was also the backdrop against which they observed and applied Shaker traditions and beliefs as they understood them at the

FIG. 6.9. Miller/Swift photographers, "Shaker Church Family Trustees' Office," 1970. The Historic American Buildings Survey photographed Bertha Lindsay and Lillian Phelps on the porch of the Trustee's Office as part of their effort to document the Canterbury Shaker Village. Courtesy Library of Congress, Prints & Photographs Division, Historic American Buildings Survey (HABS, NH, 7-CANT, 5—4).

time.[106] As historian Stephen J. Stein has shown, Shaker belief was not static: the group's theology had shifted and transformed over the centuries, and the beliefs the last sisters at Canterbury held were but one temporally grounded version of the faith.[107] As long as they were alive, though, their personal experiences, religious worldviews, and "serene presence" were what mattered most to the steady stream of visitors who returned time and again to interact with them in their residential setting.[108] The ways in which they lived and worshipped—and, perhaps most importantly, their first-person accounts of their lives and beliefs—trumped all non-Shaker interpretations of Shakerism and the Shaker past at Canterbury, no matter how nuanced, well-researched, or historically accurate.[109]

The cult of personality endured at Canterbury, in part because guides and administrators believed the focus on the village's individual residents counteracted a broader, abstracted interpretation pursued at other sites that rendered members of the faith faceless and nameless.[110] Years after the death of Ethel Hudson, the last of Canterbury's Shakers, the Canterbury tour guides reinforced perceptions of a personal connection to the sisters.[111] The gift shop stocked postcards with portraits of them. In the restored eighteenth-century dwelling house, Sister Ethel's room remains as she left it at her death.[112]

TWO LEGACIES

The ways in which these Shaker villages were interpreted to the public during their formative years as heritage sites and tourist attractions continue to influence how Americans understand the Shakers and the Shaker legacy. While Shaker architecture and material culture were presented as antecedents to American modernism in art and architecture as at Hancock, the Shakers themselves were portrayed as picturesque premodern agrarians (Pleasant Hill) and marketed as living relics (Canterbury). Visitors came away from these villages with composite impressions of the Shakers that went beyond the schematic interpretations of the sect and its legacy implemented by the site administrators and their sponsors. In collecting materials for Pleasant Hill, museum staff were drawn particularly to items that fit the modernists' interpretation of Shaker life and material culture, even when the objects did not have a Kentucky provenance. In the restoration of Hancock Shaker Village, Victorian alterations to the trustees' house were retained because Amy Bess Miller, the president of the museum's board, fondly remembered meeting there with the last Hancock sisters.[113]

To a certain extent, the outcomes at each village were a function of geography. Hancock, located in a resort community convenient to New York and Boston, was heavily influenced by major cultural institutions, including magazines like *Home and Garden* and museums such as New York's Whitney Museum of American Art and the Museum of Modern Art, and by cultural elites who were involved in international artistic movements and visual culture. Pleasant Hill, which was located in a rural agricultural region but not too far from Louisville, Lexington, and Frankfort, had access to local leaders such as Jane Bird Hutton, for whom regional economic development was a priority, as well as to urbanites like Barry Bingham and Ed Wallace, whose nostalgia for simpler times drove many of their decisions. Canterbury had the distinction of serving as the Shakers' home while simultaneously functioning as a museum. The remaining Shaker sisters shaped it in its formative years and left their enduring mark on the institution.

More broadly, however, these Shaker villages speak to larger cultural issues of the mid-twentieth century. Faith and Edward Deming Andrews, Barry Bingham, James Cogar, Jane Bird Hutton, Amy Bess Miller, Earl Wallace, Bud Thompson, and their colleagues and supporters all came to believe that the Shaker legacy was important, that Shaker villages should be preserved, and that Americans would want to visit them. The Shakers—pacifists and communitarians—resonated with them and others at a time of sweeping economic and social change. When the Shakers were presented as precursors to modernism, American culture as a whole was vindicated as being something other than crass or gauche. Shaker material culture challenged the longstanding European notion of Americans as being uncultivated vulgarians. This sect's furniture, widely recognized for its design and fine craftsmanship, was presented as proof of a distinctly American tradition in the decorative and applied arts. The reevaluation of Shaker architecture and material culture coincided with the New York School of abstract expressionism's ascendancy in the art world, and established cultural legitimacy for the United States' position as a leader on the world political stage.

When site administrators presented Shaker villages as bucolic, classless, raceless, and premodern, they were responding in part to societal anxieties about economic and social transformations. Shaker villages allowed visitors to ground themselves comfortably in a stable and unchanging past.

During this period, many Americans whose extended families might have been split by corporate relocations or rising divorce rates claimed Canterbury's surviving Shakers sisters as adoptive grandmothers.[114] Buffered from worldly affairs, living virtuous celibate lives, while seemingly financially secure, they were treated like convenient relatives whom experience-seekers could emulate and visit when they desired without being burdened by familial responsibilities.[115] The sisters projected a strong, historically grounded female identity that could not be undermined by either the new role for women posited by Helen Gurley Brown or the feminist critique of Betty Friedan's *The Feminine Mystique*. The postcards bearing their images, sold in the Canterbury gift shop, testified to their enduring value as role models.

While these Shaker villages are important as places where members of the sect lived out their communal experiment, they also have histories as museums and cultural entities. As institutions, they are significant in their own right as testaments to the ideologies and perspectives of that founding generation of curators, preservationists, and enthusiasts who, whether they realized it or not, inscribed new layers of meaning on them.

POSTSCRIPT
"BORROWED LIGHT"

....

Persistent Symptoms of Shaker Fever

Shaker fever reached a breaking point with the opening of the villages as heritage tourism sites in the middle of the 1960s. By the time that the Vietnam War, the tumultuous struggle for black equality, and the clamor of the counterculture movement traumatized the nation, the interpretive tropes that the protagonists of this volume created to describe and understand the sect were standardized, formulaic, institutionalized, and predictable. Americans broadly understood Shaker material culture to be refined, elegant, and desirable. The dance community fostered a conception of sectarian ecstatic religious release shaped by Doris Humphrey's choreography. Many individuals with a taste for folk music were able to sing from memory Joseph Brackett's "Simple Gifts" and, even if they could not name other examples, were familiar with the existence of a corpus of Shaker songs. Mainstream periodicals, government bureaucrats, and travel writers accepted and celebrated Shaker villages as sites worthy of preservation and visitation.

The flurry of innovative and transformative activity that had characterized the second third of the twentieth century subsided. Since individuals like Juliana Force, Faith and Edward Deming Andrews, and Amy Bess Miller had successfully enlisted the periodical press to publicize their activities, the Shakers no longer needed to be rediscovered; the sect existed in the national consciousness. Americans understood the Shakers to be a component of the nation's diverse historic background comparable to other quaint, slightly curious groups, like the Amish or the Moravians.

While designers, bureaucrats, curators, and preservationists in the 1930s through the 1960s had felt Shaker fever fervently, during and after the 1970s the sickness spread to a broader public who may have experienced the symptoms somewhat less intensely and for whom their predecessors had created canonical understandings and established pathways for expressing the malady's passion. Enthusiasm for Shaker history and culture was no longer an obsession of individuals or small groups but was a popular interest fostered by businesses, publications, and institutions. The later cohort of enthusiasts, who also may have been drawn to the counterculture of the 1960s and the midcentury back-to-the-land movement, found in the constructed Shaker legacy a precedent for feminism, a rejection of materialism, and an intellectual balm for the stresses of deindustrialization, national economic stagnation, and the decades of culture wars that characterized the end of the twentieth century. For a liberal, educated cognoscenti, visiting restored Shaker villages and singing about simple gifts provided comfort in an ever more uncertain world.

Although many still found beauty in the simplified forms of Shaker furniture, the religious and political contexts that made a communitarian religious organization compelling eroded. By the 1970s, the long legacy of the New Deal had faded as Lyndon Johnson's Great Society was replaced by Richard Nixon's New Federalism, which undercut a belief in group effort and led, under Ronald Reagan and the New Right, to widespread distrust of government and coordinated activity. These political ideas paralleled, and were intertwined with, changes in American religious belief. The influence of liberal Protestant denominations, including Congregationalism and Unitarianism, which have featured so prominently in this work, was replaced by the power of evangelical and conservative denominations including the Southern Baptists. The newly ascendant Christian denominations placed a greater emphasis on personal conversion and individual salvation instead of, as had the receding liberal Protestant groups, covenanted religious communities and a social gospel that sought to provide material as well as spiritual succor for all believers. Members of the new religious right found little interest in a moribund sect that celebrated a heretical female prophet, promoted family values rejecting heterosexual marriage, and encouraged communal ownership of property.

Although the foundational work of understanding and explaining the Shakers had largely been accomplished by 1970, successors to the protagonists of the preceding chapters have found support among a committed audience and persisted in presenting the sect to the public up to the present. These latter-day carriers of Shaker fever continue to be inspired by the community's furniture, music, and dance, but they have also built on the work of the popularizers who preceded them. This postscript briefly examines selected examples of how the understanding of the sect developed in the middle of the twentieth century continued to inform interpretations of Shaker furniture, Shaker music and dance, and Hancock Shaker Village. In doing so, these final pages suggest how the actions of Charles Adams, William Winter, Doris Humphrey, and their cohort continue to shape our conception of this complex pietistic sect in the twenty-first century.[1]

FURNITURE

Shaker Workshops, a business founded in 1970, has kept reproductions of the sect's furniture available to the public for almost half a century. Originally located in Concord, Massachusetts, a western suburb of Boston famed for its nineteenth-century freethinkers and Transcendentalists, the company was established by Eugene Dodd, John Cole, and Russell Beede. Dodd and Cole were both Harvard graduates who had known each other while residents of the college's Eliot House. Dodd subsequently received a doctorate in history at the University of London and served as an assistant professor at the University of California at Berkeley before joining the staff of Hancock Shaker Village as curator in 1965, a post he held for five years.[2] While at Hancock, Dodd developed a connoisseur's eye for the details of Shaker furniture but also recognized an unfulfilled desire among consumers for affordable, accurate reproductions of the sect's furnishings.[3]

Dodd reached out to Cole, who had established himself as a broker of historic homes in Massachusetts and become something of an authority on the topic. Cole offered appraisals, made suggestions on the restoration of "early houses," gave lectures on the topic, consulted with the Society for the Preservation of New England Antiquities (now Historic New England), and wrote self-promoting newspaper articles.[4] With his background in salesmanship, Cole assumed the role of president and spokesperson of Shaker Workshops.

Russell S. Beede, who graduated from Milton Academy, went to Williams College, and held an M.B.A. from Dartmouth's Tuck School, joined Dodd and Cole to assist with running the business. The scion of a prominent New England family, Beede had previously served in the navy and had worked at Price, Waterhouse & Company and the CML Group, a conglomerate specializing in leisure products.[5] Beede would subsequently serve as treasurer of Eastern Mountain Sports, an influential Boston-based retailer of camping equipment.[6]

Shaker Workshops initially created furniture to order and established a showroom in West Concord. Unlike previous furniture lines by Freda Diamond, Paul McCobb, and Kipp Stewart and Stewart MacDougall, the products of Shaker Workshops were not overtly modern designs inspired by Shaker originals. Rather, they were intended as faithful reproductions of examples made by members of the sect. In creating their product line, the company drew on Dodd's curatorial experience working in the collection at Hancock Shaker Village, which included many pieces selected and gathered by Faith and Ted Andrews. Cole explained to the *Boston Globe,* "You just can't improve on perfection."[7] Shaker Workshops offered desirable classic Shaker forms, many of which had been recorded by the Index of American Design, including slat-back chairs with seats of woven tape, rocking chairs, trestle tables, drop-leaf tables, sewing chests with drawers, candlestands, benches, towel racks, band boxes, and peg rails that could be installed on interior domestic walls.

Dodd, Cole, and Beede took advantage of inexpensive vacant industrial spaces in New England to establish workshops that could produce affordable reproductions. Initially, the furniture was manufactured by a craftsman in New Hampshire before the firm established its own shop in Tyngsboro, Massachusetts.[8] Subsequently, the firm rented space on the fourth floor of a building in Gardner, Massachusetts, a historic center of furniture production. At that point, Cole described the space as "really just a very high-powered, super basement workshop."[9]

Quickly, the firm established a mail-order trade in kits that consumers could assemble at home. In doing so, Shaker Workshops was participating in a flourishing business model of the time, which also included firms such as Yield House of North Conway, New Hampshire; Cohasset Colonials of Cohasset, Massachusetts; the Bartley Collection of Lake Forest, Illinois; and Furn-a-Kit, Inc., of Rutherford, New Jersey. Writing in the *New York Times*

in 1972, arts and culture columnist Rita Reif described furniture kit manufacturing, which had blossomed since World War II, as a "multi-million
dollar industry."[10] Assembling factory-made parts into furniture provided
personal satisfaction to urban and suburban consumers who wanted to
associate with artisanal forbears without having to develop skills, maintain
a workshop, or own an extensive set of tools, but also offered a budget alternative to home decorating during a decade when inflation eroded American prosperity.[11] Consumers across the country and around the world could
receive an illustrated Shaker Workshop catalogue by sending fifty cents to a
mailing address in Concord.

In marketing his furniture kits, Cole drew generously on the rhetoric
curators and enthusiasts had applied to Shaker furniture for decades. "They
[the Shakers] were such great craftsmen, and artists as well. Everything was
designed for function first, with a wonderful purity and simplicity of line,"
he told the *Boston Globe*.[12] Another journalist quoted Cole as saying, "Harmony and simplicity came naturally to the Shaker craftsmen. . . . He looked
upon the building of a chest, table, or chair as an inspired enterprise tem-
pered by functional need."[13] Tastemakers readily repeated Cole's opinions,
which by this time had become dogma. In introducing Shaker Workshops
to his North Carolina readers in the *High Point Enterprise*, interior design
columnist Carleton Varney asserted, "The proof of just how advanced the
Shakers really were shows in their furniture. Although designed in the 18th
and 19th centuries, Shaker furniture could be the brainchild of a designer
today."[14]

Shaker Workshops similarly took advantage of Dodd's previous status
as a museum curator and of the public's acceptance of Shaker furniture
as art. Shaker Workshops reproductions were sold at the Museum of Fine
Arts in Boston and at the Smithsonian Institution in Washington, DC.[15]
The firm's furniture was similarly retailed through Hancock Shaker Village; the museum at the Shaker village in Canterbury, New Hampshire; the
Shaker Museum at Old Chatham, New York; and the Fruitlands Museum in
Harvard, Massachusetts. The firm was eventually successful enough that it
opened a West Coast showroom on the common in Ross, California, fifteen
minutes north of the Golden Gate Bridge.[16]

In 1980, Richard Dabrowski, a graduate of the University of North Carolina who had also attended Massachusetts's Tabor Academy, purchased
Shaker Workshops.[17] Dabrowski had previously worked as the marketing

87

FIGURE P.1. Joe Isom, Benchcraft by Drexel Furniture Company, 1971. Drexel's Benchcraft line of Shaker-inspired furnishings was not as commercially successful as their earlier Declaration line. Reprinted from *Home Furnishings Ideas*, Spring–Summer 1972, 87, and published without objection from Meredith Corporation.

director at Woodcraft Supply, a retail company providing woodworking tools to craftsmen.[18] Under Dabrowski's leadership, the firm thrived, at least partly because interest in the Shakers was revived by Ken Burns's 1985 PBS documentary about the sect and an exhibition of Shaker design mounted in 1986 by the Whitney Museum, which subsequently was reinstalled in the Corcoran Gallery in Washington, DC.[19] In 1990, 250,000 Americans subscribed to the company's catalogue.[20] As the company's international trade expanded, it even published a catalogue in Japanese. In 1988, Dabrowski told the *Chicago Tribune* that his clientele was primarily urbanites. "In Manhattan," he said, "we have more customers than we have in whole states elsewhere."[21] At this writing, the company, with headquarters in Center Sandwich, New Hampshire, continues to supply Shaker reproductions and other themed items to eager consumers by maintaining both a retail store and an extensive website.[22]

While Shaker Workshops was manufacturing its reproduction Shaker furniture in the 1970s, the Drexel Furniture Company introduced a new line of Shaker-inspired home furnishings. Released in 1971, only a few years after discontinuation of the company's successful Declaration line, their new Benchcraft furniture attempted to bring Shaker design up to date. The cover of the spring–summer 1972 issue of *Home Furnishings Ideas,* a consumer magazine affiliated with *Better Homes and Gardens,* featured a trestle table and four spindle-back chairs with turned finials and trumpeted "Shaker Design Is New Again!" Benchcraft, although offering a less extensive repertoire of forms than Declaration, included bedroom, dining room, living room, and occasional furniture made of honey-toned pecan wood solids and veneers.[23] Advertising copywriters and interior decorating journalists claimed that Benchmark revived century-old Shaker traditions in time for the American bicentennial and used the concept of "Shaker workshops" to reassure consumers about the quality of American-made goods.[24]

The furniture itself displayed the awkward proportions, bizarre elongations, and ornamental decorations characteristic of 1970s design (fig. P.1).[25] Butterfly-shaped wooden inlays, for example, adorned the top of the suite's drop-leaf table and bed headboard. A tall lingerie chest featured a rolltop compartment for storage and a lift-up top that revealed a hidden mirror and a velvet-lined jewelry compartment hidden behind false drawer fronts.[26] Copywriters asserted that the furniture's "shapes clearly say Today, but in the Mellow mood of wood."[27] Selected accent pieces were available in "Shaker blue, red, green, and spice," reflecting ongoing curatorial research on Shaker furniture finishes but also expressing American consumers' love of color in the 1970s. Whereas Declaration had overlaid Shaker identity on Californian midcentury modern design, Benchmark, which was not identified with a particular designer or artistic team, appeared as eccentric or poorly executed Colonial Revival furniture.

Journalists tried their best to place Drexel's bizarre pseudo-Shaker furniture within a relevant cultural context for the fraught and transforming 1970s. Sarah Booth Conroy in the *Washington Post* explained that American designers were in a "permissive period" during which traditional and contemporary furniture design were converging.[28] Ellen Eschbach, a columnist for the *Chicago Tribune,* argued that "early American goes contemporary by dipping into the past" and attempted to situate Drexel's Shaker adaptations within expanding ideas of American multiculturalism that were incorporating American Indian, Hispanic, and African American colors, designs, and motifs into home furnishings.[29] The *Boston Globe* included pieces from Drexel's Benchmark collection, along with Asian ceramic planters, rectangular molded plastic furniture, and quilted vinyl window frames, in a feature claiming that during the "individualistic '70s," unique accessories should be combined to make rooms "unmistakably yours."[30]

While Shaker Workshops found success in marketing financially accessible quality reproductions to an urban cognoscenti, Drexel was less successful with its second mass-market group of Shaker-inspired furniture. Consumers did not embrace Benchcraft's modified modern Americana, and the company soon curtailed its marketing and production.[31] By the middle of the 1970s, many middle-class Americans no longer found a contrived Shaker mystique compelling. Consumers with an abiding interest in Shaker design could acquire museum-quality reproductions from Shaker Workshops, while those unfamiliar with the sect's material culture traditions had no reason to view this particular furniture line as distinctive.

MUSIC AND DANCE

Joel Cohen, an American conductor and early music impresario, was the most noteworthy promoter and interpreter of Shaker music in the decades surrounding the advent of the twenty-first century. Trained and educated at Brown and Harvard in the 1960s, for nearly four decades starting in 1969 Cohen served as the director of the Boston Camerata, a seminal early music ensemble established in the 1950s in association with the Museum of Fine Arts' musical instruments collection. Cohen's efforts with the Camerata brought the music of the Middle Ages and the Renaissance to an expanded audience in both the United States and Europe.[32] A self-described "human-ist Jew" who observes Shabbat and celebrates Passover with seders, Cohen has explored music based in a range of spiritual traditions including medi-eval European Catholicism, his own Jewish heritage, and even Christianity as practiced in Morocco.[33] Cohen's expansive musical vision, after exploring Medieval French, Provençal, and Iberian repertoires, eventually brought him to early American music and the Shaker musical idiom.

In 1992, Cohen, a voracious researcher, found publications of Shaker songs in the Harvard Music Library and became intrigued by the sect's eso-teric musical notation practices.[34] In a book published in Canterbury, New Hampshire, in the 1850s, Cohen found a Shaker hymn that, in his words, "had notation in letters rather than in musical notes, with rhythms indi-cated sometimes by the size of the letter and sometimes by a flag."[35] With his appetite whetted by this introduction to Shaker music, Cohen made a pilgrimage to the Shaker village in Sabbathday Lake, Maine, where a com-munity of eight individuals who self-identified as Shakers continued to live while maintaining a library and museum. Based on his research, Cohen told journalists that he believed that there were approximately ten thou-sand Shaker songs and that 99 percent of them existed only in manuscript form.[36] "This is a major current of American music, and it's almost com-pletely unknown," Cohen asserted to Brian Kellow of *Opera News,* thus devaluing the efforts of Aaron Copland, Jerome Count, Jacob Druckman, Harold Aks, Edward Deming Andrews, or Daniel Patterson, a folklorist at the University of North Carolina who published an extensive scholarly study of Shaker music in 1979.[37] In Maine, the residents of Sabbathday Lake tutored Cohen in Shaker performance practices, just as Ricardo Belden had taught folklorists and performers at the Shaker Village Work Camp decades earlier.

Cohen, following in the steps of Count and Bill Randle, made a record-ing of Shaker songs that was released in 1995 as *Simple Gifts: Shaker Chants and Spirituals* on Italy's Erato Record Label, but which received wide dis-tribution within the United States. Performed by Cohen's Boston Camerata and Schola Cantorum of Boston, a vocal ensemble that usually performed Renaissance sacred music, and augmented by members of the Sabbathday Lake Community, the thirty-four songs on the album culminate with "Sim-ple Gifts," which one review of the album identified as "Shakerism's great-est hit."[38] All the songs on the disc are performed without accompaniment, many of them in unison singing without harmony, and some wordlessly through the repetition of the syllable "lu." To add verisimilitude to the album, which was supported by a grant from the National Endowment for the Arts, the recordings were made within the Sabbathday Lake Meeting-house. The compact disc includes a sixty-four-page booklet of interpretive matter written by Cohen and Sister Frances Carr and printed in English, French, and German.

Because of Cohen's stature in the world of classical music, the album was broadly reviewed and primarily received warmly. Cohen gleaned richly from a field that previously had been harvested by groups including Clarice Carr's Enfield Shaker Singers, the choir of the Shaker Village Work Camp, and the Smith and Amherst College Glee Clubs under the direction of Iva Dee Hiatt. Brian Kellow, writing for *Opera News*, called Cohen's record-ing "a marvelous celebration of the human voice."[39] In the *Chicago Tribune*, Alan G. Artner used a facile trope to suggest that the recording was charac-terized by "a stark beauty directly comparable to the clean, naturally elegant lines of Shaker furniture."[40] Anthony Tommasini, of the *New York Times* called the music fascinating and noted particularly the selections featuring the untrained voices of the believers as contributing "an earthy authentic-ity" that was missing from the voices of the professional performers.[41] In the *American Record Guide*, Philip Greenfield was less laudatory. He called the recording "a long, long hour," though he noted that, as an educator, he had a "fairly nice time" with the recording because of its historical interest as documentation of a remarkable sect.[42]

Cohen's representation of Shaker music received similar praise when performed before a live audience. In November 1999, the impresario brought six members of the Sabbathday Lake community to New York to perform at Alice Tully Hall as part of Lincoln Center's Great Performers Music of the Spirit series.[43] The believers from Maine sang alongside seven professional members of the Boston Camerata and fifteen representatives of the Harvard University Choir. In the *Christian Science Monitor*, Gloria Goodale noted, using language that echoed the Andrewses' concern for the purity and potential contamination of Shaker culture, that Cohen sought to perform Shaker music "on its own terms, in a simple, nonexploitative context."[44] Bernard Holland of the *New York Times* observed that the voices of the three elderly women and three young men from Maine could not match the verve and professionalism of the other members of the ensemble, yet opined that the forty pieces comprising the evening were "very beauti-ful, the melodies original and self-sustaining, complete without harmony or instruments." The lyrics of the Shaker songs, Holland claimed, had a "hard-headed eloquence" that reminded him of the poetry of William Blake.[45]

Having established Shaker music as part of his cultural portfolio, in 2000 Cohen released a second album in the genre entitled *Golden Har-vest: More Shaker Chants and Spirituals.* Marketed by the Glissando label based in Hamburg, Germany, and including thirty-eight additional musi-cal compositions, this album built on the previous one by being recorded at the Sabbathday Lake Shaker Village and also including the residents' voices. *Golden Harvest,* however, further included members of the Harvard University Choir and Youth Pro Musica, a Boston-based children's choral group.[46] Created for an international market, this album contained lyrics transcribed in English and German as well as introductory essays by Cohen that were reprinted from the earlier compact disc in English, German, and French. In recording the second album of Shaker songs, Cohen attempted to make the recording sound less like a concert hall and more reminis-cent of a historical Shaker meeting. He hoped to introduce more "verve" to the product.[47] Just as in 1962 Jerome Count had included an interview with Ricardo Belden on the reverse of *14 Shaker Folk Songs* to signal the camp's proximity to the music's source, *The Golden Harvest* culminated with an eight-minute conversation between Cohen and the residents of Sabbathday Lake. This track served as Cohen's imprimatur, marking him as his genera-tion's leading interpreter of Shaker music.

Reviewers once again welcomed Cohen's product. Gilbert French in the *American Record Guide* called the recording "superb" and reported that it held him from beginning to end even though he did not usually appreciate folk music.[48] In *Fanfare,* Craig Zeichner concluded his enthusiastic review by writing, "If there is any justice in this world, this recording will sell mil-lions of copies and win a Grammy, and Joel Cohen will receive a citation from the President. . . . Buy this cd at once."[49]

SAARINEN'S BORROWED LIGHT

Cohen's exploration of the Shaker musical repertoire led to new choreog-raphy inspired by Doris Humphrey's *Dance of the Chosen.* Tero Saarinen, an accomplished Finnish dancer and choreographer, found Cohen's *Simple*

Gifts in a record store in France. Saarinen, who was interested in expressing spirituality through dance and who had studied in both Japan and Nepal, was familiar with Humphrey's canonical piece.[50] The Finn sent an email to Cohen in 2003. Based on that communication, Cohen and Saarinen collaborated to create a composition entitled *Borrowed Light,* whose title supposedly refers to a Shaker architectural practice of placing windows in interior walls to allow light to further penetrate into buildings.[51] The title thus could refer to Humphrey's *Dance of the Chosen* mediating between Saarinen's choreography and the sect's movements. In *Borrowed Light,* the choreographer and the musical impresario strived to create a performance in which the songs and the dance complemented each other to provide an integration of music and choreography.

Saarinen's composition, which included seven dancers and eight vocalists all clothed in black garments, emphasized religious struggle and aesthetic severity (fig. P.2). To the accompaniment of Shaker songs sung acapella by members of the Boston Camerata, the dancers of the Tero Saarinen Dance Company performed actions that spoke of redemption, rebellion, and community on a dark minimalist stage.[52] While not meant to be a literal representation of Shaker dance or worship, Saarinen's piece portrayed a religious community struggling with earthly travails while hoping to achieve transcendence.[53] The set, designed by Mikki Kunttu to resemble a monumental meeting room, employed ramps, stairs, and piercing beams of light to create a context for a struggle for religious transcendence.[54]

Although inspired by an American religious group, *Borrowed Light* was first performed in Europe, indicating Shaker fever's continually expanding reach. In 2004, Saarinen's group performed the piece seventeen times in six different European countries. Cohen felt that it received warm receptions in Germany and France, although, he claimed, Italian audiences found the choreography inadequately "decorative." Audiences were most enthusiastic in Stockholm, Helsinki, and London.[55] Writing in the British *Independent on Sunday,* Jenny Gilbert, although referencing Humphrey's choreography, called Saarinen's work a "discovery" and exclaimed, "I've not seen, or experienced, anything like it."[56] Sarah Frater described it as "something exceptional" in the London *Evening Standard.*[57]

The American debut of *Borrowed Light* unsurprisingly took place at Jacob's Pillow in Becket, Massachusetts. Founded in the Berkshires in 1931 by Ted Shawn, one of Doris Humphrey's mentors, Jacob's Pillow has

FIGURE P.2. Christopher Duggan, "Borrowed Light," 2012. Performance photograph of the Tero Saarinen production of *Borrowed Light* at the Ted Shawn Theatre, Jacob's Pillow Dance Festival. Saarinen found inspiration for his choreography in both Shaker dances and in Doris Humphrey's *Dance of the Chosen*. Courtesy Jacob's Pillow Dance Festival, Becket, MA.

prospered as a dance school and performance center within the same elevated and fecund cultural and financial milieu that supported the Berkshire Museum, the Boston Symphony's Tanglewood performances, and both John Williams's Shaker Museum and Amy Bess Miller's Hancock Shaker Village. The area around Jacob's Pillow might be described as ground zero for the original outbreak and continuing influence of Shaker fever. In presenting Saarinen's piece in 2006, Jacob's Pillow's programmers offered their audience of cognoscenti a new variation on a familiar local theme. The work was well received. Deborah Jowitt, dance critic of the *Village Voice*, hailed it as among "the best dances of the decade."[58]

Saarinen's work was subsequently reprised the next year to similar acclaim as part of the Next Wave Festival at the Brooklyn Academy of Music, in what one journalist described as "its New York premiere."[59] Jowitt described the performance as "beautiful" and Saarinen's choreography as "extraordinary."[60] In the *New York Times*, Claudia La Rocco reported that the dancers, by combining the Shaker heritage with a Finnish aesthetic, transported her imaginatively to a "stark wintry world, their severe but exultant rituals continuing in a landscape punctuated by bare trees and small, plain houses."[61]

Critics and journalists have been enthusiastic about Saarinen's *Borrowed Light* but find it challenging to describe the choreography. A writer for the Swedish News Service noted that the dancers "lurch about Frankenstein-like in their heavy boots . . . as though they are struggling to find their way through a muddy mine field."[62] Joyce Morgan, writing in Australia's *Sydney Morning Herald*, described the work as "a singular choreography that was more angular than fluid and rhythmic stomping," noting that "while the mood was of austerity and discipline, the piece built to the sort of hypnotic devotional intensity associated with the Sufi mystic whirling dervishes."[63] Rose Jennings of London's *Observer* claimed that the dancers offered the audience "a pretty rich array of obsessive-compulsive tics. They're constantly flicking their feet for reassurance, pulling their costumes up to their faces, throwing their arms self-flagellatingly over their shoulders, [and] running at impossible stairs where every step is the height of one's body."[64] Jennie Gilbert posited that Saarinen's "eccentric staggering steps stamped and slid through in flat black boots" might, in another context, be interpreted "as the result of binge drinking."[65]

HANCOCK IN THE NEW MILLENIA

While Cohen and Saarinen have succeeded in building on the twentieth-century fascination with the Shakers to produce popular recordings and works of choreography, the individuals responsible for preserving and interpreting the Shaker legacy at museums and historic sites have found the first decades of the twenty-first century challenging. In 1992, Hancock Shaker Village reported an annual visitation of approximately 75,000; by 2014, that number had shrunk to approximately 50,000.[66] Simultaneously, diminishing personal donations and government support following the financial downturn of 2008 forced the institution to cut its already meager budget, as did many nonprofit heritage sites nationwide.

In 2012, Hancock's board hired Linda Steigleder, an arts administrator from Virginia who had served previously as assistant director of the Storm King Art Center in New Windsor, New York, and CEO of the Hill-Stead Museum in Farmington, Connecticut, to place the institution on a stable financial basis.[67] Steigleder succeeded in getting the village functioning in the black after difficult years of running at a deficit and depleting the institution's limited endowment.[68] She helped to strengthen both earned and contributed income and also worked to attract enthusiastic and talented individuals to the Board of Trustees and to the site's corps of volunteers. However, she simultaneously explored the potential of merging Hancock Shaker Village with the Berkshire Museum, before deciding that combining the two struggling institutions would fail to render significant savings. Within five years of taking leadership of the Shaker site, Steigleder resigned, seeking more "flexibility" in her life.[69]

Jennifer Trainer Thompson, who succeeded Steigleder as Hancock's president in 2016, has worked to make the compound relevant to contemporary visitors. Thompson previously had been senior vice president of partnerships and external affairs at the Massachusetts Museum of Contemporary Art in nearby North Adams. An energetic cultural administrator, she had a twenty-eight-year career at MassMOCA, working in development, membership, and special events.[70] Under her leadership, the village has instituted new programs including nouveau American cuisine farm-to-table meals, popular music performances in the round barn, and even opportunities for visitors to practice yoga while surrounded by the institution's herd of goats.[71] For Thompson, the village's extraordinary architecture provides a context within which visitors can find compelling experiences. In the 1940s, Herbert Matter abstracted Shaker furniture design to the point that it became synonymous with modernism.[72] Similarly, in the age of smart phones and Netflix, Thompson and her staff have sought to use the Shaker village to emphasize "authenticity" as a salve for the alienation caused by globalization and digital media. For them, Shakerism has become conflated with life unencumbered by the aggravations and pretenses of modernity. In the second decade of the twenty-first century, Hancock Shaker Village, according to Carolyn Shapiro in the *New York Times,* seeks to make itself alluring to the people who currently reside and vacation in the Berkshires, particularly millennials.[73] By emphasizing living animals (with a particular emphasis on "babies" born on the property each spring), wholesome local food, and American secular music, rather than pietistic religion, communal property, and sexual self-denial, Thompson hopes to build site visitation and museum membership, thus allowing the institution to steward the Shaker compound into the future.

Like Tero Saarinen, Joel Cohen, and Richard Dabrowski, Thompson draws on Shaker history and culture to create experiences and products that are relevant for individuals in the twenty-first century. Each emphasizes the sect's sincerity, simplicity, authenticity, and spirituality to craft new cultural forms that are both evocative and economically viable. In doing so, however, these twenty-first-century culture workers build on, or borrow light from, the efforts of the many non-Shaker individuals of the twentieth century who similarly sought to make the Shakers significant for the generations of Americans whose lives were shaped by the New Deal, liberal Protestantism, and the Cold War.

Although many educated Americans, including second- and third-generation carriers of Shaker fever, are familiar with the contributions made by Faith and Edward Deming Andrews, even the cognoscenti are frequently unaware of the efforts of Charles Adams, William Winter, Ruth Reeves, Doris Humphrey, Deedy Hall, and Jerome Count. These overlooked figures are important for understanding why in the early decades of the twenty-first century, Americans associate a largely moribund, celibate, communitarian religious sect with such varied activities as assembling furniture from a kit, seeing Finnish dancers in black lurch about in a manner reminiscent of revenants, practicing yoga amid goats at a historic site, or listening to a musical piece by a composer of movie soundtracks written for the inauguration of the first African American president of the United States. Between 1925 and 1965, these individuals, among many others, radically reshaped the nation's understanding of the Shakers and their history, music, and material culture to serve their own cultural, economic, political, and artistic purposes. Although Shaker fever may not currently be as virulent or contagious as it was in the middle decades of the twentieth century, the efforts of the people under its thrall during those years continue to shape our national understanding of Mother Ann Lee and her followers.

NOTES

....

ABBREVIATIONS

AA   Andrews Archives, Edward Deming Andrews Memorial Shaker Collection, Winterthur Library, Winterthur Museum and Gardens, Winterthur, DE

ATSB   Ann Tarney Scrapbook, formerly located at the Enfield Shaker Museum, Enfield, NH, currently unlocated

CC   Count Collection, Shaker Museum | Mount Lebanon, Old Chatham, NY

CCP   Clarice Carr Papers, in private hands

CSC   Charles Sheeler Collection File, Curatorial Files, Hancock Shaker Village, Pittsfield, MA

DBPC   Daniel and Beverly B. Patterson Collection, Collection No. 20026, Southern Folklife Collection, Louis Round Wilson Special Collections Library, University of North Carolina, Chapel Hill

DHC   Doris Humphrey Collection, New York Public Library for the Performing Arts Dance Collection, New York

DMP   Dorothy Miller Papers, Archives of American Art, Smithsonian Institution, Washington, DC

HCP   Holger Cahill Papers, Archives of American Art, Smithsonian Institution, Washington, DC

HPCP   H. Phelps Clawson Papers, Central Library: Rare Book Room, Buffalo
       and Erie County Public Library, Buffalo, NY

IAD   Index of American Design Archives, National Gallery of Art Archives,
       National Gallery of Art, Washington, DC

MACP   Miriam Anne Cramer Papers, MSS. 4233, Western Reserve Historical
       Society, Cleveland

NCP   Nina C. Collier Papers, Archives of American Art, Smithsonian Institu-
       tion, Washington, DC

PMF   Papers of the Melcher Family, Small Special Collections Library, Universi-
       ty of Virginia, Charlottesville

PMJN   Papers of Neal, Mary Julia, 1905–1995 (MSS4), Manuscripts and Folklife
       Archives, Western Kentucky University, Bowling Green

SMD   New York State Division of Science and State Museum, State Museum
       Director's, State Geologist's, and State Paleontologist's Correspondence
       Files, New York State Archives, Albany

SUSV   Library Collection, South Union Shaker Village, Auburn, KY

YUA   Yale University Archives, New Haven, CT

INTRODUCTION: SHAKER FEVER

1. Daniel J. Wakin, "Frigid Fingers Played It Live," *New York Times,* January 23, 2009;
Daniel J. Wakin, "Actually Live Debut Set for Inaugural Composition," *New York
Times,* January 24, 2009. In the *Washington Post,* reviewer Anne Midgette referred
to the quartet as spanning "a Benetton range of generational, ethnic, and gender
bases." Midgette, "Music Review: John Williams's 'Air and Simple Gifts' at the Obama
Inauguration," *Washington Post,* January 21, 2009.

2. "Questions from the News," *Wilmington [NC] Star-News,* March 12, 2009. See
also Phillip George, "Quartet for the Beginning of Office," *21st Century Music* 16, no.
3 (March 2009): 1.

3. Gail Levin, "Visualizing Modernity and Tradition in Copland's America," *Institute
for Studies in American Music Newsletter* 30, no. 1 (Fall 2000): 6–7, 15. Ethnomusicologist Roger Lee Hall notes that the song was first introduced to the twentieth-century
public by Edward Deming Andrews in 1937, thus making it available to Copland. Hall,
"'Simple Gifts': The Discovery and Popularity of a Shaker Dance Song," *Communal
Societies* 36, no. 2 (2016): 99. See also Edward D. Andrews, "Shaker Songs," *Musical
Quarterly* 23, no. 4 (October 1937): 491–508.

4. Roger L. Hall, "'Simple Gifts' Tune Was Appealing to Aaron Copland," *Shaker
Messenger* 3, no. 4 (Summer 1981): 7.

5. Midgette argues that Williams's use of "Simple Gifts" "merely evoked a well-worn idea of clean, honest, all-American values." Midgette, "Music Review."

6. Robert Kimball, a journalist employed by the *Berkshire Eagle* in Pittsfield, Massachusetts, coined the term "Shaker fever" to describe his own enthusiasm. See Kimball to Dorothy Miller, November 6, 1959, folder 20.4, DMP.

7. Joel Cohen, the influential twenty-first-century choral conductor and impresario, has noted that Americans have claimed the Shakers as "part of our collective self-image." "Joel Cohen: Beyond Borrowed Light," *Early Music America* 14, no. 4 (Winter 2006): 37.

8. An extensive current literature exists concerning the Shakers, their history, and their culture. Notable works include Stephen J. Stein, *The Shaker Experience in America* (New Haven, CT: Yale University Press, 1992); Elizabeth A. De Wolfe, *Shaking the Faith: Women, Family, and Mary Marshall Dyer's Anti-Shaker Campaign, 1815–1862* (New York: Palgrave, 2002); Priscilla J. Brewer, *Shaker Communities, Shaker Lives* (Hanover, NH: University Press of New England, 1992); Clarke Garret, *Spirit Possession and Popular Religion: From the Camisards to the Shakers* (Baltimore: Johns Hopkins University Press, 1987); John T. Kirk, *Shaker World* (New York: Harry N. Abrams, 1997); Scott T. Swank, *Shaker Life, Art, and Architecture: Hands to Work, Hearts to God* (New York: Abbeville Press, 1999); Julie Nicoletta, *The Architecture of the Shakers* (Woodstock, VT: Countryman Press, 1995); and Suzanne Thurman, *"O Sisters Ain't You Happy?": Gender, Family, and Community among the Harvard and Shirley Shakers, 1781–1918* (Syracuse, NY: Syracuse University Press, 2002). The range of documentary materials available for the study of Shaker history is indicated in Mary L. Richmond, *Shaker Literature: A Bibliography*, 2 vols. (Hanover, NH: University Press of New England, 1977). For concise statements concerning the Shakers, see Stephen J. Stein, "Shakers," in *Encyclopedia of American Studies*, ed. George Thomas Kurian (New York: Grolier Educational, 2001), 4:109–110; Lewis Perry, "Shakers," in *Dictionary of American History*, 3rd ed., ed. Stanley J. Kutler (New York: Charles Scribner's Sons, 2003), 7:333–335; and Gerard C. Wertkin, "Shakers," in *Encyclopedia of American Folk Art* (New York: Routledge, 2004), 479–482. For a southern regional perspective on the sect, see Charles Reagan Wilson, "Shakers," in *The Encyclopedia of Southern Culture*, ed. Charles Reagan Wilson and William Ferris (Chapel Hill: University of North Carolina Press, 1989), 1329.

9. Stein, *Shaker Experience*, 356–370.

10. "The Approaching End of the 'Shakers,'" *Literary Digest* 74 (September 30, 1922): 37.

11. Karl Schriftgiesser, "Alfred Sad as Shakers Pack Up to Leave Old Home Forever," *Boston Evening Transcript*, April 25, 1931.

12. Stein, *Shaker Experience*, 360. The causes of the Shakers' collapse are treated at length by Stein, Thurman, and others.

13. The status of these final believers is problematic since the Shaker Central Ministry broke with the Sabbathday Lake Shakers in the years between 1960 and 1990. See Stein, *Shaker Experience*, 384–394.

14. Elizabeth Stillinger, "From Attics, Sheds, and Secondhand Shops: Collecting Folk Art in America, 1880–1940," in *Drawing on America's Past: Folk Art, Modernism, and the Index of American Design*, ed. Virginia Tuttle Clayton (Washington, DC: National Gallery of Art, 2002), 45–59; James M. Lindgren, "'A Spirit That Fires the Imagination': Historic Preservation and Cultural Regeneration in Virginia and New England, 1850–1950," in *Giving Preservation a History: Histories of Historic Preservation in the United States,* ed. Max Page and Randall Mason (New York: Routledge, 2004), 107–129. See also Michael Kammen, *Mystic Chords of Memory* (New York: Vintage, 1991); and Thomas J. Schlereth, "Material Culture Studies in America, 1876–1976," in *Material Culture Studies in America*, ed. Thomas J. Schlereth (Nashville: American Association for State and Local History, 1982), 1–75.

15. Although Shaker fever resulted in artistic production in a wide range of media, sculpture is notably absent. Few if any sculptural works on a Shaker theme were produced during this time.

16. Hugh Howard and Jerry V. Grant, "Reinventing the Shakers," *Eastfield Record* 11 (Winter 2002–2003): 4.

17. Kory Rogers, "In the Spirit: Twentieth-Century and Contemporary Shaker-Inspired Design," in *Shaker Design: Out of This World*, ed. Jean M. Burks (New Haven, CT: Yale University Press, 2008), 188.

18. Stephen J. Stein, "Andrews, Edward Deming," in *American National Biography,* ed. John A. Garraty and Mark C. Carnes (New York: Oxford University Press, 1999), 1:494. See also Stillinger, "From Attics, Sheds, and Secondhand Shops," 47–48. Scott F. DeWolfe similarly emphasizes the role of the Andrewses in his important study, "Simply Shaker: The Rise and Development of Popular Images of the Shakers" (M.A. thesis, University of Southern Maine, 1991).

19. For the fullest self-congratulatory account of their career, see Edward Deming Andrews and Faith Andrews, *Fruits of the Shaker Tree of Life* (Stockbridge, MA: Berkshire Traveller Press, 1975). Christian Goodwillie recently has served as the couple's apologist. See Goodwillie, "Foundation Pillars: The Gifts of the Andrewses to Shaker Scholarship," in *The Andrews Shaker Collection* (Marlborough, MA: Skinner, 2014), 140–147.

20. Edward Deming Andrews, "Open Letter," undated, box 21, folder WPA Project, AA.

21. Andrews and Andrews, *Fruits of the Shaker Tree of Life,* 193. See also Ruth Reeves

to Holger Cahill and Adolph Glassgold, memorandum, August 10, 1936, series 2, reel 5285, frame 1165, HCP.

22. Mario S. De Pillis, "The Edward Deming Andrews Shaker Collection: Saving a Culture," in Mario S. De Pillis and Christian Goodwillie, *Gather Up the Fragments: The Andrews Shaker Collection* (New Haven, CT: Yale University Press, 2008), 1.

23. See Robert F. W. Meader to Daniel Patterson, August 30, 1962, series 3.1, folder 80, DBPC. See also Meader to Patterson, September 6, 1962, series 3.1, folder 80, DBPC.

24. I do not attempt, for instance, to discuss the impact of Shaker fever on American gastronomy, even though the enthusiasm resulted in at least three cookbooks and numerous recipes published in newspapers. See Caroline B. Piercy, *The Shaker Cook Book* (New York: Crown, 1952); *Shaker Desserts and Sweets: A Volume of Shaker Recipes* (Pittsfield, MA: Shaker Village Work Group, 195[?]); and Amy Bess Miller and Persis Wellington Fuller, eds., *The Best of Shaker Cooking* (New York: Collier, 1970).

25. For creating semiotic interpretations of culture, see Clifford Geertz, "Thick Description: Toward an Interpretive Theory of Culture," in *The Interpretation of Cultures* (New York: Basic, 1973), 3–30. See also Arthur Asa Berger, *What Objects Mean,* 2nd ed. (Walnut Creek, CA: Left Coast Press, 2014), 46–60.

26. Henry Glassie, "Meaningful Things and Appropriate Myths: The Artifact's Place in American Studies," in *Material Life in America, 1600–1860,* ed. Robert Blair St. George (Boston: Northeastern University Press, 1988), 64.

27. This work is also situated within the tradition of American Studies. See Philip J. Deloria and Alexander I. Olson, *American Studies: A User's Guide* (Oakland: University of California Press, 2017), 115–127.

28. Glassie, "Meaningful Things and Appropriate Myths," 65.

CHAPTER 1: VISUALIZING THE SHAKERS

1. Stephen J. Stein, *The Shaker Experience in America* (New Haven, CT: Yale University Press, 1992), 376; Stephen Bowe and Peter Richmond, *Selling Shaker: The Commodification of Shaker Design in the Twentieth Century* (Liverpool: Liverpool University Press, 2007), 20–30; Elizabeth Stillinger, *A Kind of Archeology: Collecting American Folk Art, 1876–1976* (Amherst: University of Massachusetts Press, 2011), 114–120.

2. See, for example, Kristina Wilson, "Ambivalence, Irony, and Americana: Charles Sheeler's 'American Interiors,'" *Winterthur Portfolio* 45, no. 4 (Winter 2011): 263.

3. "Harvard Man Heads N.Y. State Museum," *Boston Herald,* April 2, 1926.

4. Ralph S. Palmer, "Dr. Charles C. Adams," *Bulletin of the Ecological Society of America* 37, no. 4 (December 1956): 103.

5. Paul B. Sears, "Charles C. Adams, Ecologist," *Science,* new ser., 123, no. 3205 (June 1,

1956): 974. See also Richard Harmond, "Adams, Charles Christopher," in *Biographical Dictionary of American and Canadian Naturalists and Environmentalists,* ed. Keir B. Sterling et al. (Westport, CT: Greenwood, 1997), 8–9.

6. Charles C. Adams, *Guide to the Study of Animal Ecology* (New York: Macmillan, 1913).

7. Palmer, "Dr. Charles C. Adams."

8. Hugh M. Raup, "Charles C. Adams, 1873–1955," *Annals of the Association of American Geographers* 49, no. 2 (June 1959): 164–166.

9. Charles C. Adams, et al., "Plants and Animals of Mount Marcy, New York, Part I," *Ecology* 1, no. 2 (April 1920): 71–94; Charles C. Adams et al., "Plants and Animals of Mount Marcy, New York, Part II," *Ecology* 1, no. 3 (July 1920): 204–233; Charles C. Adams et al., "Plants and Animals of Mount Marcy, New York, Part III," *Ecology* 1, no. 4 (October 1920): 274–287.

10. Adams et al., "Plants and Animals of Mount Marcy, New York, Part I," 71.

11. Harmond, "Adams, Charles Christopher"; "Death Takes Dr. Adams," *Daily Illinois State Journal* (Springfield), May 23, 1955. See also "Charles Adams, Headed Museum," *New York Times*, May 23, 1955.

12. Theodore Roosevelt, "Productive Scientific Scholarship," *Science* 45, no. 1149 (January 1917): 7. For a somewhat expanded text of Roosevelt's speech, see Theodore Roosevelt, "Productive Scientific Scholarship," *University of the State of New York Bulletin*, no. 634 (March 1, 1919): 30–44. Charles C. Adams, "Twenty-Second Report of the Director," *New York State Museum Bulletin* 279 (January 1929): 14.

13. Charles C. Adams, "Twenty-Third Report of the Director of the Division of Science and the State Museum," *New York State Museum Bulletin* 284 (December 1929): 15.

14. Adams, "Twenty-Third Report," 18–19. See also Charles C. Adams, "Reorganization of Physical and Economic Geology," August 17, 1927, box 41, folder 1927 H–S Jan.–Dec., SMD.

15. Adams, "Reorganization of Physical and Economic Geology."

16. Charles C. Adams, "Memorandum to the Museum Committee," July 30, 1927, box 41, folder 1927 T–Z Jan.–Dec., SMD; Mrs. LeGrand Spicer, "Interesting Shaker Documents," *Troy [NY] Record,* June 25, 1927. For Flick, see "Dr. Flick to Retire as State Historian," *New York Times*, April 11, 1939. Caroline Mallary Marvin Spicer also was active in the Philip Schuyler Chapter of the Daughters of the American Revolution in Troy.

17. For a brief account of Adams's interest in the Shakers, see John L. Scherer, ed., *A Shaker Legacy: The Shaker Collection at the New York State Museum*, rev. ed. (Albany: University of the State of New York, the State Education Department, 2000), xi–xii; and A. D. Emerich and A. H. Benning, eds., *Community Industries of the Shakers: A*

New Look (Albany, NY: Shaker Heritage Society at Watervliet, 1983). Scott F. De Wolfe also touches lightly on Adams and his development of the Shaker collection at the New York State Museum in "Simply Shaker: The Rise and Development of Popular Images of the Shakers" (M.A. thesis, University of Southern Maine, 1991).

18. Stuart Murray, *Shaker Heritage Guide Book* (Spencertown, NY: Golden Hill Press, 1994), 157.

19. "County Commissioner," *Repository* (Canton, OH), December 14, 1929; Adams, "Twenty-Third Report," 12; Charles C. Adams, "The New York State Museum's Historical Survey and Collection of the New York Shakers," *New York State Museum Bulletin* 323 (March 1941): 94.

20. Charles C. Adams, "Carpenter and Labor on the Shaker Collection," November 22, 1927, box 41, folder 1927 A–G Jan.–Dec., SMD.

21. Adams, "Memorandum to the Museum Committee."

22. Adams, "Carpenter and Labor on the Shaker Collection"; Adams, "Memorandum to the Museum Committee."

23. Charles C. Adams to William Leland Thompson, October 28, 1927, box 41, folder 1927 T–Z Jan.–Dec., SMD. The 1930 U.S. Census records Stein as a thirty-three-year-old male employed as a draftsman for the State Museum. 1930 U.S. Census, Population Schedule, Albany, New York, 18th Ward, Sheet 76A. See also *Albany and Rensselaer, N.Y. Directory for the Year Ending July, 1932* (Boston: Sampson and Murdock, 1931), 883.

24. Charles C. Adams to William Leland Thompson, November 14, 1927, box 41, folder 1927 T–Z Jan.–Dec., SMD.

25. For McClean and Cathcart, see Stein, *Shaker Experience*, 370–372. For Sears, see Cynthia H. Barton, *History's Daughter: The Life of Clara Endicott Sears Founder of Fruitlands Museum* (Harvard, MA: Fruitlands Museum, 1988). See also Stillinger, *A Kind of Archeology*, 101–108.

26. Clara Endicott Sears, *Gleanings from Old Shaker Journals* (Boston: Houghton Mifflin, 1916).

27. See Sears, "Charles C. Adams."

28. Adams, "Twenty-Third Report," 13.

29. Adams, "The New York State Museum's Historical Survey and Collection of the New York Shakers," 132. The New York State Museum subsequently provided a number of Stein's images to the Historic American Building Survey. As components of the holdings of that federal agency, some of these photographs are available online through the Library of Congress, https://www.loc.gov.

30. Adams, "Twenty-Third Report," 13.

31. Charles C. Adams, "Twenty-Fourth Report of the Director of the Division of Science and the State Museum," *New York State Museum Bulletin* 288 (July 1931): 23.

32. "Y.W.C.A. to Give Seventh Annual Drama Tourney," *East Hampton [NY] Star,* March 31, 1933; "Wm. Lassiter, Author of Article on 'Shakers,'" *East Hampton Star,* February 22, 1945; "Complete Alumni Register 1812–1922," *Hamilton College Bulletin* 6, no. 1 (November 1922): 220; Cornell University, *Directory of the University, Second Term, 1921–22* (Ithaca, NY: Cornell University, 1922), 62.

33. Charles C. Adams to William L. Lassiter, June 24, 1931; William L. Lassiter to Charles C. Adams, March 10, 1931, both box 42, folder 1931 L–Z, SMD.

34. Gerard C. Wertkin, "William Lawrence Lassiter (1896–1977)," in *Important Shaker Furniture and Related Decorative Arts: The William L. Lassiter Collection* (New York: Sotheby Parke Benet, 1981), n.p.; Adams, "Twenty-Third Report," 19; Adams, "Twenty-Fourth Report," 28.

35. Gus Nelson, "Lassiter Sale Puts Shaker on Its Way," *Shaker Messenger* 4, no. 2 (Winter 1982): 24–25; Charles C. Adams, "Twenty-Fifth Report of the Director of the Division of Science and the State Museum," *New York State Bulletin* 293 (June 1932): 28.

36. Adams, "The New York State Museum's Historical Survey and Collection of the New York Shakers," 93. See also Milton Sherman, *Shaker: The William F. Winter, Jr. Collection of Shaker Photographica, Books, and Ephemera* (Armonk, NY: Milton Sherman, [1989?]).

37. Adams, "The New York State Museum's Historical Survey and Collection of the New York Shakers," 135. The standard history of General Electric is John Winthrop Hammond, *Men and Volts: The Story of General Electric* (Philadelphia: J. B. Lippincott, 1941).

38. 1920 U.S. Census, Schenectady, New York, Ward 11, Sheet 7B. See also *Schenectady Directory, 1920* (Schenectady, NY: H. A. Manning, 1920), 626.

39. 1930 U.S. Census, Population Schedule, Schenectady, New York, Ward 11, Sheet 16B; Adams, "The New York State Museum's Historical Survey and Collection of the New York Shakers," 135.

40. Adams, "The New York State Museum's Historical Survey and Collection of the New York Shakers," 93, 135.

41. *Manning's Schenectady and Scotia (New York) City Directory for Year Beginning March 1933* (Schenectady, NY: H. A. Manning, 1933), 674.

42. David A. Schorsch, *The Photographs of William F. Winter, Jr.* (New York: David A. Schorsch, 1989).

43. David E. Nye, *Image Worlds: Corporate Identities at General Electric, 1890–1930* (Cambridge, MA: MIT Press, 1985), 38–39, 49.

44. For an influential overview of this aesthetic, see Karen Tsujimoto, *Images of America: Precisionist Painting and Modern Photography* (Seattle: University of Washington Press, 1982). See also Theodore E. Stebbins, Jr., and Norman Keyes, Jr., *Charles Sheeler: The Photographs* (Boston: Museum of Fine Arts, 1987).

45. John T. Kirk, *The Shaker World: Art, Life, Belief* (New York: Abrams, 1997), 240–241.

46. William F. Winter, "Shaker Portfolio," *U.S. Camera* 1, no. 3 (March–April 1939): 25.

47. Schorsch, *Photographs of William F. Winter,* 5–6; Sherman, *Shaker,* n.p.

48. In 1939, Winter reported that he had used two cameras in producing his Shaker images: a Zeiss Ikon Ideal B, 9 x 12 cm, with a 15-cm F/4.5 Tessar, and a Korona View, 5 x 7 in., with a lens of 4¼, 6, 9⅛, 13¼, or 18¾ focal length. See Winter, "Shaker Portfolio," 24.

49. Adams, "The New York State Museum's Historical Survey and Collection of the New York Shakers," 135.

50. Nye provides a useful overview of how photographers for General Electric created their images; see Nye, *Image Worlds,* 40–45.

51. My reading of the relationship between Winter and Faith and Edward Deming Andrews differs from that presented by the couple themselves and from that of Kristina Wilson. As John Kirk notes, the Andrewses wished the world to believe that they were responsible for the success of Winter's photographs. See Kirk, *Shaker World,* 242. In an article about Charles Sheeler's Shaker interiors, Wilson accepts the primacy of the Andrewses. Wilson, "Ambivalence, Irony, and Americana,'" 263–264.

52. Wilson reads this image differently, ignoring its abstraction and arguing that its range of tonalities indicate that Winter's aesthetic derived from the Andrewses. Wilson, "Ambivalence, Irony, and Americana," 263.

53. Sherman, *Shaker,* n.p.

54. As Faith and Edward Deming Andrews are the most analyzed figures in the historiography of the Shakers, a full biography of them is not attempted here. Rather, their actions are discussed in relation to their contemporaries. For useful entries into the bibliography concerning the couple, see Stillinger, *A Kind of Archeology,* 109–123; and Stein, *Shaker Experience,* 372–384.

55. Faith and Edward Deming Andrews, *Fruits of the Shaker Tree of Life: Memoirs of Fifty Years of Collecting and Research* (Stockbridge, MA: Berkshire Traveller Press, 1975), 145; Sherman, *Shaker,* n.p.

56. Christian Goodwillie, "The Andrewses and the Shakers," in *Gather up the Fragments: The Andrews Shaker Collection,* ed. Mario S. De Pillis and Christian Goodwillie (Hancock, MA: Hancock Shaker Village, 2008), 73.

57. Stephen J. Stein, "Andrews, Edward Deming (6 Mar. 1894–6 June 1964)," in *American National Biography,* ed. John A. Garraty and Mark C. Carnes (New York: Oxford University Press, 1999), 1:493–494; "Edward D. Andrews," *New York Times,* June 13, 1964.

58. Goodwillie, "The Andrewses and the Shakers," 61. For insight into the antiques market in the Berkshires at this time, see Charlotte Emans Moore, "Another Generation's Folk Art: Edward Duff Balken and His Collection of American Provincial

Paintings and Drawings," in *A Window into Collecting American Folk Art: The Edward Duff Balken Collection at Princeton* (Princeton, NJ: The Art Museum, Princeton University, 1999), 11–28.

59. Andrews and Andrews, *Fruits of the Shaker Tree of Life,* 22; Goodwillie, "The Andrewses and the Shakers," 61.

60. For an overview of the development of the markets for American antiques in the decades preceding the Andrewses' entry into the field, see Elizabeth Stillinger, *The Antiquers* (New York: Knopf, 1980). See also Jeffrey Trask, *Things American: Art Museums and Civic Culture in the Progressive Era* (Philadelphia: University of Pennsylvania Press, 2012); and Briann G. Greenfield, *Out of the Attic: Inventing Antiques in Twentieth-Century New England* (Amherst: University of Massachusetts Press, 2009), 1–89.

61. Goodwillie, "The Andrewses and the Shakers," 62. The story about the loaf of bread is repeated in many sources with various dates. For example, a short article in *Time* magazine from 1940 dates it as having happened in 1920. See "Shaker Art," *Time,* August 26, 1940, 38. See also "Shaker Historian Faith E. Andrews Dies," *Shaker Messenger* 12, no. 2 (1990): 2; and Alice Scott Ross, "Shaker-Made Loaf of Bread Leads Couple to New Life," *Springfield [MA] Union,* October 16, 1957.

62. Stein, *Shaker Experience,* 397.

63. Dorothy Miller to Beverly Hamilton, February 12, 1981, box 17, folder B20.26, DMP.

64. For a laudatory overview of their career by one of their admiring associates, see Mario S. De Pillis, "The Edward Deming Andrews Shaker Collection: Saving a Culture," in De Pillis and Goodwillie, eds., *Gather up the Fragments,* 1–59.

65. Edward Deming Andrews, "The Shakers in a New World," *Magazine Antiques* 72, no. 4 (October 1957): 340. In retrospect, Irene Zieget noted that she and her husband originally purchased from the Andrewses a bed and low-backed dining room chair, which she believed would be "perfect" as a dressing table chair. Irene N. Zieget, "Our Shaker Collection and How It Started," *Yankee Magazine,* April 1970, 126.

66. For insight into the Andrewses' continued activities in the antiques business in the 1930s, see Homer Eaton Keyes to Kate Perkins, January 13, 1938, box 5, Correspondence, AA.

67. B. Altman display advertisement, *New York Herald Tribune,* February 13, 1944. For antiques retailed in department stores, see Greenfield, *Out of the Attic,* 8. For another example of an antiquer's collection being presented by B. Altman, see Seth C. Bruggeman, "'A Most Complete Whaling Museum': Profiting from the Past on Nantucket Island," *Museum History Journal* 8, no. 2 (July 2015): 198.

68. Dorothy Miller to Beverly Hamilton, February 12, 1981, box 17, folder B20.26, DMP.

69. Kirk, *Shaker World,* 128.

70. "City Doctor, Wife Experts on Vanishing Shakers," *New Haven [CT] Register,* May 28, 1962. It is worth noting that although Faith Andrews donated voluminous holdings of Ted Andrews's papers related to his writing and museum activities to the Winterthur Library after his death, few records of their activities as dealers and wholesalers have survived and become accessible to scholars.

71. Andrews and Andrews, *Fruits of the Shaker Tree of Life,* 22.

72. Clara Endicott Sears to Edward Deming Andrews, December 5, 1926, SA 1295.1, AA.

73. For Keyes, see Stillinger, *The Antiquers,* 197–200.

74. Kirk, *Shaker World,* 239–240.

75. Keyes contributed an extended headnote about the history of the sect for the first article.

76. Edward A. Andrews and Faith Andrews, "Craftsmanship of an American Religious Sect: Notes on Shaker Furniture," *Magazine Antiques* 14, no. 2 (August 1928): 132. These works articulate the understanding of folk art as the unconscious expression of a group identity that was developing at the time. For a near contemporary statement of this idea, see Holger Cahill, "Folk Art: Its Place in the American Tradition," *Parnassus* 4, no. 3 (March 1932): 2.

77. Edward D. Andrews and Faith Andrews, "The Furniture of an American Religious Sect," *Magazine Antiques* 15, no. 4 (April 1929): 296.

78. Kirk, *The Shaker World,* 239–240.

79. Andrews and Andrews, "Craftsmanship of an American Religious Sect," 136.

80. Andrews and Andrews, "The Furniture of an American Religious Sect," 296.

81. See, for example, the images reproduced in De Pillis and Goodwillie, eds., *Gather up the Fragments,* 99. The Edward Deming Andrews Memorial Shaker Collection at Winterthur includes a number of informal snapshots of Shaker furniture that may have been used to document pieces for sale by the dealers. Images SA620a and SA620b present a slant-top desk photographed in front of a similarly wrinkled sheet used as a backdrop.

82. Homer Eaton Keyes to Edward Deming Andrews, May 12, 1931, box 6, folder Correspondence, AA.

83. Adams, "Twenty-Fifth Report," 20.

84. Stein, "Andrews," 493. Material derived from his doctoral dissertation about the history of public schools in Vermont appeared as Edward Deming Andrews, "The Country Grammar Schools and Academies of Vermont," *Proceedings of the Vermont Historical Society* 4, no. 3 (1936): 117–211.

85. In 1931, Andrews wrote to Adams, "Unfortunately Mrs. Andrews and I are not in the position of scholars whose leisure is free to spend on such interesting activities."

Edward Deming Andrews to Charles C. Adams, February 4, 1931. In the summer
of 1931, Adams attempted to assist Andrews in securing a teaching position at the
Illinois State Normal University in Normal, Illinois. See Adams to Andrews, July 19,
1931; Andrews to Adams, July 18, 1931; Adams to President H. A. Brown, July 17, 1931;
William L. Lassiter to Adams, March 10, 1931; Adams to Lassiter, June 24, 1931, all box
42, folder 1931 A–K, SMD.

86. Charles S. Adams, "Twenty-Sixth Report of the Director of the Division of Science and the State Museum," *New York State Bulletin* 298 (April 1933): 19.

87. Goodwillie, "The Andrewses and the Shakers," 72.

88. Adams, "Twenty-Sixth Report of the Director of the Division of Science and the State Museum," 19; William Lassiter to Charles C. Adams, memorandum entitled "Report of Work Done on Historical Collection between May 15 and August 16, 1930," box 42, folder 1930 L–Z, SMD.

89. Walter Rendell Storey, "Hand-Weavers Show Their New Fabrics," *New York Times,* December 31, 1933.

90. Andrews as quoted in Adams, "Twenty-Fifth Report," 23–24.

91. Bowe and Richmond, *Selling Shaker,* 22.

92. Edward D. Andrews, *The New York Shakers and Their Industries* (Albany: New York State Museum, 1930).

93. Adams, "The New York State Museum's Historical Survey and Collection of the New York Shakers," 129.

94. Edward Deming Andrews to Charles C. Adams, February 4, 1931, SMD.

95. Charles C. Adams to Edward D. Andrews, February 9, 1931, SMD.

96. Although this volume was cited repeatedly in subsequent works about the Shakers and still appears on bibliographies of recommended reading on the subject, it received remarkably little notice on publication. See Storey, "Hand-Weavers Show Their New Fabrics"; and "*The Community Industries of the Shakers* by E. D. Andrews," *New York History* 15, no. 1 (January 1934): 93–94.

97. Andrews and Andrews, *Fruits of the Shaker Tree of Life,* 145.

98. Edward D. Andrews, *The Community Industries of the Shakers* (Albany: New York State Museum, 1933), 13. See Stein, *Shaker Experience,* 373.

99. Andrews, *Community Industries,* 265.

100. Andrews, *Community Industries,* 11.

101. Andrews, *Community Industries,* 265.

102. The photograph of the spinning wheel appears as figure 34 on page 153.

103. Design historian Maggie Taft notes that Winter's "suggestive staging" of furniture and textiles in a spare architectural space approximates interior design exhibition practices used by the Danish Cabinetmaker's Guild. See Taft, "Morphologies and

Genealogies: Shaker Furniture and Danish Design," *Design and Culture* 7, no. 3 (2015): 317.

104. While Bragg, Winter, and the Andrewses were planning their exhibition at the Berkshire Museum, Lassiter installed a show at the New York State Museum, which was on view from September 1, 1932, to July 1, 1933. See Adams, "The New York State Museum's Historical Survey and Collection of the New York Shakers," 129. See also William L. Lassiter to Charles C. Adams, memorandum entitled "Work Done on the Historic Collection between July 1, 1932 and September 1, 1932," December 14, 1932, box 43, folder L–Z 2, SMD.

105. Bragg's standard biography is Louise Anderson Allen, *A Bluestocking in Charleston: The Life and Career of Laura Bragg* (Columbia: University of South Carolina Press, 2001). For Bragg's obituary, see "Laura Mary Bragg, Cultural Leader, Dies," *Charleston News and Courier*, May 17, 1978.

106. "Head of Museum Takes New Post," *Charleston News and Courier*, March 31, 1931; "Z. M. Crane Dead, Paper Firm Head," *Boston Globe*, April 30, 1936.

107. "Berkshire Athenaeum and Museum," *American Magazine of Art* 23, no. 4 (October 1931): 335.

108. Allen, *A Bluestocking in Charleston*, 13–17; Eleanor P. Hart, "Weighing Her Merits," *Preservation Progress* 10, no. 1 (January 1965): 2; Louise Anderson Allen and James T. Sears, "Laura Bragg and Her 'Bright Young Things': Fostering Change and Social Reform at the Charleston Museum," in *Renaissance in Charleston: Art and Life in the Carolina Low Country, 1900–1940*, ed. James M. Hutchinson and Harlan Greene (Athens: University of Georgia Press, 2003), 156.

109. Allen, *A Bluestocking in Charleston*, 23.

110. Rowena Wilson Tobias, "Laura M. Bragg, Rejuvenator of Museums, Returns to Charleston after Retirement," *Charleston News and Courier*, January 28, 1940.

111. Allen, *A Bluestocking in Charleston*, 51.

112. James Sears and Louise Allen indicate that Bragg had "romantic friendships with several aristocratic Southern ladies." James T. Sears and Louise A. Allen, "Museums, Friends, and Lovers in the New South: Laura's Web, 1909–1931," *Journal of Homosexuality* 40, no. 1 (2000): 107.

113. Allen and Sears, "Laura Bragg and Her 'Bright Young Things,'" 155.

114. Tobias, "Laura M. Bragg, Rejuvenator of Museums"; "Tour of Museums through South," *Charleston News and Courier*, December 18, 1924; "Will Lecture at Columbia U.," *Charleston Evening Post*, May 20, 1927; "Cooperation of Schools," *Charleston Evening Post*, August 25, 1927.

115. "Museum Head in Savannah," *Charleston Evening Post*, January 11, 1927.

116. Robert R. Weyeneth, "Ancestral Architecture: The Early Preservation Movement

in Charleston," in *Giving Preservation a History: Histories of Historic Preservation in the United States,* ed. Max Page and Randall Mason (New York: Routledge, 2004), 260–262. See also "Charleston Birthplace of the Museum Idea in America," *Charleston Evening Post,* April 3, 1923.

117. Allen, *A Bluestocking in Charleston,* 137–140. For the fullest current discussion of Drake, see Leonard Todd, *Carolina Clay: The Life and Legend of the Slave Potter Dave* (New York: Norton, 2008).

118. "Contemporary Art at Pittsfield Museum," *Springfield [MA] Republican,* September 17, 1931.

119. "Berkshire Athenaeum and Museum"; "Art Show in Pittsfield," *New York Times,* September 1, 1931.

120. "Reception Opens Berkshire Art Show," *New York Times,* August 10, 1932.

121. Lewis Mumford, "The Art Galleries," *New Yorker,* September 23, 1933, 49–50.

122. Mario De Pillis indicates that the dealers "instantly understood the importance of Laura Bragg's social and professional connections for the future acceptance of Shaker art and artifacts." De Pillis, "The Edward Deming Andrews Shaker Collection," 18.

123. "Shaker Exhibition at Museum Opens with Large Reception," *Berkshire Eagle* (Pittsfield, MA), October 11, 1932.

124. Invitation to Opening Reception of Shaker Exhibition at the Berkshire Museum, box 15, folder Misc. Reviews and Exhibits and Clippings, AA.

125. Bowe and Richmond offer a cursory analysis of this exhibition. Bowe and Richmond, *Selling Shaker,* 25–26.

126. These temporary installations were created in the midst of a period that David L. Barquist has dubbed the golden age of period rooms in American art museums. Barquist, "Period Room Architecture in American Art Museums," *Winterthur Portfolio* 46, nos. 2–3 (Summer–Autumn 2012): 113.

127. Walter Rendell Storey, "Native Art from Old Shaker Colonies," *New York Times,* October 23, 1932.

128. See Storey, "Native Art from Old Shaker Colonies." Years after the exhibition closed, the *Springfield [MA] Sunday Union and Republican* ran photographs of it to accompany an article celebrating the Andrewses' collection. "Mode of Shaker Life Preserved in Museum," *Springfield Sunday Union and Republican,* February 11, 1934.

129. Storey, "Native Art from Old Shaker Colonies."

130. Charles M. Stowe, "Shaker Furniture," *New York Sun,* December 3, 1932. For Stowe, see "Antique Authorities to Be Party Guests," *Sunday Morning Star* (Wilmington, DE), December 4, 1938.

131. "Shaker Exhibition at Museum Opens with Large Reception"; "Library to Publish Frost Bibliography," *Springfield Republican,* February 25, 1937; "Panelists at Williams

Laud Modern Science Creativity," *Springfield Union*, October 8, 1958; "Former Berkshire Woman Alienations Suit Principal," *Springfield Union*, May 29, 1951. For Little, see Stillinger, *A Kind of Archeology*, 123–132. See also Elizabeth Stillinger, "Edna Greenwood and Everyday Life in Early New England," *Magazine Antiques* 162, no. 2 (August 2002): 62–71.

132. "Museum Director Dinner Hostess," *Berkshire Eagle*, October 11, 1932. For Sawyer, see Marjorie L. Harth, "Charles Sawyer (1906–2005): A Star in the Museum Firmament," *American Art* 19, no. 3 (Fall 2005): 94–96.

133. Andrews and Andrews, *Fruits of the Shaker Tree of Life*, 146–147.

134. "Society to Preserve Shaker Antiquities May Be Formed," *Berkshire Eagle*, October 28, 1932.

135. "Shaker Exhibition at Museum Opens with Large Reception."

136. "Mount Lebanon Shakers Speak Here in Appropriate Setting," *Berkshire Eagle*, October 15, 1932.

137. "Society to Preserve Shaker Antiquities May Be Formed."

138. Bragg was premature. Her vision of institutions in the Berkshires preserving Shaker "antiquities" subsequently come to fruition. See chapters 4 and 6.

139. Avis Berman, "Force, Juliana Rieser (1876–1948)," in *Encyclopedia of American Folk Art*, ed. Gerard C. Wertkin (New York: Routledge, 2004), 171. For Whitney, see Joan Marter, "Whitney, Gertrude Vanderbilt," *American National Biography Online*, February 2000, http://www.anb.org.

140. Hermon More and Lloyd Goodrich, "Juliana Force and American Art," in *Juliana Force and American Art: A Memorial Exhibition* (New York: Whitney Museum of American Art, 1949).

141. Flora Miller Biddle, *The Whitney Women and the Museum They Made: A Family Memoir* (New York: Arcade, 1999), 72.

142. Avis Berman, "Juliana Force and Folk Art," *Magazine Antiques* 136, no. 3 (September 1989): 543–553.

143. Avis Berman, *Rebels on Eighth Street: Juliana Force and the Whitney Museum of American Art* (New York: Atheneum, 1990), 147. See also Stillinger, *A Kind of Archeology*, 175–178.

144. Wanda Corn, *The Great American Thing: Modern Art and National Identity, 1915–1935* (Berkeley: University of California Press, 1999), 321.

145. Stillinger, *A Kind of Archeology*, 150–152.

146. Berman, "Force, Juliana Rieser"; Stillinger, *A Kind of Archeology*, 152–155.

147. Although Berman suggests that Sheeler influenced Force's taste for Shaker material, Dorothy Miller, who knew both figures, indicated that Force acquired her Shaker furniture before meeting Sheeler. See Dorothy Miller to Beverly Hamilton, February 12, 1981, box 17, folder B20.26, DMP.

148. Constance Rourke, *Charles Sheeler: Artist in the American Tradition* (New York: Harcourt, Brace, 1938), 141; Corn, *The Great American Thing*, 337; Martin Friedman, *Charles Sheeler* (New York: Watson-Guptil, 1975).

149. Andrews and Andrews, *Fruits of the Shaker Tree of Life*, 147. This dealer was likely Archibald E. Horne, a Tasmanian-born dealer in antiques who immigrated to the United States in 1910. 1930 U.S. Census, Ridgefield Village, Fairfield County, Connecticut, Sheet 13B. See also Stillinger, *A Kind of Archeology*, 178. With the help of Andrews, Force held an auction of her Shaker furniture in 1937. See *Catalogue of a Private Sale of Shaker Furniture, from the Collection of Mrs. Willard Burdette Force, at "Shaker Hollow," South Salem, Westchester County, N.Y., May 18 and 19, 1937* ([New York?]: N.p., [1937]).

150. "How the Idea of the Whitney Museum Has Developed—Old Whitney Studio Club," *New York Times*, November 15, 1931.

151. Edward Allen Jewell, "What Is American Art?" *New York Times*, November 15, 1931. See also Forbes Watson, "The Growth of the Whitney Museum," *Magazine of Art* 32 (October 1939): 558–567, 606–607.

152. Berman, *Rebels on Eighth Street*, 287; Corn, *The Great American Thing*, 297.

153. *Shaker Handicrafts* (New York: Whitney Museum of American Art, 1935), 11–14.

154. Exhibition Checklist, box 3, Shaker Handicrafts, folder 9, Planning, Exhibitions, 1931–2000, Whitney Museum Archives, New York.

155. *Shaker Handicrafts*, 15.

156. Homer Eaton Keyes, "The Coming Shaker Exhibition in Manhattan: A Gallery Note," *Magazine Antiques* 28, no. 5 (November 1935): 205.

157. Since their public debut at the Whitney, each of these genres has attracted significant scholarship. Noteworthy titles include David Sellin, "Shaker Inspirational Drawings," *Philadelphia Museum Bulletin* 57, no. 273 (Spring 1962): 93–99; Edward Deming Andrews and Faith Andrews, *Visions of the Heavenly Sphere: A Study in Shaker Religious Art* (Charlottesville: University Press of Virginia, 1969); Daniel W. Patterson, *Gift Drawing and Gift Song: A Study of Two Forms of Shaker Inspiration* (Sabbathday Lake, ME: United Society of Shakers, 1983); Jane F. Crosthwaite, "The Spirit Drawings of Hannah Cahoon: Window on the Shakers and Their Folk Art," *Communal Societies* 7 (1987): 1–15; Robert P. Emlen, *Shaker Village Views: Illustrated Maps and Landscape Drawings by Shaker Artists of the Nineteenth Century* (Hanover, NH: University Press of New England, 1987); Sally M. Promey, *Spiritual Spectacles: Vision and Image in Mid-Nineteenth-Century Shakerism* (Bloomington: Indiana University Press, 1993); and Jane F. Crosthwaite, *The Shaker Spiritual Notices of Eleanor Potter* (Clinton, NY: Richard W. Couper Press, 2013).

158. Edward Deming Andrews, introduction, in *Shaker Handicrafts*, 5, 9, 7, 8.

159. "Art of Shakers to Be Exhibited," *New York Times*, November 11, 1935.

160. Keyes, "The Coming Shaker Exhibition in Manhattan," 104. See also "Whitney Museum Opens Its Season," *Springfield Republican*, October 20, 1935.

161. Harriet Dyer Adams, "Whitney Museum Shows Shaker Handicrafts," *Brooklyn Daily Eagle*, November 24, 1935. Harriet Dyer Adams had an extensive career as an art historian, curator, and librarian. For her obituary, see "Adams, Harriet Dyer," *Times Union* (Albany, NY), September 27, 2005, https://www.legacy.com. See also "Curator Is Named for UNC Gallery," *Greensboro [NC] Daily News*, January 21, 1945.

162. "The Shakers," *New York Herald Tribune*, November 17, 1935. See also "Shaker Craft on Exhibit at Museum Here," *New York Herald Tribune*, November 12, 1935.

163. Helen Johnson Keyes, "Thus Spoke Shaker Crafts," *Christian Science Monitor*, November 30, 1935.

164. Walter Rendell Storey, "Folk Art Inspires the Designer," *New York Times*, November 24, 1935.

165. "Shaker Handicrafts," *Art News* 34, no. 9 (November 30, 1935): 20; Henry McBride, "Early Communist Art: Shaker Arts and Crafts Displayed at the Whitney Museum," *New York Sun*, November 16, 1935; "Crafts of Shakers, Nantucketers, Reveal Two Kinds of Americans," *Springfield Union and Republican*, November 24, 1935; "Area Shakers' Handiwork Exhibited in N.Y. City," *Albany Times Union*, November 12, 1935; William Germain Dooley, "Communist Art of the Early Shaker Groups," *Boston Evening Transcript*, November 23, 1935. See also "Shaker Handicrafts at Whitney Museum," *Springfield Republican*, November 17, 1935.

166. "Whitney Museum Holds Handicrafts Exhibition," *Dallas Morning News*, November 21, 1935.

167. "Shaker Art," *New York Times*, November 17, 1935.

168. Adams, "Whitney Museum Shows Shaker Handicrafts."

169. M.D.S., "Shaker Crafts Exhibited Here," *New York Sun*, November 16, 1935.

170. The museum did not produce installation photographs of the show. See Juliana Force to H. M. Lydenberg, director, New York Public Library, December 23, 1935, box 3, Shaker Handicrafts, folder 9, Planning, Exhibitions, 1931–2000, Whitney Museum Archives. See also Edmund Archer, associate curator, to William Sumner Appleton, corresponding secretary, Society for the Preservation of New England Antiquities, December 9, 1935, box 3, Shaker Handicrafts, folder 8, Publicity, Exhibitions, 1931–2000, Whitney Museum Archives.

171. Stillinger, *A Kind of Archeology*, 120.

172. Nye, *Image Worlds*, 56.

173. Kirk, *Shaker World*, 240.

CHAPTER 2: "A NATIVE TRADITION WITH A FUTURE"

1. Nancy E. Allyn, *The Index of American Design* (Washington, DC: National Gallery of Art, 1984), n.p. See also Nancy Elizabeth Allyn, "Defining American Design: A History of the Index of American Design, 1935–1942" (M.A. thesis, University of Maryland, 1982). A brief overview of the Index of American Design is also offered in Milton Meltzer, *Violins and Shovels: The WPA Arts Projects* (New York: Delacorte Press, 1976), 81–84.

2. Virginia Tuttle Clayton, "Picturing a 'Usable Past,'" in *Drawing on America's Past: Folk Art, Modernism, and the Index of American Design*, ed. Virginia Tuttle Clayton (Washington, DC: National Gallery of Art, 2002), 4–7. See also Holger Cahill, "Introduction," in Erwin O. Christensen, *The Index of American Design* (New York: Macmillan, 1950), ix–xii.

3. Whitney Blausen, "Reeves, Ruth," in *Dictionary of Women Artists*, ed. Delia Gaze (London: Fitzroy Dearborn, 1997), 2:1152. See also Sarah Burns, "Fabricating the Modern: Women in Design," in *American Women Modernists: The Legacy of Robert Henri, 1910–1945*, ed. Marian Wardle (Brunswick, NJ: Rutgers University Press, 2005), 32–38. In the 1910s and 1920s, Reeves executed fashion illustrations for *Women's Wear Daily*; some of her drawings are reproduced in Morris De Camp Crawford, *One World of Fashion* (New York: Fairchild, 1946).

4. Reeves's married name was Mrs. Donald R. Baker. An overview of her career appears in Ralph M. Pearson, *The Modern Renaissance in American Art* (New York: Harper and Brothers, 1954), 184–193. Walter Rendell Storey, "New Styles in Decorative Glassware," *New York Times*, December 20, 1931. See also Roger Gillman, "The International Exhibition of Metalwork and Textiles," *Parnassus* 2, no. 8 (December 1930): 46.

5. Walter Rendell Storey, "Arts and Crafts Attuned to the Hour," *New York Times*, May 3, 1931; Rita Susswein, "The AUDAC Exhibition at the Brooklyn Museum," *Parnassus* 3, no. 5 (May 1931): 14–15; Walter Rendell Storey, "Frontier Touches for Summer Homes," *New York Times*, June 21, 1931; "Museum Has Show of Utilitarian Art," *New York Times*, Oct. 13, 1931.

6. Storey, "New Styles in Decorative Glassware"; Storey, "Frontier Touches." See also "Going Native," *House Beautiful*, March 1935, 23.

7. Ruth Reeves, "Seeking Design Inspiration in the Americas," *Interior Decorator* 94 (March 1935): 18–20, 41–42.

8. Edward Alden Jewell, "Guatemalan Work in Textiles Show," *New York Times*, February 16, 1935; Walter Rendell Storey, "Folk Motifs for Textiles," *New York Times*, February 17, 1935; Frank Johnson, "Art Forum," *New York Times*, August 19, 1934; Mary Margaret McBride, "New Ideas for Industry Brought Back from Jungle by

Designing Explorers," *New York Sun*, February 22, 1935; "Guatemala Inspires New Fabric Designs," *New York Sun*, February 20, 1935; Ruth Reeves, *Guatemalan Exhibition of Textiles and Costumes* (New York: National Alliance of Art and Industry, 1935).

9. Marta K. Sironen, *A History of American Furniture* (East Stroudsburg, PA: Towse, 1936), 147.

10. Mary Roche, "Museums Called Vital for Designs," *New York Times*, November 30, 1945; "Fabrics Offered in Maori Designs," *New York Times*, June 10, 1950; "Guggenheim Fund Helps 73 Scholars," *New York Times*, April 8, 1940; Adelaide Kerr, "Mummies and Jungles to Give Woman Designer New Patterns for Moderns," *St. Petersburg [FL] Times*, August 5, 1940; "Ruth Reeves, 74, a Crafts Expert," *New York Times*, December 24, 1966. Reeves went to India in 1956 as a Fulbright Scholar but stayed on with support from the Ford Foundation and the All-India Handicrafts Board. She studied many aspects of Indian crafts and published extensively on these topics in the 1960s.

11. Elisabeth Luther Cary, "Textiles Shown in the Industrial Arts Exposition," *New York Times*, April 8, 1934; Joseph Downs, "An Exhibition of Glass and Rugs," *Bulletin of the Pennsylvania Museum* 25, no. 131 (January 1930), 17; Pearson, *Modern Renaissance in American Art*, 186.

12. Blausen, "Reeves, Ruth," 2:1153; Walter Rendell Storey, "Metals and Fabrics from Many Lands," *New York Times*, November 30, 1930; C. Louise Avery, "The International Exhibition of Decorative Metalwork and Cotton Textiles," *Metropolitan Museum of Art Bulletin* 25, no. 12 (December 1930): 265; Pearson, *Modern Renaissance in American Art*, 186–188. See also Pan Wendt, "Ruth Reeves, Designer, Length of Fabric, 'Manhattan Pattern' (also called 'Canyons of Steel')," in *A Modern World: American Design from the Yale University Art Gallery, 1920–1950*, ed. John Stuart Gordon (New Haven, CT: Yale University Art Gallery, 2011), 151.

13. Marion Clyde McCarroll, "Textile Designs Created for Draperies and Upholstery for Each Room in the House Are Shown by Ruth Reeves," *New York Evening Post*, December 17, 1930.

14. Storey, "Metals and Fabrics"; Storey, "New Styles in Decorative Glassware."

15. Mary Schoeser and Whitney Blausen, "'Wellpaying Self Support': Women Textile Designers," in *Women Designers in the USA, 1900–2000: Diversity and Difference*, ed. Pat Kirkham (New Haven, CT: Yale University Press, 2000), 148. In 1931, Reeves's fabrics also were shown in Chicago and Pittsburgh. See Eleanor Jewett, "Block Prints upon Textiles Delight Critic," *Chicago Tribune*, February 5, 1931; "Ruth Reeves Fabric Designs Shown Here," *Pittsburgh Press*, May 3, 1931; and Wendt, "Ruth Reeves, Designer," 135.

16. Cary, "Textiles Shown in the Industrial Arts Exposition."

17. Walter Rendell Storey, "Beauty Linked Firmly to Design," *New York Times*, April

1, 1934; "As the Modernist Sees the Hudson," *House and Garden,* September 1934, 87; Elinor Hillyer, "Scenic Fabrics Revived," *Arts and Decoration* 41 (May 1934): 8–10. See also "Art in Industry," clipping from unidentified textile industry publication, dated May 1934, in Ruth Reeves's scrapbook, Ruth Reeves Papers, reel 3093, Archives of American Art, Washington, DC.

18. "Hudson Prints on View," *New York Times,* April 3, 1934.

19. McCutcheon's advertisement, *New York Times,* April 1, 1934.

20. "New Hudson River Art," *Literary Digest* 117 (April 14, 1934): 26.

21. Romana Javitz to Holger Cahill, April 29, 1949, reel 5286, frame 1064, HCP. Javitz's name frequently appears in sources inaccurately transcribed as Ramona. For example, see Gayle R. Davis, "Gender and Creative Production: A Social History Lesson in Art Evaluation," in *The Material Culture of Gender: The Gender of Material Culture,* ed. Katherine Martinez and Kenneth L. Ames (Winterthur, DE: Winterthur Museum, 1997), 55. See also Sanka Knox, "Fashions Live Forever in Wardrobe of Pictures," *New York Times,* August 30, 1958.

22. Luica S. Chen, "From Picture Collection to Picture Collection Online," *Collection Building* 23, no. 3 (2004): 139–140. See also Knox, "Fashions Live Forever in Wardrobe of Pictures." For Javitz's death notice, see "Javitz—Romana," *New York Times,* January 27, 1980.

23. Frank Kingdon, *John Cotton Dana: A Life* (Newark, NJ: The Public Library and Museum, 1940), 53. For insight on the management of picture collections at the time, see John Cotton Dana, *The Picture Collection,* 4th ed., revised by Marcelle Frebault (New York: H. W. Wilson, 1929).

24. Anthony T. Troncale, "Worth beyond Words: Romana Javitz and the New York Public Library's Picture Collection," New York Public Library, 1995, https://www.nypl.org.

25. Javitz to Cahill, April 29, 1949, reel 5289, frames 1062–1063, HCP.

26. Javitz to Cahill, April 29, 1949, frame 1064.

27. Romana Javitz, "The Public Interest," in *Work for Artists: What? Where? How?,* ed. Elizabeth McCausland (New York: American Artists Group, 1947), 27–35.

28. For insight concerning Javitz's administration of the NYPL's Picture Collection, see Celestine Frankenberg, "Specialization: Pictures: A Dialogue about the Training of Picture Librarians," *Special Libraries* 56 (January 1965): 16–19.

29. Phyllis Crawford to Holger Cahill, March 18, 1949, reel 5286, frame 971, HCP.

30. Ruth Reeves to Holger Cahill, April 15, 1949, reel 5286, frame 1031, HCP

31. Phyllis Crawford to Holger Cahill, March 18, 1949, reel 5286, frames 972, 978, HCP.

32. Phyllis Crawford, oral history interview, August 27, 1964, Archives of American Art.

33. Carl Tranum to Romana Javitz, July 11, 1935, reel 5286, frame 1055, HCP; Tranum to Javitz, July 15, 1935, reel 5286, frame 1056, HCP; Javitz to Cahill, April 29, 1949, reel

5286, frames 1064, 1065, HCP. See also Ruth Reeves to Nina P. Collier, "Decoration Day Weekend" 1950, reel 1, frames 64–67, NCP; Reeves to Collier, June 16, 1950, reel 1, frames 68–71, NCP; Reeves to Collier, September 1, 1950, reel 1, frames 72–75, NCP.

34. Frances M. Pollak to Holger Cahill, April 24, 1949, reel 5286, frame 1038, HCP.

35. Phyllis Crawford to Holger Cahill, March 18, 1949, reel 5286, frame 971, HCP; Romana Javitz to Cahill, April 29, 1949, reel 5289, frame 1065, HCP. Crawford would later become a popular, award-winning author of novels for teens. See "Crawford, Phyllis," in *Current Biography: Who's News and Why, 1940,* ed. Maxine Block (New York: H. W. Wilson, 1940), 203–204.

36. Of her financial situation at the time, Reeves later reported, "The depression was going full tilt, the textile manufacturers thought my fabric designs too avant garde, and as a result I found myself lining up just any old industrial design job." Reeves to Cahill, April 15, 1949, reel 5286, frame 1031, HCP. Pearson chronicles Reeves's struggles to find appreciative manufacturers for her designs. Pearson, *Modern Renaissance in American Art,* 184–193.

37. The details of Cahill's youth are unclear and disputed. See Cheryl Rivers, "Cahill, Holger," in *Encyclopedia of American Folk Art,* ed. Gerard C. Wertkin (New York: Routledge, 2004), 79–80; Barbara Blumberg, "Cahill, Holger," in *American National Biography,* ed. John A. Garraty and Mark C. Carnes (New York: Oxford University Press, 1999), 4:183–184; Wendy Jeffers, "Holger Cahill and American Art," *Archives of American Art Journal* 31, no. 4 (1991): 2–11. See also John Michael Vlach, "Holger Cahill as Folklorist," *Journal of American Folklore* 98, no. 388 (April–June 1985): 149–151.

38. Vlach, "Holger Cahill as Folklorist," 149–150. For Skansen, see William J. Murtagh, *Keeping Time: The History and Theory of Preservation in America,* 3rd ed. (Hoboken, NJ: Wiley, 2006), 77–79.

39. Diane Tepfer, "Edith Gregor Halpert and the Downtown Gallery: Downtown, 1926–1940; A Study in Patronage" (Ph.D. diss., University of Michigan, 1989), 8; Beatrix T. Rumford, "Uncommon Art of the Common People: A Review of Trends in the Collecting and Exhibiting of American Folk Art," in *Perspectives on American Folk Art,* ed. Ian M. G. Quimby and Scott T. Swank (New York: Norton, 1980), 23–25. See also Eugene W. Metcalf, Jr., and Claudine Weatherford, "Modernism, Edith Halpert, Holger Cahill, and the Fine Art Meaning of American Folk Art," in *Folk Roots, New Roots: Folklore in American Life,* ed. Jane S. Becker and Barbara Franco (Lexington, MA: Museum of Our National Heritage, 1988), 145–147. For a journalistic biography of Halpert, see Lindsay Pollock, *The Girl with the Gallery: Edith Gregor Halpert and the Making of the Modern Art Market* (New York: Public Affairs, 2006).

40. See also Carol Troyen, "After Steiglitz: Edith Gregor Halpert and the Taste for Modern Art in America," in *The Lane Collection: 20th Century Paintings in the American Tradition* (Boston: Museum of Fine Arts, 1983), 34–57.

41. Tepfer, "Edith Gregor Halpert and the Downtown Gallery," 31.

42. Vlach, "Holger Cahill as Folklorist," 151. For Field, see Doreen Bolger, "Hamilton Easter Field and His Contribution to American Modernism," *American Art Journal* 20, no. 2 (1988): 79–107.

43. William Zorach, *Art Is My Life: The Autobiography of William Zorach* (Cleveland: World Publishing, 1967), 88.

44. Wanda Corn, *The Great American Thing: Modern Art and National Identity, 1915–1935* (Berkeley: University of California Press, 1999), 321.

45. John D. Bardwell, *Ogunquit-by-the-Sea* (Charleston, SC: Arcadia, 1994), 78.

46. Constance Rourke, *Charles Sheeler: Artist in the American Tradition* (New York: Harcourt, Brace, 1938), 133.

47. Martin Friedman, *Charles Sheeler* (New York: Watson-Guptill, 1975), 92–95.

48. Avis Berman, "Halpert, Edith Gregor, (1900–1970)," in Wertkin, ed., *Encyclopedia of American Folk Art*, 219–220. See also Avis Berman, "Pioneers in American Museums: Edith Halpert," *Museum News*, November–December 1975, 35.

49. Paul Marchand, "The Picture Market," *Creative Art*, July 1928, 40.

50. Quoted in Tepfer, "Edith Gregor Halpert and the Downtown Gallery," 180. William Zorach remembered, "At first they expected the antiques to carry the art." Zorach, *Art Is My Life*, 88.

51. Edith Halpert to Holger Cahill, February 3, 1940, series 2, reel 5286, frames 170–171, HCP; Halpert to Cahill, December 15, 1940, series 2, reel 5286, frame 308, HCP; "American Folk Art on View," *New York Times*, September 22, 1931.

52. Tepfer, "Edith Gregor Halpert and the Downtown Gallery," 49.

53. Rumford, "Uncommon Art of the Common People," 32–35.

54. Rourke, *Charles Sheeler*, 141; Corn, *The Great American Thing*, 293–337; Friedman, *Charles Sheeler*.

55. Vlach, "Holger Cahill as Folklorist," 153–154. See also Barbara Lipton, *John Cotton Dana and the Newark Museum* (Newark, NJ: The Newark Museum, 1979).

56. Carol Duncan, "John Cotton Dana's Progressive Museum," in *Self and History: A Tribute to Linda Nochlin*, ed. Aruna D'Souza (London: Thames and Hudson, 2001), 131; "Art for the People's Sake: The Newark Museum's Idea," *New York Times*, April 20, 1924; "News and Comment: John Cotton Dana and the Newark Museum," *Magazine of Art* 37, no. 7 (November 1944): 268–275. See also Kingdon, *John Cotton Dana*, 104.

57. Nicholas Maffei, "John Cotton Dana and the Politics of Exhibiting Industrial Art in the US, 1909–1929," *Journal of Design History* 13, no. 4 (2000): 301–317.

58. Holger Cahill, *American Design: An Address by Holger Cahill Made at the Opening of the Exhibit "Old and New Paths in American Design"* (Newark, NJ: Newark Museum, 1936), 3.

59. Jennifer Marshall, "Common Goods: American Folk Crafts as Sculpture at the Museum of Modern Art, New York City, 1932–33," *Prospects* 27 (2002): 447–465.

60. Warren I. Sussman, "The Thirties," in *The Development of an American Culture,* ed. Stanley Coben and Lorman Rather (Englewood Cliffs, NJ: Prentice-Hall, 1970), 189.

61. Henry G. Alsberg, circular letter, January 1936, series 2, reel 5285, frames 922–923, HCP.

62. "Index of American Design," September 16, 1937, series 2, reel 5285, frame 1462, HCP.

63. Ruth Reeves to Holger Cahill, memorandum, February 4, 1936, series 2, reel 5285, frame 940, HCP. See also Nina Collier to Cahill, Alexander Williams, and Adolph Glassgold, field report, February 13, 1936, series 3, reel 1107, frames 1008–1009, HCP; and Reeves to Cahill, field report, March 23, 1936, series 2, reel 5285, frames 1036–1037, HCP. For a list of contacts at museums and historical associations, see reel 1, frames 48–63, NCP.

64. Holger Cahill to Francis Pollak, January 29, 1936, series 2, reel 5285, frames 935–936, HCP.

65. Nina Collier to Holger Cahill, Alexander Williams, and Adolph Glassgold, field report, February 18, 1936, series 3, reel 1107, frame 1012, HCP. A copy of this field report is also located in box 21, WPA Project Folder, AA.

66. Ruth Reeves to Richard Morrison, memorandum, August 1, 1936, series 2, reel 5285, frame 1155, HCP.

67. Ruth Reeves to Holger Cahill, memorandum, February 26, 1936, series 2, reel 5285, frames 995–996, HCP.

68. Reeves to Cahill, memorandum, February 26, 1936. See also Reeves to Cahill and Adolph Glassgold, memorandum, March 3, 1936, series 2, reel 5285, frame 1015, HCP; and Reeves to Cahill and Glassgold, memorandum, March 26, 1936, series 2, reel 5285, frames 1041–1042, HCP. For Benson's obituary, see "Rita Romilly Benson Dead at 79," *New York Times,* April 7, 1980. For Benson and Gurdjieff, see Paul Beekman Taylor, *Gurdjieff's America: Mediating the Miraculous* (London: Lighthouse Editions, 2004).

69. Ruth Reeves to Holger Cahill and Adolph Glassgold, field report, June 17, 1936, series 2, reel 5285, frame 1122, HCP.

70. By this time the Shaker village of Watervliet, outside Albany, which had been central to the construction of the New York State Museum's Shaker collection, had been converted to an airport and a county poor farm.

71. Ruth Reeves to Holger Cahill and Adolph Glassgold, field report, April 17, 1936, series 2, reel 5285, frames 1061–1062, HCP.

72. The idea of moving the Andrewses' collection to Boston for recording purposes was proposed as early as February 14, 1936. See Nina Collier to Holger Cahill,

memorandum, February 14, 1936, series 3, reel 1107, frame 1010, HCP; Ruth Reeves to Cahill and Adolph Glassgold, memorandum, April 22, 1936, series 2, reel 5265, frame 1065, HCP.

73. Frank W. Sterner to Edward Andrews, January 9, 1936; Sterner to Andrews, January 20, 1936; Holger Cahill to Andrews, March 9, 1936, all box 21, folder WPA Project, AA.

74. Ruth Reeves to Holger Cahill, May 7, 1936, series 2, reel 5285, frame 1090, HCP.

75. Ruth Reeves to Holger Cahill and Adolph Glassgold, field report, May 24, 1936, series 2, reel 5285, frame 1096, HCP. See also Reeves to Cahill, Thomas Parker, and Glassgold, memorandum, August 5, 1936, series 2, reel 5285, frame 1160, HCP.

76. Constance Rourke, "The Early American Mind in the Making," *New York Herald Tribune Books,* March 12, 1933. For Rourke, see Joan Shelley Rubin, "Rourke, Constance Mayfield," in Garraty and Carnes, eds., *American National Biography,* 18:951–952. For one analysis of Rourke's efforts to define American culture, see Michael Kammen, *Mystic Chords of Memory* (New York: Vintage, 1993), 411–415. See also Victoria Grieve, *The Federal Art Project and the Creation of Middlebrow Culture* (Urbana: University of Illinois Press, 2009), 116–130.

77. Ruth Reeves to Holger Cahill and Adolph Glassgold, field report, June 17, 1936, series 2, reel 5285, frame 1121, HCP. See also Phyllis Crawford, oral history interview. For Rourke and Sheeler, see Joan Shelley Rubin, "A Convergence of Vision: Constance Rourke, Charles Sheeler, and American Art," *American Quarterly* 42, no. 2 (June 1990): 191–222; and Rourke, *Charles Sheeler.*

78. Ruth Reeves to Holger Cahill, Thomas Parker, and Adolph Glassgold, memorandum, August 5, 1936, series 2, reel 5285, frame 1160, HCP.

79. Ruth Reeves to Holger Cahill and Adolph Glassgold, memorandum, July 23, 1936, series 2, reel 5285, frame 1141, HCP.

80. Ruth Reeves to Richard Morrison, memorandum, August 1, 1936, series 2, reel 5285, frame 1156, HCP. For Moutal and Smith, see "Appendix 1: Artists' Biographies," in Clayton, ed., *Drawing on America's Past,* 248.

81. For Vincentini, see Nina Collier to Frances Pollak, January 14, 1936, series 2, reel 5385, frame 924, HCP. See also Melissa A. McEuen, *Seeing America: Women Photographers between the Wars* (Lexington: University Press of Kentucky, 2000), 279. Reeves and Vincentini had served together on the faculty of the Design Laboratory, a WPA-funded art school in New York City. "WPA Establishes Free Art School," *New York Times,* December 2, 1935. For Herlick, see "Human Element Important," *New York Times,* October 31, 1935; and "Federal Gallery Show," *New York Times,* May 12, 1937. See also *Photographs: Sheldon Memorial Art Gallery Collections, University of Nebraska-Lincoln* (Lincoln: Nebraska Art Association, 1977), 154–155. Herlick also took photographs for the Historic American Buildings Survey, which are now in the

Library of Congress. See "Sea and Land Church, Henry and Market Streets, New York County, NY," Library of Congress, https://www.loc.gov.

82. Lesley Herzberg, *A Promising Venture: Shaker Photographs from the WPA* (Clinton, NY: Richard W. Couper Press, 2012), 13–14.

83. Lesley Herzberg and the Hancock Shaker Village have provided a great service by making these images readily available in her book *A Promising Venture.*

84. Lawrence W. Levine, "The Historian and the Icon: Photography and the American People in the 1930s and 1940s," in *Documenting America, 1935–1943*, ed. Carl Fleischhauer and Beverly W. Brannan (Berkeley: University of California Press, 1988), 28.

85. Ruth Reeves to Richard Morrison and Gordon Smith, memorandum, July 10, 1936, series 2, reel 5285, frame 1135, HCP. See also Reeves to Holger Cahill and Adolph Glassgold, memorandum, series 2, reel 5285, frame 1140, HCP.

86. Virginia Heckert, "237. Charles Sheeler," in Maria Morris Hambourge et al., *The Waking Dream: Photography's First Century* (New York: Metropolitan Museum of Art, 1993), 360; Charles Millard, "The Photography of Charles Sheeler," in *Charles Sheeler* (Washington, DC: Smithsonian Institution Press, 1968), 81–86; Karen Mae Lucic, "The Present and the Past in the Work of Charles Sheeler" (Ph.D. diss., Yale University, 1989), 112–125.

87. See for example, "Bucks County Barn" and "Side of White Barn," both from 1917, reproduced in Theodore E. Stebbins, Jr., and Norman Keyes, Jr., *Charles Sheeler: The Photographs* (Boston: Museum of Fine Arts, 1987); and Paul Strand, *Time in New England* (New York: Oxford University Press, 1950).

88. Levine, "The Historian and the Icon," 33–37.

89. Ruth Reeves to Richard Morrison and Gordon Smith, memorandum, July 10, 1936, series 2, reel 5285, frame 1136, HCP.

90. Ruth Reeves to Holger Cahill and Adolph Glassgold, field report, June 17, 1936, series 2, reel 5285, frame 1123, HCP.

91. Sharon Long Baerny, "Yvonne Twining Humber: An Artist of the Depression Era," *Woman's Art Journal* 16, no. 2 (Autumn 1995–Winter 1996): 16–23. See also Edith A. Tonelli, "The Avant-Garde in Boston: The Experiment of the WPA Federal Art Project," *Archives of American Art Journal* 20, no.1 (1980): 18–24. For Twining's obituary, see Regina Hackett, "Yvonne Twining Humber: Her Love of Art Never Diminished," *Seattle Post-Intelligencer*, May 18, 2004, http://seattlepi.nwsource.com.

92. Howard Devree, "Young American Artists," *New York Times*, February 9, 1934; Howard Devree, "Galleries," *New York Times*, January 7, 1934.

93. "Berkshire People Represented in Williams Exhibit," *Berkshire Eagle* (Pittsfield, MA), June 16, 1939; "Paints South Egremont Scene," *Berkshire Eagle*, August 13, 1938; "Stockbridge Tea Opens Art Exhibit," *New York Times*, September 8, 1935; "Art Prizes in the Berkshires," *New York Times*, September 7, 1935.

94. D. A., "Four New England Painters," *Christian Science Monitor,* December 21, 1937.

95. Ruth Reeves to Richard Morrison, memorandum, August 1, 1936, series 2, reel 5285, frame 1156, HCP.

96. Reeves also apparently produced an oil painting of a Shaker subject, which she described as being in a "primitive style." In her final culminating memo to Richard Morrison on her departure from Pittsfield, she indicated that it was incomplete. If it exists, this work is unlocated. Ruth Reeves to Holger Cahill and Adolph Glassgold, field report, June 17, 1936, series 2, reel 5285, frame 1123, HCP. See also Reeves to Cahill and Glassgold, memorandum, July 23, 1936, series 2, reel 5285, frame 1141, HCP; and Reeves to Richard C. Morrison and Gordon M. Smith, field report, August 16, 1936, series 2, reel 5285, frame 1169, HCP.

97. Ruth Reeves to Holger Cahill, Thomas Parker, and Adolph Glassgold, memorandum, August 5, 1936, series 2, reel 5285, frame 1161, HCP.

98. Ruth Reeves to Holger Cahill and Adolph Glassgold, memorandum, July 23, 1936, series 2, reel 5285, frame 1139, HCP.

99. Edward Deming Andrews and Faith Andrews, *Fruits of the Shaker Tree of Life* (Stockbridge, MA: Berkshire Traveller Press, 1975), 154. See also Ruth Reeves to Holger Cahill and Adolph Glassgold, memorandum, August 10, 1936, series 2, reel 5285, frame 1166, HCP.

100. Ruth Reeves to Richard Morrison and Gordon Smith, memorandum, July 10, 1936, series 2, reel 5285, frame 1134, HCP.

101. Ruth Reeves to Holger Cahill and Adolph Glassgold, memorandum, July 23, 1936, series 2, reel 5285, frame 1141, HCP. The Andrewses also may have been jealous of Sheeler's close relationship with Juliana Force, who was their client and patron.

102. Ruth Reeves to Holger Cahill, memorandum, August 10, 1936, series 2, reel 5285, frame 1164, HCP; Avis Berman, *Rebels on Eighth Street: Juliana Force and the Whitney Museum of American Art* (New York: Atheneum, 1990), 317. See also Reeves to Cahill and Adolph Glassgold, field report, July 23, 1936, series 2, reel 5285, frames 1139–1141, HCP. See also Mario S. De Pillis, "The Edward Deming Andrews Shaker Collection: Saving a Culture," in *Gather up the Fragments: The Andrews Shaker Collection,* ed. Mario S. De Pillis and Christian Goodwillie (Hancock, MA: Hancock Shaker Village, 2008), 20–24.

103. Edward Deming Andrews and Faith Andrews, *Shaker Furniture: The Craftsmanship of an American Communal Sect* (New Haven, CT: Yale University Press, 1937). See also Stephen J. Stein, *The Shaker Experience in America* (New Haven, CT: Yale University Press, 1992), 375.

104. Richard C. Morrison, oral history interview, June 8, 1965, 7, Archives of American Art. In a report to Morrison, Ruth Reeves indicated that Vincentini also harbored

resentments against the Andrewses. See Reeves to Morrison and Gordon M. Smith, memorandum, August 16, 1936, series 2, reel 5285, frames 1169–1170, HCP.

105. Ruth Reeves to Holger Cahill, Thomas Parker, and Adolph Glassgold, memorandum, August 5, 1936, series 2, reel 5285, frame 1160, HCP. Surprisingly, only four days earlier in a memo to Richard Morrison, Reeves had dismissed the whole matter as "one of those little things which, if allowed to go on, causes a tension that snaps the main currents." See Reeves to Richard Morrison, memorandum, August 1, 1936, series 2, reel 5285, frame 1156, HCP.

106. Marguerite Frost to Marguerite Melcher, April 19, 1943, Marguerite Melcher Papers, Shaker Manuscripts, reel 9, New York Public Library; Ruth Reeves to Holger Cahill and Adolph Glassgold, field report, May 24, 1936, series 2, reel 5285, frame 1096, HCP; Adele Brandeis, oral history interview, June 1, 1965, Archives of American Art. See also Reeves to Cahill and Glassgold, memorandum, August 10, 1936, series 2, reel 5285, frame 1166, HCP.

107. Ruth Reeves to Holger Cahill and Adolph Glassgold, field report, June 17, 1936, series 2, reel 5285, frame 1122, HCP. See also Reeves to Cahill and Glassgold, memorandum, August 10, 1936, series 2, reel 5285, frame 1166, HCP. For Weld, see "Appendix I: Artists' Biographies," in Clayton, ed., *Drawing on America's Past,* 248.

108. "Appendix II: Annotated List of State Projects," in Clayton, ed., *Drawing on America's Past,* 250; Sandra Shaffer Tinkham, ed., *The Consolidated Catalog to the Index of American Design* (Teaneck, NJ: Somerset House, 1980), 12A–16E.

109. Constance Rourke to Holger Cahill, report, September 19, 1936, series 2, reel 5285, frame 1210, HCP; Adele Brandeis, oral history interview. For Brandeis, see document dated August 30, 1935, series 3, reel 1107, frame 39, HCP. See also Erika Doss, "Regional Reputations, Modern Tastes, and Cultural Nationalism: Kentucky and the Index of American Design, 1936–1942," in *Kentucky by Design: The Decorative Arts and American Culture,* ed. Andrew Kelly (Lexington: University Press of Kentucky, 2015), 19–22.

110. For an overview of the Index of American Design in Kentucky, see Kelly, ed., *Kentucky by Design.*

111. Tinkham, *Consolidated Catalog to the Index of American Design.* For Isenberg, see William D. Moore, "'United We Commemorate': The Kentucky Pioneer Memorial Association, James Isenberg, and Early Twentieth-Century Heritage Tourism," *Public Historian* 30, no. 3 (Summer 2008): 51–81.

112. The Andrewses' grievances against all aspects of the Index of American Design are catalogued fully in a letter to Richard Morrison dated October 15, 1936. Faith and Edward Deming Andrews to Morrison, October 15, 1936, box 31, folder WPA Project, AA. See also "Open Letter," n.d., box 21, folder WPA Project, AA.

113. Ruth Reeves to Richard C. Morrison and Gordon M. Smith, memorandum, August 16, 1936, series 2, reel 5285, frames 1169–1170, HCP. See also draft of letter from Edward Deming Andrews to Mr. M, n.d., box 21, folder WPA Project, AA.

114. Richard C. Morrison to Edward Andrews, September 12, 1936, box 21, folder WPA Project, AA.

115. Adolph Glassgold to Constance Rourke, October 1, 1936, series 2, reel 5285, frames 1223–1224, HCP.

116. Harry L. Kinnear to Edward Andrews, October 20, 1936, box 21, folder WPA Project, AA.

117. Andrews and Andrews, *Fruits of the Shaker Tree*, 154.

118. Constance Rourke to Holger Cahill, memorandum, October 19, 1936, series 2, reel 5285, frame 1229, HCP.

119. Constance Rourke to Holger Cahill, report, January 10, 1937, series 2, reel 5285, frames 1305–1308, HCP. For Reeves's subsequent activities with the Southern Highlanders, Inc., see Jane S. Becker, *Selling Tradition: Appalachia and the Construction of an American Folk, 1930–1940* (Chapel Hill: University of North Carolina Press, 1998), 114–115, 192–193.

120. Adolph Glassgold to Holger Cahill, memorandum, August 4, 1937, series 2, reel 5285, frames 1399–1402, HCP.

121. Jerry V. Grant and Douglas R. Allen, *Shaker Furniture Makers* (Hanover, NH: University Press of New England, 1989), 136–163.

122. For additional examples of beds with ornamental turnings crafted by Emmory Brooks, see Fran Kramer, *Simply Shaker: Groveland and the New York Communities* (Rochester, NY: Rochester Museum and Science Center, 1991), 84–85. See also John T. Kirk, *The Shaker World: Art, Life, Belief* (New York: Abrams, 1997), 207–214.

123. Gerrie Kennedy, Galen Beale, and Jim Johnson, *Shaker Baskets and Poplarware* (Stockbridge, MA: Berkshire House, 1992), 86–89; June Sprigg, *By Shaker Hands* (New York: Knopf, 1975), 138–319; Beverly Gordon, *Shaker Textile Arts* (Hanover, NH: University Press of New England, 1980), 45–48, 216–223. See also M. Stephen Miller, "Designed for Sale: Shaker Commerce with the World," in *Shaker Design: Out of This World*, ed. Jean M. Burks (New Haven, CT: Yale University Press, 2008), 83–85.

124. Gordon, *Shaker Textile Arts*, 204; Beverly Gordon, "Victorian Fancy Goods: Another Reappraisal of Shaker Material Culture," *Winterthur Portfolio* 25, nos. 2–3 (Summer–Autumn 1990): 115.

125. A Shaker fancywork sewing stand was recorded in Kentucky by Eugene W. McGill. Possibly distance from New York made the Kentucky WPA administrators less cognizant of the modernist ideology. See Jean M. Burks, "A Shaker Poplar Sewing Stand," in Kelly, ed., *Kentucky by Design*, 97–99.

126. For references to noncanonical decorations within Shaker villages, see John Harlow Ott, *Hancock Shaker Village: A Guidebook and History,* 4th ed. (Hancock, MA: Shaker Community, 1976), 105–107; and Julie Nicoletta, *The Architecture of the Shakers* (Woodstock, VT: Countryman Press, 1995), 81–87.

127. *New Horizons in American Art* (New York: Museum of Modern Art, 1936).

128. See, for example, Helen Johnson Keyes, "Artists Record American Handiwork," *Christian Science Monitor,* October 3, 1936.

129. William Germain Dooley, "Graphic Survey Is Being Made of Shaker Culture," *Boston Evening Transcript,* September 19, 1936. See also, William Germain Dooley, "Early American Design's Index Shows Progress," *Boston Evening Transcript,* September 19, 1936. Dooley seems to have lifted the quoted words directly from a press release prepared by the Museum of Modern Art. See "Shaker Art Revealed," folder B20.7, DMP.

130. "Shaker Crafts Unique Contribution," *Berkshire Eagle,* October 7, 1936.

131. "The Art of the American Shakers," *New York Herald Tribune,* September 13, 1936.

132. William Germain Dooley, "Textiles and Shaker Arts Featured in Index Exhibit," *Boston Evening Transcript,* January 30, 1937; *Index of American Design Exhibition* (Cambridge, MA: Fogg Museum of Art, Harvard University, 1937).

133. "Here and There," *New York Times,* January 30, 1938. See also Carl Greenleaf Bede, "Artists Record American Handicrafts," *Christian Science Monitor,* April 2, 1938.

134. Edward Alden Jewell, "WPA Art Is Shown at Exhibition Here," *New York Times,* March 15, 1939; Edward Alden Jewell, "Saving Our Usable Past," *New York Times,* March 19, 1939.

135. Walter Rendell Storey, "Our Colonial Craft a Source of Modern Design," *New York Times,* July 3, 1938. For images of this installation at Macy's, see series 3, reel 1108, frames 305–318, HCP.

136. "An Exhibition That Makes American History Come Alive," *Chicago Daily Tribune,* March 16, 1937.

137. Arthur Millier, "American Design Recorded by Federals," *Los Angeles Times,* March 27, 1938.

138. Walter Rendell Storey, "Antique Exhibits: Auctions," *New York Times,* March 28, 1943.

139. "President Roosevelt's Message to Congress on the State of the Union," *New York Times,* January 7, 1941.

140. Benjamin Knotts, "Hands to Work and Hearts to God," *Metropolitan Museum of Art Bulletin* 1, no. 7 (March 1943): 236.

141. Index of American Design Archives, WPA Records, box 23, folder Ohio State Museum, National Gallery of Art, Washington, DC. See also Will Adams, "Rise and

Fall of the Shaker Empire: Museum Shows Mementos of Sect," July 20, 1947, Index of American Design Archives, WPA Records, box 20, folder Shakers—Articles and Clippings, National Gallery of Art.

142. Betty Lee Mastin, "Something for Everyone at Shakertown Festival," *Lexington [KY] Sunday Herald-Ledger,* October 8, 1961; "Shakertown Festival to Feature Exhibits, Items," *Harrodsburg [KY] Herald,* September 29, 1961; "Shakertown Fall Festival Is in Progress," *Harrodsburg Herald,* October 6, 1961.

143. "Checklist of Shaker Material Shown at the Philadelphia Museum of Art, April 19–May 20, 1962," *Philadelphia Museum of Art Bulletin,* 57, no. 273 (Spring 1962): 114.

144. "Smithsonian Shaker Show on View Here," *Berkshire Eagle,* July 21, 1962.

145. Rita Wellman and Holger Cahill, "American Design," *House and Garden,* July 1938, 15–16; "Index of American Design: A Portfolio," *Fortune* 15 (June 1937): 103–110. In 1950, sixteen Shaker images were included in Christensen, *The Index of American Design.*

146. Elizabeth McCausland, "The Shaker Legacy," *Magazine of Art* 37, no. 8 (December 1944): 287–291.

147. "Shaker—Pattern of Practical Beauty—Modern Then and Now," *House and Garden,* March 1945, 36–45.

148. It also included an article entitled "The Shaker Legacy" by William Lassiter of the New York State Museum.

149. Andrews and Andrews, *Fruits of the Shaker Tree,* 61, 82.

150. See Ruth Green Harris, "The Federal Arts Projects Explore Folkways," *New York Times,* January 8, 1939. For a brief discussion of the impact of the Index of American Design on subsequent modern furniture, see Jean M. Burks, "The Shakers and Modernism," in *The Andrews Shaker Collection* (Marlborough, MA: Skinner, 2014), 134–139.

151. Don Wallance, *Shaping America's Products* (New York: Reinhold, 1956), 110–111. For Diamond, see Cherie Fehrman and Kenneth Fehrman, *Postwar Interior Design: 1945–1960* (New York: Van Nostrand Reinhold, 1987), 78–79. See also Ella Howard and Eric Setliff, "'In a Man's World': Women Industrial Designers," in Kirkham, ed., *Women Designers in the USA,* 279–280. Diamond's papers at the Archive Center of the Smithsonian Institution's National Museum of American History contain photographs from the Index of American Design. Freda Diamond Papers, box 3, folder 10, Archive Center, National Museum of American History, Smithsonian Institution, Washington, DC.

152. Regina Lee Blaszczyk, *Imagining Consumers: Design and Innovation from Wedgwood to Corning* (Baltimore: Johns Hopkins University Press, 2000), 249–252. See also "Group to Push Art in Lines for Home," *New York Times,* April 6, 1940.

153. Elizabeth MacR. Boykin, "Shaker Furniture of Last Century Adapted to Modern

Apartments," *New York Sun,* October 4, 1937; Freda Diamond, "The Pendulum Swings to Informal Furniture," *Furniture World* 146, no. 13 (December 30, 1937): 45; Katharine Hill, "Shaker Furniture Vies with Modern," *Herald Examiner* (Chicago, IL), January 30, 1938; Lynn Hardesty, "Simple Settings Fit New Types of Furniture," *Washington Post,* January 2, 1938; J. W. Robinson Company Display Advertisement, *Los Angeles Times,* November 22, 1938.

154. *"Shaker" Takes a Worldly Turn,* pamphlet in the Freda Diamond Collection, box 4, folder 10, Archive Center, National Museum of American History.

155. Herman Miller Furniture Company, *We Present Shaker Furniture* (Zeeland, MI: Herman Miller Furniture Company, 1938).

156. Margaret White, "You'd Swear They Were Modern," *Better Homes and Gardens,* November 1937, 34.

157. Elizabeth McRae Boykin, "Shaker Furniture in Modern Setting Is Naively Sophisticated," *Atlanta Constitution,* November 2, 1937. See also Lynn Hardesty, "Simple Settings Fit New Types of Furniture," *Washington Post,* January 2, 1938.

158. Lenore Kent, "Shaker-Type Furniture in Tryout Stage," *Washington Post,* September 11, 1938. See also Helen Johnson Keyes, "Sophistication Adopts Shaker Simplicity," *Christian Science Monitor,* December 18, 1937.

159. Boykin, "Shaker Furniture of Last Century."

160. Millier, "American Design Recorded by Federals."

161. "Religious Simplicity in Shaker Modern," *Furniture Index* 74, no. 3 (February 1938): 20–21.

162. Homer Eaton Keyes to Edward Deming Andrews, October 8, 1937, box 5, Correspondence, Freda Diamond, AA.

163. Edward Deming Andrews to Barry Bingham, September 8, 1961, box 18, folder Pleasant Hill (1): Correspondence, Pamphlets, etc., AA.

164. Adolph Glassgold to Parker, memorandum, July 12, 1937, series 2, reel 5285, frame 1352, HCP.

165. Betty Pepis, "New Designs on the Shaker Scene," *New York Times,* October 21, 1951; Betty Pepis, "Shaker Reproductions," *New York Times,* June 16, 1955; Barbara Plumb, "Shaker Furniture Is Revived in Copies," *New York Times,* May 27, 1963; Mary Roche, "Useful Then, Useful Now," *New York Times,* December 12, 1948; Kory Rogers, "In the Spirit: Twentieth-Century and Contemporary Shaker-Inspired Design," in *Shaker Design: Out of This World,* ed. Jean M. Burks (New Haven, CT: Yale University Press, 2008), 187–204. For George Nakashima, see Wallance, *Shaping America's Products,* 149–151.

166. O. Gueft, "McCobb's Predictor Solves Many Problems, *Interiors* 111 (October 1951): 126.

167. Fehrman and Fehrman, *Postwar Interior Design,* 81–82; Kathryn B. Hiesinger

and George H. Marcus, *Landmarks of Twentieth-Century Design: An Illustrated Handbook* (New York: Abbeville, 1993), 361. See also Mel Byars, *The Design Encyclopedia* (London: Laurence King, 1994), 367; and "Paul McCobb, Modern Designer, Dies," *New York Times*, March 12, 1969.

168. Louis Hagen, "Best in Design Quiet, Stays in Background," *Dallas Morning News,* January 12, 1952.

169. W. & J. Sloane's advertisement, *Sunday Star* (Washington, DC), February 12, 1952; Maison Blanche advertisement, *New Orleans Times-Picayune*, May 5, 1953; Bloomingdale's advertisement, *New York Times*, October 28, 1951. See also Pepis, "New Designs on the Shaker Scene."

170. Gloria Bernard, "New Group Makes Debut," *Boston Traveler,* April 24, 1952.

171. Betty Ann, "Modern Reflecting the Past," *Milwaukee Journal,* December 26, 1951.

172. Elizabeth Hillyer, "American Furniture Goes Native," *Sunday Journal-Star* (Peoria, IL), October 21, 1951.

173. "This Furniture Designed Locally for Tomorrow," *Boston Evening American,* March 15, 1952.

174. Pepis, "New Designs on the Shaker Scene."

175. For Drexel, see Wiley J. Williams, "Drexel Furniture Company," in *Encyclopedia of North Carolina*, ed. William S. Powell (Chapel Hill: University of North Carolina Press, 2006), https://www.ncpedia.org. See also Allen C. Irvine, *Sixty Years of Progress in the Making of Fine Furniture: Drexel Enterprises, Inc., 1903–1963* (Drexel, NC: Drexel Enterprises, 1963?). Drexel had previously had success with a line entitled "American Traditional" and acquired the name and designs of the Wallace Nutting Company. Irvine, *Sixty Years of Progress,* 36.

176. Jeanne Barnes, "New Furniture Group Creates Wide Interest," *Dallas Morning News*, May 25, 1958. For an illustration of the variety of forms offered, see "Kornmyer's Presents Declaration by Drexel," *Morning Advocate* (Baton Rouge, LA), April 26, 1959. An advertisement for Milwaukee's Kunzelmann-Esser furniture store claims that they were offering "over 66 pieces for your living room, bedroom, dining room and occasional pieces." "Opening Sale of America's Newest and Smartest Modern Walnut Fashion for 1958," *Milwaukee Journal*, March 16, 1958.

177. Drexel Furniture Company, "Presenting Declaration by Drexel," *Los Angeles Times,* March 2, 1958.

178. Betsy Marsh, "It's American Contemporary," *News and Observer* (Raleigh, N.C.), March 9, 1958.

179. "Local Boys Make Good: Here Is the Work of Kipp Stewart and Stewart Mac-Dougall," *Los Angeles Times,* January 30, 1955.

180. Marsh, "It's American Contemporary"; Grace Holm, "Pacesetters in Design: Two Newcomers," *Oregonian* (Portland), January 22, 1956; "3 Young Designers: Logic and

Decoration," *Los Angeles Times*, January 30, 1955. See also George Beronius, "A Way of Life . . . a Way of Design," *Los Angeles Times*, March 2, 1958.

181. Abraham & Straus, "Starts Monday . . . 'Declaration' . . . by Drexel," *New York Times,* January 26, 1958.

182. Bloomingdales, "Half-Yearly Sale of Furniture and Rugs," *New York Times,* February 12, 1961. Stewart had earlier experimented with case pieces as room dividers in his Criterion Collection. See Virginia Stewart, "Design for '53," *Los Angeles Times*, November 15, 1952.

183. Abraham & Straus, "Starts Monday."

184. Drexel Furniture Company, "Presenting Declaration by Drexel."

185. Braslau Furniture Company, "Declaration by Drexel," *Corpus Christi [TX] Caller-Times*, October 27, 1959. "Assert your own American good taste" also appears in this advertisement. See also Braslau Furniture Company, "A New Frontier in Furniture Fashion," *Corpus Christi Caller-Times*, April 18, 1959. This advertisement asserts that "Declaration's selection is as wide as America's Boundaries."

186. Barnes, "New Furniture Group."

187. Motorola, "New Motorola Stereo Hi-Fi Has the Difference You Can Hear!" *Life Magazine,* October 24, 1960, 129.

188. Stevens Shopping Centers, "Motorola Television," *New York Times,* October 23, 1959. See also B. Altman & Company, "Motorola Console TV," *New York Times*, December 3, 1959. By 1965, the Declaration line was being used to house color televisions. See "Motorola TV Lines Feature Elegant Cabinets by Drexel," *Dallas Morning News,* October 15, 1965.

189. Irvine, *Sixty Years of Progress*, 38.

190. For the Brussels World's Fair and the Moscow trade fair, see Robert H. Haddow, *Pavilions of Plenty: Exhibiting American Culture Abroad in the 1950s* (Washington, DC: Smithsonian Institution Press, 1997). See also Robert W. Rydell, "'This Is America': The American Pavilion at the 1958 Brussels World's Fair," in *Modern American Landscapes*, ed. Mick Gidley and Robert Lawson-Peebles (Amsterdam: VU University Press, 1995), 197–218; and *This Is America: Official United States Guide Book Brussels World's Fair 1958* (New York: Office of the United States Commissioner General, 1958).

191. Haddow, *Pavilions of Plenty,* 157.

192. Irene Zieget, "Our Shaker Collection and How It Started," *Yankee Magazine,* April 1970, 126.

193. John Wanamaker Department Store, "Shaker Simplicity," *New York Times,* January 19, 1939. See also John Wanamaker Department Store, "Shaker Simplicity," *New York Herald Tribune*, January 23, 1939.

194. Woodward & Lothrop, "'Modern Shaker' Neckwear Frills," *Washington Post*, March 1, 1939.

195. New York Public Library, "André Studios: 1930s Fashion Drawings and Sketches in the Collections of FIT and the New York Public Library," http://andrestudios.nypl .org. See also New York Public Library, "André Studios, 1930–1941: Fashion Drawings and Sketches in the Collections of FIT and the New York Public Library," http:// andrestudios.nypl.org.

196. For Naylor, see "Genevieve Naylor, 74, Photographer Dies," *New York Times,* July 25, 1989; For Gill, see W. L Broecker, "The Elegant Eye of Leslie Gill," *Popular Photography,* September 1984, 64–71, 88–89. For Daché, see Bernadine Morris, "Lilly Daché, 97, Creator of Hats for the Fashion Set of Yesteryear," *New York Times*, January 2, 1990.

197. "The Gift to Be Simple," *Junior Bazaar,* January 1946, n.p.

198. For a popularly disseminated image of a reconstructed Shaker period room, see *America's Arts and Skills, by the Editors of Life* (New York: E. P. Dutton, 1957), 87.

199. For an example of a more recent book celebrating the constructed understanding of the Shakers, see John S. Bowman, *Shaker Style* (North Dighton, MA: JG Press, 2004).

CHAPTER 3: "USING MATERIAL FROM OUR OWN HISTORY IN THE ARTS"

1. Humphrey, in contrast, who grew up in and around Chicago seems to have been exposed to the Shakers as an itinerant professional dancer.

2. "The Shakers," *Vanity Fair,* January 1933, 20–21. The revue opened on October 18 of the previous year. See "Theatrical Notes," *New York Times,* October 18, 1932. See also the display advertisement in the same issue. For an announcement of its forthcoming premier, see John Martin, "The Dance: War Satire," *New York Times,* October 2, 1932. For an advertisement for *Americana,* see *New York Times,* October 31, 1932. Selected pages of the program for the opening night of this production are available online at *Playbill,* 2019, http://www.playbill.com.

3. Another Steichen photograph of Doris Humphrey's dancers in their Shaker costumes from *Americana* appeared in the December 15, 1932, issue of *Vogue.* Edward Steichen, "Two Doris Humphrey Dancers in the Hysterical Shaker Dance of 'Americana,'" *Vogue,* December 15, 1932, 49.

4. Don McDonagh, *The Complete Guide to Modern Dance* (New York: Doubleday, 1976), 90. For Lawrence, see "Pauline Lawrence Is Dead; Designed Limon Costumes," *New York Times,* July 31, 1971.

5. McDonagh, *Complete Guide to Modern Dance,* 90; Joseph H. Mazo, *Prime Movers: The Makers of Modern Dance in America* (New York: William Morrow, 1977), 130. For another verbal description of *The Shakers,* see Selma Jeanne Cohen, *Doris Humphrey: An Artist First* (Middletown, CT: Wesleyan University Press, 1972), 95–96.

6. Margaret Lloyd, *The Borzoi Book of Modern Dance* (New York: Knopf, 1949), 89.

7. "Summer Music," *Brooklyn Daily Eagle*, August 6, 1933. For Johnson, see Mary Frances Early, "Johnson, Hall (1888–1970)," *American National Biography*, February 2000, http://www.anb.org.

8. John Martin, "The Dance: A New Field in the Theatre," *New York Times*, October 16, 1932; Mazo, *Prime Movers*, 130. When the piece was performed in Boston in May 1935, the accordion was part of the performance, but Hall Johnson's chorus had apparently been removed. See "Repertory Theatre: Doris Humphrey, Charles Weidman and Dance Group," *Boston Globe*, March 15, 1935.

9. Mazo, *Prime Movers*, 130. In the 1940s, Shaker music was added to the performance. When the piece was performed at City Center in 1949, it was accompanied with music arranged and directed by George Wood. See Paul Affelder, "Four Modern Dance Groups Open First Season of N.Y. Dance Theater at City Center," *Brooklyn Daily Eagle*, December 15, 1949.

10. Elizabeth K. Dale, Columbus, Ohio, to Doris Humphrey, May 1943, MGZMC—Res. 3—C549.10, DHC.

11. "A Bit of Americana in the Dance," published to accompany "On with the Dance," *Literary Digest*, October 29, 1932, 17.

12. See, for example, Jill Johnston, "New England Revivals," *Village Voice* (New York), September 10, 1964. Writing in the *Cleveland Plain Dealer*, Wilma Salisbury stated simply, "'The Shakers' by Doris Humphrey is one of the classics of American modern dance." Salisbury, "'Quakers' to Shake at Museum Tonight," *Cleveland Plain Dealer*, October 11, 1974. See also Laura Shapiro, "New Group to Recreate Neo-Classics for 25th Connecticut Dance Festival," *Boston Globe*, June 25, 1972; and Eileen Sondak, "Modern Dancers Take on Classics," *Los Angeles Times*, October 27, 1987.

13. John Martin, "Novelties Presented at Dance Concert," *New York Times*, February 5, 1931; John Martin, "The Dance Theatre Opens Second Season," *New York Times*, February 2, 1931.

14. For a thumbnail biography of Humphrey, see Selma Jeanne Cohen, "Humphrey, Doris," in *American National Biography Online*, February 2000, http://www.anb.org. For an entrance into the vast bibliography related to Doris Humphrey, see Mary E. Edsall, "Shakers in Cyberspace: Electronic Resources and the Bibliography of Dance," *Dance Research Journal* 28, no. 2 (Autumn 1996): 60–74.

15. John Martin, "The Dance: A Week of Unique Programs," *New York Times*, January 5, 1930.

16. Brooks Atkinson, "Design and Dance in an 'American Revue' That Represents Modern Taste in Artistry," *New York Times*, October 6, 1932. Atkinson's words were also reported in "On with the Dance," *Literary Digest*, October 29, 1932, 17. For more mixed reviews of modern dance in "Americana," see Charlotte Michaud, "The Dance,"

Lewiston [ME] Evening Journal, November 29, 1932. Martin noted that Humphrey had successfully transplanted her earlier dances into McEvoy's revue "without despoiling them of any of their bloom." See John Martin, "The Dance: A Negro Play," *New York Times,* March 13, 1933.

17. Edward Cushing, "Music of the Day," *Brooklyn Daily Eagle,* February 2, 1931.

18. "'The Shakers' Tops the Humphrey-Weidman Final Recital," *Brooklyn Daily Eagle,* April 30, 1934.

19. See, for example, Julia L. Foulkes, *Modern Bodies: Dance and American Modernism from Martha Graham to Alvin Ailey* (Chapel Hill: University of North Carolina Press, 2002).

20. Cohen, *Doris Humphrey,* 95.

21. Marcia B. Siegel, "Shakers, The," in *International Encyclopedia of Dance,* ed. Selma Jeanne Cohen and George E. Dorris (New York: Oxford University Press, 1998), 5:57; Dorothy Stowe, *Deseret News* (Salt Lake City, UT), June 15, 1994; Yunyu Wang, "Reconstruction of Humphrey's Masterpieces in the United States and Taiwan," *Choreography and Dance* 4, no. 4 (1998): 93–107. Writing in 1974 of Humphrey's oeuvre, Deborah Jowitt asserted, "Only 'Shakers' is performed fairly regularly—usually by college groups." Jowitt, "A Feast of Brain-Teasers," *Village Voice,* December 9, 1974. For examples of revivals of *The Shakers,* see "Dance Program," *Boston Globe,* December 18, 1962; "Miss McIntosh in Sweet Briar Events," *Florence [AL] Times,* March 8, 1963; "Keuka Groups to Offer Music, Dance Programs," *Schenectady [NY] Gazette,* November 14, 1966; Margo Miller, "Subsidy of Arts Doubtful: Will Theater-Going Nixon Oblige?" *Boston Globe,* November 17, 1968; Margo Miller, "Spring in Their Feet: The Dance at Dartmouth," *Boston Globe,* August 24, 1969; "'Shakers' to Feature Pitt Dance Program," *Pittsburgh Press,* February 11, 1971; "Dance Takes Foreign Turn at Thomas Hall," *Cleveland Plain Dealer,* October 6, 1974; Christine Temin, "Post-Modern Dance Series Begins at ICA Today," *Boston Globe,* December 14, 1980; Mary Campbell, "Limon Dance Troupe Opens in New York," *Schenectady Gazette,* February 4, 1981; "Dance Company to Perform at ASU," *Schenectady Gazette,* February 13, 1981; and "Modern Dance Program Coming to Dickinson College," *Gettysburg [PA] Times,* November 10, 1986.

22. For Davis and Murphy, see Wanda Corn, *The Great American Thing: Modern Art and National Identity* (Berkeley: University of California Press, 1999), 90–133, 339–348.

23. John Martin, "On Folk Art: The Existence of an American Dance," *New York Times,* July 16, 1933.

24. Barbara Hausler, "The Influence of Francis W. Parker on Doris Humphrey's Teaching Methodology," *Dance Research Journal* 28, no. 2 (Autumn 1996): 10; Lloyd, *Borzoi Book of Modern Dance,* 79. See also "Farm and Society Evolve Art Dance," *Cleveland Plain Dealer,* April 19, 1934.

25. Foulkes, *Modern Bodies*, 133.

26. Foulkes, *Modern Bodies*, 136. For Shawn, see Chistena L. Schlundt, "Shawn, Ted," in *International Encyclopedia of Dance*, 5:583–587.

27. Martin, "The Dance: A Negro Play."

28. Doris Humphrey to her family, September 1930, (S)* MGZMC—Res. 3—C278.15, DHC.

29. Cohen, *Doris Humphrey*; Mazo, *Prime Movers*, 121.

30. Hausler, "The Influence of Francis W. Parker," 11. For Parker, see Flora J. Cooke, "Colonel Francis W. Parker: His Influence on Education," *Schools: Studies in Education* 2, no. 1 (May 2005): 157–170. For a period statement concerning the Francis W. Parker School, see Mrs. Emmons Blaine, "The Origin and Aims of the Francis W. Parker School," *Francis W. Parker School Year Book* 1 (June 1912): 5–10.

31. John Dewey, "How Much Freedom in New Schools?" *New Republic*, July 9, 1930, 204.

32. Natalie Crohn Schmitt, "Creating Community: Experiments in Drama at Francis W. Parker's School, Chicago," *Theatre Survey* 49, no. 1 (May 2008): 39–41.

33. Schmitt, "Creating Community," 41.

34. See Martha Fleming, "Purposes and Values of the Morning Exercise," *Francis W. Parker School Year Book* 2 (June 1913): 4–8.

35. For explication of how to present mathematics in this format, see Herman T. Lukens, "Preparation of an Exercise on Historical Methods in Arithmetic," *Francis W. Parker School Year Book* 2 (June 1913): 30–33. See also Raymond W. Osborne, "Morning Exercises on Science Topics," *Francis W. Parker School Year Book* 2 (June 1913): 73–80.

36. "Evaluation of Morning Exercises," *Francis W. Parker School Year Book* 2 (June 1913): 209.

37. Martha Fleming, "Speech, Oral Reading, and Dramatic Art," *Course of Study* 1, no. 1 (July 1900): 55.

38. Selma Landon Odom, "Sharing the Dances of Many People: The Teaching Work of Mary Wood Hinman," in *Proceedings of the Tenth Annual Conference of the Society of Dance History Scholars*, comp. Christena L. Schlundt (Riverside, CA: Dance History Scholars, 1987), 65–67. For Humphrey's reminiscences about her early experiences with Hinman, see Marcia B. Siegel, *Days on Earth: The Dance of Doris Humphrey* (New Haven, CT: Yale University Press, 1987), 22–24. See also Lloyd, *Borzoi Book of Modern Dance*, 79–80.

39. In her memoir *I Came a Stranger*, Hilda Satt Polacheck remembered that all the girls in her Hull House dancing class loved Hinman. She further reminisced, "She always dressed in a gray accordion-pleated skirt, with a blouse of the same material, a red sash, and gray dancing shoes. She floated around that room like a graceful bird."

Polacheck, *I Came a Stranger: The Story of a Hull-House Girl*, ed. Dena J. Polacheck Epstein. (Urbana: University of Illinois Press, 1989), 77. Folk music was such an integral part of the subsequent settlement house curriculum that Sinclair Lewis satirized it in *Ann Vickers*, his examination of progressive female reformers. Lewis, *Ann Vickers* (Garden City, NY: Doubleday, Doran, 1933), 235.

40. Selma Landen Odom, "Hinman, Mary Wood," in *International Encyclopedia of Dance*, 3:367.

41. Odom, "Hinman, Mary Wood."

42. Patricia Mooney Melvin, "Building Muscles and Civics: Folk Dancing, Ethnic Diversity and the Playground Association of America," *American Studies* 24, no. 1 (Spring 1983): 89–99.

43. Linda J. Tomko, *Dancing Class: Gender, Ethnicity, and Social Divides in American Dance, 1890–1920* (Bloomington: Indiana University Press, 1999), 194–196.

44. Thomas Winter, "'The Healthful Art of Dancing': Luther Halsey Gulick, Gender, the Body, and the Performativity of National Identity," *Journal of American Culture* 22, no. 2 (Summer 1999): 33. See also Mirjana Laušević, *Balkan Fascination: Creating an Alternative Music Culture in America* (New York: Oxford University Press, 2007), 91–95.

45. Luther H. Gulick, *The Healthful Art of Dancing* (New York: Doubleday, Page, 1910). For examples from Hinman, see photographs between pages 18 and 19, between 20 and 21, between 24 and 25, and between 28 and 29. For an image from Burchenal, see image between 32 and 33.

46. Deborah Jowitt, *Time and the Dancing Image* (Berkeley: University of California Press, 1989), 100. The choreography of *Greek Sacrificial Dance* is republished in Cohen, *Doris Humphrey*, 235–236.

47. Tomko, *Dancing Class*, 160–163.

48. Hinman was the "Master of the Pageant" for *Father Penn*, produced in 1915 at Pennsylvania State College. Naima Prevots, "University Courses in Pageantry and American Dance: 1911–1925," in *Proceedings of the Eleventh Annual Conference of the Society of Dance History Scholars*, comp. Christena L. Schlundt (Riverside, CA: Society of Dance History Scholars, 1988), 240.

49. See David Glassberg, *American Historical Pageantry: The Uses of Tradition in the Early Twentieth Century* (Chapel Hill: University of North Carolina Press, 1990).

50. *Hinman School of Gymnastic and Folk Dancing* (1917), n.p., item Res3-Z8, DHC

51. Prevots, "University Courses in Pageantry and American Dance," 247.

52. Mary Porter Beegle and Jack Randall Crawford, *Community Drama and Pageantry* (New Haven, CT: Yale University Press, 1916), 199.

53. Doris Humphrey, "Garland Dance," "Will o' the Wisp (A Dance for Young Children)," and "Daffodils," in Mary Wood Hinman, *Gymnastic and Folk Dancing* (New

York: A. S. Barnes, 1922), 3:64–66, 72–73; Doris Humphrey, "Greek Sacrificial Dance" and "Moment Musical," in Hinman, *Gymnastic and Folk Dancing,* 4:11–13, 20–22.

54. Cohen, *Doris Humphrey,* 28–30.

55. For an introduction to St. Denis, see Kristine Somerville, "The Logic of Dreams: The Life and Work of Ruth St. Denis," *Missouri Review* 36, no. 4 (2013): 123–141. See also Deborah Jowitt, "St. Denis, Ruth," in *American National Biography Online,* February 2000, http://www.anb.org.

56. Lloyd, *Borzoi Book of Modern Dance,* 26–29.

57. For period advice on producing "dance pageants" that harmonize with Humphrey's aesthetics in staging *The Shakers,* see Lucille Marsh, "Producing the Dance Pageant," *Journal of Health and Physical Education* 4, no. 5 (May 1933): 18–20, 63.

58. Peter C. Bunnell, "Introduction," in Barbara Morgan, *Barbara Morgan* (New York: Morgan and Morgan, 1972), 9.

59. Curtis L. Carter, "Barbara Morgan: Philosopher/Poet of Visual Motion," in Curtis L. Carter and William C. Agee, *Barbara Morgan: Prints, Drawings, Watercolors and Photographs* (Milwaukee: Patrick and Beatrice Haggerty Museum of Art, Marquette University, 1988), 8.

60. Elizabeth McCausland, "Books on the Dance," *Dance Observer* 8, no. 9 (1941): 120.

61. Deba P. Patnaik, "Barbara Morgan," in *Barbara Morgan* (New York: Aperture, 1999), 6. She also mounted an exhibition of Edwin Weston's modernist photographs at UCLA.

62. Carter, "Barbara Morgan," 10; Ann T. Keene, "Morgan, Barbara," in *American National Biography Online,* September 2000, http://www.anb.org. Willard Morgan would ultimately become the first photo editor of Henry Luce's *Life* magazine and the first director of the photography division of New York's Museum of Modern Art.

63. James Auer, "Revolutions Have Helped Barbara Morgan Grow," *Milwaukee Journal,* April 10, 1983.

64. For Sheeler, see Theodore E. Stebbins, Jr., and Norman Keyes, Jr., *Charles Sheeler: The Photographs* (Boston: Museum of Fine Arts, 1987). Morgan showed slides of objects in the Barnes Collection at the A.C.A. Gallery on West Eighth Street under the auspices of the Young American Artists Association on March 24, 1939. "Art Notes," *New York Times,* March 24, 1939.

65. Patnaik, "Barbara Morgan," 6; Brett Knappe, "Barbara Morgan's Photographic Interpretation of American Culture, 1935–1980" (Ph.D. diss., University of Kansas, 2008), 83.

66. Morgan quoted in Knappe, "Barbara Morgan's Photographic Interpretation of American Culture," 46. See also Barbara Morgan, "Modern Dance," *Popular Photography* 16, no. 6 (June 1945): 68.

67. Patnaik, "Barbara Morgan," 7. For Graham and Morgan, see also William A. Ewing, *Dance and Photography* (New York: Henry Holt, 1987), 25–26.

68. Quoted in Bunnell, "Introduction," 9. For more on previsualization, see Barbara Morgan, "In Focus: Photography, the Youngest Visual Art," *Magazine of Art* 35, no. 7 (November 1942): 252.

69. Patnaik, "Barbara Morgan," 8. Carter writes, "She transforms her insights into the dances into photographic works of art in their own stead." Carter, "Barbara Morgan," 18.

70. Barbara Morgan, "Dance Photography," *Complete Photographer* 10, no. 3 (March 10, 1942): 1135.

71. Patnaik, "Barbara Morgan," 7.

72. Morgan herself noted that this transformation in dance photography was due, in part, to changes in technology. See Morgan, "Dance Photography," 1133.

73. In 1941, Morgan wrote, "The best pictures in this book are portraits of energy; energy of imagination, generating motor energy and transfixed by light energy." Barbara Morgan, "Dance into Photography," *U.S. Camera*, December 1941, 104. Morgan's dance photographs were also shown at the Kamin Bookshop and Gallery on West 56th Street in Manhattan during April 1939. "Notes of Camera World," *New York Times*, April 23, 1939; John Martin, "The Dance: Miss Junger," *New York Times*, April 9, 1939.

74. Quoted in Ewing, *Dance and Photography*, 26.

75. Elizabeth McCausland, "The Shaker Legacy," *Magazine of Art* 37, no. 8 (December 1944): 287–291.

76. John Martin, "The Dance: In Praise of Argentinita," *New York Times*, January 1, 1939; "Art Brevities," *New York Times*, January 9, 1939. In January 1940, Morgan's dance photographs were exhibited at Brooklyn's Pratt Institute, School of Fine Arts. "Newly Opened Shows," *New York Times*, January 26, 1940. In December 1938, Eleanor Frampton sponsored a photographic exhibit at the Cleveland Institute of Music that may have included Morgan's photographs. See "Dance Photo Exhibit Opening in Institute," *Cleveland Plain Dealer*, December 11, 1938.

77. Elizabeth Noble, "Four Art Exhibitions," *The New Masses*, January 1939, 29.

78. John Martin, "The Dance: Americana," *New York Times*, October 27, 1940.

79. "Modern Art Museum Alters Display List," *New York Times*, March 2, 1945.

80. "A Photographic Exhibition of the Modern American Dance," *Dance Observer* 12, no. 5 (May 1945): 53–54.

81. *National Gallery of Art. Report of the Inter-American Office: National Gallery of Art, January 1944–May 1946* (Washington, DC: U.S. Government Printing Office, 1946), 1.

82. "Modern American Dance," *New York Times*, April 1, 1945.

83. "It's an Art," *New York World-Telegram*, April 6, 1945.

84. "American Modern Dance" was installed at the Museum of Modern Art between the Yalta Conference, which took place on February 4–11, 1945, and the Potsdam Conference of July 17–August 2, 1945. In the period between these two diplomatic events, the United States and the Soviet Union went from being allies to rivals.

85. "Mrs. Miriam Cramer, Sculptor, Dies at 75," *Cleveland Plain Dealer*, June 5, 1956. The Cleveland Public Library owns a sculpture from 1933–34 by the elder Cramer entitled "Jo Reads to Aunt March." This item is identified as number 119 in Karal Ann Marling, *Federal Art in Cleveland, 1933–43* (Cleveland: Cleveland Public Library, 1974).

86. "Children's Party at Heights School," *Cleveland Plain Dealer*, February 23, 1919.

87. Clarice White, "Woman's Club Will Entertain Men Tomorrow," *Cleveland Plain Dealer*, May 19, 1919; "'College Daze' Intercollegiate Midnight Frolic," *Cleveland Plain Dealer*, June 21, 1925.

88. "Play House Actress Weds Law Student," *Cleveland Plain Dealer*, June 13, 1933. For an advertisement for the Miriam Anne Cramer School of the Dance, see *Cleveland Plain Dealer*, October 17, 1937.

89. Glenn C. Pullen, "Two Instructors Join Cain Park Theater Staff," *Cleveland Plain Dealer*, June 17, 1944.

90. Judith Diehl, "Dance," *Encyclopedia of Cleveland History*, July 11, 1997, http://ech.case.edu; "Institute of Music to Open Modern School of Dancing," *Cleveland Plain Dealer*, September 13, 1931; "Eleanor Frampton, Dance Teacher, Dies," *Cleveland Plain Dealer*, October 10, 1973; "Birthday: Eleanor Frampton," *Cleveland Plain Dealer*, August 29, 1935. See also Wilma Salisbury, "Eleanor Frampton, Dance Teacher and Advocate, 1896–1973," Cleveland Arts Prize, n.d., http://clevelandartsprize.org.

91. *Cleveland Plain Dealer*, July 5, 1931; "Institute of Music Opens Season Today," *Cleveland Plain Dealer*, September 21, 1931; "Famous Dancers to Direct Opera Ballet," *Cleveland Plain Dealer*, May 23, 1932. Herbert Elwell, "Kolberg New Concertmaster, Makes Solo Debut This Week; Philadelphia Orchestra Here," *Cleveland Plain Dealer*, October 26, 1941.

92. "Frampton Concert Will Introduce Five Dancers in Little Theater," *Cleveland Plain Dealer*, November 29, 1936; "Frampton Brings Out New Ballet Tonight," *Cleveland Plain Dealer*, December 11, 1936; Herbert Elwell, "Frampton Dance Tells a Story," *Cleveland Plain Dealer*, December 12, 1936.

93. *Cleveland Plain Dealer*, June 7, 1937.

94. "Christmas Parties, Carols, and Plays Y. W. Program," *Cleveland Plain Dealer*, December 14, 1924.

95. Eleanor Clarage, "Main Street Meditations," *Cleveland Plain Dealer*, December 14, 1927.

96. Broadside for *More Love, Brother*, performed at the Eldred Theatre, April 24–29, 1945, item (S)* MGZMC—Res3—Z16.5, DHC.

97. William F. McDermott, "Community Theaters Conservative and Less Experimental Than Broadway: Cleveland Is Pointed Out as an Exception to Trend," *Cleveland Plain Dealer*, July 13, 1947; "Leatham, Barclay Spencer," *Encyclopedia of Cleveland History*, July 10, 1997, http://ech.case.edu.

98. William F. McDermott, "Cleveland Comes into Notice as Center of Hope for New Playwrights," *Cleveland Plain Dealer*, August 20, 1944.

99. Eleanor Clarage, "Main Street Meditations," *Cleveland Plain Dealer*, October 6, 1944. Cramer also unsuccessfully sought to visit the remaining Shaker villages in New England. Sister A. Rosetta Stephens wrote to her in October 1944 informing Cramer that she could not extend an invitation to visit New Lebanon since the village was in "a disturbed condition" because of recent deaths and the impact of the war. Stephen to Cramer, October 16, 1944, folder 5, MACP. See also Edward Deming Andrews to Cramer, postcard, September 28, 1944, folder 5, MACP.

100. Miriam Cramer, "The People Called Shakers," typescript of a presentation to Authors and Composers Association, November 7, 1944, folder 18, MACP.

101. Miriam Cramer to Marguerite Melcher, October 15, 1945, Literary Correspondence and Papers, box 10, PMF.

102. See, for example, Miriam Cramer Georges, "Assent," *Cleveland Plain Dealer*, February 16, 1934; Miriam Cramer Georges, "Warning," *Cleveland Plain Dealer*, December 7, 1935; Miriam Cramer Georges, "Christmas," *Cleveland Plain Dealer*, December 17, 1935.

103. *New York Times*, April 24, 1945: "Miriam Cramer to Baptize Her New Drama Wednesday," *Cleveland Plain Dealer*, April 22, 1945. See also "Drama and Gymkhana Fill Vacation Days of Flora Stone Mather Girls," *Cleveland Plain Dealer*, April 14, 1945.

104. "Dramatic Play Tells Life of Ohio Shakers," *Lima [OH] News*, February 27, 1945.

105. "W.R.U. Cast Ready for Shaker Drama," *Cleveland Plain Dealer*, April 23, 1945; Robert S. Stephan, "WTAW to Broadcast Scene of Play, 'More Love, Brother,'" *Cleveland Plain Dealer*, April 18, 1945.

106. Miriam Cramer to Marguerite Melcher, October 15, 1945, Literary Correspondence and Papers, box 10, PMF.

107. An unpaginated mimeographed script of Cramer's *More Love, Brother* is in the Manuscript Collection at the Kelvin Smith Library Special Collections, Case Western Reserve University, Cleveland. Cramer's copy of the mimeographed script is located in folder 20 of MACP.

108. Glenn C. Pullen, "Miriam Cramer's New Play Has Color and Imagination," *Cleveland Plain Dealer*, April 25, 1945.

109. "Miriam Cramer to Baptize Her New Drama Wednesday."

110. Miriam Cramer, "Shakerism Today," typescript of talk given to Women's Alliance of the Unitarian Church, January 25, 1955, folder 18, MACP.

111. Miriam Cramer, "The People Called Shakers," typescript of a presentation to Authors and Composers Association, November 7, 1944, 7–8, folder 18, MACP.

112. Pullen, "Miriam Cramer's New Play."

113. Louis Wohlgemuth, "Shaker Play in Premiere," *Cleveland Press,* April 25, 1945.

114. Glenn C. Pullen, "Broadway Producers Become Interested in Shaker Play," *Cleveland Plain Dealer,* May 1, 1945.

115. "Cain Park Prepares for Season," *Cleveland Plain Dealer,* May 11, 1945.

116. "Cain Park to Stage Shaker Play and Three Tune Shows," *Cleveland Plain Dealer,* May 30, 1945.

117. "Cain Park to Stage Shaker Play and Three Tune Shows."

118. For reminiscences of the Cain Park Theatre production, see Dina Rees Evans, *Cain Park Theatre: The Halcyon Years* (Cleveland: Halcyon, 1980), 203–205.

119. The latter image was published in the *Cleveland Plain Dealer.* See "Shaker Play at Cain Park," *Cleveland Plain Dealer,* August 5, 1945.

120. *Cain Park Theatre Program for the Week of August 5–8th Summer Season 1945* (Cleveland Heights, OH: City of Cleveland Heights, 1945), Cleveland State University Cleveland Memories Project, http://images.ulib.csuohio.edu.

121. William F. McDermott, "Play about Shakers Discovers Richness of Local Resources," *Cleveland Plain Dealer,* August 12, 1945.

122. Glenn C. Pullen, "Vividly Done Shaker Play Is Dampened Only by Rain," *Cleveland Plain Dealer,* August 8, 1945.

123. Glenn C. Pullen, "More Love, Brother," *Variety,* August 22, 1945. "Strawhat" is a theater industry name for a summer theatrical production.

124. In 1960, Miriam Cramer Andorn shared the script of *More Love, Brother* with Sister Mildred Barker, who at that time was located in Sabbathday Lake, Maine. Barker was less than congratulatory. Although she admitted that the work was "beautifully written," the Shaker sister did not approve of Cramer's representation of Shaker characters as "cold and austere." See Barker, Poland Spring, Maine, to Andorn, December 12, 1960, folder 5, MACP. For more of Barker's disapproval of theatrical representations of the sect, see chapter 5.

125. "Sidney Andorn Is Wed," *Cleveland Plain Dealer,* June 4, 1946; "Andorn-Cramer Marriage," clipping from the *Cleveland Press,* June 5, 1946, Clipping File for Miriam E. Cramer, Cleveland Public Library.

126. In 1964, the Department of Education of the Unitarian Universalist Association published and circulated nationally a Shaker Christmas pageant written by Miriam Cramer Andorn for the First Unitarian Church of Shaker Heights. See Andorn, *A Shaker Christmas* (Boston: Department of Education, Unitarian Universalist Association, 1964).

127. For an obituary of Marguerite Fellows Melcher published by her husband's firm,

see "Marguerite Fellows Melcher," *Publisher's Weekly,* June 30, 1969, 42. For a short biography of Frederic G. Melcher, see G. Thomas Tanselle, "Melcher, Frederic G. (1879–1963)," in *World Encyclopedia of Library and Information Services,* 3rd ed., ed. Robert Wedgeworth (Chicago: American Library Association, 1993), 566–568.

128. Marguerite Melcher, personal statement, ca. 1959, Literary Correspondence and Papers, box 10, PMF. See also Marguerite Melcher, "Hands to Work and Hearts to God," unpublished typescript, n.d., Writings by Marguerite Fellows Melcher, box 20, PMF.

129. Marguerite Melcher, biographical statement, January 28, 1959, Montclair Public Library, Montclair, NJ; "Melcher, Frederic G(ershom)," in *Current Biography: Who's News and Why 1945,* ed. Anna Rothe (New York: H. W. Wilson, 1945), 396.

130. "Frederic G. Melcher, 1879–1963," *Library Journal* 88, no. 7 (April 1, 1963): 1394.

131. *Current Biography* quotes Frederic Melcher as saying, "No one can be satisfied with the world as we have built it. No one nation, race, or religion can have by itself the complete solution of the problems ahead. . . . There is need to resolve that all denominations work together. There is need not only for solidarity on military and political fronts, but also on the fronts which face the big problems of life." "Melcher, Frederic G(ershom)," 397.

132. Tanselle, "Melcher, Frederic G.," 567.

133. "Party Honors Worker," *New York Times,* April 2, 1962.

134. Theatre Program for Four One-Act Plays Produced by the Smith College Theatre Workshop, March 11, 1936, Literary Correspondence and Papers, box 9, PMF; Theatre Program for "The Pulitzer Prize" by Mrs. Frederic Melcher Produced by the Unity Players, March 20, 1936, Literary Correspondence and Papers, box 9, PMF.

135. Marguerite Fellows Melcher, "Steps unto Heaven," typescript, Steps unto Heaven Folder, box 16, PMF.

136. Melcher, "Steps unto Heaven," typescript. This prophecy was actually Melcher commenting on the fact that the Enfield Center Union Church was celebrating an anniversary while the Enfield Shaker Village was empty and had been sold to a Catholic brotherhood.

137. Christmas Card 1936, box 8, Christmas Cards Sent by Marguerite (Fellows) and Frederic G. Melcher, PMF.

138. "The Shaker Adventure," typescript presentation script, Writings by Marguerite Fellows Melcher, box 20, PMF.

139. "Mrs. Clarice Carr Is Playing Consultant," *Claremont [NH] Daily Eagle,* January 12, 1949.

140. Marguerite Melcher to Kerry Shaw, March 3, 1939, Literary Correspondence and Papers, box 9, PMF.

141. Audrey Wood, Century Play Company, Inc., to Marguerite Melcher, June 21, 1935, Literary Correspondence and Papers, box 9, PMF.

142. Alexander L. Crosby to Marguerite Melcher, March 27, 1938, Literary Correspondence and Papers, box 9, PMF.

143. Oscar Hammerstein 2nd to Marguerite Melcher, February 14, 1944, Literary Correspondence and Papers, box 10, PMF.

144. Doris Frankel, Audrey Wood play broker and author's representative, to Marguerite Melcher, March 25, 1937, Literary Correspondence and Papers, box 9, PMF.

145. Joseph A. Brandt, director, Princeton University Press, to Marguerite Melcher, December 13, 1938, Literary Correspondence and Papers re. *The Shaker Adventure*, box 11, PMF. For Brandt, see "To Head Princeton Press," *New York Times*, April 22, 1938.

146. "Education: Sooner Back to Sooners," *Time*, December 2, 1940, 66.

147. Joseph A. Brandt, director, Princeton University Press, to Marguerite Melcher, December 13, 1938, Literary Correspondence and Papers re. *The Shaker Adventure*, box 11, PMF.

148. Sinclair Lewis, *It Can't Happen Here: A Novel* (Garden City, NY: Doubleday, Doran, 1935).

149. Joseph A. Brandt to Marguerite Melcher, April 22, 1939, Literary Correspondence and Papers re. *The Shaker Adventure*, box 11, PMF. Brandt also suggested that the book should be characterized by "leisureliness and informality." See Brandt to Melcher, March 20, 1940, Literary Correspondence and Papers re. *The Shaker Adventure*, box 11, PMF. See also "Notes on Books and Authors," *New York Times*, November 23, 1940.

150. Joseph A. Brandt to Marguerite Melcher, January 24, 1939, Literary Correspondence and Papers re. *The Shaker Adventure*, box 11, PMF.

151. Some of Melcher's research notes and correspondence are included on reel 9 of the New York Public Library's Shaker Manuscript Collection. Shaker Manuscript Collection, New York Public Library, microfilm, *ZL-301.

152. Marguerite Fellows Melcher, *The Shaker Adventure* (Cleveland: Press of Case Western Reserve University, 1968), 5.

153. Melcher, *Shaker Adventure*, 5.

154. Melcher, *Shaker Adventure*, 287.

155. Melcher, *Shaker Adventure*, 286.

156. Melcher, *Shaker Adventure*, 286.

157. Melcher, *Shaker Adventure*, 292.

158. Although Brandt hoped to create a series of books about American nonconformists to follow this volume, he left Princeton University Press before subsequent titles were published. Soon after *The Shaker Adventure* was published, Brandt became

president of the University of Oklahoma, then director of the University of Chicago Press, and later president of Henry Holt & Company. See "Books-Authors," *New York Times*, July 27, 1945; Kenneth C. Kaufman, "Joe Brandt," *Daily Oklahoman* (Oklahoma City), December 8, 1940; "Joe Brandt Elected President of New York Publishing House," *Daily Oklahoman*, July 22, 1945; "To Head Oklahoma University," *New York Times*, November 16, 1940; "Editing a University," *Time*, October 26, 1942, 84; "Publisher, Teacher Joseph Brandt Dies," *Los Angeles Times*, November 11, 1984; and Joseph A. Brandt to Marguerite Melcher, December 5, 1940, Literary Correspondence and Papers re. *The Shaker Adventure*, box 11, PMF.

159. For example, "The Shaker Adventure," *Springfield [MA] Weekly Republican*, April 24, 1941. See also "Review of Books at City Library," *Springfield [MA] Daily Republican*, September 8, 1941; "The Shakers," *Sunday Times-Advertiser* (Trenton, NJ), June 1, 1941; J. S., "'Shaker Adventure' Is Story of Strange Religious Society," *Greensboro [NC] Daily News*, April 6, 1941; and Ted Robinson, "'Shaker Adventure' Traces the Movement's History in America," *Cleveland Plain Dealer*, March 30, 1941.

160. Watt Stewart, "The Shaker Adventure by Marguerite Fellows Melcher," *American Historical Review* 47, no. 3 (April 1942): 625.

161. Herbert Gorman, "An Adventure in Communal Living," *New York Times*, May 11, 1941.

162. W. E. Garrison, "From Millennial Church to Gift Shoppe," *Christian Century*, April 16, 1941, 530.

163. Allan W. Eister, "The Shaker Adventure," *American Sociological Review* 6, no. 4 (August 1941): 585.

164. Sister A. Rosetta Stephens, Lebanon Shakers, to Datus C. Smith, March 31, 1941, Literary Correspondence and Papers re. *The Shaker Adventure*, box 11, PMF.

165. Prudence A. Stickney, trustee, Sabbathday Lake Shakers, to Marguerite Melcher, April 24, 1941, Literary Correspondence and Papers re. *The Shaker Adventure*, box 11, PMF.

166. Mary A. McCoy, Canterbury Shaker Village, to Marguerite Melcher, October 24, 1941, Literary Correspondence and Papers, box 9, PMF.

167. Miriam Cramer to David Stevens, Rockefeller Foundation, August 30, 1945, Literary Correspondence and Papers, box 10, PMF.

168. Edward D. Andrews to Marguerite Melcher, March 30, 1941, Literary Correspondence and Papers re. *The Shaker Adventure*, box 11, PMF.

169. Ann N. Tarney, "In Memoriam: Clarice Jennings Carr," Mount Holyoke College Archives and Special Collections, South Hadley, MA; *Vermont Marriage Records, 1909–2008*, User box PR-01921 reel s-30772, no. M-2032736, Vermont State Archives and Records Administration, Montpelier.

170. "Jennings, Clarice M.: 1923 Freshman Info. (LD 7060/6 1927)," Mount Holyoke College Archives and Special Collections.

171. Mount Holyoke College, *Llamarada* (South Hadley, MA: Mount Holyoke College, 1927), 102.

172. "Clarice Jennings (Mrs. Fred P. Carr 1929)," in *25th Reunion Mount Holyoke College, 1925–1952* (South Hadley, MA: Mount Holyoke College, 1952), 14; "Clarice M. Jennings (Mrs. Fred Parker Carr 1929)," in Mount Holyoke College, *Thirty-Third Reunion* (South Hadley, MA: Mount Holyoke College, 1960), n.p. For an obituary of Fred Carr, see "Carr—Fred Parker," *Boston Herald Traveler*, June 1, 1968.

173. Ellsworth Thayer, "Shakers, Few in Numbers, Abandon Enfield," *Boston Globe*, July 24, 1921.

174. Charles E. Clark, "Enfield Woman Preserves Dances, Songs of Religious Sect," unidentified and undated news clipping, ca. 1952, 46, ATSB.

175. Frances G. Sayward, "Enfield Woman Resurrects Shaker Lore, Group Performs at National Festivals," *Claremont Daily Eagle*, news clipping, n.d., 50, ATSB.

176. Clarice Carr, "Winter Incident at the Shakers," *Yankee Magazine*, January 1942, 19.

177. Clarice Carr to Estella Weeks, March 4, 1948, CCP. For the New Hampshire Folk Festival, see "New Hampshire Offers Varied Program for Summer Residents," *Boston Globe*, May 19, 1946.

178. Clarice Carr to Estella Weeks, March 4, 1948.

179. Sayward, "Enfield Woman Resurrects Shaker Lore." Ann Tarney passed away in Niceville, Florida, in 2008 at the age of 104. For an obituary, see "Ann (Nichols) Tarney (1904–2008)," *Northwest Florida Daily News* (Fort Walton Beach), July 24, 2008, http://www.legacy.com.

180. "Festivals in American Colleges for Women," *The Century* 49, no. 3 (January 1895): 431–432.

181. "May Day at Mount Holyoke College," typed manuscript, 1933, Mount Holyoke College Archives and Special Collections.

182. See Earl Banner, "Square Dancing Is Fun," *Boston Globe*, July 13, 1947.

183. New Hampshire Folk Federation, "Second Annual New Hampshire Folk Festival," 1947, 36, ATSB.

184. Sarah Gertrude Knott, "The National Folk Festival after Twelve Years," *California Folklore Quarterly* 5, no. 1 (January 1946): 83.

185. Rachel Clare Donaldson, *"I Hear America Singing": Folk Music and National Identity* (Philadelphia: Temple University Press, 2014), 61–65.

186. "Fourth Annual New England Folk Festival," 1947, 37, ATSB. For media coverage of this event, see Paul Kneeland, "Folk Dancing Festival," *Boston Globe*, January 4, 1948.

187. "14th Annual National Folk Festival: What Is Old Is New," 1948, 42, ATSB. For the National Folk Festival and Knott in this period, see Michael Ann Williams, *Staging Tradition: John Lair and Sarah Gertrude Knott* (Urbana: University of Illinois Press, 2006), 95–97. See also Joe Wilson and Lee Udall, *Folk Festivals: A Handbook for Organization and Management* (Knoxville: University of Tennessee Press, 1982), 6–8.

188. Knott, "The National Folk Festival after Twelve Years."

189. "Enfield Shaker Singers on Their Way to St. Louis National Folk Festival," *The Gazette*, 1948?, 40, ATSB.

190. Clarice Carr to Estella Weeks, March 4, 1948, CCP.

191. "Shaker Songs," program clipping, ATSB. The singers at this festival were Ruth Dennis, Marjorie Bascom, Dorothy Sanborn, and Ann Tarney, led by Clarice Carr.

192. "Shakers to Sing at Folk Festival," unidentified clipping, ATSB. An article appearing in the *Canaan Reporter and Enfield Advocate* in November 1950 indicates that the singers wanted to be very clear that they were not trying to "pass as Shakers." See "Singers of Shaker Songs to Entertain," *Canaan Reporter and Enfield [NH] Advocate*, November 20, 1950.

193. Williams, *Staging Tradition*, 97; "Shakers to Sing at Folk Festival."

194. Sarah Gertrude Knott to Clarice Carr, April 20, 1950, CCP.

195. *Annual Report of the Officers of the Town of Enfield, New Hampshire for the Year Ending January 31 1943* (Enfield, NH: The Advocate, 1943).

196. "Enfield's Shakers N.Y. Play Topic," *Canaan Reporter and Enfield Advocate*, December 9, 1948; "Mrs. Clarice Carr Is Playing Consultant." For the Abbe Workshop, see J. P. Shanley, "The Abbe Workshop," *New York Times*, March 5, 1950. See also Robert Wahls, "Drama Workshop Proves a $ucce$$," *New York Sunday News*, September 18, 1949; and "Robert O'Byrne: Writer and Producer, 74," *New York Times*, June 26, 1991.

197. "Gloria Monty, 84, Producer Who Resuscitated 'General Hospital,'" *New York Times*, April 5, 2006. See also George Dullea, "As Gloria Monty's World Turns," *New York Times*, July 11, 1986; and Stacy Jenel Smith, "Gloria Monty," *Cleveland Plain Dealer*, October 12, 1980.

198. Robert Garland, "An Attention Holding Off-Broadway Play," *New York Journal-American*, January 5, 1949.

199. Vernon Rice, "Off-Broadway Play Tells of Religious Sect," *New York Post*, January 7, 1949.

200. Murray Gross, "The Abbe Workshop Produces 'Rose in the Wilderness' Drama," *New York Star*, January 6, 1949.

201. William Hawkins, "'Rose of the Wilderness,' Abbe Play, Tells of Shaker Sect," *New York Telegram*, January 7, 1949.

202. "Rose in the Wilderness," *Variety*, January 12, 1949.

203. Brooks Atkinson, "Shaker Community Inquiry," *New York Times,* January 5, 1949.

204. Estella Weeks to Erwin Christensen, February 9, 1945, RG 17b, box 33—Correspondence—Alphabetical, IAD.

205. Clarice Carr to Marguerite Melcher, January 11, 1949, Literary Correspondence and Papers, box 10, PMF. Jerome Count of the Shaker Village Work Camp also attended Melcher's play. See Clarice Carr to Jerome Count, November 28, 1951, Correspondence Unprocessed Material, CC.

206. Jerome Count to Marguerite Melcher, August 28, 1950, Literary Correspondence and Papers, box 10, PMF. See also letter from Clarice Carr to Count, November 28, 1951, Correspondence Unprocessed Material, CC.

207. Charles C. Adams to Marguerite Melcher, January 15, 1949, Literary Correspondence and Papers, box 10, PMF.

208. Nancy Larrick to Marguerite Melcher, January 9, 1949, Literary Correspondence and Papers, box 10, PMF.

209. Estella T. Weeks to Mr. Christensen, February 9, 1949, RG 17b, box 33—Correspondence—Alphabetical, IAD.

210. "American Dance Festival, Eighth Season," 1955, 53, ATSB.

CHAPTER 4: INSTITUTING A SHAKER MUSEUM

1. "Mrs. J. August Linenau," *New York Times,* January 22, 1932.

2. "John S. Williams," *New York Times,* November 15, 1876; "The Late John S. Williams," *New York Times,* November 17, 1876; "Stephen Barker Guion," *New York Times,* December 20, 1885.

3. "Told 'Round the Ticker," *New York Times,* March 27, 1904; "Brokerage Houses Announce Merger," *New York Times,* July 30, 1932; "Eleven Men Forming Firm on Exchange," *New York Times,* October 6, 1934; "Rhoades, Williams to Split into 2 Firms," *New York Times,* September 28, 1934.

4. "Blair S. Williams, 81, Headed Wall St. Firm," *New York Times,* December 12, 1953.

5. "What Is Doing in Society," *New York Times,* April 19, 1899.

6. "John Stanton Williams '24," *Princeton Alumni Weekly,* September 22, 1982. See also "Shaker Museum Founder John Williams Sr. Dies," *Shaker Messenger* 4, no. 4 (Summer 1982): 13.

7. "Brokerage Houses Announce Merger."

8. "Firms Plan to Merge," *New York Times,* December 24, 1941.

9. Victor J. DiSanto, "National Register Nomination for John S. Williams House and Farm," September 30, 1996, National Park Service, U.S. Department of the Interior, Washington, DC.

10. For Polhemus & Coffin, see "Garage and Stable Group· Estate of Jesse Isidor Straus, Mt. Kisco, New York," *American Architect* 144, no. 2624 (July 1934): 33–35; "'Champ Soleil' the Country Residence of Mrs. Drexel Dalhgren at Newport, R.I.," *Country Life* 65 (1933): 47–49; "House of Allan C. Bakewell," *Architectural Record* 75 (1934): 152–155; "The Home of Mr. and Mrs. Vernon H. Brown at Southampton, L.I.," *House and Garden,* April 1933, 32–33; "Titten Hall: The Residence of C. Whitney Carpenter, Esq., at Bedford Hills, N.Y." *Country Life* 63 (1933): 47–49; "A New Jersey Residence with a River as Dooryard," *House and Garden,* October 1932, 30–31; and "The Connecticut Colonial Emigrates to Long Island," *House and Garden,* March 1933, 44–45.

11. "John S. Williams, 80, Is Dead; Founder of a Shaker Museum," *New York Times,* June 9, 1982.

12. John S. Williams, foreword, in *The Shaker Museum, Old Chatham, N.Y.* (Old Chatham, NY: Shaker Museum Foundation, 1968), n.p.

13. Robert F. W. Meader, "The Story of the Shaker Museum," *Curator* 3, no. 3 (1960): 204. See also "Shaker Museum Slates Festival," *New York Times,* July 19, 1957.

14. "Roger Williams, Shipbuilder, Dies," *New York Times,* November 29, 1959. Although the two shared a patronym and a similar socioeconomic status, they were not closely related.

15. Meader, "Story of the Shaker Museum," 204. See also *The Shaker Museum Old Chatham,* undated brochure, folder 2.19 Shaker Museum, HPCP.

16. Stephen J. Stein, *The Shaker Experience in America* (New Haven, CT: Yale University Press, 1992), 389.

17. "Forge and Blacksmith Shop," in *The Shaker Museum, Old Chatham, N.Y.*

18. Williams, foreword.

19. Stein, *The Shaker Experience,* 389.

20. Emma B. King to H. Phelps Clawson, July 27, 1954, folder 2.16 Correspondence, HPCP.

21. Museum of the American Indian, Heye Foundation, "Annual Report for the Period from April 1937 to April 1938," box 404, folder 7, Annual Reports: 1938–1941, Museum of the American Indian/Heye Foundation Records, 1890–1989, National Museum of the American Indian, https://sova.si.edu.

22. "Roger Williams, Shipbuilder, Dies." See also Frederick F. Hill, "Mariners' Museum Adds Display Space for Growing Exhibits," *Daily Press* (Newport News, VA), January 25, 1953.

23. Williams, foreword; "Shaker Museum," *Museum News* 29, no. 3 (June 1, 1951): 1. See also Kathy A. Ahearn to the Honorable Members of the New York State Board of Regents, memorandum entitled "Summary Recommendations with Respect to Charter Applications," May 28, 2004, http://www.regents.nysed.gov.

24. Jean Anne Vincent, "Shaker Sisters of Mother Ann," *Interiors* 113 (June 1954): 105.

25. Maryann Bird, "Zelina Comegys Brunschwig, Chairman of Fabric Company," *New York Times*, September 12, 1981; Clementine Paddleford, "Taste These Shakers," *Evening Star* (Washington, DC), September 21, 1958.

26. "Mortimer Brandt, Art Dealer, 88," *New York Times*, September 9, 1983; "Mortimer Brandt Ran Art Gallery," *Baltimore Sun*, September 9, 1983.

27. Meader, "Story of the Shaker Museum," 206. See also "Ex-Banker Is Curator of Museum," *Knickerbocker News* (Albany, NY), July 25, 1956. Clawson apparently moved to Columbia County as a result of marrying, in 1946, a prominent socialite divorcée. See "Mrs. Louise Taylor Wed," *New York Times*, June 14, 1946. See also "Mrs. Clawson's Services Held at St. Paul's," *Chatham [NY] Courier*, August 11, 1966; and "T. Ashley Dent Best Man at Son's Wedding," *New York Tribune*, September 29, 1920. For information about Clawson's wife's family trust fund, see "Action for Recovery of $100,000 Brought by Mrs. Louise Jongers," *Kingston [NY] Daily Freeman*, April 18, 1933.

28. "Romance of Stage Born of Old Books," *Boston Herald*, November 29, 1923; "J. L. Clawson Dies; Buffalo Merchant," *New York Times*, November 29, 1933.

29. "Actress Gets Divorce from H. P. Clawson," *New York Times*, June 19, 1927; "Shattered Romance of Poet and Russian Beauty," *San Francisco Chronicle*, June 12, 1927. For Clawson's poems, see Hamilton Phelps Clawson, *Transmutation: And Other Poems* (London: Elkin Matthews, 1923), and *Questings* (London: Elkin Matthews, 1926).

30. Chauncey J. Hamlin, the president of the Buffalo Society of Natural Sciences, was a graduate of the Hill School as well, so Clawson may have benefited from school ties as well as local connections in securing his position at the museum.

31. H. Phelps Clawson, *By Their Works: Illustrated from the Collections in the Buffalo Museum of Science* (Buffalo, NY: Buffalo Society of Natural Sciences, 1941), vii–xii. See also H. Phelps Clawson, "Pottery of Susa I," *Parnassus* 11, no. 4 (April 1939): 26–27.

32. For reviews of Clawson's book, see Sara Jones Tucker, "Review of *By Their Works*," *College Art Journal* 2, no. 2 (January 1942): 62–63; N. P., "Review: *By Their Works* by H. Phelps Clawson," *Burlington Magazine for Connoisseurs* 81, no. 476 (November 1942): 286; Cornelia Dam, "Review of *By Their Works*," *American Journal of Archaeology* 46, no. 1 (January–March, 1942): 161–162; George C. Vaillant, "A Background to Museum Exhibition," *Science*, new ser., 94, no. 2439 (September 26, 1941): 304; and "Primitive Man," *New York Times*, October 19, 1941.

33. Clawson, *By Their Works*, 2.

34. H. Phelps Clawson, "Understanding African Art: Background and Beliefs are Key," *Hobbies* 21, no. 3 (February 1941): 47–51.

35. "Old Chatham Museum Shows Tools That Made the Shakers Famous: N.Y. Regents Give Charter to a Hobby," *Berkshire Eagle* (Pittsfield, MA), August 17, 1950.

36. Meader, "Story of the Shaker Museum," 210; "Shaker Museum Installs Period Rooms," *Museum News* 30, no. 12 (December 15, 1952): 2.

37. Meader, "Story of the Shaker Museum," 208.

38. Meader, "Story of the Shaker Museum," 206.

39. Sanka Knox, "Shaker Furniture Shown in Museum," *New York Times*, June 1, 1953.

40. Inez Robb, "Shaker Museum Has Relics of Inventiveness," *Evansville [IN] Courier and Press*, August 3, 1958. This article also appeared as Robb, "Our Debt to the Shakers," *Trenton [NJ] Evening Times*, August 1, 1958.

41. "Old Chatham Museum Shows Tools That Made the Shakers Famous."; John S. Williams, *Consecrated Ingenuity: The Shakers and their Inventions* (Chatham, NY: Shaker Museum Foundation, 1957).

42. Richard Shanor, "Museum Gateway," *New York Times*, April 26, 1964; "Shaker Museum Remodels and Adds Buildings," *Museum News* 33, no. 5 (September 1, 1955): 1.

43. "Medicine Room," in *The Shaker Museum, Old Chatham, N.Y.*

44. "More Gifts for Shaker Museum," *Chatham Courier*, September 7, 1950.

45. Eva Lobdell, "Shaker Museum Buys Land for Improvement Program," *Chatham Courier*, January 8, 1955.

46. "The Shaker Museum," *Chatham Courier*, November 13, 1958.

47. Emma B. King to H. Phelps Clawson, July 5, 1950, folder 2.16 Correspondence, HPCP.

48. Emma B. King to H. Phelps Clawson, August 21, 1955, folder 2.16 Correspondence, HPCP. See also King to H. Clawson, May 22, 1960, folder 2.16 Correspondence, HPCP.

49. Robert F. W. Meader and James J. Kavanaugh, "The Shaker Museum: A Shrine of Consecrated Integrity," *Signature* (State Bank of Albany newsletter), Fall 1961, n.p., photocopy in author's possession.

50. Mary-Jane Tichenor, "Robert F. W. Meader Dies at 86; Longtime Authority on Shakers," *Berkshire Eagle*, October 26, 1994; "Shaker Authority Robert Meader Dies," *Shaker Messenger* 16, no. 3 (February 1995): 5–6. Meader was asked by Susquehanna University to find other employment at the end of the 1957–1958 academic year because of "various manifestations of poor judgement and a series of indiscretions." Susquehanna University Executive Committee, minutes, November 25, 1957, Susquehanna University Archives, Selinsgrove, PA.

51. Donald D. Housley, *Susquehanna University, 1858–2000: A Goodly Heritage* (Selinsgrove, PA: Susquehanna University Press, 2007), 279; Robert F. W. Meader, "Colonial Church Architecture in New England," *Susquehanna University Studies* 4, no. 1 (March 1949): 63–82.

52. Tichenor, "Robert F. W. Meader Dies at 86." See also Rita Reif, "Shakers Decrease, but Interest in Them Grows," *New York Times*, May 1, 1965.

53. Amy Bess Miller to Faith Andrews, November 4, 1959, box 31, folder Correspondence and Notes re. Hancock Shaker Village, 1958–1959, AA.

54. Meader and Kavanaugh, "The Shaker Museum."

55. For the role of women in American fundraising fairs, see Beverly Gordon, *Bazaars and Fair Ladies: The History of the American Fundraising Fair* (Knoxville: University of Tennessee Press, 1998).

56. "Shaker Festival to Be Held Aug. 4," *New York Times*, July 22, 1956; "63d Annual Horticultural Show Will Be Aug. 25, 26," *Springfield [MA] Union*, July 29, 1956; "Shaker Museum's First Festival to Picture Life of Vanishing Sect," *Knickerbocker News*, July 25, 1956.

57. "Shaker Museum Planning a Festival," *New York Times*, July 26, 1949.

58. "Festival on Aug. 3 Will Benefit the Shaker Museum," *New York Times*, July 21, 1969.

59. "Shaker Museum Will Be Setting of Fete Aug. 4–5," *New York Times*, July 29, 1962; "14th Festival to Aid Shaker Museum," *New York Times*, July 16, 1969.

60. Count and the Shaker Village Work Camp are addressed in detail in chapter 5.

61. "Shaker Museum Slates Festival."

62. "Festival Will Benefit Shaker Museum," *New York Times*, July 28, 1967.

63. "Festival on Aug. 3 Will Benefit the Shaker Museum"; "14th Festival to Aid Shaker Museum"; "Prepare for Shaker Museum Festival," *Springfield Union*, July 24, 1968.

64. "Shaker Museum Slates Festival."

65. "Vacationers Aid Shaker Museum in Old Chatham," *New York Times*, July 22, 1958.

66. "Esther Leeming Tuttle," *Times Union* (Albany, NY), July 14, 2015, http://www.legacy.com. See also Esther Leeming Tuttle with Rebecca E. Greer, *No Rocking Chair for Me: Memoirs of a Vibrant Woman Still Seeking Adventure in Her 90s* (New York: iUniverse, 2004), 141.

67. "Shaker Museum Will Be Setting of Antiques Sale," *New York Times*, July 31, 1966; "Franklin B. Tuttle," *New York Times*, October 1, 1987.

68. "Paul Hahn, Former President of American Tobacco, Is Dead," *New York Times*, August 10, 1963.

69. "Mrs. Nanette Hahn Wed to John Daly," *New York Times*, January 9, 1968; Douglas W. Cray, "Celanese Seeking Stein, Hall & Co.," *New York Times*, December 24, 1970.

70. The Andrewses' interaction with Yale is examined briefly in Mario S. De Pillis, "The Edward Deming Andrews Shaker Collection: Saving a Culture," in *Gather Up the Fragments: The Andrews Shaker Collection*, ed. Mario S. De Pillis and Christian Goodwillie (Hancock, MA: Hancock Shaker Village, 2008), 29–31. It is also treated in a typically self-serving manner in Faith and Edward Deming Andrews, *Fruits of*

the Shaker Tree of Life: Memoirs of Fifty Years of Collecting and Research (Stockbridge, MA: Berkshire Traveller Press, 1975), 194–196.

71. Catherine L. Whalen, "American Decorative Arts Studies at Yale and Winterthur: The Politics of Gender, Gentility, and Academia," *Studies in the Decorative Arts* 9, no. 1 (Fall–Winter 2002–2003): 109.

72. Everett V. Meeks, "Francis Patrick Garvan, 1875–1937," *Bulletin of the Associates in Fine Arts at Yale University* 8, no. 2 (February 1938): 35.

73. John M. Phillips, "The Mabel Brady Garvan Collections," *Bulletin of the Associates in Fine Arts at Yale University* 8, no. 2 (February 1938): 36–38.

74. Whalen, "American Decorative Arts Studies at Yale and Winterthur," 112.

75. Elise K. Kenney, "John Marshall Phillips, Yale University Art Gallery Director and Curator of the Mabel Brady Garvan Collection," *Yale University Art Gallery Bulletin* (2014), 93. Phillips was a representative material culture scholar of what Thomas J. Schlereth has termed "The Age of Collection." See Schlereth, "Material Culture Studies in America, 1876–1976," in *Material Culture Studies in America,* ed. Thomas J. Schlereth (Nashville, TN: American Association for State and Local History, 1982), 17–18.

76. Whalen, "American Decorative Arts Studies at Yale and Winterthur," 113–114. For "Pots and Pans," see also Robin W. Winks, *Cloak and Gown: Scholars in the Secret War, 1939–1961,* 2nd ed. (New Haven, CT: Yale University Press, 1996), 304.

77. Winks, *Cloak and Gown,* 304–305.

78. Kenney, "John Marshall Phillips," 94. See also "Changes in Staff," *Bulletin of the Associates in Fine Arts at Yale University* 16, no. 3 (July 1948): n.p.

79. "Named to Yale Art Post," *Boston Herald,* June 10, 1948.

80. Monuments Men Foundation, "Lamont Moore (1909–1988)," http://www.monu mentsmenfoundation.org.

81. For the apprenticeship program, see E. T. Booth and John Cotton Dana, *Apprenticeship in the Museum* (Newark: Newark Museum, 1928).

82. While at the Newark Museum, Moore also attended lecture courses on the history of art at New York University. See "Art Scholarships at N.Y.U. Won by 80," *New York Times,* November 29, 1936. See also "Delicate Works Copied by New Four-Cent Process," *Science News-Letter* 28, no. 758 (October 19, 1935): 247.

83. Lamont Moore, interview by Anne Ritchie, November 7, 1990, National Gallery of Art Archives, Washington, DC.

84. During this time, Moore's wife, who was also educated in Dana's program, worked at the Museum of Modern Art. Lamont Moore, interview by Anne Ritchie.

85. Lamont Moore, interview by Anne Ritchie.

86. "A New Director for the Yale University Art Gallery," *Bulletin of the Associates in Fine Arts at Yale University* 23, nos. 1–2 (February 1957): 4.

87. "Staff of the Yale University Art Gallery," *Bulletin of the Associates in Fine Arts at Yale University* 21, no. 3 (July 1955): 10.

88. Edward Deming Andrews, "Report in Chronological Outline, of Developments prior to, and during a Two-Year Appointment as Consultant in Shaker History and Culture at Yale University," April 28, 1958, box 29, folder Yale Material 1958–1961, AA.

89. Jock Reynolds, "In Memoriam: Charles Sawyer 1906–2005," *Yale University Art Gallery Bulletin* (2006), 26. See also Winks, *Cloak and Gown*, 304.

90. Sydney E. Ahlstrom, "Studying America and American Studies at Yale," *American Quarterly* 22, no. 2 (Summer 1970): 512.

91. Michael Holzman, "The Ideological Origins of American Studies at Yale," *American Studies* 40, no. 2 (Summer 1999): 77. See also Winks, *Cloak and Gown*.

92. Homer D. Babbidge, who subsequently served as the president of the University of Connecticut from 1962 to 1972, helped to found the program for foreign students. Babbidge earned his B.A., M.A., and Ph.D. at Yale and taught in the American Studies Program. See Bruce M. Stave et al., *Red Brick in the Land of Steady Habits: Creating the University of Connecticut, 1881–2006* (Hanover, NH: University Press of New England, 2006), 105–106; and Walter H. Waggoner, "Dr. Homer Babbidge Jr., 58, Noted Connecticut Educator," *New York Times*, March 29, 1984.

93. "United States of America," *Études à L'étranger* 2 (1949): 35.

94. "40 Reach Yale for Insight of American Life," *Springfield Union*, July 30, 1950. See also "Foreign Students Will Be at Yale," *Springfield Union*, July 20, 1952.

95. "40 Reach Yale for Insight of American Life."

96. "20 French Teachers Tour Mystic Seaport," *New London Evening Day*, August 10, 1954.

97. Holzman, "The Ideological Origins of American Studies at Yale," 79. For Gabriel and Williams, see Ahlstrom, "Studying America and American Studies at Yale," 501–510. For Gabriel, see "Ralph H. Gabriel, 96 Dies; Taught at Yale for 43 Years," *New York Times*, April 25, 1987.

98. Quoted in Lisa Nichols, "Wyoming as America: Celebrations, a Museum, and Yale," *American Quarterly* 54, no. 3 (September 2002): 453.

99. Holzman, "The Ideological Origins of American Studies at Yale," 81.

100. Ahlstrom, "Studying America and American Studies at Yale," 512.

101. William Devane to Charles Seymour, May 1949, quoted in Holzman, "The Ideological Origins of American Studies at Yale," 83.

102. "Yale Head Urges American Studies Plan in Universities to Fight Communist Threat," *New York Times*, February 23, 1949.

103. "Yale Head Urges American Studies Plan in Universities to Fight Communist Threat."

104. David M. Potter, "American Studies at Yale," *Yale Alumni Magazine* (January 1955): 13.

105. Potter, "American Studies at Yale," 13; "American History at Yale," *New York Times*, July 8, 1950.

106. "What Is Doing in Society," *New York Times*, May 26, 1900; "Married," *New York Times*, June 6, 1900. For Henry Rogers, see Eugene L. Huddleston, "Rogers, Henry Huttleston," in *American National Biography Online*, February 2000, http://www.anb.org.

107. "William R. Coe, 85, Sportsman, Dead," *New York Times*, May 16, 1955; "William Robertson Coe," *Newsweek*, March 28, 1955, 70. Coe's wealth was evident in the country residence created for him in an English Gothic mode in the 1920s at Oyster Bay, Long Island, by the architectural firm Walker & Gillette. See John Taylor Boyd, Jr., "Residence of William R. Coe, Oyster Bay, L.I.," *Architectural Record* 49, no. 3 (March 1921): 194–224. Coe's Oyster Bay estate, "Planting Fields," is treated in Robert B. McKay, Anthony K. Baker, and Carol A. Traynor, eds., *Long Island Country Homes and Their Architects, 1860–1940* (New York: Society for the Preservation of Long Island Antiquities, 1997), 265, 326–328, 425–427.

108. Holzman, "The Ideological Origins of American Studies at Yale," 84; "Edward B. Gallaher," *New York Times*, January 10, 1953.

109. Provost Archibald Foord to Edward Gallaher, June 6, 1950, Presidential Papers, Charles Seymour YRG 2-A-15, series I, box 15, folder 128, YUA.

110. "To Fill Yale's Coe Chair in History of America," *New York Times*, July 2, 1950; See also "Academy Graduate to Fill Coe Chair at Yale University," *Augusta [GA] Chronicle*, July 9, 1950. Daniel Horowitz offers a sensitive and nuanced portrait of Potter in Daniel Horowitz, *The Anxieties of Affluence: Critiques of American Consumer Culture, 1939–1979* (Amherst: University of Massachusetts Press, 2004), 79–101.

111. Thomas Winter, "Potter, David Morris," in *American National Biography Online*, February 2000, http://www.anb.org. Although the idea of national character suffused Potter's work, he explored the idea explicitly in an essay published in 1962. See Potter, "The Quest for the National Character," in *The Reconstruction of American History*, ed. John Higham (New York: Harper and Brothers, 1962), 197–220.

112. David M. Potter to William Rogers Coe, December 21, 1955, box 8 "Teaching Materials—Yale," folder 8 "W.R. Coe—American Studies," David Morris Potter Papers, Special Collections, Stanford University Library, Palo Alto, CA.

113. Horowitz, *Anxieties of Affluence*, 87.

114. David Morris Potter, *People of Plenty: Economic Abundance and the American Character* (Chicago: University of Chicago Press, 1954).

115. John N. Ingham, "Walgreen, Charles Rudolph," in *Biographical Dictionary of American Business Leaders* (Westport, CT: Greenwood Press, 1983), 4:1533–1534; "Walgreen Gives $550,000 for Institute at Chicago University, Which He Criticized," *New York Times*, June 6, 1937. For Walgreen's criticism of the University of Chicago, see Robert Coven, "Red Maroons," *Chicago History* 21, no. 1 (January 1992): 20–37.

116. Winter, "Potter, David Morris"; Alice Felt Tyler, "Review of *People of Plenty:*

Economic Abundance and the American Character by David M. Potter," *Annals of the American Academy of Political and Social Science* 298 (March 1955): 194–195.

117. Potter, *People of Plenty*, 89.

118. Robert M. Collins, "David Potter's *People of Plenty* and the Recycling of Consensus History," *Reviews in American History* 16, no. 2 (June 1988): 321–335.

119. Horowitz, *Anxieties of Affluence*, 100. For a useful compilation of Potter's shorter writings published after his death, see Don E. Fehrenbacher, *History and American Society: Essays of David M. Potter* (New York: Oxford University Press, 1973).

120. Horowitz, *Anxieties of Affluence*, 84. See, for example, David Potter to Dr. George Humphrey, February 12, 1956, box 8 "Teaching Materials—Yale," folder "W.R. Coe—American Studies," David Morris Potter Papers, Special Collections, Stanford University Library.

121. Deborah Hardy, *Wyoming University: The First 100 Years, 1886–1986* (Laramie: University of Wyoming, 1986), 165–167; Benjamin Fine, "American Studies Gain New Stature," *New York Times*, May 30, 1954.

122. Quoted in Holzman, "The Ideological Origins of American Studies at Yale," 87. See also "American Studies," *Charleston News and Courier*, July 5, 1954.

123. Quoted in Nichols, "Wyoming as America," 457.

124. Hardy, *Wyoming University*, 195.

125. Holzman, "The Ideological Origins of American Studies at Yale," 88. See also Nichols, "Wyoming as America," 453–456.

126. William F. Buckley, *God and Man at Yale* (Chicago: Henry Regnery, 1951), 101–103; Michael Kimmage, "Buckley Jr., William F.," in *American National Biography Online*, April 2014, http://www.anb.org.

127. Holzman, "The Ideological Origins of American Studies at Yale," 90.

128. Potter, "American Studies at Yale," 11.

129. Holzman, "The Ideological Origins of American Studies at Yale," 90.

130. Holzman, "The Ideological Origins of American Studies at Yale," 89.

131. For more about the Scarborough School, see Scarborough School, *Subject-Matter and the Program of Studies* (Scarborough-on-Hudson, NY: Scarborough School, 1920). For an advertisement for the Scarborough School, see "Scarborough School," *New-York Tribune*, September 17, 1922. See also "Scarborough School," *New York Herald*, September 10, 1922.

132. Andrews, "Report, in Chronological Outline."

133. Lamont Moore to Edward Deming Andrews, April 10, 1956, box 29, folder Yale Material 1956, AA.

134. David M. Potter to Edward Deming Andrews, November 8, 1957, box 29, folder Yale Material 1957, AA.

135. Edgar S. Furniss, "Re Andrews and Shaker," Secretary's Office, Reuben A Holden

Secretarial Records, 1901–1971, RG 19, YRG; 4-A, series 11, box 42, folder 210, Art Gallery 1953–57, YUA; "Edgar S. Furniss. Ex-Yale Provost," *New York Times,* July 19, 1972.

136. Edward Deming Andrews to Lamont Moore, draft, July 8, 1956, box 29, folder Yale Material 1956, AA.

137. Edward C. Roberts to Edgar Furniss, memorandum, August 3, 1956, box 29, folder Yale Material 1956, AA.

138. Lamont Moore to Edward Deming Andrews, June 27, 1956, box 29, folder Yale Material 1956, AA.

139. Andrews, "Report, in Chronological Outline."

140. Lamont Moore to Edward Deming Andrews, August 27, 1956; Moore to Andrews, September 10, 1956, both box 29, folder Yale Material 1956, AA.

141. Through careful word choice, this public relations statement disregarded John S. Williams's collection, which had been transferred to a nonprofit corporation.

142. Yale News Bureau, press release, September 1, 1956, Secretary's Office, Reuben A. Holden Secretarial Records, 1901–1971, RG 19 YRG: 4-A, series 11, box 42, folder 210 Art Gallery 1953–1957, YUA. See also "Shaker Collection Donated to Yale by Mass Couple," *Boston Traveller,* October 9, 1956.

143. "Yale Gets Art," *New York Times,* September 9, 1956. See also "Shaker Accessions at Yale," *Christian Science Monitor,* September 7, 1956.

144. "Public Gets Treasure of Shaker Heirlooms," *Cleveland Plain Dealer,* September 16, 1956.

145. "Outstanding Shaker Collection Is Given by Dr. Andrews to Yale," *Berkshire Eagle,* September 1, 1956; Alice Scott Ross, "Shaker-Made Loaf of Bread Leads Couple to New Life," *Springfield Union,* October 16, 1957.

146. "Shaker Collection at Yale," *History News* 12, no. 1 (November 1956): 8.

147. Faith and Edward Deming Andrews to Andrew C. Ritchie, April 30, 1957, box 29, folder Yale Material 1957, AA.

148. Andrews, "Report, in Chronological Outline."

149. "Yale Library Exhibition Gives New, Interesting Data on Shakers," *New Haven [CT] Register,* February 17, 1957; "Yale Library Exhibition Depicts Shakers from Plain to Fanciest," *Hartford [CT] Courant,* February 17, 1957.

150. Faith and Edward Deming Andrews to Andrew C. Ritchie, April 30, 1957, box 29, folder Yale Material 1957, AA.

151. Eugene Davidson, Yale University Press, to Edward Deming Andrews, September 9, 1957, box 29, folder Yale Material 1957, AA.

152. Edward Deming Andrews to Carroll L. V. Meeks, professor of architecture and history of art, memorandum, October 26, 1957, box 29, folder Yale Material 1957, AA.

153. Andrews, "Report, in Chronological Outline."

154. Edward D. Andrews, "The Shakers in a New World," *Magazine Antiques* 72, no. 4 (October 1957): 343.

155. A 1956 draft of the deed of gift is located at Winterthur. See "Instrument of Gift to Yale University of the Andrews' Shaker Collection," box 29, folder Yale Material 1956, AA.

156. Furniss, "Re Andrews and Shaker."

157. Andrews, "Report, in Chronological Outline."

158. Lamont Moore to Whitney Griswold, December 24, 1956, Secretary's Office, Reuben A. Holden Secretarial Records, 1901–1971, RG 19, YRG: 4-A, series 11, box 42, folder 210 Art Gallery 1953–1957, YUA.

159. Reynolds, "In Memoriam," 27; Marjorie L. Harth, "Charles Sawyer (1906–2005): A Star in the Museum Firmament," *American Art* 19, no. 3 (Fall 2005): 95.

160. "Yale Provost to Retire after 20 Years in Post," *New York Times,* June 24, 1957.

161. Alan Shestack, "Andrew Carnduff Ritchie 1907–1978," *Yale University Art Gallery Bulletin* 37, no. 22 (Summer 1979): 13; "Museum Aide to Head the Yale Art Gallery," *New York Times,* January 3, 1957; C. R., "A New Director for the Yale University Art Gallery," *Bulletin of the Associates in Fine Arts at Yale University* 23, nos. 1–2 (February 1957): 3–4.

162. "Yale to Display Art Acquisitions," *New York Times,* February 21, 1958. See also "Yale Gallery to Show New Art Acquisitions," *New York Times,* February 16, 1959.

163. J. R., "Mr. A.C. Ritchie," *Times* (London), August 30, 1978.

164. Furniss, "Re Andrews and Shaker."

165. In November 1957, Ritchie also hired Myeric R. Rogers, a British-born decorative arts scholar and curator, to serve as curator of the Garvan and Related Collections. "Myeric Rogers Named Art Curator by Yale," *New York Times,* November 25, 1957. For Rogers, see "Appointment of Director," *Bulletin of the City Art Museum of St. Louis* 14, no. 2 (April 1929): 18.

166. David M. Potter to Edward Deming Andrews, November 8, 1957, box 29, folder Yale Material 1956, AA.

167. E. S. Furniss to Edward D. Andrews, December 3, 1957, box 25, folder Interesting Letters, AA.

168. Andrews, "Report, in Chronological Outline"; Norman S. Buck, "Interview with Mr. and Mrs. Andrews (with R. A. Holden Present) on May 12, 1958," Secretary's Office, Reuben A. Holden Secretarial Records, 1901–1971, RG 19, YRG: 4-A, series: 11, box 42 folder 210 Art Gallery 1953–1957, YUA.

169. De Pillis, "The Edward Deming Andrews Shaker Collection."

170. James T. Babb to Edward Deming Andrews, January 27, 1958; Andrews to Babb, March 9, 1959, both box 29, folder Yale Material 1958–61, AA. See also Buck, "Interview with Mr. and Mrs. Andrews (with R. A. Holden Present) on May 12, 1958."

171. Faith Andrews to Reuben Holden, July 14, 1958; Margaret S. Rollins to Reuben Holden, October 7, 1958, both Secretary's Office, Reuben A. Holden Secretarial Records, 1901–1971, RG 19, YRG: 4-A, series 11, box 42, folder 210 Art Gallery 1953–1957, YUA.

CHAPTER 5: "REAL AMERICANA"

1. "Shakers Leave Mt. Lebanon, Merge with Hancock Group," *Springfield [MA] Republican,* December 21, 1947; "Mount Lebanon Shaker Colony to Join West Pittsfield Society," *Berkshire Eagle* (Pittsfield, MA), August 8, 1947.

2. "Shaker Property Sold for $10,000 for Dance Festival," *Berkshire Eagle,* December 25, 1945.

3. "Shaker Village Work Camp Is Novel Camping Experience," *Berkshire Eagle,* August 13, 1947.

4. For Count's own accounting of his purpose and activities, see Jerome Count, "Teen-Agers and the Shakers," *Shaker Quarterly* 1, no. 2 (Summer 1961): 84–87.

5. For Count's obituary, see "Jerome Count Dead at 67, Founded Shaker Work Unit," *Berkshire Eagle,* November 21, 1968.

6. For Holmes, see David M. Robinson, "Holmes, John Haynes," in *American National Biography Online,* February 2000, http://www.anb.org.

7. "Holmes Offers Plan to Cut Unemployment," *New York Times,* April 22, 1930; "Good-Will Judges Named," *New York Times,* February 12, 1930.

8. "Jerome Count Dead at 67"; "Church Plans Camp as Simple Refuge," *New York Times,* April 10, 1927; "Church Plans Camp as Simple Refuge," *Putnam County Courier* (Carmel, NY), April 15, 1927; "Homestead Camp Dedicated at Crafts," *Putnam County Courier,* July 8, 1927.

9. "White Breaks in on Trial of Edison Worker," *Brooklyn Daily Eagle,* December 11, 1931; "Charges Edison Defense Fails to Square with Facts," *Brooklyn Daily Eagle,* December 19, 1932; "To Dine by Candle in Edison Protest," *Brooklyn Daily Eagle,* March 1, 1933; "U.S. Court Refuses to Enjoin Edison Company Union," *Brooklyn Daily Eagle,* November 3, 1933; "Edison Denies Unfair Labor Policy Charge," *Brooklyn Daily Eagle,* January 19, 1933; "Maltbie Calls Policeman at Edison Probe," *Brooklyn Daily Eagle,* June 23, 1933; "Workers Jeer Firm's Refusal to Sign Code," *Pittsburgh Press,* August 10, 1933; "Sue N.Y. Edison System; Charge Plot to Beat NRA," *Chicago Tribune,* October 31, 1933.

10. Jerome Count, "Brooklyn Edison against the Public," *The Nation,* January 18, 1933, 56–57; Jerome Count, "The Electrical Revolution," *The Nation,* April 26, 1933, 467–469; Jerome Count, "The Utility Crisis in New York," *The Nation,* August 23,

1933, 211–223; Jerome Count, "The Power Industry Goes NRA," *The Nation,* January 31, 1934, 128–129.

11. "200 Liberals Ask for a Powerful NRA," *New York Times,* May 24, 1934.

12. Jerome Count to Captain George Egerton Harriman, August 18, 1939; Harriman to Count, August 23, 1939, both Non-Sectarian Anti-Nazi League to Champion Human Rights Records, Rare Book and Manuscript Library, Columbia University, New York; "Nazi Library Aided by Consulate Here," *New York Times,* September 14, 1940; "Jewish News," *Jewish Floridian* (Miami, FL), July 4, 1941. For the league, see Richard A. Hawkins, "The Internal Politics of the Non-Sectarian Anti-Nazi League to Champion Human Rights, 1933–1939," *Management and Organizational History* 5, no. 2 (May 2010): 251–278.

13. "East Saves 'Gas' for 1,000 Bombers," *New York Times,* February 7, 1943; "Food Dealers Here Score OPA Rules," *New York Times,* March 17, 1943; "Business World," *New York Times,* June 19, 1943; "Jelline, OPA Aide, Quits," *New York Times,* February 11, 1944. See also Jerome Count, "Flexible Pricing Is Urged," *New York Times,* August 9, 1945.

14. "Committees of City Bar," *New York Times,* July 22, 1945.

15. 1920 U.S. Census, Milford Township, Connecticut, sheet 21A.

16. *Milford Orange Directory 1935* (New Haven, CT: Price and Lee, 1935), 242.

17. "Shaker Village Work Camp Is Novel Camping Experience."

18. "Count, Sybil A. Wolfson," in *Who's Who of American Women and World Notables,* 6th ed. (Chicago: A. N. Marquis, 1969), 265.

19. "Jerome Count and Shaker Village," *Promenade: A Magazine of American Folklore* 7, no. 2 (1949): 4.

20. These work camps were one manifestation of the larger American pattern of outdoor education. For an historic overview of American outdoor education, see Paul Hutchinson, "Crafting an Outdoor Classroom: The Nineteenth-Century Roots of the Outdoor Education Movement" (Ph.D. diss., Boston University, 2015). See also Abigail A. Van Slyck, *A Manufactured Wilderness: Summer Camps and the Shaping of American Youth, 1890–1960* (Minneapolis: University of Minnesota Press, 2010).

21. Louise Evans, "Work Camps for 1,500,000 High-School Youth," *Clearing House* 15, no. 9 (May 1941): 519.

22. Harriet Eager Davis, "Work Summers for Teenagers," *Parents' Magazine* 20, no. 6 (June 1945): 128. See also Ruth and Edward Brecher, "Ambassadors in Dungarees," *Parents' Magazine and Family Home Guide* 30, no. 6 (June 1955): 48–49, 82–86.

23. American Friends Service Committee, *Work Camps for American and Philadelphia Service Group* (Philadelphia: American Friends Service Committee, 1941), n.p.

24. Davis, "Work Summers for Teenagers," 126.

25. Dorothy Barclay, "'Working' Vacations for Teen-Agers," *New York Times*, April 5, 1953.

26. Hugh B. Masters, "A Community School Camp," *Elementary School Journal* 41, no. 10 (June 1941): 739.

27. W. L. Rhyne, "Work Camps as Education," *High School Journal* 30, no. 4 (October 1947): 212–214. See also "For the Common Defense," *Time*, November 18, 1940, 60.

28. American Friends Service Committee, *Work Camps for American and Philadelphia Service Group*.

29. Marjorie Garber, *Quotation Marks* (New York: Routledge, 2003), 60.

30. Paul C. Mishler, *Raising Reds: The Young Pioneers, Radical Summer Camps, and Communist Political Culture in the United States* (New York: Columbia University Press, 1999), 106.

31. Mishler, *Raising Reds*, 101. For the Elizabeth Irwin School, see "29 Receive Diplomas," *New York Times*, June 15, 1945. The school was the high school of an institution that also had primary grades organized as the Little Red School House. See also U.S. Congress, House Committee on Un-American Activities, *Investigation of Communist Activities, New York Area. Part 5, Summer Camps Hearings before the United States House on Un-American Activities Eighty-Fourth Congress, First Session, on July 25, 28, 29, Aug. 2, 1955* (Washington, DC: U.S. Government Printing Office, 1955), 1373.

32. Norman Studer, "Work and the School Curriculum," *Childhood Education* 20, no. 1 (January 1, 1943): 217–218. For an advertisement for Camp Woodland, see "Camps," *New York Times*, May 3, 1953. In 1955, Studer testified that 160 children attended his camp. U.S. Congress, House Committee on Un-American Activities, *Investigation of Communist Activities*, 1374.

33. Norman Studer, "Catskill Folk Festival," *New York Folklore Quarterly* 1, no. 3 (August 1945): 160–166. For a later articulation of Studer's views concerning the importance of folklore, see Studer, "The Place of Folklore in Education," *New York Folklore Quarterly* 18, no. 1 (Spring 1962): 3–12.

34. Dale W. Johnson, "Camp Woodland: Progressive Education and Folklore in the Catskill Mountains of New York," *Voices: The Journal of New York Folklore* 28, nos. 1–2 (Spring–Summer 2002): 6–12.

35. Haufrecht, a composer trained at Julliard, had previously worked for the Federal Theatre Project of the WPA. See Allan Kozinn, "Pianist, Composer, Folklorist," *The Day* (New London, CT), July 3, 1998.

36. Mishler, *Raising Reds*, 102.

37. Elie Siegmeister, "Catskill Folksongs," *New York Times*, December 21, 1941; Robert Shelton, "Catskill Singers in Folk Concert," *New York Times*, April 6, 1961; Norman Studer, "Catskill Folk Festival," *New York Folklore Quarterly* 1, no. 3 (August 1945): 161–166; Norman Studer, "Folk Festival of the Catskills," *New York Folklore Quarterly*

16, no. 1 (Spring 1960): 6–10. For Cazden, see "Norman Cazden, Musicologist, Pianist, Composer and Educator," *New York Times*, August 22, 1980. See also Stephen Erdely, "Norman Cazden (1914–1980)," *Ethnomusicology* 25, no. 3 (September 1981): 493–496; and Herbert Haufrecht, "Norman Cazden, 1914–1980," *Sing Out!* 28, no. 3 (1980): 41.

38. Studer, "Folk Festival of the Catskills," 8–9.

39. For Botkin, see Lawrence Rodgers and Jerrold Hirsch, *America's Folklorist: B. A. Botkin and American Culture* (Norman: University of Oklahoma Press, 2010).

40. Joanna Cazden, Letter to the Editor, *Sing Out!* 42, no. 2 (Fall 1997): 3; Mishler, *Raising Reds,* 101. For Studer's testimony, see U.S. Congress, House Committee on Un-American Activities, *Investigation of Communist Activities,* 1372–1377.

41. "Shaker Village Work Camp Is Novel Camping Experience." See also "Shaker Village Work Camp in Full Swing," *Berkshire Eagle,* July 19, 1947.

42. Shaker Village Work Camp, *What Is Shaker Village?* (New York: Shaker Village Work Camp, n.d.), promotional brochure in MACP. For a further enunciation of Count's ideas about teenage self-government, see Count, "Standards for Teenagers," *New York Times,* January 5, 1952.

43. Work Education Foundation, *Shaker Village Work Group: Program and Policy* (New Lebanon, NY: Work Education Foundation, n.d.).

44. Stu Jamieson, foreword, in *A Shaker Musical Legacy,* ed. Robert C. Opdahl and Viola E. Woodruff Opdahl (Hanover, NH: University Press of New England, 2004), xiii.

45. Jerome Count, *When Your Adolescent Resists Work and Study* (Pittsfield, MA: Work Education Foundation, 1960), 1. Apparently the teenagers enjoyed their summers at the Shaker Village Work Camp. See also Marcia Winn, "Make the Child's Household Tasks Interesting; Then He'll Do His Part," *Chicago Daily Tribune,* May 10, 1956. For contemporary accounts of their experience at the camp written by teenage participants, see Linda Louise Starr, "Shaker Village Work Group," *The Yorker* 18, no. 1 (September–October 1959): 14; and Lynne Sprichinger and Paul Holmes, "Yorkers at Shaker Village," *The Yorker* 20, no. 2 (November–December 1961): 10–15.

46. Brecher, "Ambassadors in Dungarees," 82–83.

47. Faith does not seem to have been a defining character of this camp. Based on their last names, many of the campers seem to have been from Jewish backgrounds, but children of other ethnicities also participated. B. Matthew Neiburger was kind enough to share with me a mailing list for the villagers who attended the camp in 1970, near the end of its existence. This list includes campers with last names such as Cohen, Goldfarb, Jacobs, Rokowitz, and Klein, but also individuals named McGrath, Shaw, Briggs, and Lenihan.

48. Estella Weeks to Erwin O. Christensen, October 28, 1947, box 33, folder Weeks Miss Estella, IAD.

392 NOTES TO PAGES 224–225

49. "Mrs. P" to Jerome Count, memorandum, December 18, 1946, Correspondence Unprocessed Material, CC.

50. Jerome Count to Federation of Arts, December 25, 1946; Alexander Malitsky, Fine Arts Department, Brentano's Booksellers, to Count, March 29, 1947; Alvin G. Whitney, assistant director, New York State Museum, to Count, November 6, 1946, all Correspondence Unprocessed Material, CC.

51. Jerome Count to Diamond Crystal Salt Company, December 30, 1946, Correspondence Unprocessed Material, CC.

52. B. W. Cleland, advertising manager, Diamond Crystal Salt Co., January 29, 1947, Correspondence Unprocessed Material, CC.

53. "Mrs. P." to Jerome Count, memorandum, May 28 [1947], Correspondence Unprocessed Material, CC. For Weeks, see Erwin O. Christensen to "Mr. Cairns," memorandum, February 8, 1949, box 27 Correspondence—Alphabetical, Shaker Music Project, IAD. In this memorandum, Christensen noted that Charles C. Adams of the New York State Museum believed that Weeks was the best-informed person on the subject of Shaker music alive at that time.

54. Jerome Count to Estella Weeks, May 29, 1947, Correspondence Unprocessed Material, CC.

55. Jerome Count to National Art Gallery, May 29, 1947, box 27, folder Shaker Village Work Camp, IAD.

56. Erwin Christensen to Jerome Count, June 13, 1947; Christensen to Count, October 14, 1947; Count to Christensen, December 16, 1947, all box 27, folder Shaker Village Work Camp, IAD.

57. Count's continuing liberal pacifism was demonstrated in a letter to the editor condemning Pittsfield's embrace of corporal punishment in the public schools. See "School Disciplinary Code," *Berkshire Eagle*, October 13, 1958.

58. Jerome Count, "The Shaker Folk," *Promenade: A Magazine of American Folk Lore* 7, no. 2 (1949): 3–4.

59. Robert C. Opdahl and Viola E. Woodruff Opdahl, preface, in Opdahl and Opdahl, eds., *A Shaker Musical Legacy*, xviii.

60. Mary Roche, "Object Lesson in the Integrity of Design," *New York Times Magazine*, October 23, 1949.

61. Huston Horn, "Easy Livin' and No More Bugle Calls," *Sports Illustrated*, August 6, 1962, 50; "Shaker Village Camp," *Seventeen*, August 1954, 120, 122; Ruth and Edward Brecher, "Work Can be Fun!" *Classmate* 61, no. 30 (July 1954): 6–7. See also Gail Matthews, "Teens Restoring Shaker Village," *Boston Globe*, April 3, 1962; and Gail Matthews, "Student from Sharon Helps to Restore Shaker Village," *Boston Globe*, October 14, 1962.

62. Gillian Mitchell, *The North American Folk Music Revival: Nation and Identity in the United States and Canada, 1945–1980* (Aldershot, England: Ashgate, 2007), 61–62.

63. John Martin, "The Dance: A New Center," *New York Times*, October 20, 1940; John Martin, "The Dance: Miscellany," *New York Times*, March 3, 1940; Margot Mayo, *The American Square Dance* (New York: Sentinel Books, 1943); Gertrude Prokosch Kurath, "Review of *The American Square Dance* by Margo Mayo," *Journal of American Folklore* 62, no. 244 (April–June 1949): 211. See also Margot Mayo, "Swing Your Partner," *Daily Olympian* (Olympia, WA), March 21, 1950.

64. "All-Day Meeting on Folklore Held," *New York Times*, May 5, 1946. Mayo also taught a course in folklore and folk music for the sophomore class at the Mills School for Kindergarten Teachers, which was affiliated with Adelphi College. Richard M. Dorson, "The Growth of American Folklore Courses," *Journal of American Folklore* 63, no. 249 (July–September 1950): 356.

65. Gail Gillespie, "Final Notes, Robert Stuart 'Stu' Jamieson," *Old-Time Herald* (Durham., NC), http://www.oldtimeherald.org. A recording of "Amazing Grace" sung by Seymour Mayo made on one of these collection trips is available online at Seymour Mayo, "Amazing Grace," audio, Library of Congress, http://www.loc.gov. A finding aid to the Library of Congress's Margot Mayo Collection of recordings made on Mayo and Jamieson's collection trip in 1946 is located at http://lccn.loc.gov.

66. Mayo quoted in Dorson, "The Growth of American Folklore Courses," 351.

67. "Jerome Count and Shaker Village."

68. Douglas Martin, "Walden School, at 73, Files for Bankruptcy," *New York Times*, June 23, 1997; Shawn G. Kennedy, "Margaret Naumburg, Walden School Founder, Dies," *New York Times*, March 6, 1983. For the influence of the Walden School, see B. F. Hinitz, "The Impact of Margaret Naumburg and Walden School on Early Childhood Education in the United States," in *The Hidden History of Early Childhood Education*, ed. Blythe Simone Farb Hinitz and Susan A. Miller (New York: Routledge, 2013), 181–212.

69. "Harold Aks, 78, Who Led Choral Groups," *New York Times*, July 10, 2000; "To Present Folk Music: American-Soviet Group Plans Also for Choral Program," *New York Times*, February 28, 1947.

70. Jamieson, foreword, xiv.

71. Tony Saletan, "Michael Row the Boat Ashore," *Musica International*, n.d., http://www.musicanet.org. For Saletan, see Eric Von Schmidt, *Baby, Let Me Follow You Down: The Illustrated Story of the Cambridge Folk Years* (Amherst: University of Massachusetts Press, 1994), 24; and Ray M. Lawless, *Folksingers and Folksongs in America*, rev. ed. (Westport, CT: Greenwood, 1981), 204–205. See also Pete Seeger, *Everybody Says Freedom* (New York: Norton, 1989), 163; Ted Gioia, *Work Songs* (Durham, NC:

Duke University Press, 2006), 132; and Tony Saletan, *Let's All Sing: Televised Music Instruction for Primary Grades* (Los Angeles: Western Instructional Television, 1973), iii. The sculptor, potter, and educator Henry Halem remembers Pete Seeger visiting the Shaker Village Work Camp. Henry Halem, oral history interview, May 14, 2005, Archives of American Art, Washington, DC, http://www.aaa.si.edu.

72. Jamieson, foreword, xiv; Margot Mayo to Estella Weeks, August 12, 1949, box 33, folder Correspondence Weeks Miss Estella, IAD. For Belden, see "Shaker Ricardo Belden Dies at 89," *Berkshire Eagle,* December 3, 1958. See also Magda Gabor-Hotchkiss, "Brother Ricardo Belden Revisited," *American Communal Societies Quarterly* 6, no. 1 (January 2012): 3–12.

73. Opdahl and Opdahl, preface, xviii.

74. Opdahl and Opdahl, preface, xvii.

75. William Lichtenwanger, assistant reference librarian, Music Division, Library of Congress, to Jerome Count, June 13, 1947; Count to Lichtenwanger, June 24, 1947, both Correspondence Unprocessed Material, CC. In February 2015, the microfilm that Count purchased from the Library of Congress was in the collection of the Shaker Museum|Mount Lebanon.

76. Isaac N. Youngs, *A Short Abridgement of the Rules of Music* (New Lebanon, NY: N.p., 1843); Margot Mayo to Jerry Count, memorandum, October 28, 1948, Correspondence Unprocessed Material, CC.

77. *P.O.B. Open House Program, 1948* (Pittsfield, MA: Shaker Village Work Camp, 1948), n.p., mimeographed pamphlet in CC. A stamp on the copy in the Count Collection indicates that it originally belonged to Charles C. Adams.

78. "Open House Saturday at Shaker Work Camp," *Berkshire Eagle,* August 19, 1959; Richard Happel, "Shaker Village Teen-Agers," *Berkshire Eagle*, August 6, 1960. See Henry Halem, oral history interview.

79. Happel, "Shaker Village Teen-Agers"; Richard K. Weil, "Countdown for Character," *Berkshire Week,* August 1966. Business records and lists of participants for the camp have not been located so it is impossible at this point to know exactly which communities sent their children to the Shaker Village Work Camp. However, B. Matthew Neiburger, a participant in the camp near its close, was kind enough to share with the author a 1970 mailing list for the Shaker Village Work Group. This document, admittedly an unscientific representation of who participated during the camp's existence of more than two decades, includes 196 names and addresses. Of these names, 120, or 61 percent, are associated with an address in New York State, many of them in the city and on Long Island. Thirteen New Jersey and Massachusetts addresses each compose almost 7 percent of the list. Seven addresses, or 3.57 percent, are in Maryland, and six addresses, or 3.06 percent, are in Illinois. Other locations represented in the list with fewer attendees are Alabama, California, Connecticut,

Delaware, the District of Columbia, Florida, Georgia, Indiana, Michigan, Missouri, North Carolina, Ohio, Pennsylvania, Puerto Rico, Rhode Island, Tennessee, Texas, Vermont, Virginia, and Wisconsin.

80. The first of these annual open houses was held on August 24, 1947. See "Shaker Village Work Camp Is Novel Camping Experience."

81. *P.O.B. Open House Program, 1948.*

82. "Open House at Shaker Camp," *Berkshire Sketch* (Lenox, MA), August 14, 1952. See also "Shaker Village Work Camp to Unveil Mural Saturday," *Berkshire Eagle*, August 15, 1951. For a description of a later open house, see "Open House at Shaker Village," *Berkshire Eagle*, August 17, 1957. See also "Shaker Village Brought to Life by Teen-Agers," *Springfield [MA] Union*, August 14, 1957.

83. Miriam Cramer to Jerome Count, July 1, 1949, Correspondence Unprocessed Material, CC.

84. In a letter to Marguerite Melcher, Count gave particular credit to Aks and O'Leary. See Count to Melcher, August 28, 1950, box 10, Literary Correspondence and Papers, PMF.

85. Jamieson, foreword, xv. For Estabrook, see Stephen J. Stein, *The Shaker Experience in America* (New Haven, CT: Yale University Press, 1992), 349.

86. Marguerite Melcher to Jerome Count, August 21, 1950, Correspondence Unprocessed Material, CC. In 1952, Melcher wrote to Count, "We think you are doing a very important thing there at Shaker Village. I tell people about it whenever I get a chance." Melcher to Count, August 10, 1952, Correspondence Unprocessed Material, CC.

87. "Open House Is Scheduled Saturday at Shaker Village," *Springfield Union*, August 15, 1962.

88. *Shaker Music Lives Again* (Pittsfield, MA: Shaker Village Work Camp, 1952). A copy of this four-page promotional brochure is located in box 27, Correspondence—Alphab. Shaker Village Work Camp, IAD.

89. *Shaker Music Lives Again.*

90. Bert Sonnenfeld, "Shaker Music Lives Again," *Berkshire Sketch,* August 14, 1952.

91. A parallel could be drawn between the importance of Mother's love in Shaker music to the paeans to Sweet Daddy Grace that appear in the musical repertoires of the United House of Prayer for All Peoples. See Charles Anderson et al. *A Night with Daddy Grace* (N.p.: Harlequin Records, [195-?]); and United House of Prayer for All People et al, *Saints' Paradise* (Washington, DC: Smithsonian Folkways Recordings, 1999).

92. Anthony Tommasini, "Jacob Druckman, 67, Dies; a Composer and Teacher," *New York Times,* May 27, 1996. See also Jonathan Wiener, "Druckman, Jacob," in *American National Biography Online,* July 2002, http://www.anb.org.

93. Having earned his B.S.M. and M.A. degrees at the Hebrew Union College of

Sacred Music, Conviser subsequently had a career as a cantor, serving for decades at Miami Beach's Temple Beth Shalom and directing a choir composed of cantors from all branches of Judaism. "Cantors Concert," *Miami News*, March 12, 1982; "Upcoming Holy Days, Politics Are Topics of Area Rabbis," *Miami News*, September 5, 1968.

94. David Conviser, "Remembering Jacob Druckman," *Julliard Journal*, May–August 2014, http://journal.juilliard.edu.

95. Roger Hall, "What's Your Favorite Shaker Song," *Shakers World* 1, no. 2 (August 1996): 11.

96. *The Simple Gifts: A Cantata Based on Themes of the American Shakers* (Pittsfield, MA: Shaker Village Work Camp, n.d.). A copy of this brochure is located in the University Archives, Kentucky Building, Western Kentucky University, Bowling Green, and also in the Communal Societies Collection, Rare Book Room, Hamilton College, Clinton, NY.

97. *The Simple Gifts*.

98. Roger Hall, "Singing at Shaker Village Work Camp," *Shakers World* 1, no. 3 (December 1996): 4.

99. Elaine Brown to Jerome Count, October 30, 1956, folder 333 "B" Correspondence, series 2 Correspondence, Jacob Druckman Papers, 1928–1999, Classmark JPB 00–1, Music Division, New York Public Library for the Performing Arts. For Elaine Brown and Singing City, see J. Michele Edwards. "Brown, Elaine (i)," in *Grove Music Online*, *Oxford Music Online*, January 31, 2014, https://www.oxfordmusiconline.com.

100. Harold Aks, arranger and ed., *O Brethren, Will You Receive, from Three Shaker Songs* (Melville, NY: Edward B. Marks Music, 1957); Harold Aks, arranger and ed., *O, the Beautiful Treasure* (Melville, NY: Edward B. Marks Music, 1957). At the time of this writing, a performance by the Brooklyn Community Chorus of Aks's arrangements of "Come to Zion, Sin-Sick Souls" and "O Brethren, Will You Receive" is available online on YouTube.

101. "Interracial Chorus to Sing Haydn's Theresian Mass," *Brooklyn Eagle*, May 13, 1950; "Inter-Racial Group to Hold Meeting," *Brooklyn Eagle*, December 8, 1951; "Plans Completed for Interracial Fellowship Rally," *Brooklyn Eagle*, April 22, 1948; "The Easter Dawn Will Find Borough Folk at Worship," *Brooklyn Eagle*, April 12, 1952.

102. In 1954, the camp had previously published a similar ring-bound mimeographed book of recipes adorned with silk-screened covers and illustrations. *Recipes of the Shakers* (Pittsfield, MA: Shaker Village Work Camp, 1954).

103. Charles Nordhoff, *The Communistic Societies of the United States* (New York: Harper and Brothers, 1875), 144.

104. The image was also subsequently reproduced on page 7 of the second edition of *Songs of the Shakers*, discussed below.

105. Jerome Count to Mrs. Curry Hall, August 20, 1962, SUSV.

106. John S. Williams to Jerome Count, July 13, 1955, Shaker Museum Foundation Correspondence, CC.

107. "Shaker Museum Festival Aug. 4," *Berkshire Eagle,* July 14, 1956; "Shaker Museum Fete Is Aug. 4," *Berkshire Eagle*, July 24, 1956. See also "63rd Annual Horticultural Show Will Be Aug. 25, 26," *Springfield Sunday Republican*, July 29, 1956.

108. "Shaker Festival to Be Held Aug. 4," *New York Times,* July 22, 1956.

109. John S. Williams to Board of Trustees of the Shaker Museum, memorandum, April 20, 1956, Shaker Museum Foundation Correspondence, CC.

110. John S. Williams to Jerome Count, August 19, 1956, Shaker Museum Foundation Correspondence, CC.

111. "Teen-Age Group to Dance Saturday at Museum Festival," *Berkshire Eagle,* August 1, 1957. See also "Shaker Museum Festival to Be Event of Early August," *Schenectady [NY] Gazette,* July 18, 1957.

112. "Shaker Museum's Annual Festival Set for Aug. 6," *Berkshire Eagle,* July 14, 1960; "Shaker Museum Event Draws 2,212 Persons to Old Chatham," *Berkshire Eagle*, August 5, 1963; "Shaker Museum Festival Slated at Old Chatham," *Schenectady Gazette*, July 28, 1965.

113. "Shaker Work Camp Plans Open House Saturday Night," *Berkshire Eagle,* August 13, 1963.

114. John S. Williams to Jerome Count, August 10, 1960, Shaker Museum Foundation Correspondence, CC. For publicity concerning the 1960 Shaker Festival, see "Shaker Festival Set in Chatham," *Springfield Union,* July 7, 1960. See also "Great Barrington Church Will Have Fair Saturday," *Springfield Sunday Republican*, July 24, 1960.

115. Erin Beisel to Miriam Cramer Andorn, January 11, 1961, folder 5, MACP. Similarly, Garber indicates that a work camp, and the Shaker Village Work Camp in particular, was "a relatively idyllic, and unquestionably expensive, summer retreat for the hip, progressive, guitar-playing red-diaper-baby set" where teenagers "wore denim and flannel shirts and learned about folk songs, barn construction, leftist politics, poetry, and sex." Garber, *Quotation Marks,* 60.

116. Jerome Count to Nancy T. Leach, February 6, 1952, box 27, folder Shaker Village Work Camp, IAD.

117. Jerome Count to E. O. Christensen, March 24, 1955, box 27, folder Shaker Village Work Camp, IAD.

118. See "Shaker Exhibition Opens Here Today," *New York Times,* October 8, 1949.

119. *New Lebanon Shaker Village Catalog* (Pittsfield, MA: Shaker Village Work Camp, ca. 1950). A copy of this mimeographed catalogue produced by the campers is in CC.

120. Moses Asch to Jerome Count, May 28, 1958, Folkways Production Files, box 22, folder 35, MFAC.

121. Tony Olmsted, *Folkways Records: Moses Asch and His Encyclopedia of Sound* (New York: Routledge, 2003), 61–74.

122. Moses Asch to Jerome Count, May 6, 1958, Folkways Production Files, box 22, folder 35, MFAC.

123. Moses Asch to Jerome Count, June 5, 1958, Folkways Production Files, box 22, folder 35, MFAC. A first payment of one hundred dollars appears to have been Asch's standard practice. See Olmsted, *Folkways Records*, 74.

124. Jerome Count to Moses Asch, June 4, 1958, Folkways Production Files, box 22, folder 35, MFAC.

125. "The Shakers and Their Music," n.d., Folkways Production Files, box 22, folder 36, MFAC. See also Jerome Count to Moses Asch, June 14, 1958, Folkways Production Files, box 22, folder 35, MFAC.

126. Moses Asch to Jerome Count, October 24, 1958; Asch to Count, September 4, 1959, both Folkways Production Files, box 22, folder 35, MFAC.

127. Jerome Count to Moses Asch, February 27, 1959; Count to Asch, September 1, 1959, Folkways Production Files, box 22, folder 35, MFAC.

128. Jerome Count to Moses Asch, March 22, 1960, Folkways Production Files, box 22, folder 35, MFAC.

129. "Shaker Ricardo Belden Dies at 89," *Berkshire Eagle*, December 3, 1958; Stein, *Shaker Experience*, 364.

130. "Eldress Estabrook, 89, Dies; Last Hancock Shaker Leader," *Berkshire Eagle*, September 20, 1960.

131. John S. Williams to Jerome Count, January 16, 1962, Shaker Museum Foundation Correspondence, CC.

132. *Songs of the Shakers* (Pittsfield, MA: Work Education Foundation, 1962).

133. *Songs of the Shakers*, 5; Jerome Count to Mrs. Curry Hall, August 20, 1962, SUSV.

134. Hall, "Singing at Shaker Village Work Camp," 5. In their bibliography, Opdahl and Opdahl conflate the 1952 and 1962 records and give them an incorrect date of 1957. "Works Cited," in Opdahl and Opdahl, eds., *A Shaker Musical Legacy*, 295.

135. Shaker Village, *14 Shaker Folk Songs* (Pittsfield, MA: Shaker Village Work Group, 1962).

136. "Songs of Early America," *Boston Globe*, April 21, 1963; Percy Shain, "Earp Myth Buried Again—By Brinkley," *Boston Globe*, April 16, 1963. For a listing of some of these shows, including the Shaker program, see "Educational TV Programs," *Reading [PA] Eagle*, July 9, 1967. See also "Folksinger," *Jewish Advocate*, January 19, 1967.

137. This film may also have been shown in 1965 on the CBS affiliate in Pittsfield, Massachusetts, as part of a documentary called, unsurprisingly, "Simple Gifts." See "Shaker Village Work Group," *Berkshire Eagle*, September 9, 1965.

138. Hall, "Singing at Shaker Village Work Camp," 5.

139. Stein, *Shaker Experience*, 367.

140. Mildred Barker, Sabbathday Lake, to Helen Upton, February 22, 1967, Lib 89.2.2.55b, Upton Papers. Shaker Museum|Mount Lebanon, Old Chatham, NY.

141. Robert Meader to Brother Thomas Whitaker, May 19, 1967, Papers of Francis J. Whitaker, 1916–1994 (MSS 406), box 1, folder 8, Manuscripts and Folklife Archives, Western Kentucky University.

142. "800-Acre Shaker Land Sale in New Lebanon Recorded," unidentified clipping, June 4, 1970, Shaker Village Work Camp File, Vertical Files, Berkshire Athenaeum, Pittsfield, MA.

143. "(Scenario* of) Children of the Free Woman. (A Shaker Folk-Play)," n.d., box 19, folder Children of the Free Woman, AA; "The Blue Cloak A Shaker Folk Opera (In Three Acts, with Prologue)," n.d., box 19, folder Blue Cloak, AA; "The Shakers Shaken: An American Opera," n.d., box 19, folder Blue Cloak, AA; "THE BLUE CLOAK or COME LIFE, SHAKER LIFE A Shaker Folk Opera (In Three Acts, with Prologue)," November 19, 1956, box 19, folder Blue Cloak, AA; "COME LIFE, SHAKER LIFE (A folk play, with music, in three acts and prologue)," March 24, 1957, box 19, folder Blue Cloak, AA; "COME LIFE, SHAKER LIFE," March 24, 1957, box 19, folder Blue Cloak, AA; "COME LIFE, SHAKER LIFE A Folk Play, with Music, in Three Acts and Prologue," November 27, 1957, box 19, folder Blue Cloak, AA.

144. Box 19, Correspondence re: Shaker Opera, AA.

145. Thornton Wilder to Edward Deming Andrews, November 19, 1956, copy, box 19, Correspondence re: Shaker Opera, AA.

146. Douglas Moore to Edward Deming Andrews, June 22, 1958, box 19, Correspondence re: Shaker Opera, AA. For Moore, see Andrew Stiller, "Moore, Douglas S.," in *Grove Music Online, Oxford Music Online*, January 20, 2001, https://www.oxfordmusiconline.com.

147. Edward Deming Andrews to Doris Humphrey, July 9, 1957, box 19, Correspondence re: Shaker Opera, AA.

148. Doris Humphrey to Edward Deming Andrews, July 29, 1957, box 19, Correspondence re: Shaker Opera, AA.

149. Edward Deming Andrews to Doris Humphrey, August 9, 1957, box 19, Correspondence re: Shaker Opera, AA.

150. Doris Humphrey to Edward Deming Andrews, August 14, 1957, box 19, Correspondence re: Shaker Opera, AA.

151. Catherine White to Edward Deming Andrews, n.d., box 19, Correspondence re: Shaker Opera, AA.

152. "Smith Appoints Director of College Art Museum," *New York Times,* May 22,

1955. See also "Parks Heads Smith College Art Museum," *Springfield Sunday Republican*, May 22, 1955. For an obituary of Parks, see "Robert O. Parks," *Chicago Tribune*, August 5, 1998, http://articles.chicagotribune.com.

153. *The Work of Shaker Hands* (Northampton, MA: Smith College Museum of Art, 1961), n.p.

154. *Shaker Studies at Smith: Exhibition, Lecture, Symposium, Concert* (Northampton, MA: Smith College Museum of Art, 1960), n.p.

155. Robert Rosenblum, "With an Eye to American Art: Dorothy C. Miller '25, L.H.D.," *Smith Alumnae Quarterly* 76, no. 4 (Summer 1985): 26–27.

156. Margaret Rollins to Frederic G. Melcher, January 14, 1961, box 11, The Shakers Correspondence, 1961–1963, PMF.

157. Robert O. Parks to Miss Vaun Gillmor, Bollingen Foundation, Inc., March 9, 1960, folder B 20.8, DMP.

158. Robert O. Parks to Dorothy Miller, March 5, 1960, folder B 20.8, DMP. See also "Smith College Lists Many Events in Shaker Festival," *Springfield Sunday Republican*, January 1, 1961.

159. *Shaker Studies at Smith.* See also "Shaker Festival, January 4–20," *Smith Alumnae Quarterly* 52, no. 2 (Winter 1961): 93.

160. Kay Pollock, "Society Revives Old Traditions, Properties, Endeavors to Recapture Authentic Character," *The Sophian*, December 15, 1960, 4. Potter had also been instrumental in bringing Andrews and his collection, however fleetingly, to Yale and served on the board of the Hancock Shaker Village.

161. Edward Deming Andrews to Robert O. Parks, March 8, 1960, box 21, folder Smith College Festival, AA.

162. Shaker Village, *14 Shaker Folk Songs.*

163. Robert Miller, "Iva Dee Hiatt," *Smith Alumnae Quarterly* 71, no. 2 (February 1980): 61–62; "Iva Dee Hiatt, 60, Smith Choral Head," *Daily Hampshire Gazette* (Northampton, MA), January 7, 1980.

164. "Elected to Princeton Council," *New York Times*, December 14, 1950. The next summer Hiatt and Alexander took singers from Smith and Amherst on a goodwill tour of Europe with performances in Madrid, Naples, Rome, and Paris. Peter Schrag, "Singing Students," *New York Times*, July 23, 1961.

165. Charlotte Fitch, "Edith Burnett," *Smith Alumnae Quarterly* 29, no. 4 (Summer 1998), 70; Dorothy Potter, "Pioneer in Teaching Dancing for Academic Credit," *Daily Hampshire Gazette*, April 6, 1956; "Students at Smith to Dance a Drama," *New York Times*, May 1, 1938.

166. Robert O. Parks to Edward Deming Andrews, November 23, 1960, box 21, Smith College Festival, AA.

167. Fitch, "Edith Burnett"; Potter, "Pioneer in Teaching Dancing."

168. Ken Meyers, "Millionaire DJ Loves School, Fame, the Law," *National Law Journal* 15 (February 22, 1993): 45.

169. D. K. Wilgus, "Record Reviews," *Journal of American Folklore* 75, no. 295 (January–March 1962): 88.

170. His dissertation is available through the Case Western Reserve University Library. William McKinley Randle, "History of Radio Broadcasting and Its Social and Economic Effect on the Entertainment Industry, 1920–1930" (Ph.D. diss., Case Western Reserve University, 1966).

171. William M. Randle, "The Shaker Heritage," *Cleveland Plain Dealer,* November 26, 1961.

172. Robert Parks to Dorothy C. Miller, January 18, 1960, folder BoZo.8, DMP.

173. Carolyn Dickey and Merellyn Gallagher, "Choirs and Dancers Perform at Festival," *The Sophian,* January 10, 1961, 4. See also "Shaker Dance," *Berkshire Eagle,* January 11, 1961.

174. Margaret Rollins to Marguerite F. Melcher, January 14, 1961, box 11, The Shakers Correspondence, 1961–1963, PMF.

175. "Shaker Festival, January 4–20," *Smith Alumnae Quarterly* 52, no. 2 (Winter 1961): 93.

176. Robert Parks to Dorothy C. Miller, January 18, 1960, folder BoZo.8, DMP. For a thumbnail portrait of Mendenhall, see Barry Werth, *The Scarlet Professor* (New York: Nan A. Talese, 2001), 211–212.

177. Faith Andrews to Mrs. Curry Hall, March 21, 1961, M94–650, SUSV.

178. Edward Deming Andrews to "Miss Burnett," draft, January 10, 1961, box 21, Smith College Festival, AA.

179. Edward Deming Andrews to Hugh Ross, Manhattan School of Music, January 13, 1961, carbon copy, box 21, folder Smith College Festival, AA.

180. Edith Burnett to Faith and Edward Deming Andrews, January 12, 1961, box 21, folder Smith College Festival, AA.

181. For London, see David Cope, "London, Edwin," in *Grove Music Online, Oxford Music Online,* January 20, 2001, https://www.oxfordmusiconline.com. Although London subsequently lived by coincidence in Shaker Heights, Ohio, he did not complete any compositions based on Shaker themes. Grant Segall, "Edwin W. London Created the Cleveland Chamber Symphony," *Cleveland Plain Dealer,* January 31, 2013, http://www.cleveland.com. Vincent Brann was an instructor in speech at Smith College. See "News of Colleges," *Springfield Sunday Republican*, May 12, 1957.

182. Darryl Thompson, preface, in *Let Zion Move: Music of the Shakers,* ed. Roger L. Hall (Cambridge, MA: Rounder Records, 1999), 9.

183. For Johnson, see Flo Morse, "Brother Theodore E. Johnson Dies," *Shaker Messenger* 8, no. 3 (Spring 1986): 12. See also Stein, *Shaker Experience,* 385–394.

184. *The Shaker Heritage,* produced by Bill Randle (Cleveland: Press of Western Reserve University, 1961). See also "News and Notes," *Shaker Quarterly* 1, no. 1 (Spring 1961): 27. Selections from these recordings were rereleased in 1999 by Rounder Records on compact discs under the guidance of ethnomusicologist and Shaker music scholar Roger L. Hall. See Hall, ed., *Let Zion Move.*

185. "Smith College Director to Give Talk," *Pittsburgh Press,* March 13, 1966.

186. Robert O. Parks to Edward Deming Andrews, March 7, 1961, box 21, folder Smith College Festival, AA.

187. Edward Deming Andrews to Robert O. Parks, March 10, 1961, box 21, folder Smith College Festival, AA.

188. Robert O. Parks to Edward Deming Andrews, April 4, 1961, box 21, folder Smith College Festival, AA.

189. Julia Neal to E. L. McCormick, ca. 1960, M00-102hh, SUSV.

190. Mario De Pillis to Edward Deming Andrews, April 10, 1961, box 21, folder Smith College Festival, AA.

191. Werth, *The Scarlet Professor,* 271.

192. "Smith Prof Accused in Morals Case," *Springfield [MA] Daily News,* April 15, 1961; "Smith Professor Pleads Innocent in Morals Case," *Springfield Republican,* April 16, 1961.

193. See typescript reproduction of article from *Springfield Republican,* April 16, 1961, box 21, folder Smith College Festival, AA.

194. T. C. Mendenhall to the Visiting Committee of the Smith College Museum of Art, May 4, 1961, folder B20.32, DMP.

195. Amy Bess Miller to Faith and Edward Deming Andrews, April 19, 1961, box 31, folder Correspondence and Notes re: Hancock Shaker Village, 1961 (1), AA.

196. Margaret Rollins to Marguerite Melcher, May 28, 1961, box 11, The Shakers Correspondence, 1961–1963, PMF.

197. "Art Museum Here Names New Curator," *Sarasota [FL] Journal,* September 7, 1961. See also "Smith Teacher to Run Museum," *Boston Traveler,* September 8, 1961; "Parks Is Named," *Springfield Union,* September 15, 1961. In 1962, Vincent Brann reported in a letter to Faith and Ted Andrews that Edith Burnett and Marion DeRonde had visited Parks in Sarasota. Brann wrote, "She mentioned how sorry she felt for both Bob and Ann, and how she fears the many Smith folk in the area know all about Bob and his history, and that it will always be tough for him there." Brann to Faith and Edward Deming Andrews, March 28, 1962, box 21, folder Smith College Festival, AA.

198. Vincent Brann to Faith and Edward Deming Andrews, October 10, 1961, box 21, folder Smith College Festival, AA.

199. Vincent Brann to Edward Deming Andrews, May 22, 1962, box 21, folder Smith College Festival, AA. Brann also served as program coordinator of WFCR,

the educational radio station operated jointly by Smith College, Amherst College, Mount Holyoke College, and the University of Massachusetts. "Program Coordinator Named for WFCR," *Springfield Union*, May 11, 1961.

200. Mildred Barker to Julia Neal, April 10, 1961, PMJN.

201. Vincent R. Tortora to Moses Asch, September 11, 1976, Folkways Production Files, box 22, folder 35, MFAC.

202. The Glee Clubs of Smith and Amherst College, *Music of the Shakers,* comp. Vincent R. Tortora (New York: Folkways, 1976).

203. Timothy F. Washburn to Folkways Records, March 22, 1977, Folkways Production Files, box 22, folder 35, MFAC.

204. Vincent C. Brann to Faith and Edward Deming Andrews, n.d. but likely from spring 1961, box 21, folder Smith College Festival, AA. See also Brann to Faith and Edward Deming Andrews, September 24, 1961, box 21, folder Smith College Festival, AA.

205. Vincent Brann to Faith and Edward Deming Andrews, March 28, 1962, box 21, folder Smith College Festival, AA.

206. For outdoor dramas, see Cecelia Moore, "Outdoor Dramas," *NCPedia,* 2006, http://ncpedia.org. See also David Glassberg, *American Historical Pageantry: The Uses of Tradition in the Early Twentieth Century* (Chapel Hill: University of North Carolina Press, 1990), 275–276. For a pictorial overview of this type of popular outdoor drama, see Mary Nordstrom, *Outdoor Drama* (Chapel Hill, NC: North South Artscope, 1985). For a biographical celebration of Green, see John Gassner, "Paul Green: Playwright on Native Ground," in Paul Green, *Five Plays of the South* (New York: Hill and Wang, 1963), ix–xii. See also John Herbert Roper, *Paul Green: Playwright of the Real South* (Athens: University of Georgia Press, 2003).

207. Vincent Brann to Faith and Edward Deming Andrews, July 6, 1961, box 21, folder Smith College Festival, AA.

208. Charles G. Zug III, "Folklore and the Drama: The Carolina Playmakers and Their 'Folk Plays,'" *Southern Folklore Quarterly* 32, no. 4 (December 1968): 280.

209. Frederick H. Koch, ed., *Carolina Folk-Plays* (New York: Henry Holt, 1922), xii.

210. Walter Spearman, *The Carolina Playmakers: The First Fifty Years* (Chapel Hill: University of North Carolina Press, 1970), 52.

211. Lynn Moss Sanders, "'The People Who Seem to Matter Most to Me': Folklore as an Agent of Social Change in the Work of Howard W. Odum and Paul Green," *Southern Literary Journal* 24, no. 2 (Spring 1992): 62–75.

212. Paul Green, "Symphonic Drama," *English Journal* 38, no. 4 (April 1949): 183. For a scholarly analysis of Green's symphonic dramas, see Carolyn Leech, "Paul Green, Symphonic Drama, and Popular Culture" (Ph.D. diss., West Virginia University, 1993). See also Vincent S. Kenny, *Paul Green* (New York: Twayne, 1971), 92–146.

213. John Gassner, "Outdoor Pageant-Drama: Symphony of Sight and Sound," *Theatre Arts* 38, no. 8 (July 1954): 80.

214. William J. Free and Charles B. Lower, *History into Drama: A Source Book on Symphonic Drama Including the Complete Text of Paul Green's* The Lost Colony (New York: Odyssey Press, 1963), 100.

215. Martha Pingel, "The Stephen Foster Story: A Symphonic Drama," *North Carolina Historical Review* 37, no. 3 (July 1960): 424–425.

216. Vincent C. Brann, Edith Burnett, and Edwin London, "An Outdoor Pageant Drama of the Shakers for Shaker Community, Inc., Hancock, Massachusetts: Outline of a Proposal Submitted to the Board of Trustees," November 25, 1961, box 19, folder Proposal. AA.

217. Brann, Burnett, and London, "An Outdoor Pageant Drama of the Shakers," 1.

218. Brann, Burnett, and London, "An Outdoor Pageant Drama of the Shakers," 3.

219. Brann, Burnett, and London, "An Outdoor Pageant Drama of the Shakers," 1. For a rhapsodic description of the importance of a proper open-air amphitheater, see Gassner, "Outdoor Pageant-Drama," 81.

220. Samuel Selden, "Davis, Harry Ellerbe," *NCPedia,* January 1, 1986, http://ncpedia .org.

221. In 1962, Philip G. Hill, in contrast, wrote in the *Educational Theatre Journal* that an outdoor theater for a historical drama probably could not be built for less than $200,000, not including the cost of land or equipment subsequently installed. See Hill, "A Theatre for the Outdoor Historical Drama," *Educational Theatre Journal* 14, no. 4 (December 1962): 317.

222. Brann, Burnett, and London, "An Outdoor Pageant Drama of the Shakers," 7.

223. Catherine White to Vincent Brann, August 24, 1961, box 21, folder Smith College Festival, AA.

224. Amy Bess Miller to Catherine White, February 12, 1962, box 31, folder Re: Hancock/Shaker Community, Inc., 1962 (1), AA.

225. Amy Bess Miller to Margaret Rollins, February 23, 1962, box 31, folder Re: Hancock/Shaker Community, Inc., 1962 (1), AA.

226. Amy Bess Miller to Catherine White, February 23, 1962, box 31, folder Re: Hancock/Shaker Community, Inc., 1962 (1), AA.

227. Edward Deming Andrews to Vincent Brann, April 1, 1962, box 21, folder Smith College Festival, AA.

228. Vincent Brann to Faith and Edward Deming Andrews, March 28, 1962, box 21, folder Smith College Festival, AA.

229. Edward Deming Andrews to Vincent Brann, April 1, 1962, box 21, folder Smith College Festival, AA.

230. Amy Bess Miller to Marguerite Melcher, August 12, 1964, box 11, The Shakers Correspondence, 1964–1968, PMF.

231. Amy Bess Miller to Members of the Pageant Committee, memorandum, June 7, 1962, box 31, folder Correspondence and Notes re: Hancock Shaker Village, 1962(2), AA. For Glover, see "Shaker Community, Inc. Names Dr. Glover Executive Director," *Berkshire Eagle*, March 31, 1962. For Spinney, see Eric Page, "Frank Spinney, Museum Innovator, Dies at 93," *New York Times*, June 23, 2002. For Crimmin, see "Race Track Sanitation Questioned," *Berkshire Eagle*, September 29, 1960; "Unitarian Church Plans Canvass of Members," *Berkshire Eagle*, May 15, 1956; "Unitarian Church Plans Jazz Service, Flower Festival," *Berkshire Eagle*, June 18, 1965; and *Manning's Pittsfield (Massachusetts) Directory for Year Beginning July, 1961* (Greenfield, MA: H. A. Manning, 1961), 309.

232. Wilbur H. Glover, "Minutes of the Meeting of the Pageant Committee," July 28, 1962, box 31, folder Correspondence and Notes re: Hancock Shaker Village, 1962 (2), AA.

233. The eldresses here may have been thinking of Druckman's *The Simple Gifts*. Amy Bess Miller and Wilbur Glover, "Memorandum for the File: Conversation with Eldress Emma King and Eldress Gertrude Soule at Hancock Shaker Village," July 30, 1962, box 31, folder Correspondence and Notes re: Hancock Shaker Village, 1962(2), AA.

234. Vincent Brann to Edward Deming Andrews, Faith Andrews, and Catherine White, August 10, 1962, box 21, folder Smith College Festival, AA. A copy of Glover's letter to Brann letting him down easily is in the archives of the Hancock Shaker Village, in a file marked "Wilbur H. Glover." Brann continued to hope that such a drama could be produced, possibly at another site, and schemed for at least another year. See Brann to Faith and Edward Deming Andrews, April 8, 1963, box 21, folder Smith College Festival, AA. In 1980, Brann was an associate professor at the University of Massachusetts. "Regional Theaters to Compete," *Springfield Sunday Republican*, May 11, 1980.

235. "Shakertown," *Louisville Courier-Journal*, September 17, 1922; Stein, *Shaker Experience*, 254–255. See also Sue McClelland Thierman, "Shaker Postscript," *Louisville Courier-Journal*, August 21, 1955; and Robyn L. Miner, "Shaker Festival," *Park City [KY] Daily News*, June 21, 1991.

236. "The Guiding Lights to South Union's Preservation," *Shaker Messenger* 2, no. 3 (Spring 1980): 3–5. See also William R. Black, "Went off to the Shakers: The First Converts of South Union" (M.A. thesis, Western Kentucky University, 2013), 132–140.

237. "Revisiting the Shakers," *Courier-Journal Magazine* (Louisville, KY), July 21, 1963; Tommy Hines, "South Union Museum Founder Dies," *Shaker Messenger* 14, no. 4 (January 1993): 16. Mrs. Hall also owned at least one significant Civil War artifact,

a Confederate battle flag descended from her great-grandfather. See Evans Donnell, *Daily News* (Bowling Green, KY), January 12, 1994.

238. Ray Glenn, "Shaker Museum Dedication Is Scheduled for May 28," *Park City Daily News,* May 1, 1960.

239. Marion Porter, "Dedication of Shaker Museum Recalls Flourishing Auburn Colony," *Louisville Courier-Journal*, May 29, 1960.

240. Dan Coleman, "Logan's Shaker Remnants May Go into Museum," unidentified clipping, box 16, folder Shaker Articles by Others, AA.

241. Ray Glenn, "Museum Opened Saturday at Auburn," *Park City Daily News*, May 29, 1960.

242. Cola Turner, "700 Registered at Shaker Museum," *Park City Daily News,* undated clipping, box 16, folder Shaker Articles by Others, AA.

243. Jane Morningstar, "First Shaker Festival Is Set for New Weekend at Auburn," *Park City Daily News,* July 15, 1962.

244. Virginia Hutcheson to Brown Lee Yates, April 15, 1960, SUSV.

245. Wilson W. Wyatt to Mrs. Curry Hall, May 25, 1961, SUSV.

246. "Miss Neal Retires as Library Director," *Daily News* (Bowling Green, KY), August 1, 1972. See also Tommy Hines, "A Tribute to Julia Neal," *Shaker Messenger* 17, no. 2 (November 1995): 5–6.

247. Julia Neal, "Shakertown of Long, Long Ago," *College Heights Herald* (Bowling Green, KY), January 14, 1926.

248. Gordon Wilson, Western Kentucky Teachers College, letter of reference, July 7, 1938, box 1, folder 1, Correspondence July 1938–December 1968, PMJN.

249. "Miss Neal Retires as Library Director." For American Studies at Michigan at this time, see Alexander I. Olson and Frank Kelderman, "Ad Hoc American Studies: Michigan and the Hidden History of a Movement," *American Studies* 55, no. 1 (2016): 107–131; and "Evaluation of America's Culture to Be Central Theme of Summer Session," *Michigan Alumnus* 46, no. 22 (June 8, 1940): 462.

250. Julia Neal, "Shakerism in the United States," paper written for a seminar in American Culture at the University of Michigan, summer 1940, box 6, folder 16, PMJN.

251. Olson and Kelderman, "Ad Hoc American Studies," 115.

252. Dianne Watkins, "Julia Neal Showed Early Interest in Kentucky Shakers," *Shaker Messenger* 11, no. 4 (Summer 1989): 9. For Cowden, see "Directs the Machinery of the Hopwood Awards," *Michigan Alumnus* 40, no. 28 (September 15, 1934): 530.

253. "1945 Hopwood Winners Announced at Lecture," *Michigan Alumnus* 51, no. 23 (July 14, 1945): 443. For the Hopwood Award, see Nicholas Delbanco, "75, and Counting," in *The Hopwood Awards: 75 Years of Prized Writing*, ed. Nicholas Delbanco, Andrea Beauchamp, and Michael Barrett (Ann Arbor: University of Michigan Press, 2006), 1–6.

254. Julia Neal, *By Their Fruits: The Story of Shakerism in South Union, Kentucky* (Chapel Hill: University of North Carolina Press, 1947).

255. W. Francis English, "Review of *By Their Fruits: The Story of Shakerism in South Union, Kentucky* by Julia Neal," *Mississippi Valley Historical Review* 34, no. 4 (March 1948): 684–685.

256. R. E. E. Harkness, "Review of *By Their Fruits: The Story of Shakerism in South Union, Kentucky* by Julia Neal," *Annals of the American Academy of Political and Social Science* 253 (September 1947): 259–260. Similar points are made in "Review of *By Their Fruits*," *Book List* 3, no. 3 (September 1947), 253.

257. Adele Brandeis, "Shaker Record Enlightening," *Louisville Courier-Journal,* May 18, 1947. See also Adele Brandeis to Julia Neal, May 19 [no year], box 1, folder 1, Correspondence July 1938–December 1968, PMJN.

258. Julia Neal to E. L. McCormick, n.d. but ca. spring 1960, Collection Moo-102jj, SUSV; Neal to McCormick, postmarked April 7, 1960, Collection Moo-102kk, SUSV.

259. Julia Neal, "Report on Work Done, Submitted to the Southern Fellowship Fund," box 1, folder 1, Correspondence July 1938–December 1968, PMJN.

260. Glenn, "Shaker Museum Dedication Is Scheduled for May 28."

261. Jane Morningstar, "First Shaker Festival Is Set for Next Weekend at Auburn," *Park City Daily News,* July 15, 1962; "Russell H. Miller to Direct Shaker Pageant," *College Heights Herald,* July 18, 1962.

262. Cyndi M. Chaffin, "Russell Miller and His Contributions to the Theatre in Bowling Green from 1947–1968," typescript research paper, Archives, Western Kentucky University.

263. Ray Gaines, "Park Row Paragraphs," *Park City Daily News,* May 30, 1955; "Miller's Ph.D. Termed Unique," undated clipping, Western Players Scrapbook, 1963–1964, Archives, Western Kentucky University; Russell H. Miller, "Giants Lie Sleeping" (Ed.D. thesis, Teachers College, Columbia University, 1963). A typescript of this work is Catalog no. 1963.4.1 in the Western Kentucky University Archives. For Kramer, see Beverly Whitaker Long, "Magdalene Kramer, 1947 President, National Communication Association," *Review of Communication* 6, no. 3 (July 2006): 174–176.

264. Chaffin, "Russell Miller and His Contributions," 6.

265. *Shakertown Revisited,* typescript play script, n.d., Russell Hale Miller Papers, box 1, folder 6, Western Kentucky University Archives.

266. "Russell H. Miller to Direct Shaker Pageant."

267. O. J. Stapleton, "Night of Music Planned to Honour Ruth Morriss," *News-Democrat and Leader* (Russellville, KY), April 21, 2015; Edward Coffman, Jr., "A Tribute to Ruth Morriss," *News-Democrat and Leader,* May 5, 2015.

268. Tommy Hines, "Ruth Morriss and Her Legacy of Shaker Music," *Logan Journal,* May 2015, http://www.theloganjournal.com.

269. Bertha Lindsay to Mrs. Curry Hall, June 29, 1962, box 4, folder 3, PMJN.

270. Julia Neal, "Shaker Festival," *Kentucky Folklore Record* 8, no. 4 (1962): 127; "First Shaker Festival Opens Friday at Auburn," *Park City Daily News*, July 19, 1962.

271. Cola C. Turner, "Ringing Praises for Producers of Fine Festival," *Auburn News* (Auburn, KY), July 25, 1962.

272. Neal, "Shaker Festival," 128.

273. "J. Granville Clark, South Union Drama Actor, Dies," *Shaker Messenger* 8, no. 3 (Spring 1986): 29.

274. Cola C. Turner, "Shaker Pageant's Final Performance Set," *Park City Daily News*, July 22, 1962.

275. Turner, "Ringing Praises for Producers of Fine Festival."

276. "Festival a Civic Triumph," *News-Democrat,* undated clipping, Western Players Scrapbook, Summer 1962.

277. George M. Chinn to Russell Miller, July 12, 1963, SUSV.

278. Edward Deming Andrews to Barry Bingham, August 10, 1963, box 18, folder Pleasant Hill (1) Correspondence, Pamphlets, Clippings, AA.

279. Al Smith, "'Shakertown Revisited' Like Seeing an Old Friend," *News-Democrat,* July 11, 1963.

280. Lin Abt to Mrs. W. Gaston Coke, April 4, 1963, SUSV.

281. "Top Ten Events of USA Include Shaker Festival," *Auburn News,* June 28, 1965.

282. Judith B. Brinkman to Deedy Hall, July 24, 1965, SUSV.

283. Deedy Hall to Martin Williams, September 9, 1963, SUSV.

284. Hines, "South Union Museum Founder Dies"; "The Guiding Lights to South Union's Preservation"; Laura Nealy Burks, "Reliving the History at South Union, Kentucky," *Shaker Messenger* 11, no. 4 (Summer 1989): 18; Julia E. Morgan, "South Union's Long Road to Preservation," *Shaker Messenger* 17, no. 1 (July 1995): 11–14.

285. Hines, "Ruth Morriss and Her Legacy of Shaker Music"; "Shaker Singers to Perform," *Daily News* (Bowling Green, KY), September 25, 1980; "Old Memories Return to Life in Shaker Music," *Daily News*, November 18, 1982; "Coming Attractions," *Daily News*, October 3, 1985; "Christmas at Shakertown," *Daily News*, November 30, 1988.

286. New England Voices, *River of Love: Music of the Shakers and Music Based on Shaker Themes* (Albany, NY: Albany Records, 2007).

CHAPTER 6: OPENING THE VILLAGES TO THE PUBLIC, 1955–1965

1. Richard Shanor, "Shaker Country," *Travel* 118 (July 1962): 50.

2. The public's sustained interest in these complexes is indicated by the publication of Stuart Murray, *Shaker Heritage Guidebook* (Spencertown, NY: Golden Hill Press, 1994). For a discussion of the shaping of a didactic historic landscape, see James

W. Baker, "'As Time May Serve': The Evolution of Plimoth Plantation's Recreated Architecture," *Old-Time New England* 74, no. 261 (Spring 1996): 49–74. See also Barbara Burlison Mooney, "Lincoln's New Salem; or, The Trigonometric Theorem of Vernacular Restoration," *Perspectives in Vernacular Architecture* 11 (2004): 19–39. For a brief discussion of Shaker sites as tourist attractions in New England, see David L. Richards, "Shaker Villages," in *Encyclopedia of New England,* ed. Burt Feintuch and David H. Watters (New Haven, CT: Yale University Press, 2005), 1493.

3. See, for example, correspondence between Barry Bingham and Edward Deming Andrews while Bingham was planning the restoration of Kentucky's Pleasant Hill and Andrews was involved in establishing Massachusetts's Hancock Shaker Village as a museum. Box 18, folder Pleasant Hill (1) Correspondence, Pamphlets, Clippings, AA.

4. "Shaker Project in Kentucky Plans $1.5 Million Restoration," *Berkshire Eagle* (Pittsfield, MA), November 11, 1961.

5. Sociologist James Loewen indicates that every historic site tells the story of two distinct historic eras. See James Loewen, *Lies across America* (New York: Simon and Schuster, 1999), 36–43.

6. Diane Lea, "America's Preservation Ethos: A Tribute to Enduring Ideals," in *A Richer Heritage: Historic Preservation in the Twenty-First Century,* ed. Robert E. Stipe (Chapel Hill: University of North Carolina Press, 2003), 8–10. See also William J. Murtagh, *Keeping Time,* rev. ed. (New York: Preservation Press, 1997), 39–61. For the Civil War centennial, see Michael Kammen, *Mystic Ties of Memory: The Transformation of Tradition in American Culture* (New York: Vintage, 1993), 590–610.

7. "Shaker Property Sale for Museum Approved," *Berkshire Eagle,* July 18, 1960; Eric Pace, "Amy Miller, 90, a Founder of Shaker Village," *New York Times,* February 26, 2003; Ruth Bass, "Amy Bess Miller: A Believer in Shakers," *Berkshire Eagle,* August 8, 1964. See also Stephen J. Stein, *The Shaker Experience in America* (New Haven, CT: Yale University Press, 1992), 364–366. For an appreciation of Lawrence K. Miller, Amy Bess Miller's husband, see Robert C. Achorn, "Lawrence K. Miller," *Proceedings of the American Antiquarian Society* 101, no. 2 (1991): 245–247.

8. Bob Kimball to Dorothy Miller, November 6, 1959, folder 20.4, DMP; "Berkshire Art Group Elects New Officers," *Springfield [MA] Union,* August 25, 1955; Mrs. Alfred S. Beach, "New Ashford," *North Adams [MA] Transcript,* May 3, 1949; "Kimball Upsets Forrest White for Selectman in New Ashford," *Berkshire Eagle,* February 5, 1957.

9. Amy Bess Miller, *Hancock Shaker Village/The City of Peace: An Effort to Restore a Vision, 1960–1985* (Hancock, MA: Hancock Shaker Village, 1984), 18.

10. Faith Andrews to Amy Bess Miller, October 20, 1959, folder 20.4, DMP. See also Jean Lipman to Dorothy Miller, May 17, 1960, copy, folder B20.8, DMP; and Andrews to Philip Guyol, October 13, 1959, box 31, folder Correspondence and Notes re Hancock Shaker Village, 1958–1959, AA.

11. "Carl Rollins, 80, Type Expert, Dies," *New York Times,* November 21, 1960. For an overview of Rollins's career, see Katherine McCanless Ruffin, "Carl Purlington Rollins and the Bibliographical Press at Yale University" (Ph.D. diss., Simmons College School of Library and Information Science, 2015).

12. Miller, *Hancock Shaker Village/The City of Peace,* 164–165.

13. Faith and Edward Deming Andrews to Amy Bess Miller, November 17, 1959, box 31, folder Correspondence and Notes re Hancock Shaker Village, 1958–1959, AA.

14. Amy Bess Miller to Dorothy C. Miller, n.d., probably enclosed with letter dated June 1, 1960, folder B20.8, DMP.

15. Amy Bess Miller to Dorothy C. Miller, August 9, 1961, folder B 20.9, DMP. Conflict inevitably erupted between the Andrewses and Miller and the village's administration. See Mario S. De Pillis, "The Edward Deming Andrews Shaker Collection: Saving a Culture," in *Gather up the Fragments: The Andrews Shaker Collection,* ed. Mario S. De Pillis and Christian Goodwillie (Hancock, MA: Hancock Shaker Village, 2008), 31–40.

16. For a description of one such figure, see Charlotte Emans Moore, "Another Generation's Folk Art: Edward Duff Balken and His Collection of American Provincial Paintings and Drawings," in *A Window into Collecting American Folk Art: The Edward Duff Balken Collection at Princeton* (Princeton, NJ: The Art Museum, Princeton University, 1999), 16–23. Balken is described as a potential patron of the Hancock Shaker Village in a letter from Bob Kimball, of the *Berkshire Eagle,* to Dorothy Miller. Kimball to Miller, November 6, 1959, folder 20.4, DMP.

17. "The Shakers," *Time,* July 28, 1961, 53.

18. Moore, "Another Generation's Folk Art," 15; "Berkshires Live Anew: Old Colonists' Love of the Hills Is Shown in the Spread of Cultural Projects," *New York Times,* July 28, 1935.

19. Bob Kimball to Dorothy Miller, November 6, 1959, folder 20.4, DMP.

20. Miller, *Hancock Shaker Village/The City of Peace,* 20.

21. See Blanchette F. Rockefeller to Edward Deming Andrews, June 27, 1958, copy, folder 20.5, DMP. For Fahs, see "Charles Fahs, Authority on Japan," *New York Times,* March 6, 1980. Blanchette Ferry Rockefeller was the wife of John D. Rockefeller III and a patron of the Museum of Modern Art. Items from their collection of Shaker furniture were shown in an exhibition entitled *The Shakers: Their Arts and Craft* at the Philadelphia Museum of Art in 1963. See *Philadelphia Museum Bulletin* 57, no. 273 (Spring 1962): 66.

22. Walter Muir Whitehill to Margaret Rollins, March 25, 1961, box 31, folder Correspondence and Notes re: Hancock Shaker Community, 1961(1), AA.

23. Richard Howland to Carroll L. V. Meeks, November 25, 1957, box 20, folder Misc. Hancock Material, AA.

24. *A Proposal to Save the Shaker Community at Hancock Massachusetts: Its Importance as Part of the American Heritage* (N.p: Connecticut Printers, 1960), n.p.

25. Faith Andrews and Edward Deming Andrews, "Sheeler and the Shakers," *Art in America* 1 (1965): 91–93.

26. Richard Happel, "'Miracle' in Hancock," *Berkshire Eagle,* July 1, 1961.

27. The dwelling house first opened to the public in June 1961. See "Shaker Community Museum Opening Monday Represents Work of More Than 50 Persons," *Berkshire Eagle,* June 29, 1961; and Happel, "'Miracle' in Hancock."

28. Richard Shanor, "Berkshire Shaker Village to Be Museum Town," *New York Times,* June 18, 1961. See also Richard V. Happel, "Shaker Simplicity—A Modern Trend," *Berkshire Eagle,* August 24, 1963.

29. Susan L. Buck, "Interpreting Paint and Finish Evidence on the Mount Lebanon Shaker Collection," in Timothy D. Rieman, *Shaker: The Art of Craftsmanship* (Alexandria, VA: Art Services International, 1995), 46–57; Rita Reif, "Even before the Movies, the Shakers Had Technicolor," *New York Times,* November 5, 1995.

30. Amy Bess Miller to Charles Sheeler, May 29, 1962, CSC. For a list of the items Sheeler lent to the Philadelphia Museum of Art, see "Furniture," *Philadelphia Museum of Art Bulletin* 57, no. 273 (Spring 1962): 101–107. For "The Shakers: Their Arts and Craft," see Stephen Bowe and Peter Richmond, *Selling Shaker* (Liverpool: Liverpool University Press, 2007), 97–99.

31. Charles Sheeler to "Mrs. Miller," June 11, 1962; Sheeler to Miller, October 2, 1962; Wilbur Glover to Edith Halpert, November 13, 1962; Halpert to Glover, November 26, 1962; Glover to Halpert, November 30, 1962; Amy Bess Miller to Glover and the file, memorandum, December 7, 1962, all CSC. For Glover, see "Shaker Community, Inc. Names Dr. Glover Executive," *Berkshire Eagle,* March 31, 1962.

32. Amy Bess Miller to John McAndrew, February 14, 1964, CSC. See also Amy Bess Miller to Dorothy C. Miller, December 9, 1963; and Amy Bess Miller to Dorothy C. Miller, December 29, 1963, both folder B20.12, DMP.

33. Amy Bess Miller to William LaVenture, October 22, 1965, CSC.

34. "In Albany Exhibition," *Berkshire Eagle,* April 14, 1965.

35. Nancy Liddle, "Special Exhibits on Animals and Shakers," *Knickerbocker News* (Albany, NY), April 20, 1965; Andrews and Andrews, "Sheeler and the Shakers," 91.

36. John Harlow Ott, *Hancock Shaker Village: A Guidebook and History,* 4th ed. (Hancock, MA: Shaker Community, 1976), 125–126.

37. Andrews and Andrews, "Sheeler and the Shakers."

38. "Eric Sloane," *Current Biography Yearbook, 1972* (New York: H. W. Wilson, 1973), 395; James William Mauch, *Aware: A Retrospective of the Life and Work of Eric Sloane* (Laurys Station, PA: Garrigues House, 2000). Beinecke is probably best known for

establishing the Beinecke Rare Book and Manuscript Library at Yale University. See "Frederick Beinecke, 84, Dead; Gave Rare Manuscripts to Yale," *New York Times*, August 1, 1971; "Frederick Beinecke Dies at 84; Aided Many Berkshire Institutions," *Berkshire Eagle*, August 2, 1971; and G. E. Kidder Smith, *Source Book of American Architecture* (New York: Princeton Architectural Press, 1996), 171. Smith, an architect and architectural historian, calls the round barn "one of the country's greatest autochthonous buildings."

39. Eric Sloane, *An Age of Barns* (New York: Funk and Wagnalls, 1966). For Sloane, see Douglas McGill, "Eric Sloane, Who Celebrated Early Americana in Paintings," *New York Times*, March 8, 1985. The Green River Gallery, in Millerton, New York, owns a Sloane painting of the structure from approximately the same time entitled *Round Barn, Hancock, Mass.*

40. Paul Grimes, "Shaker Village Sets the Table for Tourists," *New York Times*, July 4, 1965. Other midcentury architects who notably created round or curved buildings include W. A. Sarmiento and Geddes, Brecher, Qualls & Cunningham.

41. For a critique of Sloane's nostalgic vision of American rural landscapes, see Helen A. Harrison, "Lost America—or Is It?," *New York Times*, June 15, 1980.

42. John Brannon Albright, "New England Shaker Village," *New York Times*, June 2, 1968. See also Ott, *Hancock Shaker Village*, 88–93.

43. Russell Lynes, "Movers and Shakers," *Harper's Magazine*, December 1966, 38.

44. Janet Malcolm, "About the House," *New Yorker*, August 8, 1970, 65.

45. In subsequent decades, Hancock Shaker Village worked to revise its earlier interpretation. See Matthew Cooper, "Representing Historic Groups Outside the Mainstream: Hancock Shaker Village," *CRM* 24, no. 9 (2001): 36–37.

46. Richard D. Starnes, introduction, in *Southern Journeys: Tourism, History, and Culture in the Modern South*, ed. Richard D. Starnes (Tuscaloosa: University of Alabama Press, 2003), 5.

47. For Kentucky's Pioneer Memorial State Park, see William D. Moore, "'United We Commemorate': The Kentucky Pioneer Memorial Association, James Isenberg, and Early Twentieth-Century Heritage Tourism," *Public Historian* 30, no. 3 (August 2008): 51–81. See also "James L. Isenberg," *Register of Kentucky State Historical Society* 37, no. 118 (January 1939): 59–64.

48. "James Isenberg Taken by Death," *Lexington [KY] Herald*, November 1, 1938. See also "Harrodsburg Pays Tribute to Historian," *Lexington [KY] Leader*, November 2, 1938; and "Kentucky Progress Commission and Staff Executives," *Kentucky Progress Magazine* 6, no. 3 (Spring 1934): 105.

49. "James Isenberg Taken by Death"; "The Sacred 'Yea' and 'Nay' of the Shakers Remained in Mercer's Heart," *Harrodsburg [KY] Herald*, Bicentennial Edition, June 1974, D-11. A copy of this special commemorative bicentennial edition of the

Harrodsburg Herald from June 1974 is located at the Filson Historical Society, Louisville, KY.

50. Sandra Shaffer Tinkham, ed., *The Consolidated Catalog to the Index of American Design* (Teaneck, NJ: Somerset House, 1980), 12A7, 12A8, 12B9, 13D6, 13D8.

51. Carolyn H. Grimes, "Isenberg . . . Leader and Citizen." *Harrodsburg Herald*, Bicentennial Edition, June 1974, AA-5; "City Joins Shakertown Subsistence Plan; Isenberg Tells of Shakertown Industry Plan," *Danville [KY] Daily Messenger*, February 19, 1935, 1. The Shakers abandoned Pleasant Hill in the 1920s. See also Moore, "'United We Commemorate.'"

52. "City Joins Shakertown Subsistence Plan"; "Federal Aid on Home Industry Plain [*sic*] Is Sought," *Kentucky Advocate* (Danville), June 28, 1935. See also "To Ask Federal Funds for Home Industry Plan," *Danville Daily Messenger*, June 29, 1935.

53. "Home Industry Plan Explained to Local Body," *Kentucky Advocate*, February 19, 1935.

54. "500 Expected at Onward Kentucky Council," *Danville Daily Messenger*, May 23, 1935.

55. "City Joins Shakertown Subsistence Plan." See also "Shakertown Plan to Be Launched in City," *Danville Daily Messenger*, May 2, 1935. Isenberg's plan is reminiscent of the Southern Highland Handicraft Guild established in 1929 to assist Appalachian mountaineers to market their crafts to urban consumers. See Jane Becker, *Selling Tradition: Appalachia and the Construction of an American Folk, 1930–1940* (Chapel Hill: University of North Carolina Press, 1998).

56. "Dr. Turck Made Chairman; Isenberg Tells of Plan," *Kentucky Advocate*, May 25, 1935.

57. "Isenberg's Dream," *Danville Daily Messenger*, February 19, 1935.

58. "Dr. Turck Made Chairman."

59. "City Joins Shakertown Subsistence Plan."

60. "Home Industry Plan Explained to Local Body."

61. "Shakertown Industries," *Danville Daily Messenger*, May 23, 1935. See also "Industries Plan Offers Opportunity," *Danville Daily Messenger*, May 2, 1935.

62. "Dr. Turck Named Chairman of New Promotion Group," *Kentucky Advocate*, May 24, 1935; "Dr. Turck Is Chairman of Shakertown Group; Many Attend Meeting," *Danville Daily Messenger*, May 25, 1935. Turck, who had served as president of Centre College since 1927, subsequently resigned his position at the college to serve on the state's tax commission. See "Dr. Turck Resigns as President of Centre," *Danville Daily Messenger*, June 15, 1936.

63. "Promotion of State Is Topic at Conference," *Lexington Herald*, June 29, 1935; "Isenberg Outlines Plan to Bluegrass Delegates," *Lexington Leader*, May 25, 1935. For McVey, see Erica A. Moyen, *Frank L. McVey and the University of Kentucky: A*

Progressive President and the Modernization of a Southern University (Lexington: University Press of Kentucky, 2011).

64. James Speed, "Old Dwellings of Shakertown Possess Quiet Comfort of Builders' Own Spirit," *Herald-Post* (Louisville, KY), March 4, 1934.

65. Before marrying Frank McVey in 1923, Frances Jewell was an assistant professor of English and dean of women at the University of Kentucky. A native of the Bluegrass State, she attended Vassar College and earned an M.A. at Columbia University. "Death Claims Mrs. McVey," *Lexington Herald*, June 14, 1945; "Frances Jewell McVey Portrait to Be Unveiled at University," *Herald-Leader* (Louisville, KY), May 12, 1946; "Mrs. Frank L. M'Vey, Kentucky Educator," *New York Times*, June 14, 1945.

66. "Home Industry Plans Formed," *Lexington Leader*, June 28, 1935.

67. "Promotion of State Is Topic at Conference," *Lexington Herald*, June 29, 1935.

68. Frances Jewell McVey, "Shaker Chronicles of Pleasant Hill," *Kentucky Progress Magazine* 5, no. 4 (Summer 1933): 16.

69. McVey, "Shaker Chronicles of Pleasant Hill," 47.

70. "Home Crafts Show Starts at Frankfort," *Lexington Leader*, June 5, 1936.

71. For an inventory of the variety of groups involved in the exposition, see James L. Isenberg, "An Appreciation," *Lexington Leader*, June 30, 1936.

72. "Discuss Plans for Exposition," *Lexington Herald*, May 30, 1936; "Cookery Arts Exhibited," *Lexington Leader*, May 8, 1936. See also "Onward Kentucky Exhibition," *Register of Kentucky State Historical Society* 34, no. 107 (April 1936): 214.

73. "Cookery Arts Exhibited."

74. "Onward Kentucky Exhibition," *Register of the Kentucky State Historical Society* 34, no. 108 (July 1936): 309.

75. As part of Isenberg's promotion of heritage tourism in the region, Hutton had also written and published guides to Harrodsburg and Fort Harrod. For Hutton, see Moore, "'United We Commemorate.'"

76. Daniel Mac-Hir Hutton, *Old Shakertown and the Shakers* (Harrodsburg, KY: Harrodsburg Herald Press, 1936).

77. "James L. Isenberg Reported Very Ill," *Lexington Leader*, August 13, 1936.

78. "James Isenberg Taken by Death."

79. "The Sacred 'Yea' and 'Nay' of the Shakers," D-11. For an obituary of Bingham, see Alex S. Jones, "Barry Bingham, Sr. Is Dead at 82; Louisville Newspaper Publisher," *New York Times*, August 16, 1988. For an institutional history of the preservation of Shakertown that privileges the role of Earl Wallace, see Thomas Parrish, *Restoring Shakertown: The Struggle to Save the Historic Shaker Village of Pleasant Hill* (Lexington: University Press of Kentucky, 2005).

80. "Earl D. Wallace," *Louisville Courier-Journal*, April 4, 1990.

81. Ed Ryan, "Of Shakertown Savior Wallace," *Louisville Courier-Journal,* October 23, 1982.

82. Earl D. Wallace, *Shakertown at Pleasant Hill: The First Fifteen Years* (Harrodsburg, KY: Shakertown at Pleasant Hill, n.d.), 3–6.

83. For a thoughtful history of the Colonial Williamsburg restoration, see Anders Greenspan, *Creating Colonial Williamsburg* (Washington, DC: Smithsonian Institution Press, 2002).

84. "Williamsburg Curator to Restore Shakertown Village," *Harrodsburg Herald,* June 22, 1962. See Barry Bingham, Sr., to Frederick Haupt III, National Trust for Historic Preservation, nominating James Cogar for the Crowninshield Award, February 26, 1971, Barry Bingham Papers, MSS A B613a 816, Filson Historical Society.

85. "Present Shaker Story Simply, Consultant Says," *Harrodsburg Herald,* July 20, 1962. For Brown, see Norman Tippens, "Peter Brown, CW Visionary, 79," *Daily Press* (Williamsburg, VA), October 26, 2002.

86. For a celebratory history written by Pleasant Hill's director of marketing and public relations, see Diana B. Ratliff, "The Preservation of Pleasant Hill," *CRM* 24, no. 9 (2001): 38–40.

87. "Harrodsburg's 188th Birthday Celebrated at Shakertown," *Harrodsburg Herald,* June 22, 1962.

88. For lovely, luminous photographs presenting the restored Pleasant Hill as a premodern utopia, see Ross Bennett, ed., *Visiting Our Past: America's Historylands,* rev. ed. (Washington, DC: National Geographic Society, 1986), 220–229.

89. "Shakertown a Must," *Harrodsburg Herald,* August 11, 1961; "Mercer's Part in Shaker Project Is Explained," *Harrodsburg Herald,* August 18, 1961; "Mass Meeting on Shakertown," *Harrodsburg Herald,* August 25, 1961. See also "Full Scale Drive to End Rural Poverty," *Harrodsburg Herald,* August 18, 1961.

90. "What Others Think," *Harrodsburg Herald,* November 17, 1961.

91. "Shakertown Support Urged," *Harrodsburg Herald,* December 29, 1961.

92. "$2-Million Loan Approved for Restoration Project," *Harrodsburg Herald,* January 10, 1964. In the late 1980s, the site reportedly had an annual visitation of approximately 250,000. See "Earl D. Wallace," *Louisville Courier-Journal,* April 4, 1990.

93. Robert F. W. Meader to Brother Thomas Whitaker, August 31, 1964, Francis J. Whitaker Papers (MSS 407), box 1, folder 8, Archives, Western Kentucky University, Bowling Green.

94. Bertha Lindsay to Julia Neal, February 4; June 30; November 13, 1962, box 4, folder 2, PMJN. See also Earl O. Anderson, "Shakers Dwindling but Impact Still Felt," *New Hampshire Sunday News* (Manchester), September 24, 1961.

95. Bertha Lindsay to Julia Neal, November 1, 1964, box 4, folder 2, PMJN.

96. William R. Bibber, "The Amazing Shakers," *Boston Sunday Herald,* September 20, 1964.

97. Marguerite Melcher to Clarice Carr, February 17, 1957, CCP; Bertha Lindsay to Julia Neal, November 1, 1964, box 4, folder 2, PMJN; Robert Meader to Brother Thomas Whitaker, September 27, 1964, Francis J. Whitaker Papers (MSS 407), box 1, folder 8, Archives, Western Kentucky University; June Sprigg, *Simple Gifts: A Memoir of a Shaker Village* (New York: Knopf, 1998), 23.

98. Anderson, "Shakers Dwindling," 13. For reminiscences of living in the Shaker village by Darryl Thompson, Charles Thompson's son, see Linda Landry, *Classic New Hampshire: Preserving the Granite State in Changing Times* (Hanover, NH: University Press of New England, 2003), 150-154.

99. Earl O. Anderson, "NH Shakers Turn Village into a National Shrine," *New Hampshire Sunday News,* August 6, 1970.

100. N. Morrison, "Shakers Open Museum of Old Craftsmanship in Canterbury," *Concord [NH] Monitor,* June 7, 1960; M. S. King, "Shaker Village [Canterbury, N.H.]," *Boston Sunday Globe Magazine,* September 4, 1960; Sprigg, *Simple Gifts,* 43.

101. Anderson, "Shakers Dwindling," 20.

102. David Strickler, "Last of Shakers Sure Faith Will Live On," *New Hampshire Sunday News,* April 17, 1966.

103. Alex Ghiselin, "Gentle N.H. Lady Relives the Days of Shaker Sect," *Boston Globe,* February 22, 1970.

104. Sprigg's *Simple Gifts* is a book-length exposition of her personal experience with this phenomenon.

105. Although visitors were welcomed to the village and encouraged to tour the museum set up in the meetinghouse, they were usually barred from entering the sisters' dwelling house. See Sprigg's glowing account of her 1972 tour of the dwelling house led by Sister Ethel Hudson. Sprigg, *Simple Gifts,* 139-147.

106. Jane O'Shea, "Canterbury Shaker Village Is Ghost of Earlier Days," *Manchester [NH] Union Leader,* August 7, 1959; Strickler, "Last of Shakers Sure Faith Will Live On."

107. Stein, *Shaker Experience,* 353.

108. Jeanette Prosser, "The Shakers of Canterbury," *New Hampshire Profiles,* August 1960, 26-31.

109. Archeologist David R. Starbuck has long challenged the dominant interpretation of Canterbury. See Starbuck, *Neither Plain nor Simple: New Perspectives on the Canterbury Shakers* (Hanover, NH: University Press of New England, 2004).

110. See Felice Belman and Mike Pride, eds., *The New Hampshire Century:* Concord

Monitor *Profiles of One Hundred People Who Shaped It* (Hanover, NH: University Press of New England, 2001), 179–180.

111. Based on the author's personal observations. David R. Starbuck and Paula J. Dennis bemoan the creation of a "bland, homogenized, androgynous Shaker" in an image that is a "colorless image [which] has the men wearing broad-brimmed hats and the women wearing bonnets, modestly covered from head to toe, but otherwise portrayed as indistinguishable from each other." Starbuck and Dennis, "The Dynamics of a Shaker Landscape in Canterbury, New Hampshire," in *Archaeology and Preservation of Gendered Landscapes,* ed. S. Baugher and S. M. Spencer-Wood (New York: Springer, 2010), 241.

112. The room was retained as part of an expensive and extensive restoration of the dwelling house under the administration of Scott Swank and Sheryl Hack at the beginning of the twenty-first century.

113. Miller, *Hancock Shaker Village/The City of Peace,* 19.

114. Sprigg, *Simple Gifts,* 9; Landry, *Classic New Hampshire,* 152.

115. Irene N. Zieget, "Our Shaker Collection and How It Started," *Yankee,* April 1970, 126–127; Helen Meritt Upton, "Collecting Shaker," *Russell Sage Alumnae Quarterly* 34, no. 2 (Winter 1964): 4–5; Charles and Helen Upton, "Living with Antiques," *Antiques* 90, no. 1 (July 1966): 85.

POSTSCRIPT: "BORROWED LIGHT"

1. I am grateful to Darryl Thompson for his insights on the periodization of Shaker fever.

2. "Adams Study Club to Hear Curator of Shaker Village," *North Adams [MA] Transcript,* December 30, 1967.

3. Jane Pierce, "Shaker Craft Stands Out by Contrast," *Boston Globe,* March 12, 1971.

4. Marilyn Hoffman, "Losing a Heart to Shaker Simplicity," *Daily Messenger* (Canandaigua, NY), August 19, 1975; "Craftsman Revives Art of Shakers," *Bucks County Courier Times* (Levittown, PA), September 7, 1975; "House of the Shakers," *Boston Globe,* June 24, 1967; John F. Cole, "The Peaslee Garrison," *Boston Globe,* November 12, 1967.

5. "Personal and Social," *Providence [RI] Journal,* January 1, 1959; "Miss Fleet, Mr. Beede Are Married," *Boston Herald,* May 17, 1959; Donald White, "CML Group—Leisure Bent," *Boston Globe,* March 6, 1970.

6. Jean Dietz, "EMS—A Growing Mecca for Outdoor Lovers," *Boston Globe,* November 13, 1977.

7. Pierce, "Shaker Craft Stands Out."

8. Polly Long, "Shaker Furniture Labor of Love," *Boston Herald Traveller,* December 7, 1971.

9. Eve Goodman, "Cash-and-Carry Kit Furniture: Put It Together, Take It Apart," *Boston Herald American,* March 8, 1979.

10. Rita Reif, "Do-It-Yourself Furniture Kits: Hobby and Creative Outlet," *New York Times,* May 30, 1972.

11. Lynda Graham Barber, "Furniture Kits: Do-It-Yourself Reproductions," *New York Times,* February 1, 1979.

12. Pierce, "Shaker Craft Stands Out."

13. "Craftsman Revives Art of Shakers."

14. Carleton Varney, "Shaker Genius Displayed in Furniture," *High Point [NC] Enterprise,* July 3, 1974.

15. "Shaker Furniture Reproductions on Sale," *Berkshire Eagle* (Pittsfield, MA), May 29, 1973.

16. "Authentic Reproductions," *San Francisco Chronicle,* May 26, 1974.

17. Richard Dabrowski, LinkedIn, https://www.linkedin.com.

18. Christian Becksvoort, *The Shaker Legacy: Perspectives on an Enduring Furniture Style* (Newtown, CT: Taunton Press, 2000), 28–29.

19. Leslie Garisto, "Documentarians with a Difference," *New York Times,* August 4, 1985; Stephen Bowe and Peter Richmond, *Selling Shaker: The Commodification of Shaker Design in the Twentieth Century* (Liverpool: Liverpool University Press, 2007), 181–184. See also Vanessa Williams Snyder, "Shaker Items Available as Kits," *News Record* (North Hills, PA), March 28, 1993; and Lisa Wren, "Looking for Furniture That's Simple yet Quite Graceful? Try Shaker," *Fort Worth [TX] Star-Telegram,* September 2, 1989.

20. Jo Werne, "Simple Shaker Furniture Has Glamorous Following," *The Advocate* (Stamford, CT), October 18, 1990.

21. Mary Daniels, "Armchair Shopping: Catalogues Give Country Style Their Stamp of Approval," *Chicago Tribune,* November 6, 1988. In 1981, Suzanne Slesin suggested that Shaker reproduction furniture was suited for use in apartments because its compact design was "inspirational and eminently practical." See Slesin, "Bringing Shaker-Style Furniture Back to Life," *New York Times,* November 5, 1981.

22. Shaker Workshops, "Shaker Workshops, Makers of Fine Shaker Furniture and Accessories," https://www.shakerworkshops.com.

23. "New Furniture Captures Beauty of Shaker Past," *Home Furnishings Ideas,* Spring–Summer 1972, 86–87. See also J. H. Bigger advertisement, *Los Angeles Times,* September 23, 1971.

24. See, for example, June Hill, "Contemporary's Link with Past," *Chicago Tribune,* September 26, 1971.

25. "Americana," *Boston Globe*, April 1, 1973. See also June Hill, "Eye on Furniture," *Chicago Tribune*, September 26, 1971.

26. "A Shaker Simplicity," *Los Angeles Times*, September 19, 1971. See also June Hill, "Cabinetry," *Chicago Tribune*, September 26, 1971.

27. "Troost Bros. Furniture," *News Palladium* (Benton Harbor, MI), October 1, 1971.

28. Sarah Booth Conroy, "Furniture Forecast: Old and New," *Washington Post*, January 21, 1973.

29. Ellen Eshbach, "The New Americana: It's More than Colonial. Other Heritages Are Surfacing, Too," *Chicago Tribune*, October 7, 1973.

30. "The Spark of Elegant Accents," *Boston Globe*, September 30, 1973.

31. The 1977 Drexel Heritage catalogue does not include Benchcraft furniture. Many of Benchcraft's characteristics and forms were continued, without the Shaker identification, in the firm's Consensus and Accolade Collections. Drexel Heritage, *Lifestyles* (Drexel, NC: Drexel Heritage Furnishings, 1977).

32. Howard Schott and Andrew Shenton, "Cohen, Joel (Israel)," *Grove Music Online*, *Oxford Music Online*, October 16, 2013, https://www.oxfordmusiconline.com.

33. Caroline Lagnado, "Simple Gifts; Complex Spirituality," *New York Jewish Week*, November 2, 2007, 41; "Joel Cohen: Beyond Borrowed Light," *Early Music America* 12, no. 4 (Winter 2006): 36–38. See also Allan Kozinn, "Discovering the New World Anew," *New York Times*, December 21, 1994.

34. Brian Kellow, "Notebook," *Opera News* 60, no. 5 (November 1995): 10. Cohen's discovery of Shaker music in Harvard's libraries echoes Tony Saletan's finding of "Michael Row the Boat Ashore" in the same institution decades previously.

35. Allan Kozinn, "Music Notes," *New York Times*, November 29, 1994.

36. Kozinn, "Music Notes"; Kellow, "Notebook"; Craig Zeichner, "Joel Cohen and the Shakers of Sabbathday Lake," *Fanfare* 24, no. 2 (November 2000): 150.

37. Kellow, "Notebook"; Daniel W. Patterson, *The Shaker Spiritual* (Princeton, NJ: Princeton University Press, 1979). One review of *The Shaker Spiritual* noted that it was an "encyclopedic work" which marked the culmination of "many years of meticulous labor." Susan Dwyer-Shick, "Review of *The Shaker Spiritual*," *American Anthropologist* 83, no. 2 (June 1981): 442.

38. Philip Greenfield, "Collections—Simple Gifts: Shaker Chants by Boston Camerata, Schola Cantorum of Boston and Shakers of Sabbathday Lake under Joel Cohen," *American Record Guide* 59, no. 2 (March 1996): 248. The Boston Camerata included Anne Azéma, Margaret Swanson, Elizabeth Anker, William Hite, Daniel McCabe, and Joel Frederiksen. The Schola Cantorum of Boston, directed by Frederick Jodry, was composed of Alice Dampman, Sherri Dietrich, Megan Henderson, Paul Cummings, and Stephen Falbel, assisted by Mary Ann Valaitis, Robert Dodson, and Arthur

Rawding. The recording does not enumerate the individual members of the group identified as "The Shaker Community of Sabbathday Lake, Maine."

39. Kellow, "Notebook."

40. Alan G. Artner, "Simple Gifts: Shaker Chants and Spirituals," *Chicago Tribune*, November 19, 1995.

41. Anthony Tommasini, "Simple Gifts: Shaker Chants and Spirituals," *New York Times*, January 7, 1996.

42. Greenfield, "Collections—Simple Gifts."

43. Lawrence Van Gelder, "Footlights," *New York Times*, November 17, 1999.

44. Gloria Goodhue, "Shakers Step Up to a New York Stage," *Christian Science Monitor*, October 22, 1999.

45. Bernard Holland, "A Window into a Past of Singing and Dancing," *New York Times*, November 19, 1999.

46. The Boston Camerata, at this point, included Anne Azéma, Margaret Frazier, Deborah Leath Rentz, Timothy Leigh Evans, Dan Hershey, David Wilkinson, and Joel Frederiksen. The members of the Harvard University Choir, under the direction of Murray Forbes Somerville, who performed on the recording included Deborah Abel, Meagan Anderson, Elizabeth Rogers, Victoria de Menil, Carolyn Szal, Anna Engstrom, Alice Farmer, Michael Cedrone, Edward Chiu, Wesley Chinn, Edward Jones, and Daniel Roihl. Under the direction of Hazel Somerville, Youth Pro Musica was composed of Kate Nyhan, Amanda Savitt, Johanna Murphy, Eliza Murphy, McCurdy Miller, Owen Callen, Ruthanne Callen, Rachel Sklar, Sarah Sklar, Leah Sakala, Megan Hughes, Allison Condon, John Sullivan, John Arida, Alexander Caruso, Taylor Dunn, and Nalini Margaitas. While Cohen's *Simple Gifts* had not identified the individual residents of Sabbathday Lake who participated, the liner notes to *The Golden Harvest* listed Frances Carr, Marie Burgess, June Carpenter, Arnold Hadd, Wayne Smith, and Douglas Anthony.

47. Craig Zeichner, "Joel Cohen and the Shakers of Sabbathday Lake," *Fanfare* 24, no. 2 (November 2000): 150–156.

48. Gilbert French, "The Golden Harvest," *American Record Guide* 64, no. 2 (March–April 2001): 229.

49. Zeichner, "Joel Cohen and the Shakers of Sabbathday Lake," 156.

50. Jack Anderson, "From Finland, Wearing Large Tutus," *New York Times*, March 26, 2006. See also Inka Juslin, "Nordic Dance Performances in the North American Marketplace," in *Nordic Dance Spaces: Practicing and Imagining a Region*, ed. Karen Vedel and Petri Hoppu (Farnham, Surrey, England: Ashgate, 2014), 166–168.

51. Anderson, "From Finland."

52. Claudia LaRocco, "Brooklyn Convention of Shakers (and Movers)," *New York Times*, November 9, 2007.

53. "Joel Cohen: Beyond Borrowed Light," 36.

54. Deborah Jowitt, "Soul Shakers," *Village Voice,* November 21–27, 2007.

55. "Joel Cohen: Beyond Borrowed Light," 37.

56. Jenny Gilbert, "Dance: And Then, Right, He Only Goes and Drives a Train through Her Tummy," *Independent on Sunday* (London), April 10, 2005. For a less positive review that claims that the work is twice as long as it should be, see Judith Mackrell, "Dance: Tero Saarinen: Queen Elizabeth Hall, London, 3/5," *The Guardian* (London), April 8, 2005.

57. Sarah Frater, "Moved by a Sense of Wonder," *Evening Standard* (London), April 7, 2005.

58. Deborah Jowitt, "The Decade's Best Dance," *Village Voice,* December 23–29, 2009.

59. Joel Lobenthal, "Illuminating a Dark Tradition," *New York Sun,* November 10, 2007.

60. Jowitt, "Soul Shakers."

61. Claudia La Rocco, "Brooklyn Convocation of Shakers (and Movers)," *New York Times,* November 9, 2007.

62. "Sublime Light."

63. Joyce Morgan, "All Dressed Up and Ready to Come Out," *Sydney Morning Herald,* March 14, 2008.

64. Rose Jennings, "Critics, More Critics: Dance: The Light Fantastic," *The Observer* (London), April 10, 2005.

65. Gilbert, "Dance."

66. Sherry Marker, "Visiting the Past in Massachusetts," *New York Times,* August 30, 1992; Brian Shaeffer, "A Shaker Village Finds Enterprise Is Not So Simple," *New York Times,* December 21, 2014.

67. "Hancock Shaker Village Appoints President and CEO," iBerkshires.com, July 2, 2012, http://www.iberkshires.com.

68. Shaeffer, "A Shaker Village Finds Enterprise," C8.

69. Phil Demers, " Hancock Shaker Village CEO Linda Steigleder to Step Down in November," *Berkshire Eagle,* March 4, 2016.

70. Jenn Smith, "Hancock Shaker Village Names Jennifer Trainer Thompson as New Leader," *Berkshire Eagle,* September 14, 2016.

71. Carolyn Shapiro, "Bringing the Past into the Present," *New York Times,* March 15, 2018.

72. See chapter 2.

73. Shapiro, "Bringing the Past into the Present."

INDEX

....

Aaron, Daniel, 258
Abbe Practical Workshop, 180–182
Adams, Charles C., 3, 8, 14, 182; education
  and background, 15–16; the New York
  State Museum and, 15–22
Adams, Harriet Dyer, 30, 66–67
Addams, Jane, 148
Adix, Vern, 165
"Air and Simple Gifts" (J. Williams), 1–2
Aks, Harold, 226, 229–230, 232–233, 259,
  321
Albany Institute of History and Art, 196,
  295
Alexander, J. Heywood, 260
Alexander, Pearl Levy, 130, 133–134
Alexandre, Anna R., 195
Alfred Shaker Village, Maine, 4, 53, 83
Alsberg, Henry G., 87
Americana (McEvoy), 141–142, 144
Americana (Sheeler), 83–85, 107
American Friends Service Committee,
  220–221
American Museum in Britain, 137
American Studies, 2, 10, 202–210, 212,
  258–259, 261, 278, 290
Amherst College, 260

André, 130
Andrews, Edward Deming, 8, 124, 172,
  175, 217, 285, 321; *The Community
  Industries of the Shakers*, 42–49
Andrews, Faith, 31, 263, 267
Andrews, Faith and Edward Deming,
  242, 279, 290–297, 316; as antique
  dealers, 30–37; early articles by, 33–35;
  historiographical emphases upon, 6–7;
  the Index of American Design and,
  88–114; pattern of interaction with
  collaborators, 7, 15, 210, 214, 259, 267;
  The People Called Shakers, 236; *Shaker
  Furniture: The Craftsmanship of an
  American Communal Sect*, 110; Shaker
  pageantry and, 253–269; "Sheeler and
  the Shakers," 296; Yale University and,
  201, 207–214
Anstatt, Isaac, 22
Antiques. See *Magazine Antiques*
Appalachian Spring (Copland), 2, 231,
  259–260
Asch, Moses, 243–248, 269

B. Altman & Co., 32
Barker, Mildred, 251–252, 266, 269

Becker, Joseph, 235–236

Beede, Russell, 315–316

Beinecke, Frederick and Carrie Regina
    Sperry, 296

Beisel, Erin, 242

Belden, Ricardo, 188–189, 226–232,
    239–241, 249–250, 261, 321, 323

Benchcraft furniture, 318–320

Benson, Rita Romilly, 88–89, 113

Berkshire Museum, 8, 13–14, 49–56, 327;
    Shaker exhibition at, 52–55, 201–202

Bingham, Barry, 285, 305–306

Borrowed Light (Saarinen), 324–326

Boston Camerata, 320–324

Bowe, Stephen, 41

Brackett, Joseph, Jr., 1, 313

Bragg, Laura, 14, 49–56, 80, 201

Brandeis, Adele, 110, 279

Brandt, Joseph A., 172–173

Brandt, Mortimer, 189

Brann, Vincent, 265–266, 268–275

Brooklyn Academy of Music, 325–326

Brooks, Emmory, 115, 137

Brown, Elaine, 233

Brown, Peter A. G., 305

Brunschwig, Zelina, 189

Brussels World's Fair, 129

Buck, Norman S., 213

Buck, Susan L., 295

Buckley, William F., 206

Burchenal, Elizabeth, 148–149

Burnett, Edith, 260–266, 268–269, 271

Burns, Ken, 318

Bussell, Joshua, 60, 64

*By Their Fruits: The Story of Shakerism
    in South Union, Kentucky* (Neal),
    278–280, 283, 285

Cahill, Holger, 9, 82–90, 114, 117, 290

Cain Park Theater, 162–167, 180

Callan, Judith Lee Davenport, 195

Camp Woodland, 221–222

Canterbury Shaker Village, New Hamp-
    shire, 10–11, 110, 175–176, 239, 249, 265,
    279–280, 288–289, 307–312, 317

Carr, Clarice Jennings, 9, 139–140,
    175–182, 261

Carr, Frances, 266, 322

Case, Anna, 38, 60, 62

Cathcart, Wallace, 17

Cazden, Norman, 222

Charleston Museum, 49–50

Childers, William Paul, 299

Christensen, Erwin O., 225

Christiana, Helen Pitcher, 195, 239

Clark, J. Granville, 277, 283

Clawson, Hamilton Phelps, 189–194, 197,
    215

Cleveland Institute of Music, 159

Coe, William Robertson, 204–208

Coffin, William Sloane, 203

Cogar, James, 305–307

Cohen, Joel, 320–324

Cold War, 128–129, 156–158, 179–180,
    202–207, 214

Cole, John, 315–317

Collier, Nina, 87–88

Collins, Sarah, 25, 56, 103–104, 107

Colonial Revival, 5, 187, 320

Colonial Williamsburg, 305–306

*Communistic Societies of the United
    States, The* (Nordhoff), 235

Community Industries of the Shakers, The
    (E. D. Andrews), 42–49, 66; photo-
    graphs by Winter for, 43–49, 72

*Community Industries of the Shakers,
    The* (exhibition at the New York State
    Museum), 37–49

Congregationalism, 2, 9, 139, 314

Conviser, David, 232

Copland, Aaron, 1–2, 231–232, 259–260,
    321

Corcoran Gallery, 319

Count, Ellen, 242–248

Count, Jerome, 6, 10, 182, 217–253, 273,
    276, 321, 323; the Shaker Museum at
    Old Chatham and, 196–197; Unitarian-
    ism and, 218, 225

Count, Sybil A. Wolfson, 219–220, 252

counterculture, 174, 242, 314

Cramer, Miriam, 6, 9, 139–140, 158–168,
    175, 242; *More Love, Brother*, 160–168,
    228–229, 261

Crane, Zenas Marshall, 49, 55

Crawford, Phyllis, 81–82
Crimmin, Charles R., 274
Cronk, Lon, 111–112, 299–300

Dabrowski, Richard, 317–319
Dale, Elizabeth K., 142
Daley, Margaret Fraser, 196
Dana, John Cotton, 2, 79, 86, 117, 200
Dance of the Chosen (Humphrey),
    141–146, 261, 323–324
Darrow School, 188
Dartmouth College, 172, 176
Davis, Harry E., 272
Davis, Stuart, 57, 145, 255
Declaration by Drexel (Stewart &
    MacDougall), 127–129, 319
de Mille, Agnes, 143, 162, 254
Denishawn dancers, 159
Denishawn School, 143, 145, 150–151, 155
Dennis, Ruth, 177
De Pillis, Mario S., 7, 213, 258, 267
DeRonde, Marion, 260, 265–266
Devane, William C., 203, 206
Dewey, John, 2, 50, 147–148, 221, 223, 226
Diamond, Freda, 122–125, 128, 171
Diamond Crystal Salt Company, 224
Dodd, Eugene, 315–317
Doody, Leo M., 17
Downtown Gallery, 84
Drexel Furniture Company, 127–129,
    318–320
Druckman, Jacob, 232–233, 259, 287, 321
Dyer, Caleb, 171

Elam, Aida, 266, 308
Enfield, New Hampshire, 168–169,
    171–172, 175–176, 179–180
Enfield Shaker Singers, 175–180, 182, 261,
    322
Enfield Shaker Village, New Hampshire,
    168, 171, 176
Epstein, William, 249
Estabrook, Fannie, 60, 230, 249

Faison, S. Laine, 290
fashion, Shaker-inspired, 130–136, 196
Federal Art Gallery, Boston, 119

Federal Art Gallery, New York City, 119
Federal Art Project, 74, 81–82, 90
Fisher, Thomas, 115
Flick, A. C., 17
Flinn, Eleanor T., 158
Flora Stone Mather College, 159
Fogg Art Museum, 119
folk art, American, 57–58, 60, 66, 82–87
folk dance, 148–150, 177–180, 225–226,
    230
folk music revival, 10, 177–180, 216
folk opera, 182, 253, 269–276
Folkways Records, 243–249, 269
Force, Juliana, 14, 56–59, 82, 110
Foster, Lawrence, 90
14 Shaker Folk Songs (Shaker Village
    Work Group), 249–250, 323
Frampton, Eleanor, 159
Francis W. Parker School, 146–148, 151
freedom of religion, 119–120, 170
Frost, Marguerite, 265, 308
Fruitlands Museum, 317
Furniss, Edgar S., 208, 211, 213

Gabriel, Ralph Henry, 203–204, 213
Gallaher, Edward Beach, 204–205
Garvan, Francis Patrick, 199–200
General Electric, 22–24
Ger, Anne, 90
Gessert, Robert, 258
Gill, Leslie, 133
gift drawings, 60, 63, 65, 89, 133, 228, 255
Glassgold, Adolph, 112, 114, 124
Glover, Wilbur H., 274–275, 295
*Golden Harvest: More Shaker Chants and
    Spirituals* (Boston Camerata), 323
Gomer, T. Hal, 283
Goodwillie, Christian, 31
Goodwin, Phyllis, 177
Gleanings from Old Shaker Journals
    (Sears), 18
Graham, Martha, 1, 143, 145, 154–155, 231
Green, Henry, 115
Green, Paul, 270–271, 280
Griswold, Alfred Whitney, 206–207
Gulick, Luther Halsey, 148–149
Guyol, Philip, 291

Hadden, Eloise, 277, 283
Hahn, Nanette Hogan Wells, 196
Hall, Deedy, 10, 263, 276–278, 285–286
Hall, Frances, 290
Halpert, Edith, 82–87, 295
Hancock Shaker Village, Massachusetts,
    10–11, 89, 107, 120, 137, 188, 217, 239,
    279, 288–298, 315–317, 325–327;
    symphonic drama at, 270–276
Hartnagel, Chris A., 16–17
Harvard University Choir, 322–323
Haufrecht, Herbert, 222
Healy, Dale, 128
heritage tourism, 217, 271, 277–278,
    287–289, 292, 298–299, 306, 308
Herlick, George, 90, 97–106
Herman Miller Company, 122–125
Heston, Herbert, 266
Heye Foundation, 187, 190
Hiatt, Iva Dee, 259–260, 265, 269, 322
Hinman, Mary Wood, 146, 148–150, 226
historic preservation, 289–290, 292–295
Holden, Reuben, 213
Holmes, John Haynes, 218
Howland, Richard, 292
Hudson, Ethel, 310
Hull House, 148–149
Humphrey, Doris, 9, 140–159, 182, 218,
    222, 313; Andrews, E. D., and, 254–255;
    background and education, 146–150;
    Dance of the Chosen, 141–146, 261, 323–
    324; *Greek Sacrificial Dance*, 149–150;
    The Shakers, 141–146, 160
Humphrey-Weidman Troupe, 159–160
Huntington, Gertrude, 258
Hutcheson, Virginia, 277
Hutton, Daniel Mac-Hir, 304–305
Hutton, Jane Bird, 305–306

Index of American Design, 9, 15, 74–122,
    210, 224–225, 242, 271, 290, 295, 316;
    artwork exhibited at department
    stores, 119; artwork exhibited at
    museums, 120, 177, 255, 285
Isenberg, James L., 111, 298–305
isolationism, 169–170

Jacob's Pillow Dance Festival, 324–325
Jamieson, Robert Stuart, 226, 229
Javitz, Romana, 75–82
Johnson, Hall, 142, 145
Johnson, Theodore, 265
Junior Bazaar, 121, 133, 135–136

Kelleher, John, 90, 93
Kenyon, Cecelia M., 258
Keyes, Homer Eaton, 33, 35, 41, 53, 66, 124
Kimball, Robert, 195, 290
King, Emma B., 188, 194, 266, 275, 280,
    290
Kirk, John, 33, 71
Knott, Sarah Gertrude, 179–180
Knotts, Benjamin, 119–120
Koch, Frederick, 270–271
Kowal, T., 237–238
Kramer, Magdalene, 280
Kunttu, Mikki, 324

Landesman, Geoffrey, 163–165
Larkin, Oliver W., 258
Lassiter, William L., 20–22, 38, 60, 90,
    279
Lawrence, Pauline, 141–142
Leatham, Barclay, 160
Lee, Mother Ann, 3, 280
Lewis, Sinclair, 172
Lindsay, Bertha, 265, 282–283, 307–309
Little, Bertram, 291
London, Edwin, 265–266, 269, 271, 274

Ma, Yo-Yo, 1
Mabel Brady Garvan Collection, 199–
    201, 210
MacDougall, Stewart, 127–128
Magazine Antiques, 33–37, 53, 66, 72
mail-order furniture, 316–317
Mann, Arthur, 258
Mantz, Harold C., 165
Mariners' Museum, 189
Marks, Gerald, 249
Matter, Herbert, 121–122, 327
Mayo, Margot, 225–229
McGill, Anthony, 1

McCausland, Elizabeth, 120, 154–156
McClean, John Patterson, 17
McCobb, Paul, 125–128
McCoy, Mary A., 175
McDowell, Nancy, 287
McEvoy, J. P., 141–142
McVey, Frances Jewell, 303–304
McVey, Frank L., 302
Meacham, Joseph, 3
Meader, Robert F. W., 7, 194–195, 197, 215, 249, 251–252, 291, 307
Melcher, Marguerite Fellows, 9, 139–140, 168–175, 230, 262–263, 268; background and education, 168; *Rose in the Wilderness*, 170–171, 180–182; *The Shaker Adventure*, 173–175, 279–280; *Steps unto Heaven*, 168–170
Mendenhall, Thomas C., 263, 268
Metropolitan Museum of Art, 119, 137
midcentury modernism, 125, 127
Millennial Laws, 3–4, 53
Miller, Amy Bess, 15, 195, 251, 258–259, 268, 273–276, 290–293, 295
Miller, Donald, 291
Miller, Dorothy C., 31–32, 117, 256–258, 290–291
Miller, Lawrence K., 291
Miller, Russell H., 280–281, 283, 285–286
modern dance, 143–146, 228, 260
modernism, 12; American nationalism and, 114; compared to Shaker design, 55, 66–67, 116–119, 120–121, 124, 294–295; in dance photography, 153
Montero, Gabriela, 1
Monty, Gloria, 180–181
"Monuments Men," 200–202, 212
Moore, Douglas, 253–254
Moore, Lamont, 200–201, 207–208, 211–212
More Love, Brother (Cramer), 160–168, 229, 261
Morgan, Barbara, 24, 151–158
Morrison, Richard C., 109–110, 114
Morriss, Ruth, 282–283, 285–286
Mount Holyoke College, 146, 176, 178
Mount Lebanon Shaker Village, New York, 10, 89, 91, 188, 217, 237, 279
Moutal, Elizabeth, 90, 92
Muollo, Victor, 90, 94
Museum of Modern Art (MOMA), 86, 117–118, 156–157, 211–212, 256, 290
Museum of the American Indian, 187, 189
Music of the Shakers (Folkways Records), 269

National Educational Television, 251–252
National Endowment for the Arts, 322
National Folk Festival, 179–180
National Gallery of Art, 201, 224, 242
national identity, 2–3, 5–6, 88, 158, 172, 204–205, 251
nationalism, 12, 135–137, 179, 199–213
National Trust for Historic Preservation, 289, 292
nativism, 304
Naylor, Genevieve, 133, 135–136
Neal, Julia, 10, 267, 269, 278–280, 307; *By Their Fruits*, 278–280, 283, 285
Neale, Emma, 38, 56, 188–189
Neale, Sadie, 38, 56, 60–61
Newark Museum, 86–87, 117, 200
New Deal, 2, 5, 9, 74, 173, 204–205, 218, 301–303
New England Folk Festival, 179
New Hampshire Folk Festival, 177–179, 261
New Horizons in American Art (exhibition at the Museum of Modern Art), 117
New York Public Library, 172, 224, 228; picture collection of, 77–82
New York Shakers and Their Industries, The (New York State Museum), 42
New York State Museum, 3, 13–14, 80, 224, 228, 279; the creation of a Shaker collection and, 17–22; first Shaker exhibition at, 37–49; historical collections of, 16–17
Non-Sectarian Anti-Nazi League, 219, 224
Nordhoff, Charles, 235

North Union Shaker Village, Ohio, 165
Nowak, Lionel, 159
Nunn, Louie B., 286

Obama, Barack, 1–2
O'Byrne, Robert, 180
Odum, Howard W., 270–271
O'Hearn Manufacturing Company, 125
Ohio State Museum, 120
Oklahoma (Rodgers & Hammerstein), 162, 182
Old Shakertown and the Shakers (D. M.-H. Hutton), 304–305
O'Leary, Johnny, 226, 229
On a Shaker Theme (Sheeler), 255–256, 295
Onward Kentucky Movement, 300–304
Opdahl, Robert C., 226

pageantry, 148–51, 178, 260, 271
Parker, Francis W., 147
Parks, Robert O., 255–268, 290, 295
Patterson, Daniel, 321
Peacock, Eleanor, 279
Pearson, Norman Holmes, 202–203, 206, 213
People Called Shakers, The (Andrews & Andrews), 236
Perlman, Itzhak, 1
Phelps, Lillian, 266, 308–309
photographic conventions, modernist, 23–30
Philadelphia Museum of Art, 120, 137, 295
Phillips, John M., 200–201
Pleasant Hill Shaker Village, Kentucky, 10–11, 111, 120, 137, 288–289, 299–302, 303, 305–307
Poland Hill Shaker Community, Maine, 64
Pollak, Frances M., 81–82
poplarware, 115–117, 137
Potter, David, 5, 202–207, 211–213, 258–259, 290
Predictor Group (McCobb), 125–127
Princeton University, 187
Princeton University Press, 172–175
Pullen, Glenn, 162, 166–167

Randle, William, 260–261, 265–269, 321
Reeves, Ruth, 9, 75–114
religious right, 314
Richmond, Peter, 41
Ritchie, Andrew Carnduff, 211–213
Rockefeller, Abby Aldrich, 84, 306
Rockefeller, Blanchette Ferry, 292
Rockwell, Norman, 196
Rollins, Carl, 262, 290–291
Rollins, Margaret, 262–263, 268, 273–274
Rose in the Wilderness (Melcher), 170–171, 180–182
Round Stone Barn (Sloane), 297
Rourke, Constance, 90, 110, 114, 119

Saarinen, Tero, 323–326
Sabbathday Lake Shaker Village, Maine, 5, 110, 239, 249, 251, 265, 279, 321–323
Saletan, Tony, 226, 251
Sanborn, Dorothy, 177
Sawyer, Charles, 56, 201, 207, 211
Schnakenberg, Henry, 57
Schola Cantorum, 321
Sears, Clara Endicott, 17–18, 32
Seckler, Beatrice, 152–153
Seeger, Pete, 222, 226, 244
Seymour, Charles, 203
Shaker Adventure, The (Melcher), 173–175, 279–280
Shaker Buildings (Sheeler), 296
Shaker Community, Inc., 10, 256–258, 270–276
Shaker dance, 161, 181, 217, 226–228, 239–242, 272, 285
Shakeress at Her Loom (Twining), 107–108
Shaker Farm, 133, 135–136
Shaker fever, 2, 12, 290, 314–315
Shaker Folk Songs (Shaker Village Work Camp), 231–232, 235
Shaker Furniture: The Craftsmanship of an American Communal Sect (Andrews & Andrews), 110
Shaker Handicrafts (exhibition at the Whitney Museum), 59–70, 82, 88, 201–202, 256
Shaker Heights, Ohio, 158, 160
Shaker Legacy, The (Randle), 266

Shaker Museum, Auburn, Kentucky, 10, 263, 276–278; Shaker festival at, 280, 283, 285

Shaker Museum at Old Chatham, 5, 175, 186–198, 291, 295, 317, 325; summer festivals at, 195–197, 239–242, 275, 279, 282–283

Shaker music, 10, 160, 163–164, 181, 217, 226–228, 233–242, 269, 272, 282

Shakers, The (Humphrey), 141–146, 151–153, 160

Shakers: Their Arts and Crafts, The (exhibition at the Philadelphia Museum of Art), 295

Shakertown Countryside Industries, 301–305

Shakertown Revisited (R. H. Miller), 10, 276, 280–286; recording of, 285

Shakertown Revisited, Inc., 285–286

Shaker villages: collapse of, 4–5, 171; prosperity of, 4. See also Alfred Shaker Village, Maine; Canterbury Shaker Village, New Hampshire; Enfield Shaker Village, New Hampshire; Hancock Shaker Village, Massachusetts; Mount Lebanon Shaker Village, New York; North Union Shaker Village, Ohio; Pleasant Hill Shaker Village, Kentucky; Poland Hill Shaker Community, Maine; Sabbathday Lake Shaker Village, Maine; South Union Shaker Village, Kentucky; Watervliet Shaker Village, New York

Shaker Village Work Camp, 10, 182, 217–253, 259, 261, 263, 275, 321–322; 14 Shaker Folk Songs, 249–250; participation at Shaker Museum summer festivals, 196, 239–242, 249, 282–283; Shaker Folk Songs, 231–232; Songs of the Shakers, 233–239, 249–250

Shaker Workshops, 315–319

Shawn, Ted, 143, 145, 150, 324

Sheehan, Donald, 266

Sheeler, Charles, 24, 57, 88–89, 97, 295–297; Americana, 83–85, 107; as collector of Shaker items, 82–83; his collection of Shaker items, 110–111, 113, 295; On

a Shaker Theme, 255–256, 295; Rourke and, 90, 110; Shaker Buildings, 296

"Sheeler and the Shakers" (Andrews & Andrews), 296

"Simple Gifts" (Brackett), 1, 232, 251, 259, 313, 321

Simple Gifts, The (Druckman), 232–233, 259, 287

Simple Gifts: Shaker Chants and Spirituals (Boston Camerata), 321–324

Sloane, Eric, 196, 296–297

Smith, Alfred, 90–91, 110, 113

Smith, Irving, 90

Smith College, 2, 168, 217, 268; American Studies at, 258–259; Shaker festival at, 259–265

Smith College Art Museum, 10, 290, 296; The Work of Shaker Hands at, 255–258

Songs of the Shakers (Shaker Village Work Camp), 233–239, 249–250

Sonnenfeld, Bert, 232

Soule, Gertrude, 275

South Union Shaker Singers, 286

South Union Shaker Village, Kentucky, 4, 217, 252, 276, 286

Spayde, Sydney H., 162

Speed, James, 302–303

Spicer, Caroline Mallary Marvin, 17

Spinney, Frank O., 274, 291

St. Denis, Ruth, 143, 150, 155

Steichen, Edward, 141, 155

Steigleder, Linda, 326–327

Stein, Edwin J., 17–20, 26

Stephens, A. Rosetta, 56, 174

Steps unto Heaven (Melcher), 168–170

Stewart, Kipp, 127–128

Stickney, Prudence A., 174

Stillinger, Elizabeth, 70

Strand, Paul, 24, 97

Studer, Norman, 221–222, 226

Sullivan, C. B., 299–300

Sunami, Soichi, 142, 155, 157, 261

symphonic dramas. See folk opera

Tarney, Ann, 177

Thompson, Charles "Bud," 265, 280, 307–308

Thompson, Jennifer Trainer, 327
"Three Shaker Songs" (Aks), 233, 259
Tranum, Carl K., 81
Turck, Charles J., 302
Tuttle, Esther Leeming, 196–197
Twining, Yvonne, 105–109; *Hancock Shaker Village*, 108–109; *Shakeress at her Loom*, 107–108

Unitarianism, 2, 139, 158, 168, 173, 218, 225, 274, 314
University of Kentucky, 302–303, 305
University of Michigan, 2, 278–279
University of North Carolina, 270–272
University of Wyoming, 205–206
Upton, Helen, 251

Vezolles, George V., 111, 113, 299
village views, 60, 64
Vincentini, Noel, 90, 97–106, 110
Voice of America, 180

Walden School, 226
Wall, Miriam, 266
Wallace, Earl, 305–306
Wanamaker's Department Store, 123, 130–131, 171
Watervliet Shaker Village, New York, 17, 24, 38
Weeks, Estella, 181, 224
Weidman, Charles, 143, 145, 159
Weir, Thomas, 171
Wells, Jennie, 38
Western Kentucky State College, 10, 217, 278–283
Western Reserve Historical Society, 17, 160
Western Reserve University, 159–163, 261; press of, 175, 266, 268
Western Shaker Singers, 286
Weston, Edward, 24
Whitaker, Thomas, 251–252
White, Catherine, 255, 273–274
Whitehill, Walter Muir, 292

Whitney, Gertrude Vanderbilt, 56–59
Whitney Museum of American Art, 8, 13–14, 56–71, 319; *Shaker Handicrafts* at, 59–71, 256
Wilder, Thornton, 253–254
Williams, John, 1–2; "Air and Simple Gifts," 1–2
Williams, John S., 5, 9, 186–198, 214–215, 249, 275, 291–292, 307; background and education, 186–187
Williams, Roger, 187, 189
Wilson, Delmer, 115
Wilson, R. Marvin, 165–166
Winter, William F., Jr., 8, 13–15, 128, 255, 262; education and background of, 22–23; influence on Vincentini and Herlick, 97–103; as photographer at General Electric, 23–24; photographic portraits of Shaker sisters, 60–62, 67, 257; photographs by, 23–30, 67–71, 110, 115, 292–294; photographs exhibited at the Berkshire Museum, 52; photographs exhibited at the Whitney Museum, 60; photographs for *The Community Industries of the Shakers*, 42–49
Winterthur Museum, 137
Wood, Grant, 59, 107
Woodward & Lothrop, 130, 132–133
work camps, 220–222
Work of Shaker Hands, The (exhibition at Smith College Museum of Art), 255–258
Wyatt, Wilson W., 277

Yale University, 2, 10, 15, 198–214, 297; American decorative arts at, 199–202, 210; American Studies at, 202–210
Yale University Art Gallery, 200–201, 207–213, 293
Young, Isaac Newton, 228
Youth Pro Musica, 323

Zorach, Marguerite Thompson, 84
Zorach, William, 57, 83–84